C000276738

Frege: Making Sense

FREGE
Making Sense

Michael Beaney

Duckworth

First published in 1996 by
Gerald Duckworth & Co. Ltd.
The Old Piano Factory
48 Hoxton Square, London N1 6PB
Tel: 0171 729 5986
Fax: 0171 729 0015

© 1996 by Michael Beaney

All rights reserved. No part of this publication
may be reproduced, stored in a retrieval system, or
transmitted, in any form or by any means, electronic,
mechanical, photocopying, recording or otherwise,
without the prior permission of the publisher.

A catalogue record for this book is available
from the British Library.

ISBN 0 7156 2712 0

Typeset by Ray Davies
Printed in Great Britain by
Redwood Books Ltd, Trowbridge

Contents

Preface

This book is concerned with the origins, development and coherence of Frege's conception of sense. The centrality of this conception to Frege's philosophy has entailed discussion of most of the main elements of Frege's thought – his logic, philosophy of mathematics, and ideas in the philosophy of logic and language and in epistemology and metaphysics; and in writing this book, I have also tried to present a balanced and accessible account of Frege's philosophy as a whole. On many topics (logicism, Platonism, vagueness, indexicality, for example), I cannot claim to have provided more than an exposition of Frege's ideas and to have identified some of the problems raised; but I hope that this in itself will encourage a deeper appreciation, even amongst those who are familiar with his ideas, of the organic unity and dynamic development of Frege's philosophy. The emergence of Frege's distinction between sense and reference marks the transition from Frege's early to his later work, and is fundamental to an understanding of the origins of analytic philosophy, yet the distinction is too frequently discussed outside the context of Frege's creation of modern logic, his attempts to think through its philosophical implications, and his overriding aim to demonstrate the logicist thesis – that arithmetic is reducible to logic. The different demands that Frege made on his notion of sense, and the resulting tensions in his philosophy, have also been insufficiently appreciated. What is located at the heart of the account offered here is an issue that has been relatively underexplored in relation to Frege's philosophy – the nature of analysis. For it was the problem of the status of Frege's logical and logicist analyses that motivated the distinction between sense and reference, and the tensions that remained in his philosophy are a result of failing to provide a satisfactory answer to the problem.

Writing about Frege is a hazardous undertaking. At least since Michael Dummett's *Frege: Philosophy of Language*, first published in 1973, and despite the hopes of creating a consensus that he expressed in the preface to its second edition, the interpretation of Frege's philosophy has become highly controversial. Part of the reason for this is Frege's status as one of the founders of analytic philosophy. Analytic philosophers not only use his ideas, but claim his authority for developing them in certain directions. But a lot has happened in the last hundred years, and the dangers of interpreting Frege anachronistically have increased. I have attempted to avoid these dangers here by approaching Frege's work from the ideas of his predecessors and the problems that they posed, trying to understand Frege's motivations and seeing how his views developed through the course of his work. I confront the methodological issues that such 'historical philosophizing' raises in the introduction. I have also sought to keep the main text free of engagement with the burgeoning secondary literature, to enable as clear a picture of Frege's philosophy to emerge as possible. But I have not been hesitant to make use of notes, indicating some of the many debts that I owe to previous writers on Frege, marshalling additional evidence and support for my account, clarifying my position in relation to some of the debates within recent scholarship, and commenting on connected issues. The task of the historical philosopher is to carve their own way through the forest, not to map all the possible paths, parallel routes or picnic spots; but I hope that I have charted enough of the terrain in the notes to enable others to find their bearings and explore it for themselves. (For the policy adopted throughout the text concerning references, see the Bibliography.)

This book began life as an Oxford B.Phil. thesis, which developed into a D.Phil. thesis submitted in 1990. Of the latter, which contained chapters on Aristotle, Frege and Wittgenstein, only the first three chapters survive in any recognizable form, as the introduction and first two chapters of the present book, although material from the fourth chapter of the thesis has been reworked. The majority of the book has been written over the last three years, as the need to provide a detailed account of the development of Frege's conception of sense and its role in Frege's philosophy as a whole became clear. The influence of Wittgenstein on the present work has been far more profound than the number of references to him might suggest; and I hope to return to the story of the evolution of his own thought in due course.

Many people – supervisors of my graduate work as well as friends, colleagues and students of the less distant past and present – have helped shape my ideas since I first began research in the history of analytic philosophy; and I would like to take this opportunity of thanking the following, in particular: J.L. Ackrill, David Bell, Geoffrey Cantor, Wonbae Choi, Martin Davies, Dorothy Edgington, Anthony Grayling, Peter Hacker, Jonathan Hodge, Peter Millican, Peter Mott, Gianluigi Oliveri, Peter Simons, John Skorupski, Barry Smith, Roger White, David Wiggins, Adrian Wilson, and two anonymous readers of the penultimate version. Some may be horrified at the result of their influence, and no one bears more than a tiny responsibility for the deficiencies of the book; but I have been grateful for their comments, criticism and encouragement. I would also like to thank the students at Sheffield, Birkbeck and more recently at Leeds who have attended my lectures and classes on Frege over the last nine years and whose questions have made me more aware of what needs to be explained and how best to go about it. I owe a particular debt to Colin

Haycraft, who encouraged the book from the beginning and whose tragic death 18 months ago deprived the academic world of a publisher whose personal interest and commitment was deeply appreciated. I am grateful to Deborah Blake and Anthony Grayling for overseeing the latter stages of publication.

My greatest debt is to Sharon Macdonald, whose intellectual influence and practical support has been enormous, and to whom this book is dedicated, and our three children, Tara, Thomas and Harriet. They have all suffered, and the family time that was lost in the writing of this book is not easy to justify. The two eldest children would occasionally read sentences from pages left lying around and in baffled amusement pronounce them 'nonsense'; but I have been able to draw some comfort in the confirmation it provided of just what lengthy initiation into logic and philosophy is required to even start to appreciate what 'sense' involves.

January 1996   Michael Beaney

To Sharon, with love

Introduction

Lack of historical sense is the family failing of all philosophers ... what is needed from now on is *historical philosophizing*, and with it the virtue of modesty. (Nietzsche, 'Of First and Last Things' (1878), §2; *Human, All Too Human*, p. 13.)

Analytic philosophy is now firmly established as the central philosophical tradition in the English-speaking world; yet it is only recently, with the centenaries of its seminal publications already upon us, that investigation of its historical origins and development has been seriously advocated and pursued. This may not be extraordinary in itself, since any successful research programme, in either its pioneering infancy or its dominant maturity, will be more concerned with results than with the source and evolution of its assumptions and methods; but it does deserve explanation when set against the emerging appreciation in the 19th century of the importance of an historical understanding of the formation and articulation of our intellectual beliefs (to which Nietzsche, amongst others, gave such eloquent – though in Nietzsche's case, sometimes also ironic – expression). Any attempt to inject historical self-consciousness into the analytic tradition, then, has to face the apparent tension between the development of analytic philosophy itself and its own intellectual context.

The explanation of this must inevitably focus on the revolution in logic instigated, in particular, by Gottlob Frege, and consolidated, most notably, by Bertrand Russell and Ludwig Wittgenstein. The invention of a new and much more powerful conceptual system is bound to lead its early proponents to occupy themselves primarily with its *use* – reformulating and providing fresh solutions to old and intractable problems. Only when those solutions have been properly developed, and their range and implications appreciated, can questions be raised about their own dependence on the new conceptual system, and the origins, nature and value of that system as a whole. Historical questions may justifiably be submerged in the euphoria of actually operating the new system, but as that system itself comes under scrutiny, they will reappear in a more urgent form.

The short answer to the apparent tension noted above, then, is that we are only now in a position to attempt the relevant historical investigation; and it is one aim of the present work, in providing an account of Frege's philosophy, to make a contribution to this. But there is clearly more to say about the tension itself, and the longer answer can only be provided by actually pursuing this investigation in an appropriately self-conscious way. In this introductory chapter, I briefly consider the general issue as to the relationship of analytic philosophy to the history of philosophy, outlining my own historiographical stance (§0.1), before locating Fregean logic in the picture, and highlighting the main themes of my account – in particular, my central concern with Frege's conception of sense (§0.2). In the final section, I show how Frege's own repudiation of the historical approach is misguided, and comment on the implications for the project pursued here (§0.3).

0.1 Analytic Philosophy and History

Analytic philosophy has frequently been criticized not simply for its lack of interest in its own origins and development, but more fundamentally, for its explicit repudiation of considerations that are 'merely historical'. The criticism involved here raises deeper issues than the tension we initially described might suggest. For analytic philosophy has been seen not merely as *ahistorical*, but as *anti-historical*. Analytic philosophy did not simply arise from the endeavours to make use of a new and more powerful logical system. From the beginning, these endeavours were embedded in a distinctly philosophical project, which involved the forthright rejection of certain preceding views, amongst them the historicism that had emerged in the 19th century, whilst attempting to demonstrate the objective foundations of various philosophical disciplines, through the employment of a robust sense of realism inspired by the successes of the physical sciences. To an extent, the 'revolution' that occurred was very Cartesian, an essentially foundational project fostered, in this case, by the new logic, just as Descartes had been motivated by the new mathematical physics of the 17th century. Analytic philosophy offered another fresh start – a further break with the past – and since it was based on *logic*, which was assumed to be *a priori*, the dismissal of historical considerations could be taken as justified.

However, just as in the case of Descartes, the supposed break with the past turned out to be much less extensive than initially thought. If Descartes made use of certain scholastic ideas and principles in his arguments (notably in his proof of the existence of God in the third Meditation), then Frege and Russell equally took over terminology and conceptions that were then part of the standard philosophical tradition.[1] The Kantian co-ordinates of *a priori / a posteriori* and *analytic / synthetic* were only slightly modified to accommodate the new logic (the disagreement with Kant over the status of arithmetic operated *within* this framework); and in particular, the fundamental conception of logic as a priori and absolute was never questioned. Analytic philosophy may have seen itself as ahistorical, then, but this does not mean that it cannot itself be understood historically. Indeed, some sense of its historical presuppositions is required if it is to be understood at all.

But is it the task of an *analytic* philosopher to engage in this historical investigation? This raises the question as to the relationship between analytic philosophy and the history of philosophy. Analytic philosophers themselves, of course, have written extensively on their great predecessors, both within and without their own tradition. But they have often been criticized for lacking any genuine historical sense; and a distinction has come to be drawn between *rational reconstructions*, which present the thought of a past philosopher as coherently as possible from a modern perspective, selecting those topics that remain of relevance today, and *historical reconstructions*, which attempt to see the issues as they were then perceived, being as sensitive as possible to the wider social, cultural and intellectual environment of the philosopher.[2] But does this then not present a dilemma to the historian of philosophy? Which endeavour should they undertake?

One's immediate thought, however, is that the dilemma is spurious. As Richard Rorty has put it, 'We should do both of these things, but do them separately' (1984: p. 49). Given the ever increasing academic division of labour, there would seem to be no reason why philosophers should not be free simply to choose which enterprise to engage in. But this relativist ploy only delays the problem. For any useful historical reconstruction requires skill in contemporary rational argument, and any convincing rational reconstruction requires sensitivity to the historical context. Rorty himself later admits that 'the two genres can never be *that* independent', and notes that the kinds of concern that each involves 'should be seen as moments in a continuing movement around the hermeneutic circle, a circle one has to have gone round a good many times before one can begin to do *either* sort of reconstruction' (1984: p. 53, n. 1). However, if the two enterprises are, after all, mutually dependent, then there is no real sense in which they can be done separately. A rational reconstruction is better the more it is historically informed, and vice versa; so that ideal work in the history of philosophy combines both.

However, whilst the dilemma can be 'solved' at the level of the ideal ('We should do both of these things, and do them together'), there is, I think, a more manageable project that offers a practical solution to the dilemma. Let us call this project (albeit somewhat *im*modestly) *dialectical reconstruction*, which, in alluding to an Hegelian conception of the history of philosophy, also suggests that what is required is a *synthesis* of rational and historical reconstruction. The guiding idea is that any philosophical system is an attempt to reconcile certain fundamental tensions in our natural ways of looking at the world, ourselves and their interrelationships. Philosophizing is by its very nature *dialectical*, a process of synthesizing some particular viewpoint and what appears to be in conflict with it. Given that philosophizing is a conceptual process, then two features deserve emphasis. Firstly, as a *process*, it has an essentially *historical* dimension, in the sense that it *develops* through time. Philosophers can make improvements on their predecessors by furthering the dialectical process. Philosophical positions are not eternally given, towards which different philosophers take up varying attitudes and for which they construct better or worse arguments.[3] Those positions themselves evolve, and need to be understood as historical phenomena. Secondly, as a *conceptual* activity, philosophy leads – to some extent – an independent and autonomous existence, grounded in, but not determined by, the wider social and cultural environment. It may not be necessary to know the full details of a philosopher's life, and the influences upon them, to grasp the essential structure of their thought. Provided there is some minimum shared background (which may be partly constituted by a similar philosophical training – immersion in the same literature, for example), then a careful reading of the key texts may be all that is needed to appreciate the fundamental problems that a philosopher was grappling with and the conflicts that motivated them. This may be sufficient both to expound their thought fairly and also to carry the debate further.

Doing justice to both of these features, then, dialectical reconstruction will involve tracing the *development* of certain themes and ideas in the history of philosophy whilst allowing that their *selection* may be justifiably governed by present concerns (philosophy being a reasonably continuous and autonomous discipline). By focussing on the *tensions* within philosophical systems, one can appreciate both the drive of philosophical theorizing, as well as the strengths and weaknesses of their attempted resolution.[4] However many 'influences' on a philosopher's thought one considers (and more will require study the less there is a shared background), in the end it is the issues themselves – as they are found in the texts – that demand careful analysis and assessment. But the result of this must not be a series of loosely related essays on topics that the philosopher treats, but a presentation that exhibits the dynamic development of their thought, the interconnections between its elements, and the underlying tensions that motivated it and might still remain.[5] If these requirements are fulfilled, dialectical reconstruction can succeed in being both *historical* (appreciating the *evolution* of ideas, though not necessarily every aspect of the social and cultural context) and *rational* (*thinking through*, rather than merely reporting, the issues), whilst remaining on a modest scale.

It may have been Hegel who introduced the dialectical method into the history of philosophy, at the beginning of the 19th century, but his own application of it was vitiated by his combination of historical determinism and absolute idealism, reflected in his belief that history embodied the inevitable progress to self-consciousness of the universal *Geist*.[6] It was against this Hegelian historicism that Nietzsche for one reacted in the latter half of the 19th century. In one of his earliest essays, 'On the uses and disadvantages of history for life' (1874), Nietzsche asserts, in a remark that would be warmly endorsed by the contemporary analytic philosopher: 'If you are to venture to interpret the past you can do so only out of the fullest exertion of the vigour of the present' (p. 94). However, whilst analytic philosophy emerged outrightly opposed to any form of historicism, Nietzsche was more concerned with striking a balance: 'the unhistorical and the historical are necessary in equal measure for the health of an individual, of a people and of a culture' (ibid., p. 63). In his later work, it is an historicism aimed at revealing our present condition that guides his thought. In *Human, All Too Human* (as the quote at the beginning of this introduction shows), Nietzsche condemns the lack of historical sense of most philosophers, and commends instead *historical philosophizing*, pursued with the awareness that there is no overarching perspective or ultimate goal. It is this rationally moderated and non-teleological historicism that the project of dialectical reconstruction must attempt to encapsulate.

Since Hegel, historical philosophy (in varying forms) has always maintained a strong presence in Continental Europe, especially in Germany, from Marx, Dilthey and Nietzsche through Heidegger to Gadamer and modern hermeneutics. In Britain, Collingwood was the most prominent in advocating an historical approach to philosophy, but his work was largely eclipsed by the dominance of the analytic movement.[7] More recently, however, philosophers brought up *within* the analytic tradition have begun to write the kind of historical philosophy endorsed here;[8] and this is particularly significant, for it suggests that the gulf between analytic philosophy and 'continental' thought may finally be bridged. Certainly, the clarity and rigour of analytic philosophy combined with the historical sensitivity and critical self-consciousness of hermeneutics should make for a powerful new force. Whether such an approach could be applied in the field of *logic* – which might seem especially resistant to historical treatment – will be considered in the next section.

0.2 The Development of Fregean Logic

Ever since Aristotle first carved it out, logic has always had a unique but contested relationship with philosophy as a whole. Logic has been seen as the foundation of philosophy, as a branch of philosophy, or as merely a tool of philosophy (cf. §1.3 below). The dispute over the *status* of logic depends, of course, on the debate about its *nature*. Conceived as simply the study of valid reasoning, for example, logic might indeed seem useful merely as a *tool* of philosophy. Conceived as providing us with the 'laws of thought', with knowledge of the workings of our 'reason', it might count as a *branch* of philosophy. Conceived as both of these things, together with the assumption that reason itself (reflected in thought and language) mirrors the structure of the world, it might be regarded as the *foundation* of philosophy.

Clearly, the answer that is given here determines the shape and content of a *history of logic*. If logic were either a branch or the foundation of philosophy, then the history of logic could be investigated in exactly the same way, and be as philosophically relevant, as the history of philosophy generally. If logic were merely the study of valid reasoning, on the other hand, and assuming that our patterns of reasoning have not significantly changed over the last two and a half millennia (perhaps because the structure of language, or the world itself, has not substantially changed), then there would be no reason to suppose that logic possessed an *essentially* historical dimension. It might well be that our *theories* have improved over the years, but this would simply mean that they have come to encompass greater areas of our reasoning, so that a history of logic would just be the story of our progress towards a more comprehensive theory. As many are tempted to think in the case of science, knowledge of the history of the subject would not be necessary either to understand logical theory or to use or develop it effectively.

However, even a brief acquaintance with textbooks on logic shows that philosophical assumptions are made in formalizing arguments, and that there is often disagreement on how particular types of proposition or argument *should* be characterized. The proliferation, since the time of Frege, of various non-classical logics (such as intuitionistic and quantum logic) reveals, even more fundamentally, profound disagreement over the logical laws themselves. Logic as it is now practised covers not only formalization and proof, but also their justification, and the critique of alternative theories. Modern logic now involves not only formal logic, but also mathematical logic, philosophical logic, philosophy of logic, philosophy of language, philosophy of mathematics and philosophy of science, although all of these areas overlap with one another and cannot actually be defined independently. Even in its infancy, logical formalization revealed philosophical preconceptions, though these were not always explicitly recognized to the extent that would justify regarding, say, Aristotle as himself a philosopher of logic or language. (I take up this controversial issue in chapter 1.) Any history of logic, then, would not simply involve the story of the development of a more and more comprehensive logical theory, or set of logical theories, but also, more importantly, provide an account of our changing *conceptions* of logic – the philosophical assumptions involved, the perceived nature and value of logic, and its evolving place within philosophy as a whole.

Any position that might be adopted on the debate over the nature and status of logic, then, would itself embody philosophical assumptions, so that a history of logic could hardly eschew philosophical discussion – clarifying and tracing the evolution of these assumptions. (In the same way, the history and philosophy of science are intimately related, each involving the other to the extent that they are frequently treated as just one discipline.) Indeed, the very fact that this debate has been so fiercely contested since the time of Aristotle, and that logic has now become so inseparable from many contemporary philosophical projects, suggests that a study of its history would pay rich philosophical dividends. But this is not to say that one's own conception of logic cannot itself help shape the way the historical investigation is pursued. Here in particular, a project of dialectical reconstruction might prove effective. The evolution of ideas can be elucidated from one's current perspective, and that current perspective can in turn be refined by the investigation of its historical development, in the 'continuing movement around the hermeneutic circle' to which Rorty referred.

There is, though, a deeper reason why an appreciation of the history of logic is philosophically enriching. For the evolution of ideas never proceeds in a linear fashion, each stage emerging smoothly out of the previous one. There are often major discontinuities, and whilst some tensions and confusions may be removed at each stage, yet further ones will appear, and it is rarely the case that a later conception is superior in every respect to an earlier one. (This is precisely the message of the dialectical process.) More importantly, it is only through an awareness of the advantages and disadvantages of both the earlier and later conceptions (the 'thesis' and 'antithesis') that a better conception (a 'synthesis') can be attained, locating both in a broader perspective that offers some kind of resolution of the differences. In logic, as in philosophy generally, reflecting carefully on past achievements is itself to extend our understanding.

In the history of logic there have been two dominant logical systems – Aristotelian logic (syllogistic theory) and Fregean (modern) logic. The relationship between them is by no means simply that of primitive to more sophisticated (though modern logic is indeed more sophisticated), nor is it simply that Fregean logic *replaced* traditional logic, rebuilding from scratch and ignoring all the old ideas. Modern logic is neither completely different nor a straightforward expansion of the old, and a detailed comparison of the two yields valuable insights. The transition from one conceptual 'paradigm' to another is always fascinating, and the overthrow of syllogistic theory by Fregean logic is as important in logic as the Copernican revolution in astronomy or the change from Newtonian to quantum mechanics in physics. To appreciate the emergence of modern logic, we clearly need to recover the previous 'paradigm'; and I provide an account of Aristotelian logic in chapter 1. Not only does this provide the background against which the merits and superior power of modern logic can be exhibited, but also, more importantly, it allows us to approach modern logic from the right direction, helping us to avoid *reading into* its origins our own more fully developed conceptions. Those conceptions can *guide* us in our investigation, informing us where to look, but we must clearly be as sensitive to what a theory does *not* involve as we are to what it does.[9] Appreciating just what was new in the emergence of Fregean logic is the aim of chapter 2.

Why, in particular, though, might our understanding of the emergence of modern logic be obscured by our present conceptions? One characteristic feature of recent analytic philosophy has been its concern with *theories of meaning*, which take for granted a *semantic* conception of logic, seen as originating in Frege's work. In his pioneering book on Frege, Michael Dummett went so far as to *identify* Fregean logic with the theory of meaning (see e.g. 1981a: p. 669). In order to develop his logical system, Dummett argued, Frege had to give a semantic, and not merely a syntactic, analysis of our language, and hence had to provide 'the foundation of a theory of meaning' (ibid., p. 2). But these remarks are, at the very least, misleading, for most of Frege's reflections on language (even supposing they amount to a 'theory of meaning') occurred *after* the development of his 'Begriffsschrift', and as we shall see, even his later ideas were not fully thought through.[10] Care is needed, therefore, in tracing the *evolution* of Frege's ideas; and it is one of the aims of this work to explore in some detail the relationship between the development of a logical system and the achievement of semantic insights. Here too there is a hermeneutic circle in play, so that whilst it would be wrong to denigrate Dummett's 'rational reconstructions', we must nevertheless avoid barging into the circle with our modern semantic baggage.

It is, however, fair to say that it is only in Frege's work that a *semantic* conception of sense emerged. On this conception, two propositions have the same 'sense' – or 'content' as Frege called it in his early work – iff (if and only if) they are *logically equivalent*. As I show in §1.4, this apparently natural conception of sense was not one that Aristotle possessed, despite the fact that he recognized that members of certain pairs of propositions could be inferred one from the other. The conception emerged in Frege's work when he felt the need to *justify* his logical theory, the use of function-argument analysis yielding different results from that of traditional subject-predicate analysis. Subject/predicate position, Frege argued, was of no *logical* significance: all that was important was that feature of the meaning of a proposition that was relevant to its logical implications, and this feature Frege called its 'conceptual content'. Even after his early notion of 'conceptual content' had given way to the notions of 'Sinn' and 'Bedeutung', Frege continued to insist on the distinction between that part of the meaning of an expression with which logic is concerned – its 'sense' – and what he called 'illumination' ('Beleuchtung') or 'colouring' ('Färbung').[11]

However, the very fact that Frege's notion of 'content' did later give way to the notions of 'Sinn' and 'Bedeutung' suggests that there is a more complex story to tell here; and in fact I shall argue that there is a fundamental *tension* in Frege's conception of sense, between a coarse-grained *semantic* and a fine-grained *epistemic* conception. Very roughly, two propositions have the same *semantic* sense iff the truth of one implies the truth of the other, and vice versa; whilst two propositions have the same *epistemic* sense iff our *recognition* of the truth of one implies our *recognition* of the truth of the other, and vice versa. To use Frege's canonical example, knowing the truth of 'The Morning Star is a body illuminated by the Sun' does not entail knowing the truth of 'The Evening Star is a body illuminated by the Sun', so that the two propositions have different epistemic senses.[12] Whilst Frege's 'official' conception was epistemic, the analyses that he provides in his work require a semantic conception, and the tension runs deep in his philosophy, being reflected, for example, in his uncertainty about the status of Axiom V of the *Grundgesetze* (which Frege held responsible for the contradiction that Russell discovered in his system; see §§ 7.2 and 8.1 below), and in the problems generated by his later account of 'timeless' thoughts (see §7.5 below). The semantic conception that emerged in Frege's work, then, was insufficiently worked through by Frege to justify attributing to him a theory of meaning in the modern sense – which is not to deny that there are elements in his thought that can be used in constructing such a theory.

The motivation behind Frege's development of his new logic came not from a desire to provide a theory of meaning for natural languages but rather from the desire to secure the foundations of arithmetic, in particular, to demonstrate logicism – the thesis that arithmetic is reducible to logic. Such a project required a more powerful logical system than was then available, and it was his development of such a logic that Frege presented in his first book, the *Begriffsschrift*, published in 1879. The importance of this work, however, was not immediately recognized; so before Frege utilized his new logical system to formally demonstrate logicism, he first provided a philosophical prolegomenon, offering a critique of previous conceptions of number, and sketching his own theory informally. This was published in 1884 as *Die Grundlagen der Arithmetik*. The detailed formal proofs were provided in *Grundgesetze der Arithmetik*, volume I appearing in 1893 and volume II in 1903. I provide an account of Frege's logicist project in chapters 3 and 4.

The *Begriffsschrift*, the *Grundlagen* and the *Grundgesetze* were the three books that Frege published in his lifetime, and their overriding goal was to establish logicism. So it is extraordinary that until very recently, discussion of Frege's philosophy – more specifically, his ideas in the philosophy of logic and language and in epistemology and metaphysics – have largely ignored his logicism. Where there has been discussion of his philosophy of mathematics, it has generally been separated off from the rest of his philosophy.[13] As well as these three books, Frege also published a number of papers, three of the most important being 'Function and Concept', 'On Concept and Object' and 'On Sense and Reference', all published in the years 1891 and 1892, i.e. after the *Grundlagen* and before the *Grundgesetze*. Their aim, though it is admittedly not explicitly stated, is to provide philosophical support to the distinctions relied upon in his logicist project; yet they are discussed as if they are entirely self-standing essays in the new field of philosophical logic.[14] By discussing these papers in the light of Frege's logicism, I hope to show just what relation they did have to the rest of Frege's work.

What will emerge from chapter 4, where I offer an exposition of the positive part of Frege's logicist project, is the fundamental role that his logical analyses and definitions of number expressions play in his logicism; and much of Frege's subsequent philosophy can be seen as attempts to answer the question as to the status of these analyses and definitions. Those analyses and definitions were already in place; the ideas of his three seminal essays were attempts to *justify* them. It may well be possible to hive off these ideas from their origins in Frege's thinking about his logicism, but any attempt to modify and develop them will be impoverished, and run the risk of seriously distorting his views, if those origins are not appreciated.

Chapter 5 is the central chapter of the book. It is here that we see how Frege's logic (discussed in chapter 2) and his logicism (discussed in chapters 3 and 4) inspired his philosophical ideas. How, for example, did his famous distinction between 'Sinn' and 'Bedeutung' arise? Given his logicism, an answer can be readily given. According to his early conception, two propositions have the same 'conceptual content' iff they are logically equivalent. If Frege's logicism is correct, however, then '$2^2 = 4$' and '$2 + 2 = 4$', for example, are logically equivalent: it can be proved purely logically that if one is true, then the other is true, and vice versa.[15] Yet what we understand by each is different, which we might well express by saying that they *lack* the same 'conceptual content'. So the notion of 'content' certainly requires disambiguation. Whilst Frege believed that arithmetic was reducible to logic, he also held that arithmetic was informative, and this required an epistemic as well as a semantic conception of 'content'.

But there is a more subtle story to be told here too. As I suggest in §5.3, the ambiguity in Frege's early notion of 'content' may well have motivated his fundamental definitions of numbers as extensions of concepts. Frege was aware that those definitions could not be *derived*, which is why he officially offered them merely as stipulations, but they nevertheless require some philosophical justification and it is clear that Frege remained concerned about their status. The distinction between *Sinn* and *Bedeutung* was intended to resolve the problem. Number statements may not seem to us to be statements about extensions of concepts, but the difference lies only at the level of *sense*, not of *Bedeutung*; numbers actually *are* extensions of (logically definable) concepts. But as Frege soon realized, in the case of identity statements that lie at the base of a theory, i.e. axioms and definitions, sameness of sense is required as well as sameness of *Bedeutung*. In his final answer to the problem, therefore, Frege argued that the task of the theorist is to *reconstruct* our notions, the aim being to provide clear senses to the relevant terms where they had no clear senses before (see §5.5 below).

In chapter 6 I discuss Frege's distinction between *Sinn* and *Bedeutung* in detail. Three particular problems stand out here. Firstly, why did Frege conceive the *Bedeutung* of a sentence as its truth-value? Secondly, what was Frege's position, with regard to names, on the issue of senses without referents? Thirdly, and relatedly, does Frege's account apply as readily to 'simple' proper names as it does to definite descriptions? In all three cases, it is Frege's conception of logic that holds the key to his views; though this is not to say that those views are thereby justified. As I show, to do justice to the issues involved here, further distinctions need to be drawn, distinctions which, whilst building on the underlying schema of the distinction between *Sinn* and *Bedeutung*, in the end require revision or rejection of some of Frege's specific ideas.

According to Frege, the difficulties that arise when applying his fundamental ideas and distinctions to ordinary language show the inadequacies of ordinary language, not the deficiencies in his own views. That he took such an attitude only reinforces the point that Frege was not concerned with developing a theory of meaning for natural language. What he wished to do instead was develop an ideal logical language to *replace* ordinary language, avoiding its inadequacies and capturing 'objective thought' more faithfully; and I discuss some of the problems generated here in chapter 7.

In the final chapter I return to the issue of the tension in Frege's conception of sense, and relate this to the other fundamental tension in his philosophy, which has been more frequently discussed, between the contextualism that was manifested in the *Grundlagen* and his later endorsement of principles of compositionality. What again deserves highlighting is the differences between Frege's own views and those of analytic philosophers who came after him. The idea of analysis as a way of eliminating certain philosophical problems – by showing, in particular, that the surface form of a proposition need not commit us to the existence of objects that are the referents of constituent terms – is notable by its *absence* in Frege's work, despite the fact that such an idea cries out to be used – for example, in showing that objects are not the referents of phrases of the form 'the concept *F*'. Frege does not, in other words, pursue the eliminativist strategy that Russell was to develop so influentially in his theory of descriptions. Once again, we see how the materials are present in Frege's work for use in projects that are now seen as characteristic of analytic philosophy; yet those projects cannot themselves be read back into Frege's own work. The importance of an historical understanding is only too clear, if a fair picture of Frege's philosophy is to be achieved.

0.3 Making Sense Historically

It is often felt that to write accurately and justly about a past philosopher requires a certain amount of sympathy with their philosophical ideas. This might not seem to create a problem for the rational reconstructor, since the aim is precisely to systematize those ideas with which one does have sympathy. But such an approach runs the risk of providing a lopsided account, or at least making it inexplicable why the philosopher could ever have had the ideas with which one does *not* have sympathy. The historical reconstructor, on the other hand, in trying to make those ideas explicable, may simply deny that sympathy is required: in locating the ideas in their original context, all that is necessary is to *report* those ideas, which requires no endorsement by the reporter. But this runs the opposite risk, of providing no *rationale* for those ideas with which one does have sympathy. The dilemma might be expressed succinctly by using a distinction that lies at the base not just of analytic philosophy but of philosophy as it has been perceived by many from the time of Socrates – the distinction between logical or rational *justification* and historical or causal *explanation* (explanation of origins). By focussing on *justification*, the rational reconstructor runs the risk of providing no explanation of certain ideas, and by focussing on *explanation*, the historical reconstructor runs the risk of providing no justification of any of those ideas.[16]

How does the dialectical reconstructor avoid these twin dangers? In telling the story of a philosopher's ideas by *thinking them through*, seeing which survive (in whatever transformed way), and which are dropped (however explicitly or implicitly), placing them in a time-frame that is somewhat broader than the life-time of the philosopher and that extends to the present, the dialectical reconstructor can be regarded as providing both rational justification (of the ideas that survive) and historical explanation (of both the ideas that are dropped and the ideas that survive).

It might be objected that what is involved here is the repudiation of the distinction between justification and explanation; and it is worth noting that the distinction between rational and historical reconstruction itself presupposes this distinction. But this distinction, at least as it has typically been understood by the analytic philosopher ('justification' being of far greater importance than 'mere' historical explanation), should certainly be repudiated. There is no such thing as *ultimate justification*: justification only operates within a conceptual framework, and at a certain point (when 'justification' of the conceptual framework itself is at issue), reasons give out – the logical spade is turned – and historical understanding takes over.[17]

But such a repudiation is certainly in conflict with one of Frege's most deeply held views. For the emphasis on the distinction between logical justification and historical explanation lay at the heart of the first of his three 'fundamental principles' laid down in the *Grundlagen*: 'There must be a sharp separation of the psychological from the logical, the subjective from the objective' (p. X); and this was a principle to which he adhered throughout his life. Frege had a particular antipathy towards *psychologism* – the view that the investigation of psychological processes held the key to the justification of our beliefs; but it is clear that he regarded *any* attempt at explaining the origin of an idea as irrelevant to issues of justification. Causal, psychological and historical factors are all lumped together into one category which is opposed to that of the logical. 'The description of the origin of an idea should not be taken for a definition, nor should the account of the mental and physical conditions for becoming aware of a proposition be taken for a proof' (ibid., p. VI). Truths, Frege believed, were independent of how anyone came to apprehend them. Were this not so, then there would be as many different truths as there were individual acts of apprehension, and objectivity would be destroyed.

> The historical mode of investigation, which seeks to trace the development of things from which to understand their nature, is certainly legitimate; but it also has its limitations. If everything were in continual flux and nothing remained fixed and eternal, then knowledge of the world would cease to be possible and everything would be thrown into confusion. We imagine, it seems, that concepts originate in the individual mind like leaves on a tree, and we suppose that their nature can be understood by investigating their origin and seeking to explain them psychologically through the working of the human mind. But this conception makes everything subjective, and taken to its logical conclusion, abolishes truth. What is called the history of concepts is really either a history of our knowledge of concepts or of the meanings [*Bedeutungen*] of words. Often it is only through enormous intellectual work, which can last for hundreds of years, that knowledge of a concept in its purity is achieved, by peeling off the alien clothing that conceals it from the mind's eye. What are we then to say when someone, instead of carrying on this work where it still seems incomplete, ignores it entirely, and enters the nursery or takes himself back to the earliest conceivable stage of human development, in order there to discover, like John Stuart Mill, some gingerbread or pebble arithmetic! It remains only to ascribe to the flavour of the cake a special meaning for the concept of number. This is surely the exact opposite of a rational procedure and in any case as unmathematical as it could possibly be. No wonder that mathematicians want nothing to do with it! Instead of finding concepts in particular purity near to their imagined source, everything is seen blurred and undifferentiated as through a fog. It is as though someone who wanted to learn about America tried to take himself back to the position of Columbus as he caught his first dubious glimpse of his supposed India. Admittedly, such a comparison proves nothing; but it hopefully makes my point. It may well be that the history of discoveries is useful in many cases as preparation for further research; but it should not aspire to take its place. (*GL*, pp. VII-VIII; cf. *RHC*, p. 109.)

If Frege is right here, then it presents an intriguing problem for the historian of philosophy. Imagine someone wanting to provide an account of Frege's ideas – in particular, let us say, of the distinction between *Sinn* and *Bedeutung*. If this distinction is valid, then its origins in the work of Frege are entirely irrelevant. What is important is its use within some fully developed and correct theory. A proper account of Frege's (correct) ideas, then, need say nothing at all about Frege himself. Such an attitude would seem particularly appropriate if, as is so in the case of the distinction between *Sinn* and *Bedeutung*, his ideas, though on the right track, require revision and development.[18]

Of course, we might mean by 'Frege's ideas' the ideas as Frege himself saw them. Using Frege's own distinction, we might suggest that whilst the analytic philosopher (or rational reconstructor) would be concerned with the *referents* of Frege's philosophical expressions, the historian of philosophy would be concerned with their *senses* – with how Frege himself apprehended those referents. But as Frege himself remarks, those referents might not necessarily have revealed themselves to their discoverer in all their purity – perhaps the discoverer only saw them through a fog dimly; so again there would seem to be little value in the historical approach so conceived.

Now Frege regarded himself, of course, not as the *originator* of a number of important ideas – ideas that were to provide the basis for the development of analytic philosophy – but as the philosopher who had finally managed to achieve knowledge of the concept of number 'in its purity'. With an Hegelian arrogance, Frege clearly saw his own work on the foundations of mathematics as the culmination of centuries of 'enormous intellectual work'. Were this true, then an account of Frege's *ideas* would indeed be an account of *Frege's* ideas. Subsequent philosophy of arithmetic would then simply consist in the exposition and preservation of these ideas. However, as we now know, in the aftermath of Russell's paradox, Frege's work turned out to be only a *starting-point* – of the new discipline of mathematical logic.

Taking the passage from the *Grundlagen* seriously, then, Frege's own work would, at best, be regarded as of only limited value to 'real' philosophical thought, and at worst, be consigned to the waste bin of intellectual life. Fortunately for Frege, however, his underlying view is mistaken. It might seem ironical that an appreciation of Frege's greatness requires the repudiation of one of his deepest beliefs, but genuine appreciation does not preclude criticism. Justification is not the transcendent activity Frege believed: it too operates in a particular context and involves presuppositions that cannot themselves be 'justified' in the same way. This is especially obvious now that the very nature of analytic philosophy is under investigation – where questions have been raised about the 'justification' of the conceptual paradigm itself. Here there is no option but to look at its whole emergence and development historically. Concepts do not exist in a Platonic realm waiting to be revealed in their purity by the culminator of centuries of intellectual effort – whether an Hegelian Titan or even the fortunate dwarf who sits on the shoulders of the giants of the past. Concepts have their life in human linguistic practices, and are *acquired* by being immersed in those practices and *explained* by understanding those practices.

Most importantly, as we noted in the previous section, logic itself is a human practice with its own historical development. In drawing his absolute distinction between logical justification and historical explanation, Frege assumed that logical laws were transcendentally given. As he famously wrote in his foreword to the *Grundgesetze*, the laws of logic, as the laws of truth, 'are not psychological laws, but boundary stones set in an eternal foundation, which our thought can overflow but not dislodge. And because of this they are authoritative for our thought if it wants to attain truth. They do not stand in the relation to thought that the laws of grammar stand to language, so that they express the essence of our human thought and change as it changes.' (*GG*, p. xvi.) However, as Wittgenstein was later to argue, the laws of logic are indeed no more than deeply entrenched rules of grammar. But this is not to say that they have no authority over us. For if we wish to engage in the practices of which they are the rules, then we must abide by them. To argue 'illogically' is not to argue at all. The bridges that hold up our mental lives collapse if the laws of logic are contradicted. Nor is it to say that they are merely 'psychological' – viz. 'subjective' – laws. Frege operated with too crude a subjective/ objective dichotomy, leaving out the whole area of the *intersubjective*, which philosophers in the 20th century have, in different ways, and with varying degrees of success, been trying to characterize in developing a more moderate form of objectivism.

But such a conception does allow that the laws of logic may change, or at least be *refined* and their applicability restricted in certain ways. Only if they were somehow repudiated overnight would Frege be right that there would ensue 'a hitherto unknown kind of madness' (ibid.). Once again, what we have here is a hermeneutic circle. We reflect on our linguistic practices, and express those reflections in grammatical and logical rules, which in turn shape and direct our linguistic practices. Perhaps when regimented in a certain way, the limitations of certain practices are seen more clearly, and as a result new practices arise, which are in turn codified and even reconciled with the original practices in some more sophisticated theory. Codification (from the writing of dictionaries to the construction of logical systems) is both descriptive and prescriptive: the very act of describing a certain practice has a prescriptive effect, feeding back into the linguistic practices. The understanding of the foundations of logic, then, cannot but be historical, attempting to recover previous practices and appreciating how new ones developed.

As we have noted, the two most significant events in the history of logic were Aristotle's and Frege's codifications. But neither gave us *the* logic, or even *part* of *the* logic, since there is no such thing as *the* logic of human discourse.[19] Of course, to understand a *particular* logical theory involves seeing how the whole system works – what its axioms and rules are, and how formalization and proof operate; and I have certainly sought to show in this book how both Aristotle's and Frege's logical systems work. But the philosophical understanding of logic itself – as opposed to particular logical systems – requires a deeper, historical understanding, though one that must undoubtedly involve the detailed appreciation of particular logical systems.

If the understanding of logic requires an historical approach, then so too does our understanding of conceptions of *sense*. Take the semantic conception once again. Two propositions have the same semantic sense iff they are logically equivalent. On the assumption that logical laws are transcendentally given, then senses too are transcendentally determined; and in his late paper, 'Thoughts', Frege did indeed draw the bizarre conclusion that senses inhabit a separate realm of their own, a view that I call in §7.5 Frege's *semainomenalism*. But if logical equivalence varies according to the logical system, then what counts as the 'sense' of a proposition will also vary. This is not to repudiate objectivity – Frege mistakenly thought that *objectivity* demanded *objects* construed Platonistically – but merely to locate that objectivity in the practices of a linguistic community.

To understand Frege's conception of sense, then, involves understanding the practice that he established; and there is no substitute for *thinking through* his ideas in their historical development. This can be regarded as compatible not with the first 'fundamental principle' of the *Grundlagen*, but with the second, the context principle: 'The meaning of a word must be asked for in the context of a proposition, not in isolation' (p. X). As it stands, this principle applies only to words; but as Frege himself was clearly aware, what *thought* is expressed by a proposition is itself dependent on its context of use. The interpretation of the principle, as well as the question as to Frege's continued adherence to it in his later work, is controversial; but it captures an important insight that has informed subsequent philosophy of language, and suitably generalized, can be regarded as motivating the present project. For it is only by considering Frege's philosophical ideas in their historical context that their content can properly be apprehended.

In seeking to understand the work of a past philosopher, then, the dialectical reconstructor must become a kind of historical anthropologist, attempting to see things as they saw them, yet expressing those perceptions and critically charting the evolution of their ideas using the resources of the present. In establishing his new logical practices, Frege was indeed *making sense* – in forging new conceptual tools, he shaped the discourse in which philosophers now talk of 'sense'; and in attempting to retrace his steps, we can both deepen our understanding of that discourse and further refine it. With the allusions in the title of this book in mind, then, in making sense of Frege's philosophy, as dialectical reconstructors, we too are making sense in qualified accord with Frege's pioneering achievements.

1. The Logical Background

O insensata cura de' mortali,
quanto son difettivi silogismi
quei che ti fanno in basso batter l'ali.
                    (Dante, *Paradiso*, XI 1-3.)

[O senseless care of mortals,
how defective are the syllogisms
which make you beat your wings down.][1]

Whilst Frege is the father of modern logic, it is Aristotle who invented logic itself. Indeed, not only did he construct the first formal system, but the system he constructed, except for a period of rivalry with Stoic logic, dominated the intellectual world for twenty-two centuries, right up until Frege's time. Any account of the revolution effected by modern logic, then, and the development of Frege's philosophy as part of this, must begin with Aristotle's theory of the syllogism. It is not just that this introduces the issues concerning the nature, role and scope of logic, which are crucial to an understanding of Frege's work; analysis of Aristotelian logic also highlights key features of Fregean logic that might not otherwise be appreciated. In particular, my aim in the next chapter is to show how Frege's early notion of 'conceptual content' was formulated through an awareness of differences between the two systems and a perceived need to *justify* the new one. Since it is 'conceptual content' that later bifurcated into 'Sinn' and 'Bedeutung', any account of these notions must be set against this logical background.

After a sketch of the emergence and nature of the syllogism (§1.1), I elucidate the operation of proof in syllogistic theory (§1.2), and then explore in turn certain epistemological and semantic aspects of Aristotelian logic (§§ 1.3 and 1.4). My purpose is to demonstrate that Aristotle developed a coherent system of logic *without* a conception of 'sense' (as that might now be understood), something that has implications for an appreciation of Frege's own work. In the final section, I leap through the intervening centuries to bring us to Frege's *Begriffsschrift*.

1.1 The Syllogism

In the *Sophistici elenchi*, Aristotle remarks that before him, logic as a discipline did not exist, and he had 'to work things out over a long time by trial and error' (183b34-184b3).[2] The core of his logical theory is contained in the *Prior Analytics*, and although scholars disagree over its dating, few deny that in its final form it is one of the mature works of his *Organon*. Certainly, the care taken in formalization and presentation suggest a long gestation. Details of this period are unknown, but it is possible to sketch some of the preceding developments that facilitated the emergence of syllogistic theory.[3]

Since logic involves reflection upon forms of reasoning, it presupposes the establishment of those forms. Over two centuries of argumentation were available to Aristotle, from Thales, whom Aristotle himself called the founder of natural philosophy (*Metaphysics*, 983b20), to Plato, under whom Aristotle studied; and by the time of Socrates, self-consciousness about reasoning had also evolved. Plato occasionally states principles in his dialogues (e.g. a principle of opposites in the *Republic*, 436b), and his characterization of the sophists as purveyors of fallacious arguments in the *Euthydemus* reveals concern with correctness of reasoning. These fallacious arguments or 'sophisms' were later analysed by Aristotle in the *Sophistici elenchi*, and he is clearly drawing on a tradition of public disputation.

Socratic enquiry and the search for definitions were also important, and these were refined by Plato into the notion of 'dialectic' explained in the later dialogues.[4] This notion, applied to the method of collection and division (*collecting* things generically, and then *dividing* them by a succession of dichotomies into species), influenced Aristotle in his invention of the syllogism by suggesting a chain of terms related by class-inclusion.[5] Aristotle saw his own procedure as an improvement on Plato's, which he criticizes in the *Prior Analytics* (I 31; 46a31-b40), calling the division by genera a 'weak syllogism, since it begs the point which it is required to prove' (46a33-4). His idea was that the division that is effected is already determined by the definition desired, and hence cannot be considered to *prove* anything. As we shall see, Aristotle regarded the ability to function as a *proof* as an essential feature of the syllogism.

Developing a logical system, however, involves more than a critique of existing forms of reasoning: it also requires formalization and axiomatization within a given area. Aristotle's *De Interpretatione* shows that he was interested in propositions which either affirm or deny that a predicate applies to a subject, and more specifically, with the relationships between universal and particular propositions ('All *A*'s are *B*' and 'Some *A*'s are *B*'), as captured in the traditional square of opposition. It was in the systematic clarification of these relationships – between what I shall call *syllogistic propositions* – that Aristotelian logic arose. (For details, see Appendix 1.)

Although Aristotle indicates at the beginning of the *Prior Analytics* (24a11) that his concern is with proof or demonstration (*apodeixis*), he in fact offers his theory of the syllogism as a characterization of valid argument in general, proof being a special kind of valid argument or syllogism where the premises are both true and grounded (cf. 24b9-10, 25b28-31), an issue taken up in the *Posterior Analytics* (see §1.3 below). Initially, Aristotle defines a syllogism as 'a form of words [*logos*] in which certain things are assumed and something other than the things assumed follows necessarily from their being so' (24b18-20; my tr.). By 'from their being so', as Aristotle himself explains, 'I mean that it is because of them that the conclusion follows; and by this I mean that there is no need of any further term to render the conclusion necessary' (24b20-2).

If we ignore limiting cases where the conclusion repeats one of the premises, what we have here is a reasonable, if informal, characterization of a valid argument with two or more premises. However, in syllogistic theory, a syllogism is more than just a valid argument: it also involves a certain relationship between its parts. It is tempting to interpret Aristotle as having in mind a further *epistemological* criterion – that in a proper syllogism the premises can be known without the conclusion being known, and hence that a syllogism may *teach* us something. This is how the Peripatetics interpreted Aristotle, as their disagreement with the Stoic logicians shows (see §1.3 below). But Aristotle himself provides a 'general principle' that is purely *logical*: 'we shall never have any syllogism proving that one term is predicated of another unless some middle term is assumed which is related in some way by predication to each of the other two' (41a2-5). This can be illustrated by considering the syllogism traditionally called *Barbara*:

(BB) All *A's* are *B*, All *B's* are *C*; therefore All *A's* are *C*.

'*B*' represents the 'middle term', which, in mediating between '*A*' and '*C*', links the premises and enables the conclusion to be derived.

According to Aristotle, syllogistic propositions are essentially of subject-predicate form. But since expressions of the form '*A* is *B*' ('*A estin B*') are ambiguous, in his formalizations Aristotle generally uses '(The) *B* applies to *A*' ('*to B tō A huparchei*') instead, to make explicit which is the subject and which the predicate.[6] Strictly speaking, then, (BB) should be rephrased thus:

(BB') *B* applies to all *A*, *C* applies to all *B*; therefore *C* applies to all *A*.

However, as we shall shortly see, it is essential to Aristotle's project that the valid syllogisms of the first figure, especially *Barbara* and *Celarent*, exhibit their validity as transparently as possible, and this entails *transposing* the premises:

(BB") *C* applies to all *B*, *B* applies to all *A*; therefore *C* applies to all *A*.

Since the transitivity of the relation *applies to* is now quite obvious, the validity of the syllogism can be immediately intuited.[7] Using the notation explained in Appendix 1, then, the correct (Aristotelian) representation of *Barbara* is as follows:

(BB†) *Abc, Aab*; therefore *Aac*.

Leaving aside qualifications concerning the ordering of the premisses, though, the syllogism can be regarded as a combination of three propositions – two premisses and a conclusion – arranged in the form of a *proof*, and obeying Aristotle's 'general principle'; and this has been the traditional conception. However, some commentators, notably Lukasiewicz (1957: ch. 1) and Patzig (1968: §2 & App.), have argued that this gives the misleading impression that the premisses are *asserted*, whereas a *valid* argument merely requires that *if* the premisses are true, then the conclusion must also be true. Instead, they propose, the syllogism should be characterized as a *single* proposition in the form of a conditional, since embedding the premisses in an *if*-clause removes any suggestion that they are asserted:

(BB#) If *Abc* and *Aab*, then *Aac*.

Now Aristotle certainly allowed that there could be legitimate syllogisms with one or both premisses false (see e.g. 54b17f.); and we have already noted that he distinguished between a *syllogism* (or *valid* argument) and a *proof* (or *sound* argument, i.e. a valid argument with true premisses). But a syllogism nevertheless has the *form* of a proof – it is still an *argument* rather than a single proposition – and construing it as a conditional obscures its *deductive structure*. An argument comprises premisses and a conclusion, and a single proposition (whatever internal complexity it may have) can hardly be regarded as *valid*.[8]

But how, then, should a syllogism be characterized, if the premisses are not to be seen as asserted? The solution is to use the modern device of the *syntactic turnstile* '⊢':

(BB*) *Abc, Aab* ⊢ *Aac*.

This is read as saying that *Aac* can be derived from *Abc* and *Aab* by the rules of the relevant logical system.[9] This preserves deductive structure, without implying that the premisses are true; it merely states that a certain conclusion can be inferred from them. Understood like this, then, there is nothing wrong with the traditional construal of the syllogism.

1.2 Proof in Syllogistic Theory

In the paragraph following his initial definition of a syllogism, Aristotle goes on: 'I call a syllogism perfect if it requires nothing, apart from what is comprised in it, to make the necessary conclusion apparent; imperfect if it requires one or more propositions which, although they necessarily follow from the terms which have been laid down, are not comprised in the premisses' (24b23-6). This distinction between perfect and imperfect syllogisms is crucial to Aristotle's procedure for *proving* syllogisms. Perfect syllogisms are those valid syllogisms of the first figure, whose validity is transparent (in the manner indicated in the last section). These, then, are the *axioms* of the system; and all other valid syllogisms can be shown to be valid by 'reducing' them to perfect syllogisms (cf. 29b1-3; 40b17ff.).[10]

Aristotle has two basic methods of 'reduction': *conversion*, constituting a direct (or ostensive) proof, and *reductio ad impossibile*, constituting an indirect proof.[11] A proof of *Cesare* (*Ecb, Aab ⊢ Eac*), for example, proceeds directly:

(CS) *Ecb*, so by conversion, *Ebc*; so with *Aab Celarent* can be reached: *Ebc, Aab*; therefore *Eac*. Hence we can conclude *Eac*. (Cf. 27a5-9.)

A proof of *Baroco* (*Acb, Oab ⊢ Oac*), by contrast, proceeds indirectly:

(BR) Suppose *Aac*, then since *Acb* it follows by *Barbara* that *Aab*; but that is impossible since *Oab*; therefore *Oac* (the contradictory of *Aac*). (Cf. 27a37-b4.)

As recent commentators agree, all valid imperfect syllogisms can be proved using one or both of these methods.[12] But what has been disputed is whether the rules that these methods embody are part of syllogistic theory. Lukasiewicz (1957: §§15-16) and Patzig (1968: §27) believe that certain theorems of *propositional* logic are presupposed by Aristotle in his methods of 'reduction' and that this contradicts his view that all proofs are syllogisms (as stated e.g. in 25b30-1). (BR), for example, would be seen as presupposing the rule of contraposition:

(CPS) $(P \rightarrow Q) \rightarrow (\neg Q \rightarrow \neg P)$.

(CPS) is not itself syllogistic in form, and according to Lukasiewicz and Patzig, in a proper axiomatization, Aristotle should have formulated *all* the rules that he was using.

However, such a criticism depends on the misguided identification of syllogisms with single propositions in conditional form. In order to *prove* one proposition from another, of course some rule of inference must be recognized; but for Aristotle, imperfect syllogisms *already* have the deductive structure of proofs. All that 'reduction' does is to fill out this deductive structure: it shows *that* a syllogism *is* a syllogism (i.e. is a valid argument).[13] The premisses (to be distinguished from suppositions) and conclusion of both (CS) and (BR), for example, are precisely the premisses and conclusion of *Cesare* and *Baroco* respectively. The deductive structure has simply been elucidated. Aristotle himself seems clear enough about this, as is suggested by both his characterization of an imperfect syllogism (24b24-6; see above), and his later remarks about the 'same conditions' governing both direct and indirect proofs (I 29; cf. 42a32-5). He writes, for example, that 'we must have regard to the same terms whether it is required to prove a conclusion ostensively or to employ reduction *ad impossibile*' (45b14-15; cf. II 14). Proofs by 'reduction', then, are indeed syllogisms themselves.

It may be helpful here to draw two distinctions. Let us first distinguish between *natural syllogisms*, which are simply valid arguments satisfying Aristotle's initial definition, and *technical syllogisms*, which constitute that subset of valid arguments that fulfil Aristotle's additional logical criterion, that is, those valid arguments that possess the form of one (or a series) of the standard syllogistic moods (as set out in Appendix 1). Such technical syllogisms already have the deductive structure of a proof; so let us call the kind of proof referred to here a *syllogistic proof* (a technical syllogism constitutes such a proof when its premisses are true). This must in turn be distinguished from a *theoretical proof* – a demonstration *that* a syllogistic proof *is* a syllogistic proof. When we talk of the proof-procedure within syllogistic theory, then, we mean the mechanism of theoretical proof *that* technical syllogisms *are* technical syllogisms.

We can now clear up the confusion in Lukasiewicz's and Patzig's criticism. Providing it is appreciated what a syllogistic proof is (i.e. that it has a deductive structure), there can be no dispute that syllogistic proofs are syllogisms (both natural and technical). Nor can it be denied that theoretical proofs are *natural* syllogisms (i.e. valid arguments). The issue hinges on whether they are also *technical* syllogisms. But if by 'technical syllogism' we mean whatever has the premisses and conclusion(s) for-malizable as one (or a series) of the syllogistic moods, then, as we have seen, theoretical proofs are indeed such syllogisms. The proof expressed in (CS) may not look like the traditional formulation of *Cesare*, nor the proof in (BR) like *Baroco*; but the difference simply consists in the degree of revelation of deductive structure.

Nevertheless, is it not the case that the theoretical proof in (BR) *presupposes* (CPS), and that it is therefore a *defect* in syllogistic theory that the rule involved is not explicitly formulated? The theoretical proof certainly makes implicit use of such a rule, but why should this amount to a *fault*? It is not that there is a missing *premiss*: the argument is valid as it stands; it is just that the relevant deductive structure could be yet further elucidated. This is hardly to charge Aristotle with any *logical error*; it is simply to accuse him, unfairly, of not having invented proposi-tional logic as well.

Lukasiewicz's and Patzig's criticism, then, involves a failure to recog-nize the deductive structure of syllogistic proofs and hence their connection with the corresponding theoretical proofs. But are they still not right in accusing Aristotle of not properly axiomatizing his system? He may not have produced the neat system that some of his successors have reconstructed;[14] but that does not mean that he did not recognize what 'reduction' involved. The rules of conversion, for example, are clearly stated (see §1.4 below); and the operation of *reductio ad impossibile* is also explained (I 23; 41a23-41). Admittedly, he did not *formalize* the propositional rule involved in indirect proof; but that does not mean that the rule is not part of syllogistic theory. The rules that his methods of 'reduction' involve are essential to the workings of his logical system, and that system is coherent and admirably axiomatized as it is.[15]

Aristotle does, in fact, provide more than just an informal characterization of *reductio ad impossibile*; he also comments on its nature and status within syllogistic theory. He talks, for example, of the 'unanalysability' of arguments which are established *per impossibile*: 'The reduction *ad impossibile* can be analysed, because it is proved by a syllogism; but the rest of the argument cannot, because the conclusion is drawn from a hypothesis' (50a29-32). *Per impossibile* arguments (proving a proposition by deriving a contradiction on the supposition of its falsity), whilst counting as *natural* syllogisms (Aristotle himself refers to them as 'syllogisms', e.g. in 50b3), do not qualify as *technical* syllogisms, and this is really what he means by calling them 'unanalysable'. Of course, they can be 'analysed' within propositional logic, but then, as we have noted, it would be unfair to construe this as a criticism of Aristotle. However, he does recognize the importance of arguments *per impossibile*, remarking that they require 'further study and clear explanation' (50a39-40); and he even promises such elucidation later (50b1-2), though this is not, unfortunately, a promise he appears to have kept.[16]

As a formal system, then, Aristotle's syllogistic theory cannot fundamentally be faulted. But this is not to say that the theory has an extensive application. Certainly, from our contemporary perspective, its limitations are obvious, since *technical* syllogisms form only a small subset of *natural* syllogisms. Propositional logic has already been mentioned, although this required, and indeed received, independent development; and hence could coexist alongside syllogistic theory. More fatally for Aristotelian logic, statements of *multiple* generality (such as 'Every *A* loves some *B*') and *relational* propositions (such as '*A* is larger than *B*') also proved resistant to 'analysis'. As we shall see, it was only with the arrival of Fregean logic that satisfying treatments of these were finally provided, and this had the effect of simply swallowing up syllogistic theory.

1.3 Aristotelian Logic and Epistemology

In late antiquity, there was a well-known dispute between the Stoics, who held that logic was *part* of philosophy, the Peripatetics, who viewed logic as an *instrument* of philosophy, and the Platonists, who maintained both.[17] Now whether or not one regards the dispute itself as in the end merely verbal, the Peripatetics do appear to be following in their master's own footsteps. Aristotle's interests were *epistemological* rather than semantic, and he developed his logic more for scientific use than for the purpose of understanding the nature of reasoning.[18] It is the aim of the next section to illustrate the negative thesis – Aristotle's relative lack of concern with semantic issues, and the task of the present section to expand on the positive thesis.

The root of the disagreement between the Stoics and the Peripatetics lay in the denial by each side that the other's syllogisms really were syllogisms. The Peripatetics held that a proper syllogism should enable us to *learn* something, and argued that in the standard cases of Stoic syllogisms, such as inferences of the form 'If P then Q; but P; therefore Q', no one could legitimately claim to know the premises without knowing the conclusion. This may well be true, but it does not imply that Aristotelian syllogisms are themselves genuinely informative. The Stoics, on the other hand, in dropping the epistemological criterion, defined a syllogism as a valid argument which could be proved within their own system – of essentially propositional logic, which they were the first to develop and explore. Since Aristotelian syllogisms could not be so proved, they in turn denied that these were proper syllogisms. Neither School, then, had a fully developed conception of a valid argument; had they done so, they would have realized that Aristotelian and Stoic logic were not rivals, but complemented one other.[19]

Was Aristotle himself clear about the nature of valid argument? *Prima facie* it would seem not, since if he had been, one would not have expected the dispute to have arisen. Yet, as we have seen, he distinguishes between validity and proof, and recognizes that not every syllogism is a *technical* syllogism. So how full an appreciation of validity did he have? There are certainly passages that support the Peripatetic interpretation. Aristotle writes, for example:

> There is no reason why a man who knows both that A applies to the whole of B and again that B applies to C should not think that A does not apply to C: e.g., if he knows that every mule is sterile, and that X is a mule, he may think that X is in foal; because he does not comprehend that A applies to C, unless he considers both premises in conjunction. (67a33-8; Loeb tr.)

This conception may well be problematic (does the person *really* know both premises?), but its implication is clear. Since the obvious way of correcting the man's faulty judgement is to get him to consider both premises 'in conjunction' by presenting him with the relevant syllogism, an epistemological role for the syllogism is indeed indicated. So did Aristotle think that it was a mark of a genuine syllogism that it could be informative?

Epistemological concerns were undoubtedly a major inspiration behind Aristotle's development of syllogistic theory. His guiding vision was of the sciences as neatly axiomatized deductive systems – arranged as chains of (technical) syllogisms. The aim of the *Prior Analytics* was to set out the necessary logical structure, whilst its companion, the *Posterior Analytics*, sought to provide the philosophical rationale for the vision itself. Divided into two parts, Book I of the *Posterior Analytics* explains Aristotle's conception of *demonstration* (the method by which the scientific system is ordered) and Book II discusses the nature of the axioms. By 'proof' or 'demonstration' (*apodeixis*), Aristotle writes, he means a 'scientific syllogism' (*syllogismos epistēmonikos*), that is, 'one in virtue of which, by having it, we understand something' (71b17-19). This understanding is effected, according to Aristotle, if the premisses of the syllogism are 'true and primitive and immediate and more familiar than and prior to and explanatory of the conclusion' (71b21-2). These fundamental premisses or principles must themselves be *non*-demonstrable, Aristotle argues, since otherwise an infinite regress threatens: if we could only understand something through demonstration, and this rested on premisses that themselves needed to be understood, then we could never understand anything (72b5-73a20). Given Aristotle's *epistemological* conception of proof, the non-demonstrability of principles clearly follows; but it should be noted that on a (modern) *semantic* conception of proof, all that is required is that the premisses be true – their epistemological status is irrelevant – in which case it would be possible to 'prove' some basic proposition from premisses that are *less primitive* (epistemologically speaking).[20] There may be nothing *incoherent* about Aristotle's epistemological conception of proof, but it does need to be recognized as such, a conception that gains its legitimacy within the context of his scientific vision.

However, it would still be misleading to attribute to Aristotle the extreme Peripatetic view that the whole purpose of demonstration is to enable us to learn things. In the very first sentence of the *Posterior Analytics* he writes: 'All teaching and all intellectual learning come about from already existing knowledge' (71a1-2). But, he goes on, 'nothing, I think, prevents one from in a sense understanding and in a sense being ignorant of what one is learning; for what is absurd is not that you should know in some sense what you are learning, but that <you should know it> in this sense, i.e. in the way and sense in which you are learning it' (71b6-9). What you learn in a syllogism, then, is not the propositions themselves, which you may already know (the verb used here is *eidenai*), but the logical relations between them. As we shall see in §5.1, it is the appreciation of the connections between propositions, in an axiomatized system, that constitutes 'scientific' knowledge (*epistēmē*).

The point deserves emphasis. The Peripatetic misunderstanding of logic is a persistent confusion in the history of philosophy. It lay behind Descartes' rejection of Aristotelian logic in the 17th century. As he put it in his *Rules for the Direction of the Mind*, the syllogistic art of reasoning 'contributes nothing whatever to knowledge of the truth' (Rule Ten; p. 36); and he advocated its abandonment in favour of his own method (see §1.5

below). Locke was even more forthright. In a famous passage of the *Essay*, he wrote: 'If Syllogisms must be taken for the only proper instrument of reason and means of Knowledge, it will follow, that before *Aristotle* there was not one Man that did or could know anything by Reason; and that since the invention of Syllogisms, there is not one of Ten Thousand that doth.' But, he went on, 'God has not been so sparing to Men to make them barely two-legged Creatures, and left it to *Aristotle* to make them Rational' (IV xvii 4). However, whilst Descartes and Locke may be right in refusing to grant syllogisms privileged status, they are wrong in their consequent rejection of logic itself. As Aristotle himself recognized, elucidating the deductive structure of a certain class of inferences has, at the very least, value in the organization and articulation of a scientific system.[21]

Nevertheless, as far as the dispute with the Stoics is concerned, it does seem that Aristotle would have sided (with some qualifications) with the Peripatetics. Since Stoic syllogisms could never constitute 'proofs' as Aristotle understood them (i.e. as potential constituents in an axiomatized deductive science), then they were not genuine (technical) syllogisms. And this is presumably why Aristotle overlooked such syllogisms, and was not led into inventing propositional logic as well. His epistemological interests also explain why Aristotle failed to appreciate certain *semantic* features of his logical theory; and I consider these in the next section.

1.4 The Semantics of Conversion

As we have seen, Aristotle's two basic methods of proof are *conversion* and *reductio ad impossibile*; and his understanding of the latter was considered in §1.2. The rules of conversion are stated in chapter 2 of Book I of the *Prior Analytics*, and can be formulated as follows:

(EC) From *Eab* infer *Eba*.
(AC) From *Aab* infer *Iba*.
(IC) From *Iab* infer *Iba*.

Although these are *logical inferences*, it should be noted that by 'conversion' (*antistrophē*) Aristotle just meant the *transition* from one syllogistic proposition to another, the term 'necessary conversion' being used for logical inference. Aristotle does not state that *Oab* is *non*-convertible, for example, merely that it is 'not necessarily convertible' (since e.g. 'Some animals are not men' does not imply 'Some men are not animals'; cf. I 2); and he writes elsewhere of propositions being 'converted' into their *negations* (e.g. in II 8). However, even suggesting that Aristotle understood 'necessary conversion' as logical inference is being charitable, since he talks of propositions themselves being 'necessarily convertible' rather than the inferences in which they are involved possessing the necessity.[22] So what exactly did Aristotle understand of the semantics of conversion?

There are three further 'rules of conversion', which, for completeness, should also be noted:

(AS)   From *Aab* infer *Iab*.
(ES)   From *Eab* infer *Oab*.
(ECS) From *Eab* infer *Oba*.

(AS) and (ES) correspond to the two traditional 'rules of subalternation', and (ECS) simply follows from (EC) and (ES). In the *Topics* Aristotle appears to appreciate the two rules of subalternation (cf. 109a3-6), but he does not discuss them when developing his theory of the syllogism in the *Prior Analytics*, and hence fails to recognize the five additional *subaltern* moods that result from their use (see Appendix 1). Aristotle's failure to formulate these further rules does not imply an incoherence in syllogistic theory itself (it merely shows that his own work was slightly incomplete), but it does suggest that he had only a partial understanding of conversion. Yet is there more to it then a mere (uncharacteristic) lapse in his systematizing efforts?

There is an important difference between (EC) and (IC) on the one hand, and (AC) – and the three further rules – on the other. The modern logician would express this by saying that in the former but not the latter case, the corresponding conditionals can be strengthened to biconditionals ('*Eab* → *Eba*' to '*Eab* ↔ *Eba*', and '*Iab* → *Iba*' to '*Iab* ↔ *Iba*'). Aristotle seems to be aware that there is a difference, but it is not obvious that he has appreciated exactly what it is:

> In universal statement the negative premiss is necessarily convertible in its terms: e.g., if no pleasure is good, neither will anything good be pleasure; but the affirmative, though necessarily convertible, is so not as a universal but as a particular statement: e.g., if every pleasure is good, some good must also be pleasure. In particular statements the affirmative premiss must be convertible as particular, for if some pleasure is good, some good will also be pleasure; ... (25a5-11; Loeb tr.)

Unlike the universal negative, which is 'necessarily convertible in its terms', the universal affirmative is 'necessarily convertible ... not as a universal but as a particular statement' ('not however universally, but in part', as the Oxford tr. puts it). The Kneales have interpreted this as showing that Aristotle *did* recognize the difference between the two cases – that the universal affirmative is only 'partially convertible' (1962: p. 58). This certainly suggests that the logical relation between *Aab* and *Iba* is *weaker* than that between *Eab* and *Eba*, as captured by the modern logician in the conditional rather than biconditional. However, what Aristotle goes on to say about the *third* rule undermines this interpretation. (IC), like (EC), is also a case where the stronger *bi*conditional can be used, so one would have thought that Aristotle would also talk of it being 'necessarily convertible in its terms'. Yet he treats it like the *second* rule:

it too is only 'convertible as particular' ('in part', as the Oxford tr. again puts it). Aristotle's own understanding of a difference is characterized in terms of the *status* of the consequent, that is, whether it is universal or particular, *not* in terms of the strength of the relation between the antecedent and consequent. The division is thus between (EC) on the one hand and (AC) and (IC) *together* on the other, *not* the distinction we wanted. (The Oxford tr. may well be responsible for the Kneales' undue charity, since the phrase 'in part' is certainly misleading.) The conclusion can only be, then, that Aristotle did *not* understand the real logical difference here.

The modern logician would explain the difference *semantically*. The Kneales, for example, in using the phrase 'strictly equivalent' to characterize the relationship between *Eab* and *Eba*, and *Iab* and *Iba*, state that 'particular affirmative and universal negative statements are *convertible* without alteration of sense' (1962: p. 57). Can Aristotle be attributed the notion of 'sense' suggested here? Aristotle could certainly have provided a purely *logical* account of the difference between the rules here (in terms of *Eab* necessarily converting to *Eba*, *Iab* necessarily converting to *Iba*, *and vice versa*; *Aab* necessarily converting to *Iba*, *but not vice versa*), but given that he did not even do this, *a fortiori* he cannot have had a *semantic* conception of the difference. If the notion of 'sense' here is introduced to characterize (or 'explain') logical equivalence, then since Aristotle failed to appreciate logical equivalence – as opposed to mere logical transition or inference – he cannot have been in a position to start thinking about 'sense'.

Admittedly, though, Aristotle's text can easily suggest otherwise – if read too quickly in the light of modern logic. In a parenthetical remark in chapter 5 of Book II, Aristotle states that 'the premiss "*B* applies to no *A*" [*Eab*] is the same as "*A* applies to no *B*" [*Eba*]' (*hē ... autē protasis to B mēdeni tō A kai to A mēdeni tō B huparchein*; 58a27-9). Does this imply an understanding of logical equivalence? Once again, any positive answer is soon undermined. In the next but one chapter, he specifically *denies* that *Iab* and *Iba* are the same, even though, as in the case of *Eab* and *Eba*, the one necessarily follows from the other: 'it is necessary, if *C* belongs to some *B*, that *B* should belong to some *C*. But it is not the same that this should belong to that, and that to this: but we must assume besides that if this belongs to some of that, that belongs to some of this' (59a10-13; Oxford tr.). I shall return to what is 'assumed' here shortly, but the message is clear. Since Aristotle again exhibits his *different* treatment of the two pairs *Eab* / *Eba* and *Iab* / *Iba*, it remains the case that he cannot be attributed a proper conception of logical equivalence.

So what *did* Aristotle understand by the 'identity' of *Eab* and *Eba*? The most plausible suggestion that I can offer (and any view must be regarded as underdetermined by the text) makes use of the possibly revealing point that in the passage where Aristotle defines his three rules of conversion (25a14-23) he in effect *proves* the second and third rules by appeal to the first.[23] Given his epistemological conception of proof, then, one might conjecture that Aristotle regards the first rule as more 'primitive and immediate' than the others, a rule, that is, that cannot itself be demonstrated. Perhaps in calling *Eab* and *Eba identical*, Aristotle is voicing this view. Two propositions are identical, according to Aristotle, if and only if the transition from one to the other is *immediate*.[24] The thought would be this: if the transition from *P* to *Q* requires some mediating assumption, then *Q* cannot be the same as *P*, since *Q* partly depends on the additional input. This is just what Aristotle thinks happens in the case of the third rule. Though also a 'necessary conversion', this rule, unlike the first rule, requires proof: some extra assumption is needed in the transition from *Iab* to *Iba*.

What *is* this assumption? Aristotle writes that 'we must assume besides that if this belongs to some of that, that belongs to some of this' (59a12-13). But this, of course, is precisely the rule that we are seeking to prove. Surely Aristotle is 'begging the question' in just the way he condemns – 'proving by means of itself that which is not self-evident' (65a24-5)? If the interpretation being offered is correct, though, what Aristotle means is that the rule must be *proved* from the more primitive first rule: the conversion is not itself an 'immediate' inference.[25] However, this merely displaces the objection that Aristotle is 'begging the question' to a different level, since it is precisely the status of the rule that is at issue. Aristotle's thesis that basic principles (in this case identities) must be *non*-demonstrable, whilst not in itself incoherent, does seem – in this particular case – to be leading him astray. That the third rule *can* be proved is no reason to deny that it encapsulates an equivalence. It is Aristotle's *epistemological* assumption, then, that appears to have blocked a *semantic* understanding.

Even Aristotle's (correct) view that *Eab* and *Eba* are identical, however, might be thought to raise a difficulty for syllogistic theory. Consider, for example, the pair of syllogisms *Celarent* (*Ebc, Aab ⊢ Eac*) and *Cesare* (*Ecb, Aab ⊢ Eac*). If Aristotle had regarded *Ebc* and *Ecb* as identical, then he would presumably not have distinguished the syllogisms, yet the former is a first figure and the latter a second figure syllogism. Michael Frede has suggested that Aristotle 'should not really want to say' that *Eab* and *Eba* are identical, noting that several of the moods would then be collapsed together (1987a: p. 114; cf. Appendix 1). However, this problem disappears once we recognize again his conception of proof. *Eab* and *Eba* are identical, according to Aristotle, because the transition from one to the other is 'immediate', but the syllogisms *Celarent* and *Cesare* are not themselves identical, since the transition is 'mediated' by the first rule of conversion. (The situation is thus the same as in the case of the third rule.) Whilst *Celarent*, as a first figure syllogism, is *non*-demonstrable, *Cesare* requires proof – the 'reduction' to *Celarent* proceeding in one step by simple conversion.[26] The difficulty for syllogistic theory is removed, then, once we appreciate that Aristotle's conception of identity was *epistemological* rather than semantic; and if we wish to talk of a correlative notion of 'sense' (two propositions having the same 'sense' if they are 'identical'), then that too must be understood as epistemological. Aristotle cannot be attributed a *semantic* conception of sense.

Aristotle's (relative) semantic naivety can be further illustrated by considering one of the standard objections to his logical system. According to (AS) above (itself derivable from (AC) and (IC), which Aristotle states), *Aab* ('All *A*'s are *B*') entails *Iab* ('Some *A*'s are *B*'). *Aab* must therefore carry *existential import* (it must imply that there is at least one *A*), in which case it cannot be the *contradictory* of *Oab* ('Some *A*'s are not *B*'), as assumed in the traditional square of opposition. Two propositions are *contradictories* if they can neither both be true nor both be false, but are merely *contraries* if they cannot both be true but may both be false (cf. *De Interpretatione*, 17b16ff.). Since *Aab* and *Oab* can both be false in the case where there are no *A*'s, they are *contraries*, not contradictories. Now although this objection can be defused once it is accepted that the system as a whole *presupposes* that there are *A*'s and *B*'s (see §2.4 and Appendix 1), Aristotle's failure to recognize the problem does suggest a lack of semantic sensitivity.

It seems fair to conclude, then, that Aristotle did not appreciate the semantics of his logical system, even though the system itself is coherent. This is not to say that Aristotle had no semantic intuitions at all, since he talks about the meanings of terms on a number of occasions. He does, for example, grasp the significance of the *scope* of the negation term.[27] But he did exhibit only a partial understanding of the semantic relations between syllogistic propositions. The failure to recognize the difference between his three rules of conversion suggests that he had no genuine conception of logical equivalence, and this implies that he lacked a semantic conception of sense. As we shall see in the next chapter, this conception had to await the work of Frege.

1.5 From Aristotle to Frege

I have considered certain aspects of syllogistic theory in some detail in this chapter, for reasons that will soon become clear. I have also mentioned some of the developments in logic, both formal and philosophical, from the time of its birth in the *Prior Analytics*, and further elements in the story will emerge in the chapters that follow; but it may be helpful here to provide a synopsis of the main events up to the time of Frege.[28]

Although syllogistic theory was the dominant force in logic until the middle of the last century, this is not to say that there were no advances at all in the twenty-two centuries that passed between Aristotle's death in 322 BC and the publication of Frege's *Begriffsschrift* in 1879. We have already mentioned the other important development in antiquity, the emergence of propositional logic in the work of the Stoics. As we saw in §1.2, Aristotle himself presupposed rules of propositional logic in the (theoretical) proofs he offered of imperfect syllogisms, and whilst he should not be condemned for failing to formulate these, this does suggest that there is a form of reasoning that is more basic than syllogistic argumentation – more basic in the sense that its codification does not itself presuppose any of the syllogistic forms of inference.[29]

Chrysippus (*c.* 280-207 BC) is generally regarded as the father of Stoic logic, though his work was shaped by the interest in dialectic transmitted by the Megarians from Zeno of Elea. Dialectical argument took such forms as 'If *P* then *Q*; but not *Q*; therefore not *P*'; and this stimulated debate about the nature of conditionals. Chrysippus formalized a number of valid inferences in propositional logic, though our knowledge of what these were can only be reconstructed from later commentators such as Alexander of Aphrodisias and Sextus Empiricus (who both flourished in the 2nd century AD). The Stoics were also more sensitive than the Peripatetics to the semantic features of language, which we might use their own term in calling *semainomena*. They distinguished, for example, between a sentence and what that sentence means or signifies – the *lekton* – such that two sentences, verbally different, may express the same *lekton*. Such a conception can be seen as a distant ancestor of Frege's later notion of a *thought* – what is expressed by a sentence on a given occasion of use – though a crucial difference is that *thoughts*, unlike *lekta*, also involve abstraction from the context of utterance.[30]

Aristotelian and Stoic logic were considered rivals in the centuries that immediately followed their emergence, for the reasons outlined in §1.3; but a process of fusion gradually took place, culminating in the work of Boethius (*c.* 480-524). Boethius provided Latin translations of Aristotle's logical works, and wrote several commentaries on them, and these were the main source for the revival of Aristotelianism after the Dark Ages. In the Middle Ages, logic established itself as a fundamental discipline, with syllogistic theory providing its framework. Abelard (1079-1142) is the major figure in early scholasticism, and Duns Scotus (*c.* 1266-1308) and William of Ockham (*c.* 1285-1349) are two of the more well-known logicians of the later period. Abelard seems to have been the first to address the issue of existential import and the coherence of the traditional square of opposition (see Appendix 1). This developed into the elaborate theory of *suppositio*, concerning the various kinds of 'suppositions' involved in using singular and general terms. Medieval logicians were hampered by failing to distinguish between the semantic roles of names and predicates, and it was only with Frege's introduction of function-argument analysis that the distinction was finally clarified.[31] Abelard was also responsible for stimulating discussion in the other main debate of scholastic logic – the theory of *consequentiae*. Abelard used the term 'consequentiae' to refer to conditional propositions, but it came to apply to any piece of valid reasoning.

Once again, great ingenuity was exhibited in drawing subtle distinctions between various kinds of *consequentiae*, but the theory was generally seen as supplementing syllogistic theory rather than embedding it in a broader framework, so that no comprehensive theory emerged in the work of any one logician. Furthermore, many thinkers only succeeded in demonstrating the difficulty involved in trying to analyse statements of generality more complex than those with which Aristotle had dealt without an adequate notation for quantification.

The frustration that this must have caused, and the elaborate distinctions that were drawn, were partly responsible for the disillusionment with logic that was increasingly felt as the movements of the Renaissance gained ground. The humanists of the late 15th and 16th centuries tended to reject logic as arid and sterile, and turned instead to classical literature – to Cicero and Plutarch rather than Aristotle – for inspiration. Those humanists who did write on logic, most notably, Ramus (1515-72), valued it purely pedagogically, as providing the framework for the classification and presentation of the knowledge that was then being recovered from antiquity. But this soon gave way to outright hostility, as the scientific revolution of the 17th century gathered momentum. Two particular features of this deserve mention. Firstly, from Francis Bacon (1561-1626) onwards, there was a growing emphasis on the role of empirical observation in the attainment of knowledge, and on inductive rather than deductive methods. Secondly, the emergence of mathematical physics in the work of Galileo (1564-1642) suggested a more powerful intellectual tool for the understanding of the world than syllogistic theory.

It was this suggestion that Descartes (1596-1650) incorporated so influentially in the new outlook that heralded the birth of modern philosophy. What may be noted here is the revised view of the roles of analysis and synthesis that this embodied. As traditionally conceived, *analysis* involved the working back to epistemologically primitive truths, and *synthesis* involved the presenting of truths in a chain of deductions from the primitive ones. Synthesis was regarded, in the Aristotelian tradition, as the more important – exemplified not only in syllogistic theory but also, paradigmatically, in Euclid's geometry. According to Descartes, however, synthesis merely reveals what 'is contained in what has gone before', and 'does not show how the thing in question was discovered'.[32] It is *analysis* that enables us to discover things; so that syllogistic theory, associated purely with synthesis, was seen as of little scientific value.

Rejection of syllogistic theory on epistemological grounds became a familiar feature of 17th- and 18th-century philosophy, the passage quoted from Locke's *Essay* in §1.3 capturing the prevailing view. It is only Leibniz (1646-1716) who stands out in this period as someone who appreciated the importance of logical theory, as well as some of the technical and philosophical problems it involved. According to Leibniz, analysis and synthesis simply reflected the two directions of movement along the same deductive chain, so that there was no genuine conflict between a 'logic of discovery' and a 'logic of proof '. Although, like the medieval logicians, he too failed to recognize that the scope of logic required *expansion* rather than mere supplementation, he did write extensively on logic and the philosophy of logic, and his vision of a *characteristica universalis*, or logical language, inspired many later thinkers, not least of all Frege himself.[33] I shall say something about this Leibnizian influence in the next chapter, and more about the issue of analysis in chapter 5.

Although his own understanding of formal logic was unsophisticated, in distinguishing between *analytic* and *synthetic* propositions, and *a priori* and *a posteriori* propositions, Kant (1724-1804) shaped philosophical debate about logic and mathematics irreversibly.[34] Within this Kantian framework, Leibniz might be characterized as holding the view that both logic and arithmetic are systems of *analytic a priori* truths.[35] Kant himself, however, whilst retaining the conception of logic, rejected the Leibnizian view of arithmetic, largely for the epistemological reason that it seemed to allow no room for the informativeness of arithmetic, and he regarded it instead as a system of *synthetic a priori* truths. The possibility of such truths, although fundamental to Kant's critical philosophy, has proved highly contentious, and in the 19th century, John Stuart Mill (1806-73), working within the British empiricist tradition, rejected both the Leibnizian and Kantian conceptions, and argued for a third position – that arithmetic consists of empirical generalizations that are *synthetic a posteriori*. It was within this Kantian framework that Frege's own project was conceived, his aim being, as we shall see in chapter 3, to substantiate the original Leibnizian view.

Despite Leibniz's pioneering attempts to link logic and mathematics, it was only in the 1840s that the 'algebra of logic' finally germinated. Boole (1815-64) is often regarded as the father of mathematical logic, with the publication of *The Mathematical Analysis of Logic* in 1847, but, as we shall see in the next chapter, this must not be allowed to obscure the far more substantial advance that Frege made in 1879, when the two parts of Boole's calculus were incorporated into one powerful and comprehensive theory, justifying Frege's claim to be the real founder of modern logic. De Morgan (1806-71), Peirce (1839-1914) and Schröder (1841-1902), amongst others, all contributed to the algebra of logic, and Frege was not only aware of these developments but also wrote several papers comparing his own system with the achievements of his contemporaries.[36]

As well as refinements of Boolean algebra, the latter third of the 19th century also witnessed a revival of Kantianism in reaction to the various forms of 'scientific philosophy' that had become dominant in the middle of the century – empiricism, materialism, naturalism, psychologism – themselves responses to the excesses of German idealism regarded as culminating in Hegel's work.[37] The Kantian dichotomies of form and content, philosophy and science, the *a priori* and the *a posteriori*, were once again emphasized. Within this scheme, the Leibnizian vision of a *characteristica universalis* became the vision of a formal logical language adequate for representing the objective contents of scientific thought. Mathematics may have been seen from the 17th century as providing the necessary framework for empirical science, but with logic (in its widest sense) now being elevated into this role, construing mathematics as part of logic seemed a natural step to take. Logicism – the thesis that arithmetic is reducible to logic – was endorsed by Lotze (1817-81) in his *Logik* of 1874, which had at least some influence on Frege's own work.[38] Frege's motivation as well as his technical ability to actually pursue a demonstration of the logicist thesis were also dependent on the developments in mathematics in the 19th century, as we shall see in chapter 3. But even though the climate was conducive, Frege's transformation of logic, which made such a demonstration feasible, was still a remarkable achievement. I discuss some of the details of this transformation in the next chapter.

2. Frege's 'Begriffsschrift'

Originality. – Not that a man sees something new as the first one to do so, but that he sees something old, familiar, seen but overlooked by everyone, *as though it were new*, is what distinguishes true originality. ...

Error of philosophers. – The philosopher believes that the value of his philosophy lies in the whole, in the building: posterity discovers it in the bricks with which he built and which are then often used again for better building: in the fact, that is to say, that that building can be destroyed and *nonetheless* possess value as material.

(Nietzsche, 'Assorted Opinions and Maxims' (1879),
§§200-1, in Human, All Too Human, p. 261.)

Despite the developments sketched in the last section, it is really only Frege who truly ushered in the age of modern logic, with the publication of his *Begriffsschrift* in 1879, which refuted once and for all the view that logic had essentially emerged fully formed in the *Prior Analytics*. The classic statement of that view had occurred in Kant's *Critique of Pure Reason*, where it had been claimed that 'since Aristotle ... logic has not been able to advance a single step, and is thus to all appearance a closed and completed body of doctrine' (B viii). Whilst there is indeed a sense in which syllogistic theory is both coherent and self-contained, as we have seen, it is plainly absurd to suggest that it provides 'an exhaustive exposition and a strict proof of the formal rules of *all* thought' (ibid., B ix; my emphasis). Frege showed definitively how wrong this was; in his work, logic took not just a step forward but a huge leap.

As the initial reviews indicate, however, the importance of the *Begriffsschrift* was not immediately appreciated.[1] The main criticism, voiced by Schröder (1880) in particular, was that Frege had simply reproduced, rather poorly, the Boolean system. This induced Frege to write a lengthy paper called 'Boole's logical Calculus and the Concept-script' (*BLC*), where he compared in some detail his system with Boole's, pointing out the advantages of his own. However, no one wished to publish this, and even a much shorter version (*BLF*) was also rejected. But a far less technical paper, 'On the Scientific Justification of a Conceptual Notation' (*SJCN*) was eventually published, and this was followed by 'On the Aim of the "Conceptual Notation"' (*ACN*), originally given as a lecture.[2] In the next two sections, I shall consider these papers, together with the *Begriffsschrift* itself, in an attempt to clarify both the Leibnizian aim of his logical project and the nature of his advance over Aristotelian and Boolean logic. In §2.3 I suggest how this advance led Frege to repudiate the subject/predicate distinction, noting the effect that this had on his reconstrual of syllogistic inferences; and in §2.4 I discuss the differences between Aristotelian and Fregean logic with regard to the issue of existential import. In the final section I explain Frege's key notion of 'conceptual content', indicating the extent of his originality in introducing it.

2.1 The Leibnizian Aim of the 'Begriffsschrift'

In his 'Preface' to the *Begriffsschrift* Frege states that the main aim of his 'conceptual notation' or 'concept-script' (as 'Begriffsschrift' has been alternatively translated) is to allow us 'to test in the most reliable way the validity of a chain of inference and to reveal every presupposition that tends to slip in unnoticed, so that its origin can be investigated'. Ordinary language is inadequate for this purpose because of its 'softness and instability': 'The forms in which inference is expressed are so varied, so loose and vague, that presuppositions can easily slip in unnoticed and then be overlooked when the necessary conditions for the conclusion are enumerated' (*SJCN*, pp. 85-6). In ordinary language, Frege writes, 'logical relations are almost always only hinted at – left to guessing, not actually expressed' (*SJCN*, p. 85; cf. *BLC*, p. 12). As we shall see in the next chapter, Frege's particular interest lay in revealing the presuppositions and logical relations involved in mathematical reasoning, but his first task was to develop a logical language in which reasoning in general could be represented, and it is this that I explore in the present chapter.

In his 'Preface' to the *Begriffsschrift*, and in the papers immediately following its publication, Frege emphasizes that he is not merely designing a calculus, which is all that Boole did, but is concerned with *content* as well as logical form. He writes:

> my aim was different from Boole's. I did not wish to present an abstract logic in formulas, but to express a content through written symbols in a more precise and perspicuous way than is possible with words. In fact, I wished to produce, not a mere *calculus ratiocinator*, but a *lingua characteristica* in the Leibnizian sense. In doing so, however, I recognize that deductive calculus is a necessary part of a conceptual notation. If this was misunderstood, perhaps it is because I let the abstract logical aspect stand too much in the foreground. (*ACN*, pp. 90-1; cf. *BLC*, p. 12; *BLF*, p. 47.)

As Leibniz had envisaged it, there were four main purposes to be served by a *characteristica universalis* or ideal logical language. It was to be:

(a) an international language,
(b) a scientific notation,
(c) an instrument of discovery,

(d) a method of proof.

(a) and (b) together constituted the 'universal character', or ideal notation, the development of which was a fairly common aspiration in the 17th century. The idea was not just of a language that everyone could use, as Latin had been (and still was then) amongst scholars, but of a scientifically structured, grammatically simple system of symbols that, at least at a basic level, would bear one-one correlations with the terms of any given natural language.[3] (c) and (d) comprised Leibniz's *calculus ratiocinator*, which was seen as bringing together both analytic and synthetic reasoning. Leibniz drew the traditional distinction between the logic of invention or discovery and the logic of judgement or proof, and his aim was to show how these complemented each other.[4]

Such a vision undoubtedly inspired Frege, but he was critical of Leibniz's own conception of the project. He writes that it was 'too grandiose for the attempt to realize it to go further than the bare preliminaries', Leibniz's enthusiasm letting him 'underestimate the difficulties that such an enterprise faces' (*BS*, 'Preface'). However, he goes on:

> even if this great aim cannot be achieved at the first attempt, one need not despair of a slow, step by step approach. If a problem in its full generality appears insoluble, it has to be limited provisionally; it can then, perhaps, be dealt with by advancing gradually. Arithmetical, geometrical and chemical symbols can be regarded as realizations of the Leibnizian conception in particular fields. The 'Begriffsschrift' offered here adds a new one to these, indeed, the one located in the middle adjoining all the others. From here, with the greatest prospect of success, one can then proceed to fill in the gaps in the existing formula languages, connect their hitherto separate fields into the domain of a single language and extend it to fields that have hitherto lacked such a language. (Ibid.)

Frege may well have been more aware than Leibniz of the effort that the development of a *characteristica universalis* would involve, but the guiding vision is hardly less ambitious. The two most important elements of Leibniz's conception, (b) and (d), are clearly also combined in Frege's mind. With the right basic terms from each scientific discipline (mathematics itself was regarded as a science), and a powerful logical calculus, not only can the arguments in each field be represented, but the various areas can even be deductively linked.

Of the remaining two elements, there is little discussion in Frege's writings of (a). Whilst it is clear from letters Couturat wrote to Frege in 1901 that Frege was sympathetic towards the idea of an international language,[5] he appears to have regarded it as incompatible with the demand for logical rigour. In a paper published in 1897, comparing Peano's system with his own, Frege suggests that the attempt to develop an international language may actually *hinder* the construction of a logic of proof. Peano's intention, he writes, 'seems orientated towards the storage of knowledge rather than towards proof, towards brevity and international intelligibility rather than towards logical perfection' (*PCN*, p. 237). Of course, in one sense, a logical language – like mathematics itself – is already an international language, but the point is presumably that, unlike say, Esperanto, such a system hardly lends itself to the easy mastery or everyday use that is one of the conditions of a workable international language.[6]

Frege draws two comparisons to elucidate his project:

> I believe I can make the relationship of my 'Begriffsschrift' to ordinary language [*Sprache des Lebens*] clearest if I compare it to that of the micro-scope to the eye. The latter, due to the range of its applicability, due to the flexibility with which it is able to adapt to the most diverse circumstances, has a great superiority over the microscope. Considered as an optical instru-ment, it admittedly reveals many imperfections, which usually remain unnoticed only because of its intimate connection with mental life. But as soon as scientific purposes place great demands on sharpness of resolution, the eye turns out to be inadequate. The microscope, on the other hand, is perfectly suited for just such purposes, but precisely because of this is useless for all others. (*BS*, 'Preface'.)

> [Problems with ordinary language] are rooted in a certain softness and instability ..., which nevertheless is necessary for its versatility and poten-tial for development. In this respect, [ordinary] language can be compared to the hand, which despite its adaptability to the most diverse tasks is still inadequate. We build for ourselves artificial hands, tools for particular purposes, which work with more accuracy than the hand can provide. And how is this accuracy possible? Through the very stiffness and inflexibility of parts the lack of which makes the hand so dextrous. Word-language is inadequate in a similar way. We need a system of symbols from which every ambiguity is banned, which has a strict logical form from which the content cannot escape. (*SJCN*, p. 86.)

Both comparisons suggest that the 'Begriffsschrift' is specially constructed to perform a task that cannot properly be done by ordinary language. Natural languages (as well as such artificial languages as Esperanto) have developed (or been developed) as highly versatile linguistic systems, but *just because of that* are hardly suitable when logical rigour is required – when arguments need to be set out perspicuously and unambiguously. The first passage suggests that the right logical system can help us discern validity; whilst the second suggests that an artificial notation must be *rigid* if this to be done effectively, an idea that will become clearer in §2.5. In both cases, the point is that the 'Begriffsschrift' is carefully designed for its *logical* purpose.

The first passage, however, also suggests something more – that the 'Begriffsschrift' is intended as an instrument of scientific discovery. The cell structure of an organism cannot be studied with the naked eye, yet with a microscope the whole realm is opened up for exploration. If this analogy is taken seriously, then (c), the remaining element in Leibniz's *characteristica universalis*, is in Frege's mind too. Yet it is hard to see how a mere notation, even combined with a logical calculus, can enable us to make scientific discoveries. Frege anticipated the objection:

> It is impossible, someone might say, to advance science with a conceptual notation, for the invention of the latter already presupposes the completion of the former. Exactly the same apparent difficulty arises for [ordinary] language. This is supposed to have made reason possible, but how could man have invented language without reason? Research into the laws of nature employs physical instruments; but these can be produced only by means of an advanced technology, which again is based upon knowledge of the laws of nature. The [apparently vicious] circle is resolved in each case in the same way: an advance in physics results in an advance in technology, and this makes possible the construction of new instruments by means of which physics is again advanced. The application [of this example] to our case is obvious. (*SJCN*, p. 89.)

However, whilst we may agree (with both Frege and Leibniz) that the *completion* of science is not necessary for the development of a useful notation,[7] it is still not clear how an adequate notation can be an instrument for making scientific discoveries, in the way that a microscope obviously is. But perhaps this is pushing the analogy too far. The comparison with language and reason may be more instructive. As we shall see, the development and use of a logical system undoubtedly shapes (and is shaped by) our *semantic* conceptions – in the same way as a dictionary refines our linguistic knowledge, or a colour chart our aesthetic perceptions. So we may, if we like, speak of making semantic, linguistic or aesthetic *discoveries* through their use – generating more sensitive representations of the world – although it might still be insisted that these are on a different level from discoveries in the physical sciences.

As far as Frege's own views are concerned, however, one final point can be made here. In his later work, Frege talked of having *discovered* two new logical objects, the True and the False, and he came to argue for the existence of a separate realm of *thoughts*; so that, in a very literal sense, he did indeed take himself to have made discoveries.[8] Whether or not this can be construed as operating a 'logic of discovery', then, Leibnizian themes certainly permeate Frege's philosophy.

2.2 Frege's Logical Achievement

As we have noted, syllogistic theory was the dominant force in logic until the middle of the last century. Even Leibniz failed to free himself from Aristotle's influence. Propositional logic had indeed emerged at the time of the Stoics, but it was not until the work of Boole and others on the 'algebra of logic' that it finally approached maturity, and even then it was regarded as only one part of Boolean algebra, dependent upon the more primary calculus of classes. One of Frege's major achievements in the *Begriffsschrift* was to give a rigorous presentation of the propositional calculus. Frege produced a neater axiomatization than Boole, in effect relying on just two connectives (negation and the conditional), two rules of inference (*modus ponens* and an implicit principle of substitution), and six axioms (numbered 1, 2, 8, 28, 31 and 41 in his book).[9] Frege was explicit about the advantages that his system had over Boole's, in the two papers where he compares the two calculi (*BLC* and *BLF* – summarized at *BLC*, p. 46). Boole's logic, he remarks, suffers from a 'superfluity of signs' (*BLF*, p. 48), whereas his own system makes do with fewer primitive signs and 'the fewer primitive signs one introduces, the fewer primitive laws one needs, and the easier it will be to master the formulae' (*BLF*, p. 50; cf. *BLC*, p. 39).

Given that Frege himself states that 'the first problem for Boole and me was the same: the perspicuous representation of logical relations by means of written signs' (*BLC*, p. 14), fewer primitives might well seem counter-productive, since proofs may be longer, resulting in a *loss* of perspicuity. Frege readily admitted, though, that 'abbreviation' will be needed in practice (*BS*, 'Preface'; *BLC*, p. 37), the short answer being that once one has an axiomatized system, it becomes clearer just what abbreviations to use, enhancing perspicuity. His deeper response, however, raises the issue of axiomatization itself:

> it is a basic principle of science to reduce the number of axioms to the fewest possible. Indeed the essence of explanation lies precisely in the fact that a wide, possibly unsurveyable, manifold is governed by one or a few sentences. The value of an explanation can be directly measured by this condensation and simplification: it is zero if the number of assumptions is as great as the number of facts to be explained. (*BLC*, p. 36.)

Since the 'explanatory power' of a logical theory is proportional to its degree of axiomatization, Frege argues, Boole's system is inferior to his own.

But why should 'explanatory power' be deemed such a virtue in a logical theory? An axiomatized system has obvious *practical* advantages: it may encourage clearer understanding, aid memory, refine analytical and prob-lem-solving skills, and facilitate the setting out and testing of arguments, all of which are worthy aims of a *characteristica universalis*. Yet Frege clearly has in mind some more *theoretical* advantage. He writes: 'it wasn't my intention to provide a sample of how to carry out ... derivations in a brief and practical way: it was to show that I can manage throughout with my basic laws' (*BLC*, pp. 37-8). The aim of his axiomatization, in other words, was to show how everything follows from just a few fundamental propositions. His system has 'explanatory power' to the extent that it achieves this goal.

This suggests that it was his *foundationalist* project that Frege particularly saw as distinguishing his work from Boole's. I shall, however, postpone discussion of this until the next chapter, since Frege's most significant logical achievement and its semantic implications have still to be explained. Frege's propositional calculus may indeed be more rigorously developed than Boole's, but the most fundamental difference between their two theories concerns Frege's introduction of the *predicate calculus*. Frege was certainly aware that his own system had a broader applicability than Boole's, but even he underestimated his achievement at the time. He briefly mentions his advance in just one of his three shorter articles (*ACN*, p. 99; but not in *SJCN* or *BLF*), and even in his longer paper, he only modestly proclaims that his concept-script, 'thanks to the notation for generality, commands a somewhat wider domain than Boole's formula-language' (*BLC*, p. 46; cf. pp. 14-15, 27, 35). Yet it was Frege's invention of the quantifier that constituted the real logical breakthrough and that inaugurated the age of modern logic.

Frege's crucial move lay in extending the idea of function-argument analysis from mathematics to logic, whilst building on the propositional calculus; and it was this that made possible a more satisfying treatment of general and existential propositions.[10] Take the following two syllogistic propositions:

(A) All *A's* are *B*.
(I) Some *A's* are *B*.

In syllogistic theory, both are treated as of subject-predicate form ('All *A's*' and 'Some *A's*' representing the subjects), and hence are seen as having similar logical forms (mirroring their similar grammatical forms). In the predicate calculus, however, they are analysed quite differently. Using modern symbolism, these can be formalized, respectively, thus:

(A*) $(\forall x)(Ax \rightarrow Bx)$.
(I*) $(\exists x)(Ax \mathbin{\&} Bx)$.

Both are represented in function-argument form, (A*) involving the universal quantifier and the material conditional, and (I*) the existential quantifier and conjunction.[11] A natural reading of these can be given as follows:

(A†) For all x, if x is an *A*, then x is a *B*.
(I†) There is some (at least one) x, such that x is an *A* and x is a *B*.

On this construal, the logical forms of the two propositions are not only different from their grammatical forms, but also from each other. What the new analysis in effect does is treat (A) and (I) as *complex* propositions, composed of two simpler or *atomic* propositions ('x is an *A*' and 'x is a *B*') linked by propositional connectives and bound by a quantifier.[12] The analysis thus depends both on the use of function-argument notation and also on the more fundamental propositional calculus. Frege's invention of the predicate calculus resulted from amalgamating the two.

It is worth indicating the significance of this synthesis in the history of logic, by comparing Frege's achievement once again with Boole's. In common with other logicians of the 19th century, Boole had drawn a fundamental distinction between the logic of *categoricals* (embracing syllogistic theory) and the logic of *hypotheticals* (encompassing the propositional calculus). His algebraic system had been devised as a means of representing both logics equally, the difference between the two being, as he put it, 'not of form but of interpretation' (1854: p. 54). Under one interpretation the result was the calculus of classes, and under the other the calculus of propositions. The underlying affinity between the two calculi was generally admitted, but there was much discussion at the time about which was the more fundamental. Boole himself viewed class logic as the more basic, stating that categoricals expressed relations between classes of *things*, whilst hypotheticals expressed relations between *propositions*. The former he termed 'primary' or 'concrete' propositions (such as 'The sun shines', i.e. 'The sun is that which shines'), whilst the latter he termed 'secondary' or 'abstract' propositions (e.g. 'If the sun shines the earth is warmed'). (Cf. 1854: pp. 52-3.) Secondary propositions could be shown to be *reducible* to primary propositions, according to Boole, by demonstrating that any system of equations was equivalent to a single equation (1854: ch. 8).

Despite this conception of reduction, however, the major problem with Boole's system lay in the impossibility of *integrating* the two calculi. If each logic constituted a *different* interpretation of the same underlying algebra, then there was no way of operating both simultaneously. Yet there are valid arguments in which both primary and secondary propositions occur. Consider the following two propositions, which Boole himself distinguishes (1847: pp. 58-9):

(P) All inhabitants are either Europeans or Asiatics.
(S) Either all the inhabitants are Europeans, or they are all Asiatics.

Since (P) is a *primary* and (S) is a *secondary* proposition, they cannot both be symbolized under the same interpretation. Whilst Boole himself stressed this, however, he seems to have failed to recognize the logical connection between the two. For (P) follows from (S); yet there is no way of representing this in the Boolean system.[13] As Frege remarked, in criticizing the distinction between primary and secondary propositions, 'Any [logical] transition from one kind of judgement to the other – which, to be sure, often occurs in actual thinking – is blocked; for we may not use the same symbols with a double meaning in the same context' (*ACN*, p. 93).

The difficulty that this generates for Boolean algebra, however, is easily dealt with in a Fregean system, which offers a straightforward formalization of the inference:

(SP) $[(\forall x)\,(Ix \rightarrow Ex) \vee (\forall x)\,(Ix \rightarrow Ax)] \rightarrow (\forall x)\,[Ix \rightarrow (Ex \vee Ax)]$.

The real difference between the two systems, Frege reports, 'is that I avoid [the Boolean] division into two parts ... and give a homogeneous presentation of the lot. In Boole the two parts run alongside one another, so that one is like the mirror image of the other, but for that very reason stands in no organic relation to it' (*BLC*, p. 14; cf. p. 18, *ACN*, p. 99). As he himself recognized, then, Frege's key logical achievement was a far more 'organic' theory, no doubt suggesting to him the real possibility of carrying through the Leibnizian project of a *characteristica universalis*. But this was not the only feature of his achievement. He also *reversed* the traditionally seen relationship between the two parts of logic: 'In contrast with Boole, I now reduce his *primary propositions* to the *secondary* ones' (*BLF*, p. 17). As we have noted, Frege's analysis of syllogistic propositions depends on the more fundamental propositional calculus; and it is this that underlies his repeated insistence that, unlike previous logicians, he proceeds from judgements (involving whole propositions) rather than concepts (see e.g. *ACN*, p. 94; *BLC*, pp. 15-16, 46).

Frege's 'Begriffsschrift' was not only successful in unifying the two parts of Boolean logic. It also resolved one of the outstanding problems that had confronted syllogistic theory – the analysis of statements of *multiple generality*. Take the following example of such a statement:

(MG) Every philosopher admires some logician.

In syllogistic theory the ambiguity that is involved here is difficult to express. Consider a modification of (MG):

(MG′) Some logician is admired by every philosopher.

The two different meanings, it might be suggested, can be represented by distinguishing (MG) and (MG′), what is taken as the *subject* of the proposition holding the key to its analysis. However, this fails to overcome the problem, since both (MG) and (MG′) can still be understood in the alternative way. The ambiguity seems not to depend on subject/predicate position. In Fregean logic, on the other hand, the ambiguity can be precisely expressed:

(MG*) $(\forall x)\,(Px \rightarrow (\exists y)\,(Ly\ \&\ Axy))$.
(MG#) $(\exists y)\,(Ly\ \&\ (\forall x)\,(Px \rightarrow Axy))$.

These can be read as follows:

(MG†) For all x, if x is a philosopher, then there is some y, such that y is a logician and x admires y.

(MG‡)   There is some *y*, such that *y* is a logician and for all *x*, if *x* is a philosopher, then *x* admires *y*.

Here it is the *scope* of the quantifiers, rather than subject/predicate position, that reflects the difference between the two meanings. Logicians, Frege remarked in a letter in 1882, 'have clung too much to the linguistic schema of subject and predicate, which surely contains what are logically quite different relations' (*PMC*, pp. 100-1). And in his 'Preface' to the *Begriffsschrift*, after a similar comment, Frege declared: 'In particular, I believe that the replacement of the concepts *subject* and *predicate* by *argument* and *function* will prove itself in the long run'. In this, Frege has certainly been vindicated; though this is not to say that philosophical problems were not generated in the process.

As far as the development of formal logic is concerned, then, the expansion that Frege brought about had a twofold significance. Not only did it unite the two parts of Boolean algebra, but it also provided a new and broader framework for syllogistic theory. Frege was clearly concerned to accommodate syllogistic theory;[14] but, as we shall now see, its assimilation within the new logic was far from straightforward.

2.3 The Assimilation of Syllogistic Theory

In §22 of the *Begriffsschrift*, Frege notes how *Felapton* (*Ebc, Aba ⊢ Oac*) and *Fesapo* (*Ecb, Aba ⊢ Oac*), in the case where the premisses take the form of singular rather than universal judgements, are not differentiated in his notation 'since no subject is distinguished' (literally, 'since the stress on a subject falls away'). To explain this, let us take Frege's own example, and consider the two respective syllogisms (with their universal forms given in brackets):

(FL)   This ostrich cannot fly   (No ostriches can fly)
       This ostrich is a bird   (All ostriches are birds)
       _____
       Some birds cannot fly

(FS)   This non-flier is an ostrich   (No fliers are ostriches)
       This ostrich is a bird   (All ostriches are birds)
       _____
       Some birds cannot fly

In Frege's system, these two syllogisms are conflated, into the following judgement:

(F)   If this ostrich is a bird and cannot fly, then it follows that some birds cannot fly.

With '*b*' referring to the particular ostrich, '*Fx*' meaning '*x* can fly', and '*Gx*' meaning '*x* is a bird', we arrive at the following formalization (cf. *BS*, §22):

(F*) $(Gb \;\&\; \neg Fb) \rightarrow (\exists x)(Gx \;\&\; \neg Fx)$.

Clearly, this is a valid theorem in the predicate calculus; and it illustrates very well what Frege meant by 'not distinguishing a subject'. With the symbolism Frege provides, (FS) cannot be formalized *without* switching around the subject and predicate of the first premiss; and this turns it into an instance of *Felapton*, thereby showing the irrelevance of subject/predicate position. All that is necessary to the validity of the argument is that there is a particular object that is an ostrich, a non-flier and a bird. 'Being an ostrich' constitutes the middle term – the one that drops out in the conclusion – and it is this that makes it the appropriate term for Frege to use to single out the object. (Of course, in one sense this then constitutes the subject, but the point is that the term does not necessarily have to occupy the subject position in each premiss.)[15]

This way of putting things, however, does suggest that it would have been possible to capture the difference between *Felapton* and *Fesapo* had we so wished. Reading 'Ox' as 'x is an ostrich', instead of using 'b' to refer to a particular ostrich, the following formalizations might be offered (phrasing them as sequents, rather than the corresponding conditionals):[16]

(FL′) $(\exists x)(Ox \;\&\; \neg Fx \;\&\; Gx) \vdash (\exists x)(Gx \;\&\; \neg Fx)$.

(FS′) $(\exists x)(\neg Fx \;\&\; Ox \;\&\; Gx) \vdash (\exists x)(Gx \;\&\; \neg Fx)$.

Both are valid sequents, and the desired distinction appears to have been captured. However, in the predicate calculus, there is no convention whereby 'Ax' in '$(\exists x)(Ax \;\&\; Bx)$' represents the *subject* of the proposition, nor does there need to be, given the obvious equivalence between '$Ax \;\&\; Bx$' and '$Bx \;\&\; Ax$'. In any case, how would the subject of the *second* syllogistic premiss be indicated here? We would clearly need to set out the two premisses separately, if we were to attempt to formalize the inferences adopting the suggested convention:

(FL″) $(\exists x)(Ox \;\&\; \neg Fx), (\exists x)(Ox \;\&\; Gx) \vdash (\exists x)(Gx \;\&\; \neg Fx)$.

(FS″) $(\exists x)(\neg Fx \;\&\; Ox), (\exists x)(Ox \;\&\; Gx) \vdash (\exists x)(Gx \;\&\; \neg Fx)$.

The problem with this, though, is that neither sequent is then valid. We can only recapture the validity of the syllogisms if we return to the *universal* form of the second premiss:

(FL†) $(\exists x)(Ox \;\&\; \neg Fx), (\forall x)(Ox \rightarrow Gx) \vdash (\exists x)(Gx \;\&\; \neg Fx)$.

(FS†) $(\exists x)(\neg Fx \;\&\; Ox), (\forall x)(Ox \rightarrow Gx) \vdash (\exists x)(Gx \;\&\; \neg Fx)$.

It might indeed now look as if the adoption of the suggested convention has succeeded in distinguishing the two inferences – except that what we have here are the forms not of *Felapton* and *Fesapo*, but rather of *Disamis* (*Ibc, Aba* ⊢ *Iac*) and *Dimatis* (*Icb, Aba* ⊢ *Iac*), respectively. In response, though, it might be pointed out that a decision as to which syllogistic mood a syllogism instantiates is never going to be clear-cut when one or both of the premisses take a *singular* form (there may be several options), and that since this difficulty arises for syllogistic theory itself, it scarcely constitutes an objection to formalizations within the predicate calculus. In any case, is it really much more of a problem than deciding whether 'Ostriches cannot fly', for example, is to be construed as 'All ostriches are non-fliers' or 'No ostriches are fliers'? As we shall see in §2.5, as far as drawing conclusions are concerned, in the end it hardly seems to matter.

However, there remains one final possibility to consider. So far, the premisses of the syllogisms have been formalized as *particular* (or in one case, as *universal*) rather than as *singular* propositions, so let us try to reinstate the singularity by modifying (FL″) and (FS″) to render them valid (retaining the use of '*b*' to pick out the individual – the ostrich/non-flier/bird – referred to):

(FL‡) $(\exists x)\,(Ox\ \&\ \neg Fx\ \&\ x{=}b),\ (\exists x)\,(Ox\ \&\ Gx\ \&\ x{=}b) \vdash (\exists x)\,(Gx\ \&\ \neg Fx).$

(FS‡) $(\exists x)\,(\neg Fx\ \&\ Ox\ \&\ x{=}b),\ (\exists x)\,(Ox\ \&\ Gx\ \&\ x{=}b) \vdash (\exists x)\,(Gx\ \&\ \neg Fx).$

Here again the two schemata could still be regarded as the forms of *other* pairs of ('singularized') syllogisms, such as *Disamis* and *Dimatis*, but they are, at least, not *obviously* the forms of any other syllogistic moods. We do finally appear to have both a pair of valid sequents and the distinction we desired, but at the cost of a certain amount of unnecessary complexity.

It is presumably with some such attempt at retaining a subject/predicate distinction in mind that Frege wrote, at the end of §3 of the *Begriffsschrift*: 'In my first draft of a formula language I was misled by the example of ordinary language into constructing judgements out of subject and predicate. But I soon convinced myself that this was an obstacle to my particular goal and only led to useless prolixity.' As we have just seen, it *is* possible to retain the distinction within the predicate calculus, but only by adopting a rather trivial convention, with the consequent sacrifice of Frege's goal of maximum simplicity. In his own 'Begriffsschrift', Frege remarked, 'I closely follow the example of the formula language of mathematics, in which subject and predicate can also be distinguished only by violating it' (ibid.).

If we accept that the suggested convention is unnecessary, treating the equivalence between '*Ax* & *Bx*' and '*Bx* & *Ax*' as obvious, then sequents such as (FL″) and (FS″) will not be taken to represent different arguments. But what are the implications of this for the issue raised at the end of the last section? How exactly was syllogistic theory assimilated? If *Iab* and *Iba* are *identical* in the new logic, then a number of syllogistic distinctions disappear – not only in cases where one or more of the premisses have *singular* contents, but also between certain pairs of syllogistic moods themselves. *Disamis* and *Dimatis*, *Darii* and *Datisi*, *Ferio* and *Ferison*, and *Festino* and *Fresison*, are all conflated in Fregean logic; and with this disappears any meaningful division of the syllogisms into *figures*. (The details of all this are provided in Appendix 1.)

This was not the only effect, however. Consider the Fregean formalization of *Felapton* (*Ebc*, *Aba* ⊢ *Oac*) in its standard universal form:

(FL*) $(\forall x)(Bx \to \neg Cx), (\forall x)(Bx \to Ax) \vdash (\exists x)(Ax \,\&\, \neg Cx).$

This sequent is *invalid*; as are the Fregean formalizations of *Darapti*, *Bamalip*, *Fesapo*, and all five subaltern moods. The reason why this is so is that, on Frege's construal of syllogistic propositions, universal propositions lack, and particular propositions carry, *existential import*. Given that 'All *A*'s are *B*' is formalized as '$(\forall x)(Ax \to Bx)$', the proposition is *true* if there are no *A*'s (in propositional logic, '$P \to Q$' is true when P is false); whilst 'Some *A*'s are *B*', formalized as '$(\exists x)(Ax \,\&\, Bx)$', is *false* if there are no *A*'s. The traditional 'rules of subalternation' (e.g. 'From *Aab* infer *Iab*') are therefore invalidated; so that the working of the (translated) Aristotelian system is undermined. (Once again, for details, see Appendix 1.)

What justification can there be for Frege's construals? Merely saying that they lead to a useful simplification is hardly enough to satisfy the critic, since it is precisely the justification for this simplification that is in question. In the next section I consider the issue of existential import; and in the final section I discuss Frege's own response, which hinges on his notion of 'conceptual content'.

2.4 Existential Import

As we have noted, Aristotelian and Fregean logic differ in their construal of syllogistic propositions. According to Frege, universal propositions, unlike particular propositions, *lack* existential import, and are *true* if the subject term fails to refer. To explore this, let us consider the following two instances of a syllogistic *A*-proposition:

(HF) All hobbits have hairy feet.
(HH) All hobbits have horns.

Now most people (familiar with Tolkien) would presumably regard (HF) as true and (HH) as false. But if *A*-propositions are formalized *without* existential import, *both* will come out as *true* – since hobbits do not, in fact, exist. So should we then construe them as *possessing* existential import? But this is no better, since both would then come out as *false*. A dilemma confronts us: a proposition either has, or does not have, existential import; but in either case we reach a counterintuitive result. Does this not constitute a serious objection to Frege's logic?

Ironically, this objection – that difficulties arise as soon as we try to pin down whether a proposition carries existential import or not – has frequently been made *by Fregeans* to syllogistic theory. As we saw at the end of §1.4, if syllogistic *A*-propositions are taken to *possess* existential import

– to validate the rule of subalternation 'From *All A's are B* infer *Some A's are B*', then they are *contraries*, not *contradictories* of *O*-propositions – since *both* will be false if there are no *A's*. More generally, it can be shown that there is *no* plausible assignment of existential import to syllogistic propositions that renders consistent *all* the relationships encapsulated in the traditional square of opposition.[17] So we appear to have an equally serious objection to Aristotle's logic!

Of course, the mere fact that we can use the idea of existential import to raise difficulties for *both* systems suggests that it may be our attitude towards existential import itself that is at the root of the problem – and this may in turn reveal an underlying misunderstanding of the nature of formal logic. Let us take as our guide the response to the charge of inconsistency, in the case of syllogistic theory, that was provided in §1.4. It was suggested that if it is a presupposition of syllogistic theory as a whole that all terms refer, then coherence is restored. If the possibility of there being no *A's* is ruled out from the start, then *A*- and *O*-propositions will remain contradictories. Of course, the objection could still be pressed: should this presupposition not have been made explicit, and does it not constitute a limitation on the system? Two points can be made in reply to this. Firstly, whatever the perceived limitations of the system, the defence of its *coherence* stands: an unarticulated presupposition does not render a theory *logically* flawed. Secondly, whilst Aristotle's logic is indeed limited, it need not be restricted by the requirement that all terms refer to actual objects; they may be allowed to refer to *fictional* entities or properties. An Aristotelian could perfectly well hold, for example, that (HF) is true, and (HH) false, whilst also maintaining that (HF) implies *both* that some hobbits have hairy feet, *and* that it is false that some hobbits do not have hairy feet – all within the mythological context of Tolkien's Middle Earth. In this case, the relevant set of propositions can be construed as possessing *fictional existential import*.

However, can we not take a context in which there are, say, *no* hobbits (our actual world, for example), and still legitimately ask whether all hobbits have hairy feet? Surely (HF) would still have *meaning* in such a context, in which case must it not be either true or false? According to the objector, if our natural inclination is to regard it as *true*, then it has to be taken as *lacking* existential import, since if it *possessed* such import, it could only be *false*. But to be drawn once again to make this distinction (between possessing and lacking existential import), the argument continues, is precisely to raise difficulties for syllogistic theory. However, the Aristotelian can simply deny the assumption on which the objector's argument is based. In a non-hobbit context, (HF) cannot actually be used to say anything judgeable as *either* true *or* false. The objector is trying to force us to decide between the following two analyses:

(A1)　'All hobbits have hairy feet' is (a) *true* if either (i) hobbits exist and they all have hairy feet, or (ii) hobbits do not exist; and is (b) *false* if hobbits exist and they do not all have hairy feet.

(A2)　'All hobbits have hairy feet' is (a) *true* if hobbits exist and they all have hairy feet; and is (b) *false* if either (i) hobbits exist and they do not all have hairy feet, or (ii) hobbits do not exist.

As we have seen, however, *both* analyses lead to counterintuitive results – where there are no hobbits, (HF) is false under proposal (A2), and (HH) is true under proposal (A1). Under both proposals, (HF) and (HH) possess the *same* truth-value, and this fails to respect the intuitive difference between them. The problems dissolve, though, if we adopt instead the following analysis:

(A3)　(i) If, in a certain context, hobbits exist, then 'All hobbits have hairy feet' is (a) *true* if all those hobbits do have hairy feet; and is (b) *false* if some hobbits do not have hairy feet.
　　　(ii) If, in a certain context, hobbits do not exist, then 'All hobbits have hairy feet' has *no informative use*.

The objector might insist, though, that even in the actual world, (HF) is still *meaningful*, and indeed is *true*, since if there *were* hobbits they *would* all have hairy feet. However, whilst we may allow that (HF) remains *meaningful* – just because there *are* contexts in which talk of hobbits makes sense, this is not to say that in every context the proposition has a *truth-value*, since truth-value depends upon *use* in a context. We would *not* intuitively regard it as true *because* there are no hobbits – the possibility opened up by clause (A1aii) above – as the counterexample of (HH) shows.[18]

If this defence of Aristotelian logic is successful, then what it suggests is that the existential import of a proposition, as used on a particular occasion, is determined by the *context*.[19] There is thus no *requirement* that a formal logic embody a means of representing it; and there is certainly no implication of *incoherence* if any system does lack such a means. However, if this strategy restores coherence to syllogistic theory, it is hardly obvious that it can also rescue Fregean logic, since Fregean logic precisely involves a distinction between universal propositions that *lack*, and particular propositions that *possess*, existential import. Given that both the proposals exemplified by (A1) and (A2) lead to counterintuitive results, why should anyone wish to offer either, and in particular, why should Frege have adopted the former? The short answer is that (A1) lends itself to a straightforward formalization, and it is this that must surely have made it compelling.

It is worth appreciating exactly why this is so in more detail. Consider the following gradual progression in the interpretation and formalization of the standard syllogistic *A*-proposition:

(A)   All *A*'s are *B*.
(A')   Every *A* is a *B*.
(A")   Whatever is an *A* is a *B*.
(A†)   If anything is an *A*, then it is a *B*.
(A‡)   For all *x*, if *x* is an *A*, then *x* is a *B*.
(A*) $(\forall x)(Ax \rightarrow Bx)$.

There is presumably nothing at all controversial about the move from (A) to (A") – all three are generally accepted synonyms. But what about from there? (A†) introduces the crucial 'if ... then ...' construction, which might already be taken to suggest hesitation about whether there really are any A's. (A‡) rewrites this in function-argument notation, and (A*) concludes the formalization by interpreting the 'if ... then ...' connective as the truth-functional material conditional. If we admit that (A†) reflects the key semantic breakthrough (even allowing its possible neutrality as regards the issue of existential import), then its subsequent formalization displays two critical features: firstly, the truth-functional character of the material conditional that is used in interpreting the 'if ... then ...' construction, which allows the complex whole to be *true* when the antecedent part is *false* (i.e. when nothing is an *A*); and secondly, the quantifier notation, which allows quantification over *all* objects, so that the use of any such general proposition is not necessarily restricted to contexts where the appropriate objects are present. The first feature generates a logical system that is both simple and powerful: as Frege himself recognized (see e.g. *BS*, 'Preface' and §5), the conditional is the key to his system. The second feature reflects his Leibnizian aspiration to develop a *universal* logical language.[20]

However, if the first feature yields counterintuitive results in the case of fictional objects, the second seems merely to accentuate the problem, since the message of our discussion seemed to be that fictional contexts *cannot* be incorporated into the Fregean system. So how can Frege aspire to having created a *universal* logic? Frege himself, though, would have been happy to *accept* such counterintuitive implications, since, as the 'Preface' to the *Begriffsschrift* makes clear, his own aims were purely 'scientific' – to develop a logical language that could unify all the various scientific domains – and as long as no truths (falsehoods) about entities that *actually* existed came out as false (true), which they would not, then problems with fictional objects were irrelevant. His logical system was indeed to be seen as universal, but its value was only to be assessed 'scientifically'.

But would it not have been possible for Frege to have provided an adequate account of fictional contexts? If we managed to restore coherence to syllogistic theory by simply recognizing the role that the relevant context plays, why cannot the same strategy be employed in the case of Fregean logic? What is wrong with allowing quantification over *fictional* objects? The difference between the two analyses offered in (A1) and (A2) fades into insignificance if hobbits do exist in a certain context, and indeed both collapse into (A3i). The answer here touches the heart of Frege's enterprise. For whilst this strategy does indeed succeed in defending Fregean logic construed as a widely applicable *formal system*, it fails to accord with Frege's *epistemological* aim – already manifest at the time of the *Begriffsschrift*, and emerging even more clearly in his later work – to *abstract* from all context-dependence. This is yet a further feature of his insistence that he starts from *judgements*, not concepts, and hence of his central concern with *content* (i.e. with the *thought* expressed on a particular occasion, as he would later characterize it). What might normally be regarded as implicit *contextual aspects* of the sense of a proposition are, in Frege's 'Begriffsschrift', to be given explicit representation ('nothing is left to guessing'; *BS*, §3).[21] It is, we may say, Frege's *decontextualism* that would have made him resistant to the strategy suggested for dealing with the counterintuitive results that his system appears to yield.

As far as Frege is concerned, then, these counterintuitive results would simply have been accepted – the inevitable price paid for a universal, decontextualized logic. However, the fact that we *can* overcome the difficulties by appreciating the role of context does suggest a rather deeper paradox in Frege's own conception of that logic. For it is only in a scientific context that Frege's project of decontextualism looks feasible; yet this context does have to be recognized as such.[22] The idea of a *presuppositionless* logic is incoherent: *any* theory has to take certain assumptions for granted. And if we admit this, then there is no reason why we should not include assumptions about *existential import* in the set of presuppositions of a logical system. Indeed, as we have shown, we *must*, if the objections we considered to both Aristotelian and Fregean logic are to be met.

As far as existential import is concerned, then, the difference between the two systems arises simply from Frege's use of the truth-functional material conditional in his formalization of the syllogistic *A*-proposition. This may in turn depend on the underlying rephrasing of 'All *A*'s are *B*' as 'If anything is an *A*, then it is a *B*', but there is no reason to suppose that it reflected any prior and deeper semantic insight about existential import itself, though it may well be that Frege's alternative analysis, together with the quantifier notation, gave credence to his project of decontextualism, towards which he might already have had Leibnizian aspirations.

It is striking that in the *Begriffsschrift* itself Frege offers little justification for his analysis. Locating the work broadly within the Leibniz-Kant tradition was assumed, perhaps, to be enough; and the issue was presumably only appreciated once Frege's formal system was in place, and the differences stood out. In his subsequent writings, however, Frege is clearly concerned to remedy the lack. With regard to syllogistic *A*-propositions, two points can be found as offering support for Frege's construal – one semantic and one epistemological. The semantic point is connected with the third of Frege's 'fundamental principles' advocated in the *Grundlagen*: 'The distinction between concept and object must be kept in mind' (p. X). The importance of this, for Frege, was recognized almost immediately after the publication of the *Begriffsschrift*. In his critique of Boole, Frege writes that on his own view 'we do justice to the distinction between concept and individual, which is completely obliterated in Boole. Taken strictly, his letters never mean individuals but always extensions of concepts. That is, we must distinguish between concept and thing, even when only one thing falls under a concept.' (*BLC*, p. 18.) He goes on to distinguish 'the case of one concept being subordinate to another from that of a thing falling under a concept' (ibid.), and this is a distinction he emphasizes throughout his later work.[23] In §47 of the *Grundlagen*, it becomes clear that Frege understands 'All *A*'s are *B*' as involving the subordination of concepts (represented by '*A*' and '*B*') rather than the subsumption of an object or objects (*All A's*) under a concept (*B*). The implication is that the proposition is not taken as entailing that there *are* any objects falling under the concepts.

Why *should* 'All *A*'s are *B*', though, be construed as involving subordination rather than subsumption? Frege argues that 'All whales are mammals' is about concepts rather than animals since if we ask of which animal we are speaking, 'there is no single one that can be picked out', and he continues:

> Even assuming that a whale is present, our proposition still asserts nothing about it. We cannot infer from it that the animal present is a mammal, without the additional proposition that it is a whale, as to which our proposition says nothing. In general, it is impossible to speak of an object without in some way designating or naming it. But the word 'whale' does not name any individual creature. (*GL*, §47.)

What is going on here, I think, is that Frege's semantic point (that 'All *A*'s are *B*' involves subordination rather than subsumption) is in turn being buttressed by a more *epistemological* consideration. As the rest of the section makes clear, Frege's thought can be expressed as follows. Whilst I may well have to observe particular animals to verify 'All whales are mammals', I can at least know what its 'content' is independently of verification; whereas I cannot even know what 'Gollum is a mammal' means, let alone whether it is true or not, unless I know to what 'Gollum' refers.[24] The implication is then that this fundamental epistemological difference is only properly captured in Frege's 'Begriffsschrift'.

In view of our discussion of the importance of context, however, both parts of this argument are questionable. Firstly, with regard to *universal* propositions, there may well be contexts in which I *am* to be construed as asserting of every member within a specific (delimited) class that it falls under a certain concept – 'All the books on my desk are works by Frege', for example. Perhaps Frege felt that, by divorcing universal propositions from any implication that there *are* certain kinds of object, he was indeed according them *universal* (decontextualized) significance – showing how they are independent of the vagaries of contingent existence. Of course, it is perfectly possible to formalize such cases – of uses of syllogistic *A*-propositions in contexts where there *is* existential import – in predicate logic:

(Ae) $(\forall x) (Ax \rightarrow Bx) \,\&\, (\exists x) Ax.$

According to Frege, what we have here are 'two distinguishable thoughts', and it is 'simplicity' that demands that 'All *A*'s are *B*' be restricted merely to the expression of the first.[25] However, considerations of 'simplicity' are notoriously system-relative, and the restriction itself counts as a presupposition in exactly the same way as it is a presupposition of syllogistic theory that all propositions *possess* existential import.[26] So whilst there may be an *explanation* of Frege's construal in terms of his symbolism, we are still left without any *philosophical justification*.

Secondly, with regard to *singular* propositions, there are also contexts in which I *can* meaningfully assert that an individual object falls under a concept even though I am not, and perhaps cannot be, acquainted with that object – 'Gollum is a slimy creature', for example. This brings us to the question as to the justification for Frege's construal of *particular* propositions, which, like singular propositions, are seen as *possessing* existential import. Of course, this immediately follows from Frege's understanding of universal propositions and the assumption (as in syllogistic theory) that *A*- and *O*-propositions, and *E*- and *I*-propositions, are *contradictories*. Since universal propositions – on the Fregean account – *lack* existential import, particular propositions must *possess* it. But once again it is just this that requires justification. In a revealing piece printed in his *Posthumous Writings*, however, dating from just after the *Begriffsschrift*, Frege discusses the issue with the theologian Bernard Pünjer. The crucial part of their dialogue runs as follows:

> *Frege*: 'Some men are Germans' means the same as 'There are German men'. As from 'Sachse is a man' there follows 'There are men' so from 'Sachse is a man' and 'Sachse is a German' there follows 'Some men are German' or 'there are German men'.
>
> *Pünjer*: 'Some men are Germans' does not mean the same as 'There are German men'. 'There are men' cannot be inferred from 'Sachse is a man' alone; you need the further sentence 'Sachse exists' as well.
>
> *Frege*: My reply to this would be: If 'Sachse exists' is supposed to mean 'The word "Sachse" is not an empty sound, but designates something', then it is true that the condition 'Sachse exists' must be satisfied. But this is not a new premise, but the presupposition of all our words – a presupposition which goes without saying. The rules of logic always presuppose that the words we use are not empty, that our sentences express judgements, that one is not playing a mere game with words. Once 'Sachse is a man' expresses an actual judgement, the word 'Sachse' must designate something, and in that case I

do not need a further premise in order to infer 'There are men' from it. (*DPE*, p. 60.)

The *epistemological* message of Frege's reply is clear. Once again we see the importance of his insistence that he starts from *actual judgements* – genuine attempts, we might say, to express *scientific knowledge*. Logic, for Frege, is not just a formal theory capable of representing certain types of propositions and inferences, but a Leibnizian *characteristica universalis* capable of representing a complete system of *truths*.[27] In this context, it is indeed a presupposition that 'the words we use are not empty'. But this context does have to be recognized as such, and Frege's 'justification' would appear in the end to amount to no more than a recommendation to confine oneself to that particular context. As we shall see in chapter 6, it was Frege's conception of logic that was responsible for his failure to fully face up to the problem of 'empty' terms when he came to consider the semantics of proper names in his later work.

In conclusion, then, we may note that the issue of existential import raises the general problem as to the justification for *any* analysis that might be offered of a particular proposition or type of proposition. We might well be able to explain how that analysis *arises* – revealing the concerns, assumptions and background theory that made its adoption natural and perhaps inevitable – but its *justification* appears continually elusive. Any attempt at providing such a justification seems finally to come down to a mere statement that the meaning of the proposition involved is being restricted in a certain way for particular purposes. I confront the general problem of analysis in chapter 5, after considering, in the next two chapters, Frege's analysis of number statements. But before this, we must explore Frege's key notion of 'conceptual content', which Frege did see as playing a justificatory role. Without an understanding of this notion, Frege's own later reflections on analysis, and the distinction between *Sinn* and *Bedeutung* that emerged as a result, cannot be appreciated.

2.5 Frege's Notion of 'Conceptual Content'

After stating that the main aim of his 'Begriffsschrift' is to enable us 'to test in the most reliable way the validity of a chain of inference', Frege goes on: 'The expression of anything that is without significance for *logical inference* [*Schlussfolge*] has therefore been eschewed. I have called, in §3, that which solely mattered to me *conceptual content* [*begrifflicher Inhalt*]. This point must therefore always be kept in mind if the nature of my formula language is to be understood correctly.' (*BS*, 'Preface'.) We have already noted how Frege saw the idea here as distinguishing his work from Boole's, and the Leibnizian motivation behind it (§2.1). Yet what exactly *is* the notion of 'conceptual content'?

In §3 of the *Begriffsschrift* Frege considers the following two propositions:

(GP) At Plataea the Greeks defeated the Persians.
(PG) At Plataea the Persians were defeated by the Greeks.

Now whilst we may be able to detect a slight difference in meaning here, it is hardly significant when compared with what the two propositions have in common. This is just Frege's point. 'I call that part of the content that is the *same* in both the *conceptual content*. Since *only this* has significance for the "Begriffsschrift", no distinction is needed between propositions that have the same conceptual content.' (*BS*, §3.) For logical purposes, Frege is suggesting, (GP) and (PG) can be crystallized together. It is this process, we may say, that produces the 'rigidity' of the 'Begriffsschrift' of which Frege spoke in comparing his system with an artificial hand (see §2.1 above). But what justifies this procedure? Frege states that 'in my formula language ... the only thing that is relevant in a judgement is that which influences its *possible consequences*' (ibid.). If two propositions have the same consequences, then as far as their representation within a logical system is concerned, they can be conflated.

To say that two propositions P and Q have the same possible consequences is to say that they are logically equivalent. For since any proposition implies itself, i.e. P is a consequence of P, P will also be a consequence of Q if P and Q have the same consequences, and vice versa, so that Q implies P and P implies Q, which is to say that they are logically equivalent. Frege's criterion for sameness of 'conceptual content' can thus be stated as follows:

(CC) Two propositions have the same *conceptual content* iff (if and only if) they are *logically equivalent* (have the same possible consequences).

What we have here, it would seem, is a perfectly natural and straightforward criterion. So in what did Frege's originality consist, and why was he led to abandon the notion of 'conceptual content' in his later work?

We can approach these questions by examining the exact nature of the relationship between 'sameness of conceptual content' and 'logical equivalence'. According to Frege, we are allowed to formalize two propositions as one if they are logically equivalent, but how is this logical equivalence to be recognized or demonstrated? If we can only do so *within* some logical system, have not the propositions to be already formalized? Yet, if §3 of the *Begriffsschrift* is our guide, the purpose of Frege's notion of 'conceptual content' is to allow us to make what we might call *pre-theoretical* conflations, simplifying the systematic representations. So is the appeal to a conception of logical equivalence that is more intuitively grounded, and is this seen as more fundamental than any appeal straight off to 'sameness of content'?

To explore this, let us return to syllogistic theory. In §1.4 it was suggested that whilst Aristotle understood logical *transition*, he failed to appreciate logical *equivalence*. It was on this basis that it seemed inappropriate to attribute to him a *semantic* conception of 'sense'. This conception, we can now see, is precisely what Frege intended by 'conceptual content'. What the case of Aristotle then suggests is that it is awareness of logical inference (logical transition) that is more primitive than semantic intuitions about 'sameness of sense'. Aristotle himself did not require such intuitions to develop his logical system; so why should the situation be any different in the case of Frege?

To answer this, let us consider the following two pairs of propositions (designated by their syllogistic formalization):

(Eab) No philosophers are logicians.
(Eba) No logicians are philosophers.

(Iab) Some philosophers are logicians.
(Iba) Some logicians are philosophers.

As we saw in §1.4, whilst Aristotle regarded (Eab) and (Eba) as 'identical', he did *not* view (Iab) and (Iba) as 'identical', and the reason for this, we suggested, was that Aristotle's conception of identity was *epistemological* rather than semantic. Whilst *both* pairs are in fact logically equivalent, Aristotle himself failed to appreciate this, since he regarded the transition from (Iab) to (Iba) as requiring *mediation*. But how do things look from a Fregean perspective? The formalizations are as follows:

(Eab*) $(\forall x)\,(Px \to \neg Lx)$.
(Eba*) $(\forall x)\,(Lx \to \neg Px)$.

(Iab*) $(\exists x)\,(Px \,\&\, Lx)$.
(Iba*) $(\exists x)\,(Lx \,\&\, Px)$.

Within Fregean logic, both (Eab*) and (Eba*), and (Iab*) and (Iba*), can be proved to be logically equivalent, '$(P \to \neg Q) \leftrightarrow (Q \to \neg P)$' and '$(P \,\&\, Q) \leftrightarrow (Q \,\&\, P)$' being theorems of the propositional calculus. But, if our earlier suggestion is right, any rationale for the appropriate judgements about sameness of 'conceptual content' must be available *before* their formalizations. So let us provide a natural language reading of the formalized propositions:

(Eab†) For all x, if x is a philosopher, then x is not a logician.
(Eba†) For all x, if x is a logician, then x is not a philosopher.

(Iab†) There is some x, such that x is a philosopher and x is a logician.
(Iba†) There is some x, such that x is a logician and x is a philosopher.

The equivalences between (Eab†) and (Eba†), and (Iab†) and (Iba†), will be appreciated precisely to the extent that the equivalences between the following are recognized: 'If *P* then not *Q*' and 'If *Q* then not *P*', and '*P* and *Q*' and '*Q* and *P*', respectively. What the natural language readings thus do is enable us to see more easily the equivalences between the original syllogistic propositions. (If anything, the latter equivalence is now more obvious than the former, reversing Aristotle's position.)

So have we shown that some more intuitive appeal to logical equivalence is sufficient to underpin a judgement about sameness of 'conceptual content'? This might well seem to hold in the first case, since understanding that 'If *P* then not *Q*' and 'If *Q* then not *P*' are equivalent does indeed appear to consist in knowing that each implies the other. But in the second case, it would be stretching the point to say that what is basic is the recognition that '*P* and *Q*' implies '*Q* and *P*', and vice versa, rather than simply the appreciation that they just do have the same 'content', that is, in some ordinary sense, 'mean' the same. And this seems even more appropriate in Frege's original example. What we have, therefore, is a *gradation* of cases. As far as (GP) and (PG) above are concerned, knowledge of their equivalence may indeed be purely semantic (resting simply on a grammatical rule); whereas in the cases we have just examined, the issue is more complex, since what semantic intuitions are needed depends on the precise logical background. Quantifier notation may provide us with a clearer representation of the identity of certain syllogistic pairs, but whilst the perceived identity of (Iab) and (Iba) requires the relatively simple intuition that '*P* and *Q* ' 'means' the same as '*Q* and *P*', in the case of (Eab) and (Eba) it is knowledge of a basic theorem of propositional logic that appears to be required.[28]

However, does not any representation of a proposition *in an alternative way* embody some semantic intuition? In formulating (Eab) as (Eab†), for example, do we not need to know that they 'mean' the same? Since trying to represent *that* equivalence would involve us in an infinite regress, must we not simply assume some basic agreement in semantic judgement? The problem is general. If a judgement about sameness of 'content' is not immediate, and requires appeal to logical equivalence, and this in turn can only be recognized by rephrasing the propositions, then we must know that the rephrasings preserve 'content', and we are back where we started. So is it that judgements about sameness of 'content' do, after all, underpin assessments of logical equivalence, rather than vice versa? As we saw in §1.1, Aristotle's own 'official' formulation of 'All *A*'s are *B*' was '*B* applies to all *A*', so that here too there must have been an assumption that the two expressions 'mean' the same. However, the key point is whether the semantic intuitions are explicitly recognized as such, and it is here that Frege's advance was made. The mere act of *formalizing* a proposition involves *some* semantic awareness; but when this results, as it does in Fregean logic, in a marked *divergence* from the proposition's grammatical form, confrontation with semantic issues is inevitable.

However, even in Frege's case, there is no reason to attribute to him any solid set of semantic intuitions *before* the initial draft of his logical theory. As §3 of the *Begriffsschrift* makes clear, the repudiation of the subject/predicate distinction occurred *after* an attempt at preserving the distinction within his calculus. Having found, as we saw in §2.3, that it could only be maintained at the cost of some prolixity, it presumably *then* occurred to him that it was unnecessary anyway. For if we agree that (GP) and (PG), for example, are just two different ways of saying the same thing, then why not extend this insight to pairs of *E*- and *I*-propositions? What Frege did was introduce a concept to *express* this insight: what the relevant pairs of propositions have in common is their 'conceptual content'. Of course, this in turn prompts further semantic questions, as we explore in the chapters that follow, but the crucial point here is to recognize the subtle interplay between semantic intuitions and logical formalizations, which shape and reinforce one another as the logical theory is developed.

This should not be taken to suggest, though, that such a semantic insight could not have arisen within alternative logical frameworks. There is no essential reason why a Boolean logician might not also have formulated such a conception. Consider, for example, the following Venn diagram:

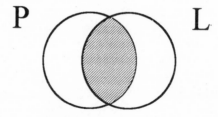

What the diagram can be taken as representing is the following proposition:

(Iv)   The intersection between the set of philosophers (P) and the set of logicians (L) is not empty.

(Iv) is equivalent to both (Iab) and (Iba), so explaining the Venn diagram would be just as good a way of proving the equivalence of (Iab) and (Iba) as the Fregean method. What is essential is just that there is *some* way of representing the identity. Here, for example, we might have said that what (Iab) and (Iba) have in common is 'pictorial content'.[29]

So did Frege's advance consist simply in the introduction of the notion of 'conceptual content' to characterize such equivalences? Consider the following passage from *The Laws of Thought*, published by Boole a quarter of a century before Frege's *Begriffsschrift*:

> the relations among [secondary propositions] are relations of coexistent truth or falsehood, not of substantive equivalence. We do not say, when expressing the connexion of two distinct propositions, that the one *is* the other, but use some such forms of speech as the following, according to the meaning which we desire to convey: "*Either* the proposition X is true, *or* the proposition Y is true"; "If the proposition X is true, the proposition Y is true"; "The propositions X and Y are jointly true"; and so on.
>
> Now, in considering any such relations as the above, we are not called upon to inquire into the whole extent of their possible meaning (for this might involve us in metaphysical questions of causation, which are beyond the proper limits of science); but it suffices to ascertain some meaning which they undoubtedly possess, and which is adequate for the purposes of logical deduction. Let us take, as an instance for examination, the conditional proposition, "If the proposition X is true, the proposition Y is true." An undoubted meaning of this proposition is, that the *time* in which the proposition X is true, is *time* in which the proposition Y is true. This indeed is only a relation of coexistence, and may or may not exhaust the meaning of the proposition, but it is a relation really involved in the statement of the proposition, and further, it suffices for all the purposes of logical inference. (1854: p. 163.)

Did Boole anticipate Frege's notion of, and criterion for, 'conceptual content'? He appears to have appreciated that logicians need only concern themselves with that part of the meaning of a proposition that is relevant to its logical implications. So was it simply that he lacked the term 'conceptual content' to express this appreciation? For Frege, to say that two propositions P and Q possess the same 'conceptual content' is to say that they are logically equivalent. Phrased in a Boolean way, it is to say that the following two conditional propositions hold: 'If P then Q' and 'If Q then P'. Yet it is clear that Boole himself would have denied that P and Q possess what he terms 'substantive equivalence'. Boole fails to explain what he means by this, but it hardly provides support for attributing to him a notion of 'conceptual content'.

For Boole, then, logical equivalence does not imply 'substantive equivalence'. But what, in any case, does Boole understand by logical equivalence? Even allowing that he can be granted *some* kind of conception of logical equivalence,[30] this would have to be viewed as more of a *temporal* than a *semantic* conception. As the above passage reveals, two propositions are 'logically equivalent' for Boole if they are, as he puts it, 'jointly true', that is, if at any particular time at which one is true, the other also is true. But this is not Frege's understanding. What Frege's notion of 'conceptual content' reflects is a *pure* conception of logical equivalence (two propositions are 'logically equivalent' simply if each implies the other), and it is the *interdependence* of these two ideas (neither of which Boole can really be considered to have shared) that constitutes the real advance.

However, if there was no essential reason why a Boolean logician could not have formulated a notion of 'conceptual content', why was it that Frege was the first to do so? The answer, as we have already suggested, lies in the radically different nature of Frege's logic. For given both the use of function-argument notation and Frege's urge to simplify, the conflation of certain pairs of syllogistic inferences emerges naturally (as we saw in §2.3). But the divergence from syllogistic theory is nevertheless so great that Frege cannot help but reflect upon the differences: the results of his formalizations make the question of justification inevitable. With the introduction of the notion of 'conceptual content' (extending the basic intuition we recognized in the case of (GP) and (PG) above), Frege has a reply: inferences such as *Disamis* and *Dimatis* can be conflated because they possess the same 'conceptual content', and 'conceptual content' is all that logicians need really concern themselves with. The awareness that his system required justification, then, may well have provided the stimulus for the introduction of the notion. But this is not to say that there is no obvious or underlying semantic insight that it reflects. As Nietzsche put it, in the maxim quoted at the beginning of this chapter, written in the very year of Frege's *Begriffsschrift*, originality consists not in seeing 'something new as the first one to do so, but [in seeing] something old, familiar, seen but overlooked by everyone, *as though it were new*'. Frege's own originality consisted in giving expression to a semantic insight in the context of a new way of pursuing logic; and it was this context that brought to the fore the insight.[31]

Returning to our earlier question, then, which do come first – semantic intuitions or logical inferences? Is it our assessments of logical equivalence that underpin judgements about sameness of 'conceptual content', or vice versa? The question itself, we can now see, masks a misunderstanding. What we might term the 'Fregean Circle' is easily dealt with.[32] As we saw in §2.1, Frege himself raised a closely related difficulty: '[ordinary] language is supposed to have made reason possible, but how could man have invented language without reason?' Rephrasing his own response, we can reply: 'The [apparently vicious] circle is resolved in each case in the same way: an advance in semantics results in an advance in logic, and this makes possible the construction of new instruments by means of which semantics is again advanced' (cf. *SJCN*, p. 89). The development or understanding of *any* logical system depends on a series of semantic insights along the way; yet those insights are themselves shaped and shown up by the grammatical or logical background.

Frege's criterion (CC), then, is not to be read as according either side of the biconditional privileged status; what it crystallizes, with the seed of the notion of 'conceptual content', is a relationship that was there to be crystallized in the flux of linguistic life. However, as formulated, it still leaves open an ambiguity, with a potential disaster threatening. For if 'logical equivalence' is captured by the *material biconditional* (which is indeed the biconditional used in Frege's 'Begriffsschrift'), then the paradox of material implication emerges to sabotage Frege's criterion. For both '$P \to (Q \to P)$' and '$Q \to (P \to Q)$', and hence '$(P \& Q) \to (P \leftrightarrow Q)$', are theorems of propositional logic; in other words, informally, if two propositions are true, then they are materially equivalent (at least, this is the material implication). So if (CC) is taken as involving material equivalence, then all true propositions turn out to possess the same 'conceptual content'![33] Clearly, this was not a result intended by Frege at the time, and indicates that (CC) must be interpreted as involving a stronger relation.

In fact, if we look more closely at how Frege introduces the notion of 'conceptual content', it might be suggested that the appropriate criterion here be formulated in terms of *provable* material equivalence. Two judgements have the same 'conceptual content' if, as Frege puts it, 'the conclusions that can be drawn from one when combined with certain others also always follow from the second when combined with the same judgements' (*BS*, §3); in other words, if they have the same possible consequences derivable from the same set of premises. If Q can be *derived* from P, and P can be *derived* from Q, utilizing the same resources, then P and Q have the same 'conceptual content'. This suggests that we need to distinguish the following two versions of (CC):

(CC#) Two propositions have the same *veritable content* iff they are *materially equivalent*.

(CC*) Two propositions have the same *logical content* iff they are *logically equivalent* (*provably* materially equivalent).

(CC#), we can note, provides just the criterion for Frege's later notion of *Bedeutung* (what I have here called 'veritable content', in other words, becoming 'Bedeutung'). According to Frege, the *Bedeutung* of a proposition is one of the two truth-values (the True or the False), and two propositions do indeed have the same truth-value iff they are materially equivalent. Given that Frege himself later talks of the bifurcation of his early notion of 'conceptual content' into 'Bedeutung' and 'Sinn' (cf. e.g. *PMC*, p. 63; *CO*, p. 47), have we therefore immediately succeeded in providing criteria for these notions? Frege does offer in one place something like (CC*) as the criterion for sameness of 'Sinn', but this cannot be taken as his 'official' view.[34] The reason is simple: there seem to be many 'logically equivalent' statements that we would not intuitively regard as possessing the same 'conceptual content'. The problem is highlighted by Frege's *logicism*, the doctrine that arithmetic is reducible to logic. For if logicism is correct, then '$2^2 = 4$' and '$2 + 2 = 4$', for example, are 'logically equivalent': it can be proved, purely logically, that if one is true, the other is true, and vice versa.[35] Yet they are not, on some understanding of this phrase, 'cognitively equivalent'. In representing them in a logical system, we would clearly not formalize them the same way – unlike, say, (GP) and (PG) above. Indeed, if the propositions of arithmetic could be seen to have the same 'content' straight off, there would be little point in seeking to *demonstrate* their 'logical equivalence'.

The differences between arithmetical propositions are therefore as important as what they have in common. Basing a criterion merely on 'logical equivalence', then, even if captured by (CC*) rather than (CC#), fails to do justice to all that seems to be involved in talk of 'conceptual content'. So let us formulate a third version of (CC):

(CC†) Two propositions have the same *cognitive content* iff they are *cognitively equivalent*.

Unlike the previous two types of equivalence, however, 'cognitive equivalence' is not itself defined, although it may be possible to illustrate what is meant, as in the example just used, in particular cases. If it is 'cognitive content' rather than 'logical content' that becomes 'Sinn', then it is precisely (CC†) that needs clarification.[36] Unfortunately, as we shall see in the second half of this book, Frege's own characterizations of 'Sinn' are not entirely consistent, and the issues involved are controversial. But before discussing this, we must first provide an account of Frege's logicist project, which was responsible not only for motivating the distinction between 'Sinn' and 'Bedeutung', but also for the tensions that nevertheless remain.

3. Frege's Critique of
Mathematical Reason

... all the things that are known have a number – for without this nothing could be thought of or known. (Philolaus, 5th century BC.)[1]

As we have seen, the main purpose of Frege's 'Begriffsschrift' was 'to test in the most reliable way the validity of a chain of inference and to reveal every presupposition that tends to slip in unnoticed, so that its origin can be investigated' (*BS*, 'Preface'). Frege's aim, more specifically, was to examine *arithmetical* chains of reasoning; and it was this that prompted the expansion of logic that allowed satisfying analyses of statements of multiple generality, statements which are clearly prevalent in mathematics (e.g. 'Every number has a successor', 'Every even number is the sum of two primes'). But, as the remark just quoted indicates, the aim was not just to test the *validity* of arithmetical chains of reasoning; it was also to identify the *assumptions* upon which those chains rested, so that their status could be ascertained. More specifically still, the aim was to reveal their *logical* status – in short, to demonstrate that arithmetic was *reducible* to logic; and it is this logicist project that I am concerned to elucidate in this and the following chapter.

In this chapter I focus on Frege's motivations and on his critique of rival conceptions of mathematics, clearing the way for an exposition of the more positive part of his programme in the next chapter. I start by sketching the developments in mathematics that form the background to Frege's thought (§3.1), and then consider his own early mathematical work (§3.2), and the analysis of mathematical induction that he provided in his *Begriffsschrift* (§3.3). In the final two sections I offer an account of the first half of Frege's *Grundlagen*, discussing, firstly, his criticisms of Kant's and Mill's views on the supposedly synthetic character of arithmetical truths (§3.4), and secondly, his attack on certain positions regarding the nature of number – empiricism, psychologism, and what he calls 'set theory' (§3.5).

3.1 The Mathematical Background

Pythagoras, reputedly, was the first to suggest that the world was governed by number and could be explained in mathematical terms. According to Aristotle's account in the *Metaphysics* (985b23-986a22), the

Pythagoreans (who flourished in the 5th century BC) believed that numbers were the basic elements of the universe. Given that numbers were conceived as the *units* of existence, this may not be as absurd a metaphysical view as one might think, and it was not until Frege that the notion of a 'unit' received the critique it required (see §§3.5 and 4.1 below). But as the quote from Philolaus at the beginning of this chapter suggests, Pythagoreanism also had an epistemological dimension – that we can have no *knowledge* of anything without ascribing it a number; and this fundamental Pythagorean belief was certainly endorsed by Frege, and given a more powerful expression by equating the laws of number which were regarded as lying at the base of our understanding of the world with the laws of logic.

Numerical relationships were seen by the Pythagoreans as underlying both music and astronomy, the latter mediated by geometry – the study of spatial properties. This might suggest that arithmetic was viewed as more fundamental than geometry, but if such a belief was ever articulated by the early Pythagoreans, it was certainly not held by the later philosophers of antiquity. Geometry, just because of its central role in the explanation of the physical universe, was regarded as the fundamental science; and it was geometry that Euclid axiomatized around 300 BC. Numbers, as the *measure* of things, were given a geometrical interpretation; and arithmetic was generally taken as playing an auxiliary role. The classical Greeks, for example, believed that no more than three numbers could be multiplied together, since space had only three dimensions; and our own talk of 'x^2' as 'x squared' and 'x^3' as 'x cubed' still reflects their original geometrical interpretation.[2]

If Pythagoreanism is right that we can have no knowledge of anything without ascribing it a number, how is it that we have knowledge of number itself? If numbers are themselves things, is there not a danger of an infinite regress? In its general form, this question greatly occupied Plato: if knowledge requires reasoning (it cannot be mere true belief), then must we not already know how to reason? Since, according to Plato, the sensible world cannot supply the forms of reasoning, due to its changing character, then we must already be in touch with an eternal world of Ideas. Such a view might seem plausible in the case of mathematics. For we seem to know what the properties of geometrical figures are, for example, *independently* of sense-experience; 'real' circles and triangles, after all, do not exist in the physical world. If epistemological Pythagoreanism is an attractive position to adopt, then there would seem to be an inevitable progression into metaphysical Platonism. As we shall see, just such a progression occurred in Frege's thought.

The ancient Greeks undoubtedly believed in the power of human reason, and as we saw in chapter 1, it was Aristotle who recognized that if knowledge is arranged in a deductive system, knowledge of the axioms must be assumed as given. The model for scientific knowledge, as propounded by Aristotle and exemplified, most famously, in Euclid's work, was thus clear: we *intuit* the axioms and *deduce* the theorems. But what deserves note is that this model was only applied, in mathematics, to *geometry*; the development of arithmetic proceeded in a more *ad hoc* and less rigorous way, governed largely by considerations of utility.

The history of the development of our conception of number is both fascinating and philosophically instructive. Take, for example, the case of irrational numbers. The Pythagoreans had discovered, and indeed proved, that there were some ratios, such as that of the hypotenuse of a right-angled isosceles triangle to one of its other sides, i.e. $\sqrt{2}$, that were incommensurable with the natural numbers, i.e. could not be represented as a ratio of natural numbers. But they were nevertheless unhappy with such irrational numbers, and it was only when Eudoxus, a younger contemporary of Plato, provided a geometrical interpretation that they began to be accepted. No purely arithmetical justification was offered. Although after the demise of Greek civilization, the Hindus and Arabs kept the torch of arithmetic alight, the logical structure of arithmetic remained unexplored until the Renaissance. The Hindus, for example, not only used irrational numbers but also introduced negative numbers, but their interest was pragmatic.[3]

During the 16th and 17th centuries, the nature and status of the various types of number began to be debated. Descartes, for example, was uneasy about negative numbers; and Pascal notoriously remarked: 'too much truth bewilders us. I know people who cannot understand that 4 from 0 leaves 0' (*Pensées*, p. 92). Complex numbers also emerged, as the roots of quadratic equations were derived; and these too were controversial. Descartes termed them 'imaginary', and Newton referred to them as 'impossible', because they lacked a physical interpretation; and once again, it was only when it had been shown how to represent them geometrically (on a plane) that their use became accepted.[4]

One of the most important developments in this period, however, was the rise of algebra, although its origins can be traced back, as in other fields, to the ancient Greeks. As we saw in chapter 1, in inventing logic, Aristotle had introduced schematic letters, or 'term variables' as they are sometimes also called, to enable the general form of a proposition to be represented (as in 'All *A*'s are *B*'); and this device was carried over into mathematics, appearing first in Euclid's *Elements* ('*AB*', for example, being used to represent a line). In the 3rd century AD, Diophantus took an important step in introducing numerical variables, corresponding to our modern symbolism of '*x*', '*x²*', '*x³*', etc.[5] But it was only in the 16th century that algebra finally got off the ground, with the publication of Cardan's *Ars Magna* in 1545, presenting various results, and Vieta's *In Artem Analyticam Isagoge* in 1591. Vieta added schematic letters to the numerical variables already being used in algebra, so that quadratic equations, for example, could be represented in the form '$ax^2 + bx + c = 0$', permitting greater generality. Vieta also distinguished between *logistica numerosa* (calculation with numbers) and *logistica speciosa* (calculation with types), the latter constituting his new algebra, concerned with the (schematized) *types* of equations.[6]

Although algebra was seen as a method of analysis rather than a discipline in itself (an 'art' rather than a 'science', as the titles of Cardan's and Vieta's books suggest), its significance should not be underestimated. Its potential was realized with the creation by Fermat and Descartes of analytic or coordinate geometry, which provided algebraic description of geometric figures. Lines could be represented in the form '$y = ax + b$', and circles of radius r in the form '$y^2 = r^2 - x^2$', for example. Since investigations could then be carried out in a more abstract and formal way, this freed mathematicians of the need to visualize everything geometrically. Euclidean geometry was still regarded as providing the fundamental framework of interpretation, but it did eventually allow the exploration of non-Euclidean geometries.

The 17th century also witnessed the rise of mathematical physics, and algebra played a further role in the formulation of the emerging laws. Galileo, for example, showed how the distance s travelled by a falling object varies according to the square of the time t taken, as given by the equation '$s = kt^2$', where k is some constant. Certain variables of a physical system were thus revealed as *functions* of one another; and the concept of a *function* was to prove of critical significance. The theory of functions became a whole branch of mathematics, and as we saw in the last chapter, it was the extension of function-argument analysis to ordinary language that instigated Frege's revolution in logic. But the most immediate development, in the 17th century, was the creation of the differential and integral calculus; and this provoked enormous controversy.

To gain a sense of the dispute, let us use the example just given. Whilst we can readily speak of the *average speed* of a falling object over a certain time ($= s/t$), we also want to know its speed at any instant t_n. To determine this, we consider the average speed in the interval immediately following t_n, i.e. between time t_n and time $t_n + \delta t$, when the object has fallen from point s_n to point $s_n + \delta s$, where δt and δs are the relevant increments.[7] Since $s = kt^2$,

$$(s_n + \delta s) = k.(t_n + \delta t)^2,$$
$$= k.t_n^2 + 2k.t_n.\delta t + k.(\delta t)^2.$$

Subtracting s_n ($= k.t_n^2$) from both sides, we obtain the formula for δs:

$$\delta s = 2k.t_n.\delta t + k.(\delta t)^2.$$

The average speed over the interval is thus given as follows:

$$\delta s/\delta t = 2k.t_n + k.\delta t.$$

As δt approaches 0, $\delta s/\delta t$ tends to $2k.t_n$, the *derivative* of kt^2 at $t = t_n$. ds/dt, the result of *differentiating* the original function $s = kt^2$, is thus $2kt$.

The problem can now be seen. For if δs and δt were indeed 0, then $\delta s/\delta t$ would be undefined, so how could its limit (ds/dt) be any number at all? And if they are not 0, but some finite quantity (however small), then it would seem that there can be no such thing, after all, as the speed of an object at an instant. Newton, who, with Leibniz, is credited with (independent) invention of the calculus, talked of 'fluxions' and 'evanescent quantities', but gave no clear account of what these were.[8] Leibniz spoke of 'infinitesimals' – magnitudes that are smaller than any given quantity, but not zero. On the supposition that 'infinitesimals' exist, we clearly arrive at a contradiction; and although Leibniz himself explicitly rejected the supposition, remarking that infinitesimals were simply 'fictions of the mind useful for calculations, of the same order as imaginary roots in algebra', he still failed to distinguish clearly enough between the differential ds and the finite variable quantity δs (to use the terminology adopted above).[9] Berkeley, in particular, was highly scornful of both Newtonian and Leibnizian conceptions, arguing that something of which one could have no idea at all (an 'evanescent quantity' or 'infinitesimal') was simply incoherent.[10]

The main problem in understanding the calculus (as Berkeley's criticisms highlighted) lay in attempting to conceive it empirically. But as Leibniz himself realized, more clearly than his contemporaries, the task was to *free* the calculus from any foundation in geometry, and to explain it in purely arithmetical and algebraic terms. This project was furthered by Euler, Lagrange and Lacroix in the late 18th century, and eventually taken up by some of the British mathematicians, such as Babbage and Peacock, having finally liberated themselves from the restrictive Newtonian tradition of seeking geometrical justifications, in the early 19th century. However, difficulties and complications kept on emerging. One assumption that had been made, for example, was that any continuous function has a derivative at each point. But this was discovered to be simply false. It might be true for functions that could be represented geometrically as 'smooth' curves, but was not true for functions with 'corners'; and in 1872 Weierstrass made public an example of a continuous function that had no derivative at any point.[11]

The concept that held the key to the interpretation of the calculus was the concept of a 'limit'. For the derivative, dy/dx, of a function relating y to x is the value that the quotient $\delta y/\delta x$ tends towards as δx approaches 0. Since δy and δx do not approach 0 *independently* of one another, their quotient does not itself approach an undefined 0/0 but rather the *limit* of the relevant series. D'Alembert was one of the few who had recognized, early on, the importance of the idea of a limit, remarking in the *Encyclopédie* that the theory of limits is the basis of the true metaphysics of the calculus.[12] But it was only Cauchy's *Cours d'Analyse*, published in 1821, that finally provided the framework for the necessary rigorization of the calculus – or *analysis*, as it came to be called. Cauchy recognized that the existence of a *limit* presupposes a *convergent* series, and he clarified the distinction between convergent and divergent series. Using the concept of a limit, he provided definitions of both the continuity and the derivative of a function.

However, Cauchy not only continued to provide geometrical interpretations but also retained the talk of *infinitesimals*, which he defined as variables whose values are less than any given quantity and which have zero for their limit. Whilst this can be interpreted harmlessly enough (as it arguably can in Leibniz's work), it is easy to slip into construing them not as *variables* but as *quantities*; and Cauchy himself did in fact trade on the ambiguity in one of his central arguments. It was only with the more refined notation (utilizing 'δ' and 'ε') introduced by Weierstrass, who is generally regarded as the founder of modern analysis, that misleading talk of infinitesimals was finally purged.[13]

Weierstrass was quite clear that if progress was to be made in areas where geometrical intuition gives out, then analysis needed to be grounded in number theory. Of course, this then meant that a rigorous understanding of *number* was required. But here too, as we have seen, there was no lack of controversy. Even in the 19th century, there were still disputes about negative numbers and complex numbers; and in 1843 Hamilton added to the problems by inventing *quaternions*, numbers of the form '$a + bi + cj + dk$', where $i^2 = j^2 = k^2 = -1$, and $jk = i$, $kj = -i$, $ki = j$, $ik = -j$, $ij = k$ and $ji = -k$. In the case of quaternions, multiplication no longer obeyed the law of commutativity. When Cayley introduced *matrices*, a further type of *hypernumber*, the moral was clear: one cannot just assume that the basic properties of one number system automatically carry over to any enlargement of that system. This raised doubts about the possibility of a *general* algebra of number, refuting Peacock's 'principle of the permanence of forms', propounded in 1833 as part of an attempt at axiomatizing algebra, which had simply *stipulated* that an algebra that covered the natural numbers also encompassed other types of number.[14]

The demands of analysis made the lack of clarity about numbers particularly pressing, since to demonstrate that a certain series has a limit, one must show that a number exists that is the value of that limit. Mathematicians had for long known that irrational numbers could be represented as sums of infinite series of rational numbers. Leibniz, for example, had shown that $\pi/4$ was equivalent to $1 - 1/3 + 1/5 - 1/7 + \ldots$[15] But no general proof had been offered that *any* convergent series of numbers has a real number as its limit. Cauchy had merely proved that convergence was *necessary* for the existence of a limit, not that it was *sufficient*. Clearly, a theory of the real numbers was called for; and the first arithmetical attempt to do so was made by Weierstrass in the 1860s, and developed, most notably, by Cantor in the 1870s. The essential strategy was to 'assign' the irrationals to convergent sequences of rationals (Cantor's 'fundamental sequences'), and then to show how the familiar properties of the real numbers could be derived. Since convergent sequences of *real numbers* (i.e. comprising the irrationals as well as the rationals) could now be constructed, one of Cantor's proofs consisted in demonstrating that the limits of these sequences were themselves real numbers (rather than yet a further type of number in turn requiring definition).[16]

A similar theory was developed by Dedekind in his *Continuity and Irrational Numbers*, published in 1872. Since the continuity of the real numbers had traditionally been represented geometrically, Dedekind started by considering what was meant by geometrical continuity, with the aim of developing an arithmetical alternative. What he noted was that if all the points of a straight line are divided into two classes such that every point in one class lies to the left of every point in the other class, then there exists one and only one point that effects this division (1872: p. 11). With this idea in mind, he then introduced the notion of a *cut* (*Schnitt*) in the series of rational numbers, dividing them into two classes A_1 and A_2 such that every number in A_1 is less than every number in A_2. For any cut (A_1, A_2), he remarked, there is a unique real number that 'corresponds to' or 'brings about' this cut (pp. 12-15).[17] Where a cut results in A_1 having a greatest number or A_2 having a smallest number, we have a rational number; where it results in neither, we have an irrational number. Like Cantor, Dedekind went on to derive the familiar properties of the real numbers, and he showed that any cut in the *real numbers* produces one and only one such number. The similarity between Dedekind's and Cantor's approaches should be clear, since any (monotonic) convergent sequence determines a unique Dedekind cut, and for any Dedekind cut one can specify a convergent sequence.[18]

These theories generate as many problems as they resolve, however, not least at the philosophical level; and I shall return to this later, since Frege's own approach involves an analogous move, identifying numbers with extensions of concepts. But here we need only note one immediate result. For both Cantor's and Dedekind's accounts involve the notion of an *infinite set* of numbers (indeed, a set that is *actually* rather than merely *potentially* infinite); and this naturally leads to questions about the properties of such sets. How do we determine, for example, whether two sets have the same number or not? Cantor suggested that the key concept here was that of one-one correspondence: if two sets, whether finite or infinite, could be put in one-one correspondence, then they should be assigned the same number. On this conception, the set of natural numbers turns out to have the same cardinality as the set of rational numbers, and Cantor denoted this by '$\aleph_0$' (aleph zero). The set of real numbers, on the other hand, proves to be larger than the set of natural numbers, and this number Cantor denoted by 'c' (the number of the continuum). Having shown that the set of all subsets of a given set is larger than the original set, since $2^n > n$, Cantor proved that c was equal to $2^{\aleph_0}$, and hypothesized that this was the next transfinite cardinal, $\aleph_1$ (aleph one) – Cantor's 'continuum hypothesis', which has still not been proved.[19] Needless to say, transfinite numbers provoked even greater controversy than other types of number; and when Cantor discovered a paradox in 1895, a chain of events was sparked off that was eventually to lead to the devastation of Frege's own work and the sophistications of modern set theory.

Controversies and further developments aside, however, by the latter half of the 19th century number theory did seem to have finally freed itself from dependence on geometry, and was generally looking in better deductive shape. But in the meantime geometry too had undergone a transformation. Euclid's work, for so long the paradigm of a rigorously axiomatized and definitive system of truths, had increasingly been the target of criticism. In particular, attention had been focussed on Euclid's notorious fifth axiom, the 'parallel postulate'. Even Euclid had been unsure about its status, and attempts to improve its formulation or derive it from the other axioms had all failed. During the 18th century it gradually dawned on mathematicians that the parallel postulate was indeed independent of the other axioms, and that a consistent geometry could be developed that denied it. During the first half of the 19th century Gauss, Lobatchevsky and Bolyai constructed the first non-Euclidean system, hyperbolic geometry, in which the angles of a triangle add up to *less* than 180°; and from the mid 19th century Riemann developed another non-Euclidean system, double elliptic geometry, in which the angles of a triangle add up to *more* than 180° and there are *no* parallel lines.

Mathematicians remained sceptical, though, as to the significance of non-Euclidean geometries, and many assumed that contradictions would sooner or later be discovered. But when double elliptic geometry was shown to be applicable to the surface of a sphere, 'lines' being interpreted as great circles, it became clear that non-Euclidean geometries were consistent if Euclidean geometry was consistent (since the configurations on which they could be mapped were Euclidean). Whilst this suggested that non-Euclidean geometries could be treated as models *within* Euclidean geometry, many mathematicians, from Gauss onwards, felt obliged to abandon the belief that Euclidean geometry was a system of absolute truths. By the end of the 19th century, Hilbert, in his own work on the foundations of geometry, was arguing that the axioms of geometry were simply formal schemata allowing a range of interpretations, but since he also proved that Euclidean geometry was consistent if arithmetic was consistent, its rigour was left untarnished.[20]

By the latter half of the 19th century, then, the Pythagorean belief in the fundamental status of the laws of number had been reinvigorated, and the traditional (classical Greek) view of the relationship between geometry and arithmetic had been inverted. Very crudely, the situation might be summarized thus. Non-Euclidean geometry could be modelled within Euclidean geometry; Euclidean geometry, through analytic geometry, could be grounded in number theory; transfinite numbers, hypernumbers, complex numbers and irrational numbers could be derived from the rational numbers; and rational numbers, both positive and negative, were definable in terms of the natural numbers. The natural numbers were still assumed as given; but with Frege, as we shall see, the final step in the reductive process was undertaken: the definition of the natural numbers in purely logical terms.

3.2 Frege's Early Work

Frege was educated at the Universities of Jena (1869-70) and Göttingen (1871-3). He took courses in mathematics and physics, but also two in philosophy (one on Kant at Jena, and the other on the philosophy of religion, taught by Lotze, at Göttingen), and submitted his doctoral dissertation, 'On a Geometrical Representation of Imaginary Forms [*Gebilde*] in the Plane' (*GR*), in late 1873.[21] Although this work is mathematical, in the Gaussian tradition then dominant at Göttingen, its philosophical motivation is worth elucidating. Gauss, who had spent almost all his mathematical career at Göttingen (he died in 1855), had been one of those responsible for legitimating complex numbers by showing how they could be represented as points on a plane.[22] In his dissertation, supervised by Schering (Gauss' official successor and editor of his works), Frege takes this a step further, by showing how imaginary forms can be represented geometrically.[23]

Frege's dissertation opens with these words:

> When we consider that the whole of geometry rests ultimately on axioms which derive their validity from the nature of our intuitive faculty, we seem well justified in questioning the sense of imaginary forms, since we attribute to them properties which not infrequently contradict all our intuitions. (*GR*, p. 1.)

The example that Frege gives is that of calculating the points of intersection of a straight line with a circle that lies outside that line, the equations for which yield imaginary points (ibid.). Such an imaginary form might strike us as simply impossible, but Frege sets out to show how the non-intuitive relations between imaginary forms can be replaced by intuitive ones (*GR*, p. 3). He considers a more familiar case to illustrate his project:

> By way of comparison let us take forms at infinity, which do not occur in the space of our intuition either. Taken literally, a 'point at infinity' is even a contradiction in terms; for the point itself would be the end point of a distance which had no end. The expression is therefore an improper one, and

it designates the fact that parallel lines behave projectively like straight lines passing through the same point. 'Point at infinity' is therefore only another expression for what is common to all parallels, which is what we commonly call 'direction'. As a straight line is determined by two points, it is also given by a point and a direction. This is only an instance of the general law that, whenever we are dealing with projective relationships, a direction can represent a point. By designating the direction as a point at infinity, we forestall a difficulty which would otherwise arise because of the need to distinguish a frequently unsurveyable set of cases according to whether two or more of the straight lines in the set were parallel or not. But once the principle of the equivalence of direction and point is established, all these cases are disposed of at one blow. (*GR*, p. 1.)[24]

Just as parallel lines, which are taken to meet at infinity, can be represented by projecting them onto the surface of a sphere, so too, Frege suggests, can a representation be found of imaginary forms (*GR*, pp. 2-3).

But if analytic geometry, utilizing the real number system, can handle standard Euclidean configurations, can it be extended by the incorporation of complex numbers to represent imaginary forms? As Frege puts it, 'It is now of the greatest importance to find out when a proposition which holds for real forms can be carried over to imaginary ones' (*GR*, p. 2). However, as Frege goes on to say, 'with few exceptions all the operations and concepts that occur in the case of real numbers can indeed be carried over unchanged to complex ones', and this 'justifies the introduction of imaginary forms into geometry' (ibid.). One concept Frege considers is that of distance. The distance r between two points (x_0, y_0) and (x_1, y_1) is given by the equation $r = \sqrt{[(x_1 - x_0)^2 + (y_1 - y_0)^2]}$. Since the use of such equations within analytic geometry involves 'operations and inferences which are equally applicable to complex numbers', they are also valid when there are complex coordinates. 'If we now take the view that what is essential to the concept of distance is not the intuitive character of a straight line but conformity to the laws of algebraic analysis, then we can apply the name "distance" also where the end points are imaginary' (*GR*, pp. 9-10). In this fashion, Frege shows, the traditional concepts of geometry can be extended to encompass imaginary forms.

Despite being a work in pure geometry, Frege's dissertation nevertheless hints at the subsequent direction of his thought. For he is clearly concerned with how results in one area can be extended into another (cf. *GR*, p. 3). What allows this is the underlying arithmetic, which can encompass the non-intuitable as well as the intuitable. That our ability to use arithmetic outstrips our powers of intuition is something that Frege emphasizes throughout his later work. Indeed, it provides the starting-point for Frege's next piece of work, his *Habilitationsschrift*, his dissertation for the *Venia docendi*, submitted in early 1874 to the University of Jena as part of his application for a teaching post.[25] Entitled 'Methods of Calculation based on an Extension of the Concept of Magnitude' (*MC*), it is in this work that Frege's foundationalist interests emerge.[26]

Frege's *Habilitationsschrift* opens with a clear indication of how it developed out of his earlier work. 'When we consider complex numbers and their geometrical representation, we leave the field of the original concept of magnitude, as contained especially in the magnitudes of Euclidean geometry: its lines, surfaces and volumes' (*MC*, p. 56). The physical interpretation of the addition of such magnitudes, in terms of the space filled, is abandoned. 'All that has remained is certain general properties of addition, which now emerge as the essential characteristic marks of magnitude. The concept has thus gradually freed itself from intuition and made itself independent. This is quite unobjectionable, especially since its earlier intuitive character was at bottom mere appearance' (ibid.). Frege suggests, for example, that someone learns what an angle is, not by being presented with one, but by being shown how to *add* angles. 'And it is clear that a concept as comprehensive and abstract as the concept of magnitude cannot be an intuition' (ibid.).

According to Frege, there is thus an important difference between arithmetic and geometry as far as their foundations are concerned:

> The elements of all geometrical constructions are intuitions, and geometry refers to intuitions as the source of its axioms. Since the object of arithmetic does not have an intuitive character, its fundamental propositions cannot stem from intuition either. And how could intuition guarantee propositions which hold for all such heterogeneous magnitudes, some species of which may still be unknown to us? (*MC*, pp. 56-7.)

Gauss, as a result of his work on non-Euclidean geometry, had departed from the traditional and Kantian view, and drawn a fundamental distinction between arithmetic and geometry, arithmetic being seen as a system of absolute truths, and geometry as an empirical discipline based on intuitions; and it might seem that Frege is endorsing that Gaussian view here. But this passage, like his remark at the beginning of his doctoral dissertation, leaves it unclear whether he thought that geometry was based on *empirical* intuitions, as Gauss himself had thought, or *a priori* intuitions, as Kant had thought.[27] Nevertheless, it is clear that by the time of the *Begriffsschrift*, Frege held a Kantian view of geometry, but, like Gauss, insisted on a separation between geometry and arithmetic, maintaining a Leibnizian view of the analytic *a priori* character of arithmetic. Only at the very end of his life did Frege propose a revision of these views.[28]

Given that the concept of magnitude is not found in intuition but created by ourselves, Frege goes on, 'we are justified in trying to formulate its definition so as to permit as manifold an application as possible, in order to extend the domain that is subject to arithmetic as far as possible' (*MC*, p. 57). The concept of magnitude cannot be grasped without the concept of addition, Frege remarks, and it is addition that is 'the subject of those fundamental propositions from which the whole of arithmetic grows as from a seed' (ibid.). All other methods of calculation derive from addition, repeated addition, for example, yielding multiplication. What is involved here, Frege suggests, is the iterative application of an operation, which can be represented by an appropriate function, such that the value of the function for a given argument can itself become the argument of that function (*MC*, p. 58). Adding 1, for example, can be represented by the successor function, $f(x) = x + 1$, adding 2 by $ff(x)$, and so on; doubling by $g(x) = x + x$, quadrupling by $gg(x)$, and so on.

What Frege is concerned with, in particular, is the magnitude that can be ascribed to operations. According to Frege, $fff(x)$, for example, has triple the magnitude of $f(x)$ (*MC*, pp. 58-9), and the main body of his *Habilitationsschrift* consists in an investigation of the relationships that hold between various types of mathematical function. But the key point to note here is the central role that the notion of a function is suggested as playing in the required theory of magnitude, making possible the connection between different areas of arithmetic (*MC*, p. 58). As we saw in the last chapter, it was Frege's development of function theory that resulted in the logic of the *Begriffsschrift*, and the envisaged unification of arithmetic that provided the nucleus of Frege's Leibnizian aspirations.

On the completion of his *Habilitationsschrift*, and on the necessary oral examination, public disputation and trial lecture, in May 1874 Frege was appointed *Privatdozent* at the University of Jena, where he stayed for the rest of his career.[29] In the first few years, his teaching load was heavy, and he only published four short pieces, three of them reviews, before the appearance of the *Begriffsschrift* in 1879.[30] In one of these, his review of H. Seeger's *Die Elemente der Arithmetik*, he notes the 'paucity of fundamental considerations', remarking that 'wherever proofs and justifications are most needed, they are found to be wanting' (*RS*, pp. 93-4); but otherwise there is no further indication of the revolution in logic and philosophy that the *Begriffsschrift* was to inaugurate.

3.3 The Analysis of Mathematical Induction

During the period between the completion of his *Habilitationsschrift* and the publication of the *Begriffsschrift*, it is almost certain that Frege read (at least some of) Hermann Lotze's *Logik*, the first edition of which was published in 1874. Lotze had taught Frege at Göttingen, and although the course Frege had followed had been on the philosophy of religion rather than logic, Frege's developing interest in logic, his earlier acquaintance with Lotze, and Lotze's own reputation, would have made Lotze's *Logik* an obvious work to have looked at.[31] It also now seems clear that one of the fragments published in his *Posthumous Writings* consists of a series of remarks inspired by the introduction to Lotze's *Logik*, the evidence suggesting that it was written sometime around 1876 or 1877.[32] Exactly what aspects of Lotze's thought influenced Frege, however, remains a matter of conjecture, but two features may be mentioned here that would have struck a sympathetic chord as Frege considered how to provide firmer foundations for arithmetic. The first is Lotze's suggestion that concepts should be treated as *functions*, rather than merely conjunctions, of component concepts.[33] Lotze developed no formal logic on the basis of this suggestion, and given that Frege himself had already appreciated the unifying potential of the notion of a function, there is no need to suppose that Lotze exerted any direct influence on Frege; but it does indicate that there was nothing unnatural, in the late 19th century, about the construal of concepts as functions.[34]

Extending the notion of a function to encompass concepts, and hence treating mathematical functions as just a specific type of function, suggests a more intimate relationship between logic and mathematics than had traditionally been conceived, and this found expression in the second feature of Lotze's thought – his view that mathematics was grounded in logic.[35] Once again there is no reason to suppose that, without Lotze, Frege would not have formulated his logicist project; and since Lotze denied that the *superstructure* of mathematics could be incorporated into general logic, there remains a difference between the two thinkers.[36] We might perhaps see Lotze as issuing a challenge to show that the whole of arithmetic was reducible to logic, and Frege as responding to this, but Frege's earlier dissertations clearly reveal that he already believed that our understanding of certain fundamental mathematical notions was conceptually (and hence logically) based rather than grounded in intuition (whether empirical or *a priori*).

Whatever the influences on Frege may have been, however, by 1879 Frege was sure what his ultimate goal was – to provide arithmetic with the strongest possible foundations. In his 'Preface' to the *Begriffsschrift*, he states that 'The firmest proof is obviously the purely logical, which, prescinding from the particularity of things, is based solely on the laws on which all knowledge rests'. Any particular truth may be established in a number of ways, some reflecting the history of its discovery, and some reflecting the psychology of the person propounding it. But the status of the truth depends on its 'most perfect method of proof' (ibid.), and hence the task is to find out if there is a purely logical method of proof. It was the project of showing that there are such methods in the case of arithmetic that Frege undertook.

Frege realized that to do this, he needed to develop a logical system that was sufficiently sophisticated to represent both arithmetical propositions and arithmetical forms of reasoning. As we saw in the last chapter, this led to the replacement of traditional subject-predicate analysis with function-argument analysis, the axiomatization of propositional logic, and the invention of the predicate calculus; and this expansion of logical theory was presented in Parts I and II of the *Begriffsschrift*. Here I shall focus on the third and final Part, entitled 'Some Elements from a General Theory of Series', in which Frege uses his logical system to provide an analysis of mathematical induction.

Proof by mathematical induction – demonstrating that a certain property holds of all the members of a given series (or that a series of objects with a certain property can be generated) – involves showing, firstly, that the property holds for the initial member of the series, and secondly, that if the property holds for any arbitrary member of the series, then it also holds for the next member of the series (or that a further member of the series can always be generated from a given member or members). Clearly, mathematical induction constitutes an important form of reasoning within mathematics, so that establishing its logical nature would go some way towards establishing the logicist thesis. But Frege's interest here had a far deeper dimension than this. For the natural number series itself is generated inductively. One starts, for example, by defining 0 and 1, stipulating that these are numbers, and then, by defining the relation of succession, or addition, shows that if n is a number, then $n + 1$ is a number. A natural number can then be specified as a member of the series recursively generated from these initial definitions. As Frege wrote in the 'Preface' to the *Begriffsschrift*, 'The course I took was first to seek to reduce the concept of ordering in a series to that of *logical* consequence, in order then to progress to the concept of number'.

Frege starts by defining the notion of an *hereditary property*. A property F is *hereditary in the f-series* if the following condition is met (formulating it in modern notation rather than Frege's own concept-script):[37]

(HP) $(\forall x) \{ Fx \rightarrow (\forall y) [f(x, y) \rightarrow Fy] \}$. (Cf. *BS*, §24, formula 69.)

'$f(x, y)$' is understood as symbolizing that 'y is a result of an application of the procedure f to x' or, equivalently, that 'y bears the f-relation to x'. (HP) can then be read as follows:

(HP†) From the proposition that x has the property F, whatever x may be, it can be inferred that every result of an application of the procedure f to x has the property F. (Cf. *BS*, §24.)

Frege gives the following example to illustrate the idea. Let '$f(x, y)$' mean that y is the child of x, and let F be the property of being a human being. Then the f-series is the series starting with x and continuing through the descendants of x, and it is clear that F is hereditary, since every child of a human being is in turn a human being (ibid.).

With the notion of an hereditary property, Frege proceeds to define the concept of *following in a series*, or as it would now be termed, the concept of the *proper ancestral* of a relation. Using (HP) to abbreviate the formula given above, 'b follows a in the f-series' can be defined thus:

(PA) $(\forall F) \{ [(HP) \& (\forall y) \{ f(a, y) \rightarrow Fy \}] \rightarrow Fb \}$. (Cf. *BS*, §26, form. 76.)

In words, this reads:

(PA†) From the two propositions that the property F is hereditary in the f-series and that every result of an application of the procedure f to a has the property F, whatever F may be, it can be inferred that b has the property F. (Cf. *BS*, §26.)

Clearly, if b does follow a in the f-series, then any hereditary property that a has will also be possessed by b, so that (PA) holds.[38] Conversely, if, whenever F is an hereditary property, and anything that is a result of an application of f to a has the property F, b also has the property F, then b must follow a in the f-series.[39] For consider the property of *following* a *in the f-series*. This clearly satisfies (HP), and hence is hereditary (cf. *BS*, §28, formula 97). Any result of applying f to a, of course, possesses this property (cf. *BS*, §28, formula 96), so that both conjuncts of the antecedent of (PA) hold. If (PA) itself holds, then (by *modus ponens*) we can deduce Fb, i.e. b has the property of following a in the f-series. So 'b follows a in the f-series' and (PA) are equivalent.

It is easy to see how a characterization of mathematical induction can now be provided. For we can immediately write down the following proposition:

(MI) [Fa & (HP) & (PA)] $\rightarrow$ Fb. (Cf. *BS*, §27, formula 81.)

From Fa and (HP) we can derive $(\forall y)\,[\,f(a, y) \rightarrow Fy\,]$, from which, with (HP) again, by (PA) we have Fb. Expressed in words, (MI) reads:

(MI†) If a has a property F which is hereditary in the f-series, and if b follows a in the f-series, then b has the property F. (Cf. *BS*, §27.)

This is precisely the key step in mathematical induction. For with the additional assumption that the first member of the f-series has the hereditary property F, we can clearly show that every member of the f-series has the property F.[40]

Frege goes on to define 'b belongs to the f-series beginning with a', that is, what we would now term the *ancestral* of the f-relation, which we can formulate, very simply, thus:

(AR) $b = a \lor$ (PA). (Cf. *BS*, §29, formula 99.)

The reading here is equally straightforward:

(AR†) b is identical with a, or b follows a in the f-series. (Cf. *BS*, §29.)

In the remainder of Part III of the *Begriffsschrift*, Frege derives further properties of series, using the notions introduced, and offers one final definition, of the *many-one* relation. A procedure f is *many-one* (*eindeutig*) if the following condition obtains:

(MO) $(\forall x)\,(\forall y)\,\{\,f(x,y) \rightarrow (\forall z)\,[f(x,z) \rightarrow z = y]\,\}$. (Cf. *BS*, §31, formula 115.)

Informally, this reads:

(MO†) From the circumstance that y is a result of an application of the procedure f to x, whatever x may be, it can be inferred that every result of an application of the procedure f to x is identical with y. (Cf. *BS*, §31.)

Although Frege does not do so in the *Begriffsschrift*, let us also formulate the condition that must be met for a relation to be *one-many*:

(OM) $(\forall x)\,(\forall y)\,\{\,f(x,y) \rightarrow (\forall w)\,[\,f(w,y) \rightarrow w = x\,]\,\}$.

A *one-one* relation, we can then say, is a relation that is both many-one and one-many, that is, that fulfils the combined condition:[41]

(OO) $(\forall x)\,(\forall y)\,[\,f(x,y) \rightarrow \{\,(\forall z)\,[f(x,z) \rightarrow z = y] \,\&\, (\forall w)\,[f(w,y) \rightarrow w = x]\,\}\,]$.

Developing Frege's earlier example, we can say that the relation of parent to eldest child is many-one, the relation of father to child (in cases where there is more than one child) one-many, and the relation of father to eldest child one-one.

Both the analysis of mathematical induction and the definition of a one-one relation played a crucial role in Frege's logicist project, as we shall see in the next chapter. But we can conclude the present section by emphasizing the important point here: what Frege had shown was that they could be given in purely logical terms.[42] Frege expressed it colourfully in his introductory remarks to Part III of the *Begriffsschrift*:

one sees [in these examples] how pure thought, regardless of any content given through the senses or even *a priori* through an intuition, is capable of bringing forth by itself, from the content which arises from its own nature, judgements which at first sight only seem possible on the basis of some intuition. This can be compared to condensation, by means of which air, which appears to a child's mind to be nothing, can be transformed into a visible fluid that forms drops. The propositions about series developed [in this Part] far surpass in generality all similar propositions which can be derived from any intuition of series. (*BS*, §23.)

The success of his initial condensations no doubt convinced Frege of the possibility of providing logical definitions of *all* arithmetical concepts and forms of reasoning. The next step was to provide definitions of the numbers themselves, and this was the task he undertook in his second book, *Die Grundlagen der Arithmetik*.

3.4 The Analyticity of Arithmetic

On the publication of the *Begriffsschrift*, and with five years of conscientious teaching behind him, Frege was promoted to *ausserordentlicher Professor* on the recommendation of Ernst Abbe, his mentor at Jena.[43] In his report on Frege's book, Abbe spoke of its 'very original cluster of ideas', but noted that 'it will probably be understood and appreciated by only a few'. Mathematics, Abbe suggested, 'will be affected, perhaps very considerably, but immediately only very little, by the inclination of the author and the content of the book'.[44] Abbe's remarks were prophetic. As we noted in chapter 2, the reviews of Frege's book were discouraging, his 'concept-script' being judged inferior to the Boolean logic of his leading contemporaries. This induced Frege to examine carefully the work of Boole, and to write several papers demonstrating the greater power of his own theory (see §2.2 above). This task occupied Frege in the three years that followed the publication of the *Begriffsschrift*, and the work analysing the concept of number, which had been heralded in the closing sentence of the 'Preface' to the *Begriffsschrift*, was consequently delayed.[45]

The criticism of the *Begriffsschrift* did, however, have one positive effect: it made Frege aware of the need to explain his ideas and sketch his proposed reduction of arithmetic to logic informally, *before* embarking on the programme of providing rigorous proofs using his 'concept-script'. He read up on the work of philosophers who had written about mathematics, and realized the importance of locating his own views against the background of the traditional disputes. The result was *Die Grundlagen der Arithmetik*, published in 1884 and recognized now, though not at the time, as a philosophical masterpiece, containing a penetrating critique of rival conceptions of arithmetic and an original account of his own. In these final two sections I shall focus on his critique of rival conceptions, and leave an exposition of his positive project until the next chapter.

Against the mathematical background sketched in §3.1, the opening passage of Frege's *Grundlagen* can be quoted without further explanation:

> After departing for a long time from Euclidean rigour, mathematics is now returning to it, and even striving to take it further. In arithmetic, simply as a result of the origin in India of many of its methods and concepts, reasoning has traditionally been less strict than in geometry, which had mainly been developed by the Greeks. This was only reinforced by the discovery of higher analysis; since considerable, almost insuperable difficulties stood in the way of a rigorous treatment of this subject, whilst at the same time there seemed little profit in the expenditure of effort in overcoming them. Later developments, however, have shown more and more clearly that in mathematics a mere moral conviction, based on many successful applications, is insufficient. A proof is now demanded of many things that previously counted as self-evident. It is only in this way that the limits to their validity have in many cases been determined. The concepts of function, continuity, limit and infinity have been shown to require sharper definition. Negative and irra-

tional numbers, which have long been accepted in science, have had to submit to a more exacting test of their legitimacy.

Thus everywhere efforts are being made to provide rigorous proofs, precise determinations of the limits of validity and, as a means to this, sharp definitions of concepts. (*GL*, §1.)

Eventually, Frege goes on, we realize that the concept of number itself requires definition, and that proofs are needed of even the simplest arithmetical propositions (§§ 2, 4).

The demand for rigour has as much a philosophical as a mathematical motivation. For in understanding how a particular truth is *justified*, we appreciate its logical status, that is, whether it is analytic or synthetic, *a priori* or *a posteriori*. I shall say much more about these distinctions in chapter 5, but let us simply note here the characterizations that Frege provides of these notions (§3):

(AN) A truth is *analytic* if its proof depends only on general logical laws and definitions.

(SN) A truth is *synthetic* if its proof cannot be given without relying on truths from a particular science.

(PR) A truth is *a priori* if its proof can be given from completely general laws, which themselves neither need nor admit of proof.

(PS) A truth is *a posteriori* if its proof cannot be given without appealing to facts, that is, to unprovable and non-general truths that contain assertions about particular objects.

These characterizations immediately rule out there being any *analytic a posteriori* truths (§12), since general logical laws and definitions are assumed to 'neither need nor admit of proof'. Analyticity implies *apriority*, in other words, but not vice versa.

There are thus three positions concerning the status of arithmetical propositions to consider. Arithmetic may be seen as a system of *analytic a priori* truths, as Leibniz can be regarded as advocating; a system of *synthetic a priori* truths, as Kant explicitly proposed; or a system of *synthetic a posteriori* truths, as Mill argued.[46] Frege endorses the Leibnizian position, though he raises some objections to Leibniz's own account. He agrees with Leibniz, for example, that numerical formulae are provable, that is, reducible via axioms and definitions to 'identities', but criticizes Leibniz's own proof that $2 + 2 = 4$ for missing out the associative law (§6). More importantly, whilst characterizing Leibniz as holding that arithmetical truths are both analytic and *a priori*, Frege recognizes that Leibniz believed that *all* truths were provable – contingent as well as necessary, threatening to collapse the distinction between necessary and contingent propositions that had been so usefully drawn (§15).[47] Frege applauds, however, Leibniz's fundamental insight: that every number can be defined in terms of its predecessor, which enables us to *conceive* very large numbers even though we can have no *idea* (*Vorstellung*) of them.[48] 'Through such definitions we reduce the whole infinite set of numbers to the number one and increase by one, and every one of the infinitely many numerical formulae can be proved from a few general propositions.' (*FA*, §6.)

What, then, is wrong with the other two positions? Frege's criticism of Kant's position is directed against what he takes as the main motivation for construing arithmetical propositions as *synthetic* truths, namely, that since they are not, typically, immediately self-evident, appeal must be made to *intuition* in any apprehension of their truth. Frege agrees that complex numerical formulae, such as 135664 + 37863 = 173527, are not self-evident, but argues that this shows, not that they are synthetic, but that they are *provable* (§5). Kant, though, talks not of proof but of *intuition* as the basis of any apprehension of truth. Kant's favourite example is 7 + 5 = 12. No amount of analysis of the concept of the sum of 7 and 5, he argues, gets us to the concept of 12; rather, we must have an *intuition* of, say, fingers or points in order to work out that 5 units added to 7 units makes 12 units.[49] Of course, appealing to fingers involves *empirical* intuition, which, as Frege recognizes, runs counter to Kant's official view. But even allowing that there could be such a thing as *pure* intuition, it is hard to see how we could have intuitions of very large numbers: 'have we, in fact, an intuition of 135664 fingers or points at all? If we had, and if we had another of 37863 fingers and a third of 173527 fingers, then the correctness of our formula, if it were unprovable, would have to be evident right away, at least as applying to fingers; but it is not.' (*FA*, §5.)

Of course, there is no reason why Kant would deny that complex numerical formulae are provable, but he would presumably still insist that the apprehension of the truth of the simplest formulae depends upon intuition. Frege's response is to point out that 'it is awkward to make a fundamental distinction between small and large numbers, especially as it would scarcely be possible to draw any sharp boundary between them'. Why should we not treat even the simplest formulae as provable? (Ibid.)[50] As Leibniz showed, even 2 + 2 = 4 is provable, so that, in Kant's own paradigm cases, there is no need to appeal to intuition. 'It is all too easy to appeal to inner intuition', Frege remarks, 'when other grounds cannot be found' (*GL*, §12).

As we have seen, Frege was adamant that the domain of arithmetic extends beyond the realm of the merely intuitable. In a letter written in 1882, after noting his departure from Kant, Frege goes on:

The field of geometry is the field of possible spatial intuition; arithmetic recognizes no such limitation. Everything is enumerable, not just what is juxtaposed in space, not just what is successive in time, not just external phenomena, but also inner mental processes and events and even concepts, which stand neither in temporal nor in spatial but only in logical relations to one another. The only barrier to enumerability is to be found in the imperfection of concepts. Bald people for example cannot be enumerated as long as the concept of baldness is not defined so precisely that for any individual there can be no doubt whether he falls under it. Thus the area of the enumerable is as wide as that of conceptual thought, and a source of knowledge more restricted in scope, like spatial intuition or sense perception, would not suffice to guarantee the general validity of arithmetical propositions. (*PMC*, p. 100.)

Frege's Pythagorean argument here is worth spelling out. Genuine thought, according to Frege, requires sharply defined concepts, which implies a determinate number of objects falling under each concept, which shows that enumerability is part of the essence of conceptual thought and hence is a purely logical matter. Since each concept has a number associated with it, Frege's subsequent definition of number in terms of the *extensions* of concepts comes as a natural move. Frege's Pythagoreanism, then, can be seen as motivating his logicist project. In §14 of the *Grundlagen* he writes: 'The truths of arithmetic govern the realm of the numerable. This realm is the broadest; for to it belongs not only the actual, not only the intuitable, but everything thinkable. Should not the laws of number, then, stand in the most intimate connection with those of thought?'

Frege's critique of Kant's position applies *a fortiori* to Mill's position, since, in also regarding arithmetic as a body of synthetic propositions, Mill narrowed its domain down even further, to the realm of the merely empirical. But, as Frege points out, we can number more than physical things. We can talk, for example, of four ideas or four concepts, or the four syllogistic figures (cf. §24). But in construing arithmetical propositions not only as synthetic, but also as *a posteriori*, Mill laid himself open to an additional barrage of criticism.

Frege again takes the case of large numbers to ridicule Mill's position. Mill accepts that we can provide definitions of natural numbers in terms of their predecessors, but remarks that 'they are definitions in the geometrical sense, not the logical; asserting not the meaning of a term only, but along with it an observed matter of fact' (*SL*, II vi 2, p. 257). But, responds Frege, 'what in the world can be the observed or physical fact, as Mill also calls it, that is asserted in the definition of the number 777864?' (§7.)[51] Of course, as in the case of Kant, we can be more charitable here and interpret Mill as allowing Leibnizian definitions of large numbers, but as still insisting on the *empirical* basis of the simplest formulae. Mill writes:

we may call "Three is two and one" a definition of three; but the calculations which depend on that proposition do not follow from the definition itself, but from an arithmetical theorem presupposed in it, namely, that collections of objects exist, which while they impress the senses thus, $^o_o{}^o$, may be separated into two parts, thus, $^{oo}\,{}^o$. This proposition being granted, we term all such parcels Threes, after which the enunciation of the above mentioned physical fact will serve also for a definition of the word Three. (*SL*, II vi 2, p. 257.)

In response to the assumed separability of the objects, Frege comments: 'It is just as well that not everything in the world is nailed down; for otherwise this separation could not be achieved, and 2 + 1 would not be 3!' (*GL*, §7.) Even granting that collections of objects are rearrangeable, there remains the problem as to how such a definition applies in other cases, say, when we speak of a clock striking three, or of three sensations of taste, or of three methods of solving an equation: 'for in none of these cases is there a sense impression as of $^0{}_0{}^0$' (ibid.).

Frege accepts that we may require experience to *learn* the truths of arithmetic, but argues that this does not make those truths *empirical* as the term 'empirical' is used in opposition to 'a priori' (§8). As Frege has already explained, the issue concerns the *justification* of arithmetical truths; and the task is to see if proofs can be found that depend solely on general laws (§3; cf. (PR) above). Whilst empirical elucidations may help us acquire knowledge of arithmetic, they are irrelevant to the question of its status. Mill always confuses, Frege remarks, the *applications* of an arithmetical proposition with the pure proposition itself. '5 + 2 = 7 does not mean that if 2 unit volumes of liquid are poured into 5 unit volumes of liquid, 7 unit volumes of liquid are obtained, but the latter is an application of the proposition, which is only admissible if no change in volume occurs as a result, say, of a chemical reaction.' And '+', for example, does not refer to a process of heaping up, since it can be applied in quite different situations. (*GL*, §9.)

However, all these considerations still leave us with the underlying issue untouched. We can allow, and Kant and Mill can also allow, that all (non-primitive) numerical formulae can be proved, and that Leibnizian definitions can be given of all the natural numbers. But for this to show that arithmetical propositions are analytic, the analyticity of the primitive truths themselves must be established. According to (AN), a truth is analytic if its proof depends only on general logical laws and definitions, and it is plainly assumed that the general logical laws and definitions are themselves analytic.[52] But the important question concerns the status of the primitive arithmetical truths. If these can be reduced to logical truths, then (with the assumption just made) the analyticity of arithmetic is assured; if they cannot, then the Kantian and Millian options remain live. The most that Part I of the *Grundlagen* establishes, then, is the conditional proposition: *if* the primitive arithmetical truths are analytic, then all arithmetical truths are analytic (since all other truths can be proved from the primitive ones).

Since Frege has already established that mathematical induction can be analysed in purely logical terms, the crucial question concerns the concept of number itself, and the definitions, in particular, of '0', '1' and 'increase by 1'. If logical definitions can also be given at this most primitive level (yielding e.g. '0 + 1 = 1'), then the logicist project is successfully launched. In Part II of the *Grundlagen* Frege criticizes the views of

previous writers on the concept of number, and in Part III he considers
views on unity (*Einheit*) and one (*Eins*). As we shall see in the next
chapter, by the end of Part III Frege's own view has emerged as a way of
resolving the difficulties he has identified in the views of others. In the
final section of this chapter, I shall simply outline Frege's criticisms.

3.5 Defective Conceptions of Number

In Part II of the *Grundlagen* Frege attacks two main positions regarding
the nature of number: empiricism and psychologism. The empiricism he
has in mind involves the conception of number as a property of external
things. Once again, Mill is the main target, and Frege offers two reasons
for not treating numbers in the same way as qualities, whether primary
qualities such as solidity or secondary qualities such as colour.[53] Firstly,
Frege argues, qualities belong to external things 'independently of any
choice of ours', whereas what number we ascribe to something depends on
our way of viewing it (§22). The *Iliad*, for example, can be thought of as
one poem, or as 24 Books, or as some large number of verses. A pile of cards
can be thought of as one pack, or as 52 cards, or as 40 points in bridge.[54]
One pair of boots can be thought of as *two* boots (§25). Secondly, Frege
argues, reiterating the point he has continually stressed, number is applicable over a far wider range than colour and solidity, and in particular,
can be applied to what is *non*-physical (§24).

If the number that can be ascribed to something depends on our way of
viewing it, then it is tempting to regard such ascriptions, and number
itself, as purely subjective. Frege quotes Berkeley as someone who re-
sponded in this way to the perceived difficulty in what is essentially
empirical realism.[55] Here is Berkeley's clearest statement of his position:

> That number is entirely the creature of the mind, even though the other
> qualities be allowed to exist without, will be evident to whoever considers,
> that the same thing bears a different denomination of number, as the mind
> views it with different respects. Thus, the same extension is one or three or
> thirty-six, according as the mind considers it with reference to a yard, a foot,
> or an inch. Number is so visibly relative, and dependent on men's under-
> standing, that it is strange to think how anyone should give it an absolute
> existence without the mind. We say one book, one page, one line; all these
> are equally units, though some contain several of the others. And in each
> instance it is plain, the unit relates to some particular combination of ideas
> arbitrarily put together by the mind. (*PHK*, §12.)[56]

To talk of ideas, understood as mental phenomena, is to suggest a *psychologistic* conception of number; and Frege is no less critical of this
alternative position:

> For number is no whit more an object of psychology or a product of mental
> processes than, let us say, the North Sea is. The objectivity of the North Sea

is not affected by the fact that it is a matter of our arbitrary choice which part of all the water on the earth's surface we mark off and elect to call the "North Sea". This is no reason for deciding to investigate the North Sea by psychological methods. In the same way number, too, is something objective. If we say "The North Sea is 10,000 square miles in extent" then neither by "North Sea" nor by "10,000" do we refer to any state of or process in our minds: on the contrary, we assert something quite objective, which is independent of our ideas and everything of the sort. (*FA*, §26.)

Anti-psychologism is one of the most dominant features of Frege's philosophy throughout his life. The principle that 'there must be a sharp separation of the psychological from the logical, the subjective from the objective' is the first of the three 'fundamental principles' he singles out in his 'Introduction' to the *Grundlagen* (p. X).[57] For Frege, the realm of the psychological or subjective is the realm of ideas, understood as private mental entities, and his fundamental objection to psychologism is that it rules out communication and makes argument pointless. 'If the number two were an idea, then it would straightaway be mine only. Another's idea is already as such another idea. We would then have perhaps many millions of twos. One would have to say: my two, your two, one two, all twos.' (§27.) If someone were then to say that $2 \times 2 = 5$, all I could do is just register that their two has one property, and mine another. Arguing that they were wrong would be futile, since we would not be speaking of the same thing.[58] But there may not only be, in some cases, many more numbers than we would normally countenance; there may also be, in other cases, none where they would be expected. '10^{10}', for example, might turn out to be an empty symbol, since there might be no being capable of having the appropriate idea (§27). In spelling out the implications of construing numbers as ideas, then, what Frege presents us with is a *reductio ad absurdum* of psychologism.

Succumbing to the temptation to treat the objective/subjective divide as corresponding to the physical/mental divide, it might be thought that, in rejecting both empiricism and psychologism, Frege has simply argued himself out of any coherent position at all. However, Frege distinguishes what is *objective* (*objectiv*) from what is *actual* (*wirklich*), the actual being the *handleable* (*handgreiflich*) or *spatial* (*räumlich*), such that what is actual (the world of material substance) is only part of what is objective. 'The axis of the earth is objective, so is the centre of mass of the solar system, but I should not call them actual in the way the earth itself is so.' (*FA*, §26.) We do, of course, speak of the equator as an *imaginary* line, but we do not mean by this that it is merely *imagined*: 'it is not a creature of thought, the product of a psychological process, but is only recognized or apprehended by thought' (ibid.). If it were *created* by thought, then we could not talk of it existing prior to its alleged creation; yet (just like gravity before Newton) the equator was around long before life on earth. What is objective, writes Frege, is 'what is subject to laws, what can be

conceived and judged, what is expressible in words', and this corresponds
to 'what is independent of our sensation, intuition and imagination', but
not, Frege goes on to say, 'what is independent of the reason, – for what
are things independent of the reason? To answer that would be as much
as to judge without judging, or to wash the fur without wetting it.' (Ibid.)
This last remark needs explanation. For how can what is objective, which
includes what is actual, depend on our reason? A physical object, for
example, can exist independently of our sensing it; and we can talk
coherently about a geometrical object such as a chiliagon even if no one
can intuit or imagine it (i.e. construct some kind of mental picture of it).
Yet neither of these is *inconceivable*, since we could not make true judgements about them without, in some sense, conceiving them; and this is all
that Frege means by saying that they are 'dependent on reason'.[59]

By the end of Part II of the *Grundlagen*, then, both empiricism and
psychologism have been rejected as offering coherent accounts of arithmetic; but we are left only with the positive assertion that numbers are
objective, though non-actual. In the final section of Part II, Frege mentions
one further position, the set theory of number, which he understands as
taking one of two forms, construing numbers either as sets of objects or as
sets of units (§28). Neither view, Frege remarks, provides an account of
the numbers 0 and 1; but the second view, he suggests, demands separate
discussion, which he takes up in Part III. In fact, however, Frege's objections to both views are clarified in this Part; and it is useful to keep them
both in mind.

Frege's critique can be presented in the form of a dilemma. Either the
things of which numbers are sets are different (as they would be if they
were different objects), or else they are identical. If they are different, then
the same problem arises that Frege posed for psychologism: there will be
as many twos, say, as there are different pairs of objects in the universe.
The first view, then, is easily demolished by *reductio ad absurdum*. Of
course, it is in the hope of avoiding this problem that the second view,
construing numbers as sets of units, seems attractive. The idea is simple.
Consider two sets of objects, both, say, with 5 members. Clearly, if numbers are *identified* with such sets, then we have two different fives. But
imagine *abstracting away* from the particular characteristics of these
objects, until all we are left with are objects that are identical with one
another. These are the *units*, and since both sets will be composed of
exactly the same units, the two sets will in fact be the same set, which can
then be identified with the number 5. However, so the objection runs, if
the units really are identical, then (so to speak) they merge into one, and
the whole theory collapses.[60]

The argument can also be run in reverse. Let us start with the fully
analysed Leibnizian definition of '5':

(5) $5 = 1 + 1 + 1 + 1 + 1.$

According to the conception of numbers as sets of units, this is to be understood as follows:

(5†) $5 = \{\, 1, 1, 1, 1, 1 \,\}$.

But if '1' is the name of an object, and each occurrence of '1' refers to the same object, then all (5†) amounts to is this:

(5‡) $5 = \{\, 1 \,\}$.

If 'and' is used as it is in talking of constructing a set (agglomeration or collection) of things out of its members (parts), then, as Frege remarks, '1 and 1 and 1 is not 3 but 1, just as gold and gold and gold is never anything other than gold' (§38), or, we might add, just as P & P in propositional logic is equivalent to P.[61] Clearly, then, '1' as it occurs in (5†) is not to be understood as the name of a particular object, *the number one*; rather, each occurrence of '1' in (5†) represents *a unit*, but a different one each time. Strictly speaking, then, (5†) should be rewritten:

(5*) $5 = \{\, 1', 1'', 1''', 1'''', 1''''' \,\}$.

But now we are back with the original problem, for this only defines *one* number five, since it differs from, say, the following definition:

(5#) $5 = \{\, 1', 1''', 1''''', 1''''''', 1''''''''' \,\}$.

As Frege remarks, 'The symbols 1', 1'', 1''' tell the tale of our embarrassment. We must have identity – hence the 1; but we must have difference – hence the strokes; only unfortunately, the latter undo the work of the former.' (*FA*, §36.) Furthermore, as Frege shows, if we carry this idea back into standard arithmetic, complete nonsense ensues (§38). $3 - 2 = 1$, for example, might be written thus:

$$(1' + 1'' + 1''') - (1'' + 1''') = 1'.$$

But now consider the following (presumably equivalent) subtraction:

$$(1' + 1'' + 1''') - (1'''' + 1''''').$$

The result here seems no more likely to be 1' than any other unit, and it is hard to see how on earth to proceed.[62] Numbers, then, cannot be construed as sets (agglomerations) of things. Whether these things are identical with one another or not, absurdity results; and calling them 'units' only serves to cover up the problem.

Frege himself offers a succinct summary of his critique:

> We are faced, therefore, with the following difficulty:
> If we try to produce the number by putting together different distinct objects, the result is an agglomeration in which the objects contained remain still in possession of precisely those properties which serve to distinguish them from one another; and that is not the number. But if we try to do it in

the other way, by putting together identicals, the result runs perpetually into one and we never reach a plurality.

If we use 1 to stand for each of the objects to be numbered, we make the mistake of assigning the same symbol to different things. But if we provide the 1 with differentiating strokes, it becomes unusable for arithmetic.

The word "unit" is admirably adapted to conceal this difficulty; and that is the real, though no doubt unconscious, reason why we prefer it to the words "object" and "thing". We start by calling the things to be numbered "units", without detracting from their diversity; then subsequently the concept of putting together (or collecting, or uniting, or annexing, or whatever we choose to call it) transforms itself into that of arithmetical addition, while the concept word "unit" changes unperceived into the proper name "one". And there we have our identity. ... The difficulty is so well hidden under the word "unit", that those who have any suspicion of its existence must surely be few at most. (*FA*, §39.)

What this suggests is that 'one' and 'unit' function in quite different ways. Whilst 'one' (i.e. '1') appears to be what Frege calls a 'proper name' ('Eigenname'), 'unit' is a concept word. I consider the issues that this raises, as well as Frege's resolution of the difficulties he has identified in the various views he has examined, in the first section of the next chapter.

4. The Logicist Project

Do not permit yourself to think you have known truth in philosophy, unless you can explain the leap in which we deduce that one, two, three, and four together make ten. (St Augustine, as quoted by Leibniz, *LS*, p. 37.)

In the last chapter I sought to clarify the background to Frege's logicist project, sketching some of the developments in the history of mathematics, revealing the motivations in his early work, and outlining his criticisms of traditional conceptions of arithmetic. In this chapter I focus on his positive programme, elucidating informally its main details. I start by explaining his construal of number statements as containing assertions about concepts, and his belief that numbers are objects (§4.1); and then provide an exposition of his argument in §§62-9 of the *Grundlagen*, which is not only fundamental to his logicism but also pivotal in the development of his philosophy, as we shall see in the next chapter. In §4.3 I clarify the moves in his logical reconstruction of the natural numbers; and in §4.4 I outline his account of other numbers, introducing his *magnum opus*, the *Grundgesetze der Arithmetik*, which presents formally what he had merely sketched informally in the *Grundlagen*. In the final section, in commenting on its plausibility, I compare Frege's own theory with the theories of Cantor and Dedekind, in particular. The developments in Frege's philosophy which the *Grundgesetze* incorporates and anticipates will be the subject of later chapters.

4.1 Numbers, Concepts and Objects

In the course of his critique of rival conceptions of arithmetic in the first half of the *Grundlagen* (§§5-44), Frege established a number of (mainly negative) preliminary points. From our exposition in the previous chapter, we can summarize these as follows:

(a) Certain traditional arguments for construing arithmetical propositions as *synthetic* truths (whether *a priori* or *a posteriori*) are flawed (§§5, 7-10, 12). The only other possible option, that they are *analytic a priori* truths, remains viable (§§3, 6, 11, 15).

(b) Numbers are not properties of external things, since ascriptions of number depend on the concepts under which the things are classified

(§§21-5). What is numerable is everything thinkable, not just the sensible or intuitable (§§14, 24, 40).

(c) Numbers are not subjective ideas; they are objective, though non-actual (§§26-7).

(d) Numbers cannot be construed either as sets of objects or as sets of 'units'. The problem as to whether to treat units as the same or different shows that 'unit' ('Einheit') and 'one' ('eins') must be distinguished. (§§28, 34-9.)

Frege offers his own review in §45, and notes that the following question has remained unanswered: in making a statement of number (*Zahl-angabe*), of what are we asserting something? He immediately proceeds to suggest the answer:

> To throw light on the matter, it will help to consider number in the context of a judgement that brings out its ordinary use. If, in looking at the same external phenomenon, I can say with equal truth 'This is a copse' and 'These are five trees', or 'Here are four companies' and 'Here are 500 men', then what changes here is neither the individual nor the whole, the aggregate, but rather my terminology. But that is only a sign of the replacement of one concept by another. This suggests as the answer to the first question of the previous section that a statement of number contains an assertion about a concept. This is perhaps clearest in the case of the number 0. If I say 'Venus has 0 moons', then there is no moon or aggregate of moons to assert anything of at all; but instead it is the concept 'moon of Venus' to which a property is ascribed, namely, that of including nothing under it. If I say 'The King's carriage is drawn by four horses', then I am ascribing the number four to the concept 'horse that draws the King's carriage'. (§46.)

In the rest of Part III of the *Grundlagen* Frege shows how this answer, treating a statement of number as asserting something about a concept, resolves the various issues he has identified. Taking the points we have just summarized in order, the following clarifications can then be offered:

(a) It is more plausible that assertions about concepts should be analytic. Whilst 'All whales are mammals', for example, might at first sight appear to be about animals (and hence be merely synthetic), in fact, Frege suggests in §47, it involves the subordination of concepts rather than the subsumption of objects under a concept. It should be construed, in other words, as 'The concept *whale* is subordinate to the concept *mammal*'. If we understand these concepts at all, we can then suggest, we will immediately recognize the truth of the proposition, which is to say that it is analytic (it is a matter of definition that a whale is a mammal).[1]

(b) We can explain how it might be thought that numbers are properties of external things, our ideas of both numbers and properties being abstracted from things themselves, just because we do in fact abstract concepts this way (though this is not the only way of acquiring concepts), the concepts then being what number statements are assertions about. We can also make sense of the universal applicability of number, since its domain is as wide as that of conceptual thought. (§§48-9.)

(c) To make assertions about concepts is not to say something about one's subjective ideas, since concepts are objective. It is an objective fact, for example, that the concept *whale* is subordinate to the concept *mammal*. (Cf. §47.)

(d) Something can only be called a 'unit' relative to a concept that precisely delimits what falls under it – what is now termed a *sortal* concept.[2] The concept *red*, for example, is *not* such a concept, since what falls under it (e.g. a surface) can be arbitrarily divided into parts all of which themselves fall under the concept. No finite number could therefore attach to this concept. The concept *moon of Jupiter*, on the other hand, *is* a sortal concept, each of the four moons of Jupiter being a unit relative to this concept. 'Units' are thus the *same* in so far as it is the same *concept* that is being applied, and *different* in so far as the *objects* numbered (falling under that concept) are different. (§54.)

Frege also suggests how his insight into the nature of number statements throws light on certain traditional problems relating to assertions of existence. The third of Frege's three 'fundamental principles' mentioned in his 'Introduction' to the *Grundlagen* is the principle that 'the distinction between concept and object must be kept in mind' (p. X), and this was a principle, as we saw in §2.4, that Frege was led to formulate as a result of his replacement of conventional subject-predicate analysis with function-argument analysis. As Frege remarked in his critique of Boolean logic, 'we must distinguish between concept and thing, even when only one thing falls under a concept' (*BLC*, p. 18). The point is stressed again in §51 of the *Grundlagen*: 'a concept does not cease to be a concept merely because only one single thing falls under it, which thing, accordingly, is fully determined by it'. Nor does a concept cease to be a concept if *nothing* falls under it, as Frege's earlier example of the concept *moon of Venus* shows (§46). What this suggests, then, is that *denial of existence* involves the assertion that the number 0 is assigned to the relevant concept, and *assertion of existence* involves the denial that the number 0 is assigned to the relevant concept (§53).

If existential statements are regarded, like number statements, as involving assertions about concepts, then, as Frege remarks, the ontological argument for the existence of God breaks down (ibid.). For existence is not a property of whatever it is that is supposed to fall under the concept *God*, that is, the concept of existence is not one of the 'characteristics' or 'marks' ('Merkmale') of the concept of God, and hence existence cannot be simply deduced by analysing the concept of God. Rather, the property of being instantiated is ascribed – rightly or wrongly – to the concept of God, and the truth of this ascription is not something that can be determined by definition. To say that God is omnipotent, for example, is to say that the concept of omnipotence is part of the concept of God; but to say that (the one true) God is existent is to say that the concept *God* is (uniquely) instantiated (i.e. that the number one is assigned to it). However, as Frege goes on to note, 'it should not be concluded that a property of a concept can never be deduced from the concept, that is, from its marks' (§53). For example, if we were to take seriously the stone paradox, that an omnipotent being cannot make a stone he cannot lift, then we might conclude that the concept of omnipotence is incoherent, and hence that the concept of God, which contains this concept, must be assigned the number 0.[3]

Denial of existence, then, need not be self-contradictory (as it would be in saying 'I do not exist'), and assertion of existence need not be uninformative (as it might be in saying 'These tame tigers exist'), and in general, existential statements need not be problematic, so long as what is involved are assertions about concepts – that certain concepts are or are not instantiated. But it remains the case that, for Frege, the use of *proper names* in logic *presupposes* the existence of objects. As we saw in §2.4, given his concept/object distinction and conception of logic, this was a natural position to adopt.[4] 'With a concept the question is always whether anything, and if so what, falls under it. With a proper name such questions make no sense.' (§51.) Whilst every sortal concept can be assigned a number from the whole range of natural numbers, in the case of proper names there is one and only one object involved.

By this point Frege has already indicated that he conceives number terms as proper names rather than concept words. In criticizing empiricism, he had rejected the view that number is a property of things, and in his discussion of 'unity' and 'one' he had added further arguments against so viewing the number one in particular (§§29-33). Firstly, since 'oneness' would presumably be a property possessed by everything, describing something as 'one' would say nothing at all. 'Only through the possibility of something not being wise does the assertion that Solon is wise gain a sense. The content of a concept diminishes as its extension grows; if the latter becomes all-embracing, then the content must be lost entirely.' (§29.) Secondly, if 'one' were a predicate, then 'Solon was one' would be just as legitimate as 'Solon was wise'. But 'Solon was one' is unintelligible on its own – without, say, 'wise man' being understood from the context. The point is even clearer in the plural case: 'Whilst we can combine "Solon was wise" and "Thales was wise" into "Solon and Thales were wise", we cannot say "Solon and Thales were one". The impossibility of this would not be perceived if "one" as well as "wise" were a property both of Solon and of Thales.' (Ibid.)

In §38 Frege makes explicit his two reasons, based on linguistic considerations, for believing that numbers are objects: firstly, that the definite article is used in constructions of the form 'the number one'; and secondly, that such number terms do not admit of plurals – we do not talk of several number ones, for example (a point, as we saw in §3.5, that played a key role in his argument against construing numbers as sets of things). 'We say "the number one" and indicate by the definite article a definite and unique object of scientific study. There are not different numbers one, but only one. We have in 1 a proper name, which as such does not admit of a plural any more than "Frederick the Great" or "the chemical element gold".' (§38; cf. §51; §68, n.)

Of course, we are entitled to ask what significance these linguistic considerations have on questions of ontology. 'Frederick the Great', after all, no longer refers to an existent object; and fictional names too show that there is no necessary connection between the use of proper names and the existence of objects. The issues involved here are controversial, not least as a matter of Fregean exegesis, and I return to them later.[5] But the explanation (though not the justification) of Frege's belief should already be clear. Since logic, according to Frege, is a system of *truths*, proper names in logic *presuppose* the existence of objects. Since logic provides the framework for conceptual thought, and the realm of the conceptual is the realm of the enumerable, numbers have a central place in logic. If number terms are proper names rather than concept words, then they too must refer to objects. Given his assumptions, it is not surprising that Frege felt that all he had to establish was that number terms *are* proper names, which does seem to be merely a linguistic matter.[6]

However, Frege was aware that questions remained; and in the first subdivision of Part IV (§§55-61), he adduces two further linguistic considerations in support of his belief that numbers are objects. The first addresses the question that immediately arises in relation to his view that statements of number contain assertions about concepts. As we have seen, existential statements can be interpreted as statements involving the number 0, and Frege himself speaks loosely of existence as a *property* of concepts (§53), which suggests that number too is a property of concepts. But surely this is incompatible with the belief that numbers are *objects*? Frege's answer is provided in §57:

> In the proposition 'The number 0 belongs to the concept *F*', 0 is only a part of the predicate, if the concept *F* is taken as the real subject. I have therefore avoided calling a number such as 0, 1 or 2 a *property* of a concept. The individual number, by forming only a part of the predicate, appears precisely as an independent [*selbständiger*] object. (§57.)

Rephrasing Frege's example as 'The concept *F* is ascribed the number 0', making 'The concept *F*' the subject term, the predicate expression is then '( ) is ascribed the number 0', so that the property that is attributed to the concept *F* is not the number 0 itself but the property of *being ascribed the number 0*.[7] Compare this with 'Alfred is the adopted son of Gottlob', where Alfred is attributed the property of being the adopted son of Gottlob, which in no way prevents 'Gottlob' from representing an independent object. A proper name can be part of a predicate expression, in other words, without impugning its own semantic role.

Frege's second, though related, linguistic consideration concerns the *attributive* use of number terms. In 'Jupiter has four moons', 'four' is being used attributively, requiring qualification by the noun that follows.[8] But this type of construction too, Frege suggests, fails to undermine the belief that numbers are objects, since it can be rephrased to exhibit the number term as a proper name.

> For example, the proposition 'Jupiter has four moons' can be converted into 'The number of Jupiter's moons is four'. Here the 'is' should not be taken as a mere copula, as in the proposition 'The sky is blue'. This is shown by the fact that one can say: 'The number of Jupiter's moons is the number 4'. Here 'is' has the sense of 'is equal to' or 'is the same as'. We thus have an equation that asserts that the expression 'the number of Jupiter's moons' designates the same object as the word 'four'. And equations are the prevalent form of proposition in arithmetic. (Ibid.)

Both these considerations come together in the process of recasting statements of number into a form that makes explicit that number terms are proper names. For Frege's first example can be rephrased as 'The concept F has 0 instances', which we may call the *adjectival* construction, which in turn can be rephrased as 'The number of instances of the concept F is the number 0', the *substantival* construction, which Frege regards as the fundamental form.[9] The importance of the process of rephrasal in Frege's philosophy cannot be overemphasized. As we shall see, not only does it play a key role in his logicist project, but it also motivates his later reflections on meaning, for it is precisely the transitions involved here that require justification. All we need note at the moment, though, is that there seems to be, as yet, no reason to treat one type of construction as more primitive than the others, as the form to which the others are *reducible*. All that comes out of §57 is the idea that since equations (e.g. $4 = 2 + 2$) are central in arithmetic, this is the fundamental form; but why should the reductive process not be reversed? Indeed, if statements of number are construed as assertions about concepts, surely it would be more natural to regard the adjectival construction as fundamental? Frege's argument does seem circular. Because numbers are independent objects, the substantival construction is fundamental; and because other constructions can be 'reduced' to this form, numbers are independent objects. I shall, however, return to these issues later.[10]

One final problem needs to be addressed here. For the obvious episte-mological objection to the view that numbers are objects is that there seems to be no way of accounting for our apprehension of such objects. Frege rejects the supposition that we can have an *idea* of a number, since, as he has argued, 'it is neither something sensible nor a property of an external thing' (§58). And even if an idea (mental picture) is called up by hearing a word, 'the idea need not correspond to the content of the word; it may be quite different in different people' (§59). Furthermore, we can often make judgements about something, such as the Earth, or the distance of the Earth from the Sun, whilst having a very inadequate idea of it, or no idea at all (§§59-60). Frege goes on:

> That no idea can be formed of the content of a word is therefore no reason for denying it any meaning or for excluding it from use. The appearance to the contrary doubtless arises because we consider the words in isolation and in asking for their meaning, look only for an idea. A word for which we lack a corresponding mental picture thus appears to have no content. But one must always keep in mind a complete proposition. Only in a proposition do the words really have a meaning. The mental pictures that may pass before us need not correspond to the logical components of the judgement. It is enough if the proposition as a whole has a sense; its parts thereby also obtain their content. (§60.)

We have already discussed the first and third of the three 'fundamental principles' Frege singled out in his 'Introduction' to the *Grundlagen*. What we have here is the second, Frege's context principle: 'The meaning of a word must be asked for in the context of a proposition, not in isolation' (p. X). Its role is not just to provide support for the rejection of the supposition (orthodox in the Lockean tradition) that the meaning of a word is the idea it stands for, but also, more positively, to justify the assignment of meaning to number terms.

The context principle is one of the most influential yet controversial elements of Frege's philosophy. Despite the stress Frege places upon it in the 'Introduction' to the *Grundlagen*, it is not formulated again in his later work, unlike the other two principles; but nor is it explicitly repudiated. Part of the explanation of this is that Frege was still operating at the time of the *Grundlagen* with an undifferentiated notion of 'content', and this is later replaced by the dual notions of 'Sinn' and 'Bedeutung', which complicates any formulation of the principle; but it is also the case that Frege's realism increasingly gains control over his ideas, submerging his contextualism. I shall, however, postpone discussion of this until further elements of the picture are in place.[11] All we need note here is the use of the principle in removing one objection to Frege's construal of numbers as objects: we know what such objects are to the extent that we can use sentences in which number words occur. 'The independence that I am claiming for number is not to be taken to mean that a number word designates something when not in the context of a proposition, but I only intend by this to exclude the use of a number word as a predicate or attribute, which rather changes its meaning' (§60).

Of course, this still provides no reason for regarding substantival constructions as more fundamental than adjectival constructions; and even if we allow that there is some sense in which numbers can be treated as objects, this still leaves open the question as to exactly what kind of objects they are. For if we admit the context principle, why do we need to suppose that numbers are 'independent' ('*selbständige*') objects? Why can we not be content with viewing them as contextually defined abstract objects? Frege's objections to this suggestion emerge in the second subdivision of Part IV of the *Grundlagen* (§§62-9), an exposition of which is provided in the next section.

4.2 Frege's Central Argument

As we have now seen, the first three Parts of Frege's *Grundlagen* (§§5-54) consist in a critique of certain traditional views of arithmetic, and the difficulties in these views are resolved, according to Frege, by treating a statement of number as an assertion about a concept. It is this construal that suggests 'so naturally' the preliminary definitions that Frege offers in the very first section of Part IV (§55), the Part that contains the constructive argument of the *Grundlagen*.

(F_0) 'The number 0 belongs to a concept F' ('There are 0 F's') is defined as 'For all x, x is not F'.

(F_1) 'The number 1 belongs to a concept F' ('There is just 1 F') is defined as 'It is not true that, for all x, x is not F; and, for all x and y, if x is F and y is F, then $x = y$'.

(F_{n+1}) 'The number $n + 1$ belongs to a concept F' ('There are $n + 1$ F's') is defined as 'There is some x, such that x is F, and n is the number that belongs to the concept *falling under F, but not x*'.

Using the modern device of the *numerical quantifier*, '$\exists_n x$' being read as 'there are n x's such that', these can be formalized thus:

(F_0*) '$(\exists_0 x) Fx$' is defined as '$(\forall x) \neg Fx$'.

(F_1*) '$(\exists_1 x) Fx$' is defined as '$\neg (\forall x) \neg Fx \ \& \ (\forall x) (\forall y) (Fx \ \& \ Fy \rightarrow x = y)$'.

(F_{n+1}*) '$(\exists_{n+1} x) Fx$' is defined as '$(\exists x) [Fx \ \& \ (\exists_n y) (Fy \ \& \ x \neq y)]$'.

What we have here, it would seem, is a logical characterization of precisely the three number statements that enable the logicist project to get off the ground; and it comes as a surprise that Frege immediately rejects them as unsatisfactory. He does, however, rightly note that (F_{n+1}) is inadequate as it stands, 'for strictly speaking the sense of the expression "the number n belongs to the concept G" is just as unknown to us as that of the expression "the number ($n + 1$) belongs to the concept F"' (§56); in other words, taking (F_{n+1}*), a definition of '$(\exists_{n+1} x) Fx$' is offered which makes use of '$\exists_n x$', which has not itself been defined. But rather than proceeding to supplement the account, he rephrases his objection to encompass what he feels is also wrong with the first two definitions, namely, that 'we can never – to take an extreme example [*krasses Beispiel*] – decide by means of our definitions whether the number *Julius Caesar* belongs to a concept, or whether that well-known conqueror of Gaul is a number or not' (§56). The example does indeed strike most people as *krass*. But from what was said in the previous section, it should be clear what Frege feels is wrong with the definitions. We have been given no explicit definition of '*the* number which belongs to the concept *F*', leaving us with no way of determining whether the number *a* which belongs to the concept *F* and the number *b* which belongs to the concept *G*, say, are the same or not, i.e., for any *a* and *b*, whether *a* = *b* or not.[12] Frege writes: 'It is only an illusion that we have defined 0 and 1; in truth we have only determined the sense of the phrases "the number 0 belongs to" [and] "the number 1 belongs to"; but this does not allow us to distinguish 0 and 1 here as independent, reidentifiable objects' (§56).

In the rest of the first subdivision of Part IV (§§57-61), as we saw in the last section, Frege proffers further support for his belief that numbers are independent objects. But as we commented, Frege's argument seems circular, and his linguistic considerations remain unconvincing. However, with the context principle formulated, Frege returns to the problem of providing adequate definitions in §62. Given that the context principle suggests a way of accounting for our apprehension of numbers without appealing to ideas or intuitions, 'It will therefore depend on defining the sense of a proposition in which a number word occurs'. He goes on:

> But we have already established that number words are to be understood as standing for independent objects. This gives us a class of propositions that must have a sense – propositions that express recognition [of a number as the same again]. If the symbol *a* is to designate an object for us, then we must have a criterion that decides in all cases whether *b* is the same as *a*, even if it is not always in our power to apply this criterion. In our case we must define the sense of the proposition
>
> > 'The number that belongs to the concept *F* is the same as the number that belongs to the concept *G*';
>
> that is, we must represent the content [*Inhalt*] of this proposition in another way, without using the expression
>
> > 'the number that belongs to the concept *F*'.
>
> In doing so, we shall be giving a general criterion for the identity [*Gleichheit*] of numbers. When we have thus acquired a means of grasping a definite number and recognizing it as the same again, we can give it a number word as its proper name. (§62.)

As §§55-6 had indicated, the task is to formulate definitions, without presupposing an understanding of the expression '*the* number that belongs to the concept *F*', which provide a means of determining, for any *a* and *b*, whether *a* = *b* or not (equations being fundamental to arithmetic).

The strategy is to find a logically definable proposition, through which 'to form the content of a judgement that can be construed as an equation on each side of which is a number' (§63). The suggestion is to use the first of the following propositions to define the second:

(Na) The concept F is equinumerous to the concept G. (There are as many objects falling under concept F as under concept G, i.e. there are just as many F's as G's.)

(Nb) The number of F's is identical with the number of G's. (The number that belongs to the concept F is the same as the number that belongs to the concept G.)

The strategy is thus to define numerical identity (*Gleichheit der Zahlen*) in terms of one-one correlation (*beiderseits eindeutige Zuordnung*) or equinumerosity (*Gleichzahligkeit*).[13] Frege notes that this strategy 'seems recently to have gained widespread acceptance amongst mathematicians' (§63), but in the course of §§63-7 raises three objections to it, the first two of which, relating to the concept of identity, he answers, and the third of which he sustains.

The first objection concerns the specificity of the definition of numerical identity. 'The relationship of identity does not only hold amongst numbers. From this it seems to follow that it ought not to be defined specially for this case.' (Ibid.) However, he responds, his aim is not to define numerical identity in particular, but 'by means of the concept of identity, *taken as already known*, to obtain that which is to be regarded as being identical' (ibid.; my emphasis). Frege switches to a geometrical example to illustrate the method:

(Da) Line a is parallel to line b.

(Db) The direction of line a is identical with the direction of line b.

Symbolically, these may be represented thus:

(Da*) $a \parallel b$.

(Db*) $\mathrm{Dir}(a) = \mathrm{Dir}(b)$.

By reconstruing (Da) with the help of the concept of identity, Frege argues, we can obtain the concept of direction: 'we replace the symbol $\parallel$ by the more general $=$, by distributing the particular content of the former to a and b. We split up the content in a different way from the original way and thereby acquire a new concept' (§64).

Frege's geometrical example raises problems of its own. As Frege recognizes, 'parallel lines are frequently defined as lines whose directions are identical', reversing what *he* sees as the relationship between (Da) and (Db). In response, Frege argues that since 'everything geometrical must surely originate in intuition', we can only start with an intuition of parallel lines, from which, 'through a mental act', we arrive at the concept of direction. (Ibid.) But this talk of intuition might itself be questioned, since any dependence on a geometrical analogy may sully the purity of the logicist project.[14] However, it is wrong to read too much into the choice of example. Frege's concern is only to illustrate the *general form* of definition; and all we need to accept is the *possibility* of defining an abstract object such as a number or direction in terms of some equivalence relation defined over objects of some other kind, and the general concept of identity.

That it is legitimate to utilize the *general* concept of identity is reinforced by considering the second doubt that Frege raises, 'as to whether such a definition might not involve us in conflict with the well-known laws of identity' (§65). Frege takes as his definition of identity Leibniz's *salva veritate* principle:

(SV) *Eadem sunt, quorum unum potest substitui alteri salva veritate.* [Those things are the same of which one can be substituted for the other without loss of truth.]

What Frege understands by this is what is often called *Leibniz's Law* – interpreted as comprising both the Principle of the Indiscernibility of Identicals (reading the equivalence from left to right) and the Principle of the Identity of Indiscernibles (reading the equivalence from right to left):

(LL) $x = y \leftrightarrow (\forall F)(Fx \leftrightarrow Fy)$.[15]

What (LL) provides is a definition of identity in purely logical terms (within second order predicate logic, i.e. where quantification over properties is allowed); and it is this that justifies Frege in taking the concept of identity as already known. Frege goes on to remark that 'in universal substitutability all the laws of identity are contained' (§65), and this is correct, so long as the substitutability is restricted to extensional contexts, something that Frege was only clear about later.[16] But in this case, as he suggests (ibid.), every result of substituting 'the direction of b' for 'the direction of a' in an expression of a geometrical truth will itself be the expression of a geometrical truth; and this is to say that the direction of a is identical with the direction of b.

In §66, however, Frege raises his third objection, which he regards as unanswerable. According to Frege, as §56 had indicated, an adequate definition must enable us to *reidentify* the object introduced. But whilst the definition of (Db) by means of (Da) allows us to determine whether the direction of a given line is the same as that of any other given line, it does not tell us exactly *what* directions are, that is, what distinguishes them from any other objects, such as, to take Frege's second *krasses Beispiel*, England (§66). The general objection here, alluding to Frege's earlier example, has come to be known as 'the Caesar problem'.[17] The appropriate *criterion of identity* (as demanded in §62) has not been properly specified. An adequate definition must enable us to determine whether the following proposition is true *for any q*:

(Dq) The direction of line *a* is identical with *q*.

According to Frege, however, the suggested definition only enables us to do this 'if *q* is given in the form of "the direction of *b*" ' (§66). Any attempt to stipulate that (Dq) can only be true if *q* is a direction would presuppose the very concept of direction that we were trying to define; and any definition of the following form would be circular:

(q)   *q* is a direction, if there is a line *b* whose direction is *q*. (Cf. §66.)

The only kind of non-circular definition that could be offered would be this:

(Dr) The direction of line *a* is whatever is in common to line *a* and any other line that is parallel to it.

Frege's point can then be put very simply: the phrase 'whatever is in common' is inadequate for singling out the kind of object that a direction is.

In §67, which is one of the important passages in the development of his views, Frege elaborates the problem further:

> If one were to say: *q* is a direction if it is introduced by means of the definition offered above [(q)], then the way in which the object *q* is introduced would be treated as a property of it, which it is not. The definition of an object asserts, as such, really nothing about it, but instead stipulates the meaning [*Bedeutung*] of a symbol. After this has been done, it transforms itself into a judgement which does deal with the object, but now it no longer introduces it but stands on the same level as other assertions about it. If this way out were chosen, it would presuppose that an object can only be given in one single way; for otherwise it would not follow, from the fact that *q* was not introduced by means of our definition, that it could not have been so introduced. All equations [identities] would then come down to this, that whatever is given to us in the same way is to be recognized as the same. But this is so self-evident and so unfruitful that it is not worth stating. Indeed, no conclusion could ever be drawn here that was different from any of the premisses. The multitude of meaningful [*bedeutsame*] uses of equations [identities] depends rather on the fact that something can be reidentified even though it is given in a different way.

In §24 of the *Begriffsschrift* Frege had talked of the *Doppelseitigkeit* of definitions, whereby an initial stipulation of the meaning of a symbol could be 'converted' into a corresponding judgement, and this has now merged with the distinction between introducing an object and asserting something *about* that object. If rephrased in terms of specifying a *Bedeutung* and expressing a *Sinn*, then the later distinction between *Sinn* and *Bedeutung* can be seen as emerging in the thinking out of the conception of the *Doppelseitigkeit* of definitions; and I shall return to this later (see especially §6.4). For the moment we need only note that what Frege realizes here is that in order for a definition to satisfy his fundamental requirement, it is essential that the object introduced be recognizable in *other* ways than that involved in the initial definition. Only then can a definition transform itself into a judgement, and play a part in a scientific system (where *truths* are established). This leads Frege to the conclusion that the attempted definition of (Db) in terms of (Da) (and hence of any similar definition of number) is inadequate; and he goes on to consider a different way.

Frege's preferred way proceeds from the recognition that (Da) holds iff the following holds:

(Dd) The extension of the concept 'line parallel to line *a*' is identical with the extension of the concept 'line parallel to line *b*'.

He then suggests the following definition:

(De) The direction of line *a* is the extension of the concept 'parallel to line *a*'.

Having indicated the idea, he then drops the geometrical example, and provides a similar definition of number:

(Ne) The number that belongs to the concept *F* is the extension of the concept 'equinumerous to the concept *F*'. (Cf. §68.)

§68 of the *Grundlagen* contains one of Frege's most fundamental moves, crucial not only to his logicist project but also to the development of his philosophy; yet the argument is astonishingly compressed. Having rejected the contextual attempt to provide an adequate definition of *direction* by means of (Da) and (Db), Frege's alternative strategy is introduced without warning, and his proffered definition sprung on us with little explanation. All we are told is that (Da) and (Dd), and the corresponding two propositions, (Na) and (Nd), are logically equivalent:

(Na) The concept *F* is equinumerous to the concept *G*.
(Nd) The extension of the concept 'equinumerous to the concept *F*' is identical with the extension of the concept 'equinumerous to the concept *G*'.

(Nd) is true, Frege writes, iff (Na) is true (§69). But our remarks at the end of chapter 2 should make us cautious about placing any weight on considerations of logical equivalence at this stage of Frege's development; and I shall provide a more detailed analysis of the relationships involved here in §5.3.

But an obvious question arises straightaway. For how does Frege's alternative definition avoid the Caesar problem? Surely (Da) and (Db) are also logically equivalent, so how can (De) be an improvement on (Dr)? The answer, stated in the footnote to §68, but not justified anywhere in the *Grundlagen*, is that we are simply assumed to have knowledge of what the extension of a concept is.[18] Whilst (Dr) contains the vague phrase 'whatever is in common', Frege takes it that there is no such indeterminacy in (De). (De) is seen not only as stipulating a meaning for 'the direction of line *a*', but also as singling out the appropriate object in such a way that it *is* possible to reidentify it, just because we already know what the object is – the extension of the concept. Again, though, this is something to which we shall return in later chapters.

4.3 The Natural Numbers

Opening the third subdivision of Part IV of the *Grundlagen*, Frege writes: 'Definitions prove themselves by their fruitfulness' (§70). He has accepted that there may be doubts about his identification of numbers with extensions of concepts (cf. §69),[19] but so long as all 'the well-known properties of numbers' can be derived, he is satisfied that his definition can be justified (§70). As we saw in §3.3, what Frege regards as important for the status of a proposition is its 'most perfect method of proof' (*BS*, 'Preface'), and if a purely logical proof *can* be provided of every arithmetical proposition, then logicism is validated.

Let us first note that from Frege's explicit definition we can immediately derive the proposition that, according to Frege, had been inadequately defined contextually. For what we have are the following two definitions:

(Ne)　The number that belongs to the concept *F* is the extension of the concept 'equinumerous to the concept *F*'.

(Nε)　The number that belongs to the concept *G* is the extension of the concept 'equinumerous to the concept *G*'.

By (Nd), stating that the two extensions are identical, itself derived from (Na), we can infer our desired identity statement (Nb). What we have done is derive (Nb) not *directly* from (Na), but *indirectly* via (Nd) and the explicit definitions. So if we felt unhappy about Frege's explicit definition, but found the contextual method legitimate, we could still accept Frege's starting-point.[20]

It remains the case, then, that (Na) and (Nb) form the basis of Frege's logicist project:

(Na)　The concept *F* is equinumerous to the concept *G*.

(Nb)　The number of *F*'s is identical with the number of *G*'s.

Since (Nb) can be derived from (Na), with (or without) the help of the explicit definition (Ne), the task is now to provide a logical characterization of (Na). What is it for two concepts to be equinumerous? The answer has already been indicated: equinumerosity can be defined in terms of one-one correlation (*GL*, §63). Frege gives an example to illustrate the idea:

If a waiter wants to be sure of laying just as many knives as plates on a table, he does not need to count either of them, if he simply lays a knife right next to each plate, so that every knife on the table is located right next to a plate. The plates and knives are thus correlated one-one, by means of the same spatial relationship. (§70.)

Generalizing from this example, then, two concepts F and G are equinumerous if there is a relation R that correlates one-one the objects falling under F with the objects falling under G. As we saw in §3.3, the logical analysis of one-one correlation had already been provided in the *Begriffsschrift*; so let us simply write down the condition as follows, 'Rxy' symbolizing that x stands in relation R to y:

(Na*) $(\forall x)\,(Fx \rightarrow (\exists y)\,[\; Gy\; \&\; (\forall z)\,(Rxz \leftrightarrow z = y)\,]\;)$
       $\&\; (\forall y)\,(Gy \rightarrow (\exists x)\,[\; Fx\; \&\; (\forall w)\,(Rwy \leftrightarrow w = x)\,]\;).$

The first conjunct says that for any F (i.e. anything that is an F), there is one and only one G to which it is R-related, and the second conjunct adds that for any G, there is one and only one F to which it is R-related. (The first clause, in other words, states the condition for the relation between the F's and the G's to be *many-one*, and the second clause the condition for the relation to be *one-many*, the two clauses providing the combined condition for the relation to be *one-one* – compare (OO) in §3.3 above.) As Frege remarks in §72 of the *Grundlagen*, in offering the same analysis there, this 'reduces one-one correlation to purely logical relationships'.

Returning to the problem that Frege felt had been unresolved in §56, we do now have a way of determining whether the number that belongs to the concept F is the same as the number that belongs to the concept G. Frege's definitions of propositions of the form 'The number n belongs to the concept F' ('There are n F's') were regarded as unsatisfactory, because they did not adequately determine the relevant objects. But propositions of this form, according to Frege, are reducible to propositions that have the preferred form of an identity statement:

(NF)   The number n is the number that belongs to the concept F.

The expression 'n is a number' is taken as equivalent to the expression 'there exists a concept such that n is the number that belongs to it'; and this is now seen as acceptable with Frege's explicit definition (Ne) in place. 'Thus the concept of number is defined, admittedly, it seems, in terms of itself, but nevertheless without error, since "the number that belongs to the concept F" is already defined [as "the extension of the concept *equinumerous to the concept F*"].' (§72.)

All that is then needed, to provide definitions of the individual numbers, is to find appropriate concepts to substitute in (NF). In the case of the number 0, Frege utilizes the concept *not identical with itself*, yielding the following definition (cf. §74):

(N0) The number 0 is the number that belongs to the concept *not identical with itself*.

In offering this, Frege writes:

> Some may find it shocking that I should speak of a concept in this connexion. They will object, very likely, that it contains a contradiction and is reminiscent of our old friends the square circle and wooden iron. Now I believe that these old friends are not so black as they are painted. To be of any use is, I admit, the last thing we should expect of them; but at the same time, they cannot do any harm, if only we do not assume that there is anything which falls under them. That a concept contains a contradiction is not always obvious without investigation; but to investigate it we must first possess it and, in logic, treat it just like any other. All that can be demanded of a concept from the point of view of logic and with an eye to rigour of proof is only that the limits to its application should be sharp, that we should be able to decide definitely about every object whether it falls under that concept or not. But this demand is completely satisfied by concepts which, like "not identical with itself", contain a contradiction; for of every object we know that it does not fall under any such concept. (*FA*, §74.)

Furthermore, the crucial point about Frege's chosen concept is that it can be specified purely logically ('$x \neq x$'). As Frege remarks, 'I could have used for the definition of nought any other concept under which no object falls. But I have made a point of choosing one which can be proved to be such on purely logical grounds; and for this purpose "not identical with itself" is the most convenient that offers, taking for the definition of "identical" the one from Leibniz given above [§65], which is in purely logical terms' (ibid.). From (Ne) and (N0) we can then formulate an explicit definition that satisfies Frege's requirements:

(E0) The number 0 is the extension of the concept 'equinumerous to the concept *not identical with itself*'.

Assuming, with Frege, that the notion of an extension is unproblematically a logical notion, then we have indeed managed to characterize the number 0 in purely logical terms.[21]

The next step in the project is to define the successor relation, relating any two adjacent members of the natural number sequence. Frege offers this definition of 'n follows in the series of natural numbers directly after m':

(SR) There is a concept F, and an object x falling under it, such that the number that belongs to the concept F is n and the number that belongs to the concept *falling under F but not identical with x* is m. (§76.)

Intuitively, this clearly gives the desired result: there is one less object falling under the latter concept than under the former, and the relationship between the two concepts can be characterized purely logically (cf. (F_{n+1}*) in §4.2 above).

Frege goes on to show how the definition yields 1 as the successor of 0 (§77). Take the concept *identical with 0*. Since one and only one object falls under this concept, namely, the number 0, the number that belongs to this concept is the number 1. The number that belongs to the concept *falling under the concept 'identical with 0' but not identical with 0*, on the other hand, is clearly 0, since nothing can fall under this concept. So the condition stated in (SR) is satisfied (taking 'F' as 'identical with 0', giving $x = 0$, $n = 1$ and $m = 0$), and we can conclude that 1 is the successor of 0. What Frege has done here, in other words, is provide a suitable concept to substitute in (NF) to generate a definition of the number 1:

(N1) The number 1 is the number that belongs to the concept *identical with 0*.

Since 0 has already been defined purely logically, and in fact is the only object that has been so defined up to this point, the concept *identical with 0* is obviously the ideal concept for Frege to take to logically define the number 1. What the argument just given then shows is that this is indeed the number that follows in the series of natural numbers directly after 0.

From (Ne) and (N1), the following explicit definition can then be offered:

(E1) The number 1 is the extension of the concept 'equinumerous to the concept *identical with 0*'.

With the numbers 0 and 1 now defined, the number 2 can then be generated in a similar way:

(N2) The number 2 is the number that belongs to the concept *identical with 0 or 1*.

(E2) The number 2 is the extension of the concept 'equinumerous to the concept *identical with 0 or 1*'.

The pattern that emerges is clear: each number can be defined in terms of its predecessor(s), since the series of natural numbers up to a given number n has itself $n + 1$ members (since it starts from 0). This suggests the following general definition:

(Nn+1) The number $n + 1$ is the number that belongs to the concept *member of the series of natural numbers ending with n*.

Of course, the concept *member of the series of natural numbers ending with n* itself needs to be defined, but once again, the materials for doing so had already been supplied in the *Begriffsschrift*. As we saw in §3.3, a logical characterization had been offered, through the notion of an hereditary property, of 'b follows a in the f-series' (cf. *GL*, §79), from which 'b is a member of the f-series beginning with a' could then be defined (cf. *GL*,

§81). Since this is equivalent to '*a* is a member of the *f*-series ending with *b*', the required logical definition can be provided. (SR) can then be used to show that (Nn+1) yields $n + 1$ as the successor of n – substituting 'member of the series of natural numbers ending with *n*' for '*F*', '*n*' for '*x*', '*n* + 1' for '*n*', and '*n*' for '*m*'.[22]

With Frege's definitions in place, it becomes possible to derive the familiar properties of the natural numbers. For example, (Nn+1) implies that every number has a successor, i.e. that no member of the series of natural numbers follows after itself, as Frege puts it in §83. In the *Grundlagen* Frege merely states a handful of theorems; the full task was to be undertaken in the *Grundgesetze*.[23] But if we grant him his assumptions, we can understand the optimism with which he faced this task. Certainly, his apparent success in generating the entire natural number series from the (purportedly logical) definitions offered would have made the logicist project look thoroughly feasible. As Frege himself concluded in Part V of the *Grundlagen*, 'I hope in this work to have made it probable that arithmetical laws are analytic judgements and therefore *a priori*. Accordingly, arithmetic would be simply a further developed logic, every arithmetical theorem a logical law, albeit a derivative one.' (§87.)

4.4 Non-natural Numbers

Most of the positive part of Frege's *Grundlagen* is concerned with showing how the natural numbers can be defined logically. Except for some brief remarks about infinite (transfinite) numbers (§§84-6), it is only in Part V, entitled 'Conclusion', that Frege addresses the question of other numbers, and even here the main thrust of the discussion seems to be to refute formalism. The formalist is understood as someone who imagines that one need only postulate that, say, the laws of addition and multiplication, as defined over the natural numbers, hold for any extension of the number system, in order to coherently investigate the properties of that extended system.[24] But, Frege argues, it is quite wrong to suppose that a concept has instances if no contradiction has yet revealed itself – not only are self-contradictory concepts admissible, but even if a concept contains no contradiction, that is still no guarantee that anything falls under it.[25] So more is needed in justifying the introduction of new numbers than the formalist would seem to imply.

Frege remarks that 'It is common to act as if mere postulation were already its own fulfilment' (§102), a criticism that later found expression in Russell's famous comment that 'The method of "postulating" what we want has many advantages; they are the same as the advantages of theft over honest toil' (*IMP*, p. 71). The real work of proving consistency cannot be shirked. 'Postulating', say, that through any three points a straight line can be drawn is simply incoherent; and as we noted in §3.1, quaternions provide just one example of numbers which fail to obey what had previously been regarded as a fundamental law, in this case concerning the commutativity of multiplication. (Cf. §102.) With the introduction of new numbers, Frege remarks, 'the meanings of the words "sum" and "product" are extended' (§100), and we cannot automatically assume that initial definitions of basic concepts remain valid in any enlarged system.[26]

But if we cannot just define new numbers into existence by specifying a list of properties that characterize them, nor arrive at them by simply extending an existing number system taking its axioms for granted, how are they then to be apprehended? In asking this question in §104, Frege answers that 'everything will depend in the end on finding a judgeable content that can be transformed into an equation [identity] whose sides are precisely the new numbers. In other words, we must fix the sense of a recognition judgement [*Wiedererkennungsurtheils*] for such numbers.' Just as it did in the project of defining the natural numbers, what underlies Frege's strategy is his adoption of the context principle, and it is worth noting here that at the very point at which Frege introduced the principle, in §60, he took the example of infinitesimals to illustrate its importance. As we saw in §3.1, if infinitesimals are understood as actually existing quantities, then a contradiction ensues, and the task seemed to be to find some way of construing them as 'useful fictions', as Leibniz had regarded them. In this respect, Frege's approach looks promising: 'It all depends on defining the sense of an equation [identity] of the form $df(x) = g(x)dx$, rather than showing that there is a line bounded by two distinct points whose length is dx' (§60, n.).

However, this only raises the question as to whether contextually defined terms nevertheless do refer to genuinely existing objects, an issue on which Frege's and Leibniz's views seem to diverge.[27] Certainly, Frege himself, in reminding us in §104 of his general strategy of 'splitting up a content' to yield an identity, immediately goes on: 'In doing so, we must heed the doubts that we discussed, in §§63-8, concerning such a transformation. If we proceed in the same way as we did there, then the new numbers will be given to us as extensions of concepts.' And these extensions, of course, are themselves regarded as objects, albeit logical ones. But since Frege says no more about infinitesimals in the *Grundlagen*, and makes only a few remarks in his later work, it is hard to be clear as to his precise position.[28]

Frege does, however, express firmer views on those numbers at the opposite end of the spectrum, namely, transfinite numbers, which he briefly discusses in the final subdivision of Part IV, immediately after his sketch of the logicist reduction of the natural numbers. The idea is simple. Consider the concept *finite number*, defined as the concept *member of the series of natural numbers beginning with 0* (cf. §83), which, as we saw in the last section, can be logically characterized and applies to all the natural numbers. The number that belongs to this concept is clearly an infinite number, and Frege symbolizes it by '∞_1'. He writes:

There is nothing at all weird or wonderful about the infinite number ∞_1 so defined. 'The number that belongs to the concept F is ∞_1' means [*heisst*] no more nor less than: there is a relation that correlates one-one the objects falling under the concept F with the finite numbers. According to our definitions, this has a perfectly clear and unambiguous sense; and that is sufficient to justify the use of the symbol ∞_1 and secure it a meaning [*Bedeutung*]. That we can form no idea of an infinite number is quite irrelevant and applies just as much to finite numbers. Our number ∞_1 is in this way just as definite as any finite number: it can without doubt be recognized as the same again and be distinguished from another. (§84.)

Frege goes on to express his agreement with Cantor that infinite numbers are as legitimate as finite numbers (§85), though he does suggest that his own method of introducing infinite numbers, through logical definition, is superior to Cantor's appeal to 'inner intuition' (§86). Furthermore, Frege notes, since numbers are characterized right from the start as belonging to concepts, there is no extension of the meaning of 'number' when infinite numbers are introduced (since they too are attached to concepts), so that worries about invalidating any fundamental laws are minimized (§85).

The case of infinite numbers suggests that if even they – amongst the most controversial of numbers – can be defined on the basis of the natural numbers, then so too can all the other numbers, and although Frege hardly mentions the real numbers in the *Grundlagen*, there is no indication that he did not regard them as similarly definable.[29] But it is only in the second volume of the *Grundgesetze*, published in 1903, that Frege finally takes up the issue; and then it comes as a surprise to learn that he believes that the natural numbers and the real numbers form quite distinct domains. This constitutes a departure from what, by the end of the 19th century, as we indicated in §3.1, had become the dominant foundationalist tradition. Frege is perfectly aware of this, and in fact introduces his own positive account of the real numbers, much as he did in the *Grundlagen* with regard to the natural numbers, with a lengthy and scathing attack on rival conceptions.[30]

Frege's main criticism of these alternative views concerns their failure to accord due weight to the *application* of real numbers. Defining real numbers in terms of converging sequences of rational numbers, for example, ignores their central role in *measurement*. Frege writes:

> it is not possible to extend the domain of natural numbers to that of the real numbers; they are quite separate domains. The natural numbers answer the question 'How many objects of a certain kind are there?', whilst the real numbers can be regarded as measurement numbers [*Maasszahlen*], which state how large a magnitude is compared with a unit magnitude. (*GG*, II, §157.)[31]

According to Frege, a real number is essentially a *ratio of magnitudes*

(*Grössenverhältnis*); and this precisely captures its role in measurement (cf. *GG*, II, §73). Such an emphasis on the *application* of numbers might seem in conflict with the attitude he revealed in the *Grundlagen* in accusing Mill of confusing the applications of an arithmetical proposition with the pure proposition itself (*GL*, §9; see §3.4 above). But Frege was quite insistent even then that a proper account of a number system should *explain* its applicability. In the case of the natural numbers, for example, it was construing them as belonging to concepts, according to Frege, that explained their own wide-ranging applicability – to both physical and mental phenomena (cf. *GL*, §48; see §4.1 above). Whilst *particular applications* of a number system are distinct from its essential functioning, its *general applicability* is not: the features responsible for those applications are fundamental.[32]

Frege remarks that 'exactly the same ratio of magnitudes, which obtains between line segments, also obtains between intervals of time, masses, intensities of light, and so on. In this way the real number is detached from these particular kinds of magnitude and is, as it were, suspended above them.' (*GG*, II, §158.) He goes on to distinguish his own position both from the old geometrical conception, which, whilst misguidedly based on spatial intuition, at least treated real numbers as measurement numbers, and from more recent accounts, in which 'measurement either fails to appear at all or else is patched on purely externally, without an inner connection grounded in the essence of number' (*GG*, II, §159). So whilst real numbers are independent of particular magnitudes, they are far from independent of magnitude in general.

Just as whatever falls under a sortal concept can be counted, then, so too whatever can be measured can be assigned a real number; and a theory of the real numbers must explain the latter just as much as a theory of the natural numbers must explain the former. Despite the difference in the roles of these two types of number, however, there are similarities in Frege's accounts of them. For just as the natural numbers are identified with extensions of logically definable concepts (functions of one argument), so too the real numbers are identified with extensions of logically definable relations (functions of two arguments).

The key notion in Frege's account of the real numbers is that of a *magnitude domain* (*Grössengebiet*).[33] A magnitude domain is any class of objects with the type of structure revealed, for example, in the domains of lengths, masses, or temperatures (cf. *GG*, II, §161). Any two objects within such a domain stand in a certain relation to one another, i.e. a ratio of magnitudes obtains; and it is the extensions of these relations that exhibit the features of the real numbers. The task is then to find an appropriate class, which Frege terms a *positive class*, possessing the required properties of a magnitude domain from which the real numbers can be defined.

The objects of the chosen class must themselves, of course, be logically definable. To indicate the feasibility of his project, Frege notes that every real number can be represented in the following form, where 'r' is understood as a non-negative integer, and 'n_1', 'n_2', etc. constitute an infinite sequence of positive integers (*GG*, II, §164):

$$r + \sum_{k=1}^{k=\infty} \frac{1}{2^{n_k}}$$

Every real number can thus be represented as an ordered pair, consisting of a natural number and a class of natural numbers excluding 0. Since the natural numbers can be defined logically, on Frege's view, so too can the ordered pairs and hence the relations between them. The extensions of these relations can then be taken as the objects of a positive class, the extensions of the relations between these objects defining the real numbers. The real numbers thus end up as the extensions of relations between extensions of relations between ordered pairs of extensions of concepts and sets of extensions of concepts. What could be more logical?

After indicating the outline of his project (*GG*, II, §§156-64), Frege spends the rest of Volume II of the *Grundgesetze* formally demonstrating the properties of a positive class. In §245 he notes his next task – to show that there exists a positive class; but with this note his constructive account ends. A third volume was clearly planned, but by this time, Frege had been informed by Russell of the paradox that effectively dealt a death-blow to his logicist ambitions.[34] Despite an appendix to the second volume, added whilst the book was in press, that sought to respond to the paradox, Frege was never able to complete the project begun so optimistically with the publication of the *Begriffsschrift* and single-mindedly pursued for over two decades with such technical and philosophical brilliance.

4.5 Unnatural Numbers?

Nine years passed between the publication of Frege's *Grundlagen* in 1884 and the appearance of Volume I of the *Grundgesetze* in 1893, and a further ten years before Volume II saw the light of day in 1903; and most of Frege's energies during this period were indeed taken up with the detailed working out of his logicist programme.[35] Volume I of the *Grundgesetze* contains 179 sections, divided into two Parts, Part I explaining his 'Begriffsschrift' – his symbolism, axioms and definitions (§§1-52), and Part II presenting formal proofs of the fundamental laws of arithmetic (§§53-179). Part I constitutes a revised and richer elaboration of the logical system introduced in the *Begriffsschrift*; and Part II demonstrates rigorously what was merely sketched in the constructive part of the *Grundlagen*. Part II, in fact, continues into Volume II of the *Grundgesetze* (§§1-54); and Part III of the *Grundgesetze*, on the real numbers, begins at §55 of Volume II. As already remarked, Frege's account of the real numbers follows the pattern of his account of the natural numbers: a critique of rival views precedes the formal presentation of his own theory.[36]

Two fundamental developments in Frege's thought between the *Grundlagen* and the *Grundgesetze* may be mentioned here, both of which are discussed in detail in the chapters that follow. Firstly, Frege introduced his distinction between *Sinn* and *Bedeutung*, and secondly, connected with this, he clarified his ontology, sharpening his views about objects and concepts. Most notably, *truth-values*, themselves admitted as objects, were taken as the *Bedeutungen* of sentences, so that concepts could be construed as functions mapping objects onto truth-values (see §6.2 below); and *extensions of concepts* too became accepted as legitimate objects, and hence as possible arguments of functions. Although Frege had introduced extensions of concepts in the *Grundlagen*, he had not at the time felt committed to their use. In a footnote to §68, for example, where he first offers his definition of number, he remarks: 'I believe that for "extension of the concept", simply "concept" could be said.' He raises two objections to this, firstly, that numbers (unlike concepts) are objects, and secondly, that concepts can have the same extension without themselves coinciding, but then immediately states without argument that both objections can be met. In reviewing his enquiry at the end of the book, he repeats that 'I attach no great importance to the introduction of extensions of concepts' (§107; see §5.5 below). In fact, far from being met, the two objections were soon sustained, as Frege thought through his own views more carefully (see §7.1 below). The result was that the definitions of the *Grundlagen* remained firmly in place. What happened between the *Grundlagen* and the *Grundgesetze*, then, can be seen as reinforcing, and indeed as offering justification for, Frege's appeal to extensions of concepts.

Frege's considered logicist position was thus that the natural numbers can be defined as extensions of concepts, and the real numbers as extensions of relations. I shall examine Frege's argument for such identifications, as originally given in the *Grundlagen*, in more detail in §5.3, and consider other aspects of his logicism in subsequent sections. But in the final section of this chapter, I want to comment on the plausibility of this account. For the obvious criticism of it is that whilst Frege may, at best, have succeeded in defining objects that have all the key properties of the relevant numbers, he has not defined the natural or the real numbers themselves. Is it not *unnatural*, we might ask, to construe the former as extensions of concepts, and *unreal* to construe the latter as extensions of relations between extensions of relations between ordered pairs of extensions of concepts and sets of extensions of concepts?

Taking the case of real numbers first, let us approach the problem by briefly comparing Frege's conception with the theories of Cantor and Dedekind mentioned in §3.1. The main difference is that whilst Cantor and Dedekind seek to define the real numbers in terms of sequences or classes of rational numbers, Frege attempts to define them using only the natural numbers, albeit in a more complicated fashion.[37] Given that the rationals can themselves be defined as ratios of natural numbers, the difference might seem of little significance. But as we saw in the last section, one of Frege's fundamental concerns was to provide an explanation of the *application* of real numbers, and according to him, Cantor's and Dedekind's theories, whatever their straightforward appeal might be, fail to do justice to the role of the real numbers as measurement numbers. Frege's 'unreal' account at least accords a central place to the idea of a 'ratio of magnitudes'.

But there is a deeper issue involved here, which surfaces in Frege's critique of Cantor's theory, in particular (*GG*, II, §§68-85). Cantor writes that he 'assigns' what he calls a 'fundamental sequence' (i.e. a convergent series of rationals) to the number b to be defined, and Frege opens his critique by quoting this remark.[38] But if 'b' simply *designates* the fundamental sequence, Frege argues, then we have not yet reached the real numbers themselves; if, on the other hand, we take it that 'b' does indeed designate a number, then are we not presupposing what it is our very task to define? The dilemma is clear: either the real numbers are *identified* with fundamental sequences, which does not, in fact, individuate them as numbers; or else they are merely *correlated* with fundamental sequences, which assumes that they are already given, a fundamental sequence simply determining *which number 'b'* is to stand for. In neither case are the real numbers adequately defined.

The obvious answer to this dilemma is to allow that we do have antecedent knowledge of what it is for a number to be the limit of a fundamental sequence – in the case of rationals. 1, for example, can be represented as the limit of the series $1/2, 2/3, 3/4, \dots \nu/(\nu+1), \dots$ (cf. *GG*, II, §84); and in general, any rational number a can be represented, trivially, as the limit of the sequence all of whose terms are a (i.e. $a, a, a, \dots$). The idea is then simple: wherever a fundamental sequence does *not* have a rational limit, *there* we have an irrational number. As Frege himself puts it, interpreting Cantor as favourably as he can, 'With every fundamental sequence there is connected a certain number, which does not need to be rational. These numbers are therefore partly new, not as yet considered, and they are to be determined precisely by the fundamental sequence with which they are connected.' (*GG*, II, §77.) Starting with the rationals, then, it would seem that we can indeed define a new set of numbers, simply adding to our existing system.

According to Frege, however, this does not avoid the underlying dilemma. For either the real numbers are assumed as given, or they are not. If they are, and we merely have a correlation established between them and fundamental sequences, then definitions are still lacking. If they are not, then this holds as much for the rational as for the irrational real numbers. There is nothing in Cantor's account to justify *identifying* the *real number* defined as the limit of a fundamental sequence such as a, a, a, ... with the *rational number* a itself. If such an identification seems obvious, then that is only because we are presupposing an understanding of a number being the limit of a series, which is precisely what requires explanation.[39]

These considerations confirm Frege in his view that the real numbers must be defined as a complete system, and not piecemeal via the rational numbers. Of course, as we have seen, Frege held this view for an independent reason, namely, that both the rational and irrational numbers are measurement numbers, and must be treated together. But if we play down the requirement that measurement be made central in any account (allowing it to be 'patched on externally'), whilst accepting the point that the real numbers form a distinct system from the rationals, then it is possible to refine Cantor's theory along otherwise Fregean lines. For Frege himself admits that Cantor adequately defines what it is for two fundamental sequences to have the same limit: two sequences (a_v) and (a'_v) have the same limit iff $(a_v - a'_v)$ vanishes (i.e. tends to 0) as v tends to infinity (cf. *GG*, II, §81). The real numbers can then be defined as *equivalence classes* of fundamental sequences using just that method of logical abstraction that Frege introduced in the *Grundlagen*.[40]

Dedekind's theory, to which similar objections can be raised, can also be refined along Fregean lines, a real number in this case being identified, say, with the lower of the two classes determined by a Dedekind cut.[41] If these refinements are made, then aside from the issue of the application of numbers, we would seem to have a variety of equally legitimate, i.e. logically acceptable, ways of introducing the real numbers, each of which identifies any given real number with a *different* class. But if this is so, then the idea of a *uniquely* correct account of the real numbers disintegrates. Indeed, it would no longer seem appropriate to talk of *the* real numbers at all; what count as the real numbers would depend on the underlying theory. As long as the objects defined – whatever classes they might be identified with – have all the right properties, then an adequate characterization is provided.

The possibility of alternative construals is clearly incompatible with Frege's conviction that each number is an individual object, as indicated, according to Frege, by the fact that we do speak of *the* number one, for example. Of course, we might allow that there can be alternative construals of the real numbers, but insist that the natural numbers, in terms of which the real numbers are defined, are unique. But since Frege's work, the development of set theory has generated a variety of reductions of the natural numbers too. Most accounts start by defining 0 as the null set, and 1 as the unit set of the null set (i.e. the set that contains the null set as its sole member); but thereafter more than one way of proceeding is possible. Zermelo (1908), for example, defined 2 as the unit set of 1, 3 as the unit set of 2, and so on (each number, except 0, being the unit set of its predecessor); whilst von Neumann (1923) defined 2 as the set composed of 0 and 1, 3 as the set composed of 0, 1 and 2, and so on (each number, except 0, being the set of its predecessors). Symbolizing the null set by 'Ø', the following two series, respectively, are thus generated:

(ZS)   Ø, {Ø}, {{Ø}}, {{{Ø}}}, ...
(NS)   Ø, {Ø}, {Ø, {Ø}}, {Ø, {Ø}, {Ø, {Ø}}}, ...

The underlying set theories will themselves have different properties and applications, but each is capable of generating a series with which the natural numbers can be identified.[42]

Frege himself would have seen these possibilities as only lending support to his own theory: what they show is that 2, for example, should be identified not with any *particular class* such as represented in (ZS) or (NS), but with the *class of all such classes* (i.e. with the class of all classes equinumerous to a given 2-membered class). Of course, this class too is a particular class, but since it comprises all 2-membered classes, and can be characterized purely logically, it accords best of all with Frege's fundamental assumption that logic is the most general of sciences, governing everything that is thinkable.[43] Unfortunately, however, Russell's paradox was to reveal the dangers involved in so naively talking of classes of classes, so that the modern set theorist is forced to abandon Frege's own definitions and follow a path such as taken by Zermelo or von Neumann.[44]

In his influential paper, 'What numbers could not be' (1965), Paul Benacerraf argues that the possibility of alternative set-theoretic reductions of the natural numbers shows that numbers *cannot* be sets. If numbers *were* sets, then it must be possible to say *which ones* they are; but a unique specification is what cannot be given. Benacerraf further argues that numbers cannot be objects at all, but this conclusion does not itself follow. What is shown, at best, is that numbers cannot be identified with objects of any other kind, such as sets, numerals, directions, or human beings, but not that they are not objects at all. Of course, as we saw in §4.2, it was the Caesar problem that led Frege to identify numbers with extensions of concepts, the criteria of identity for which we were assumed to know; but if we permit the introduction of abstract objects at all, through some kind of contextual definition, and Frege allows extensions of concepts themselves, then there is no reason, on this basis at least, why numbers should not be objects in their own right.[45]

However, there remains a problem about Frege's identification of numbers with extensions of concepts. For even if his definitions give logicism its greatest chance of success, numbers do not immediately strike anyone as extensions of concepts, as Frege himself admits.[46] It is at this point that Frege is forced to become more philosophical in his argument. As we shall see in §5.5, Frege ends up emphasizing that he is *reconstructing* the natural numbers. Prior to the rigorous development of a theory, Frege argues, the question as to which objects *the* natural numbers are has no clear sense, and it is precisely the task of the theorist to provide it with one. That numbers do not appear to us, pre-theoretically, to be extensions of concepts is not, therefore, an objection. Of course, this response generates further problems of its own, not least of which concerns Frege's notion of *sense*; and I discuss this notion in detail in chapter 6.

Here we need only note that despite Frege's later attempts at justification, there remains a crucial ambiguity in his conception of his reconstructive project. For does he regard himself as uncovering for the first time the real essence of those numbers with which we have all along been familiar, or as setting up a new system in which we have *analogues* of the natural numbers? If only the latter, can we truly say that Frege has shown that *the* natural numbers are logical objects? Although officially, Frege was undoubtedly a *realist* – mathematical objects are indeed already there waiting to be discovered and described, there are nevertheless aspects of his mathematical and semantic work that are in conflict with such a position; and I return to this issue in the final two chapters.

First, however, we must elucidate the underlying dilemma, which, in relation to Frege's logicist project, may be stated as follows. If we are to assess Frege's project, then we must clearly have a grasp of the basic properties of numbers (properties which Frege himself refers to as 'well-known'; *GL*, §70). But if we do, must we not *already know* whether numbers are extensions of concepts or not? Obviously, if they are not, then Frege's definitions are simply incorrect. But if they are, how is it that we seem not to know such a fundamental fact? What surfaces here is the so-called *paradox of analysis*, and it is the task of the next chapter to explain the general problem and the development of Frege's philosophy in response to it.

5. Analysis and Definitions

I know that these names, according to common usage, have other meanings, but it is my purpose to explain, not the meanings of words, but the nature of things, and to refer to them by words whose meanings, according to current use, are not entirely different from the meaning which I wish to attach to them: this warning should suffice once for all. (Spinoza, *Ethics* III, Defs. of the Emotions, XX, Explanation.)

In the first two chapters, we considered Frege's logical achievements, and his advance over traditional logic; and in the last two chapters, an account was provided of Frege's logicist project, and his critique of rival conceptions of arithmetic. In the second half of this book, I explore how this logical and mathematical work motivated his developing interest in semantic and epistemological issues. In this chapter I focus on his changing conceptions of the nature of analysis and the role of definitions, which introduces us to the problems concerning Frege's notions of *Sinn* and *Bedeutung*, and the relationship between logic and language, which occupy us in the final three chapters.

After a sketch of the historical background (§5.1), I examine Frege's early conception of the 'fruitfulness' of definitions (§5.2). In §5.3 I provide a detailed analysis of Frege's central argument in the *Grundlagen* (merely expounded in §4.2), and in §5.4 show how the problems that this generates require a distinction that Frege himself realized was necessary as he formulated, and attempted to respond to, the paradox of analysis. A certain tension in Frege's account, however, remains, and in the final section I discuss Frege's last and fullest treatment of the paradox.

5.1 Analysis and Synthesis

The general problem that underlies the issues addressed in the present chapter concerns the epistemological value of logic. Some of the questions involved here were raised in §1.3, in relation to Aristotelian logic; and in the present section I shall sketch further aspects of the historical background, against which Frege's own views must be set, outlining, in particular, the development of ideas about analysis and synthesis.

Let us note, first of all, that the fundamental epistemological problem was formulated even before the invention of logic. In the *Meno*, Plato articulates a general dilemma that threatens any attempt to seek knowledge. In response to a sceptical question posed by Meno, Socrates replies:

> Do you realize that what you are bringing up is the trick argument that a man cannot try to discover either what he knows or what he does not know? He would not seek what he knows, for since he knows it there is no need of the inquiry, nor what he does not know, for in that case he does not even know what he is to look for. (80E.)

Socrates' own response is to deny that in *learning* something, we come to know something that we did not already know. What we do is *recollect* (81D); and it is at this point in the dialogue that Socrates brings in the slave boy and, purely by asking questions, gets him to 'recollect' that the square on the diagonal of a given square has twice its area, a geometrical truth that the boy initially appeared not to know at all (82-5).

This famous passage of Plato's dialogues generates a whole host of problems of its own. Reading the dialogue, for example, one certainly recollects what is meant by a 'leading question'. But all we need note here is the basic strategy, for what Socrates does is draw a distinction – between 'knowledge' ('full-blown knowledge'), 'true opinion', and what we may call 'unconscious knowledge'.[1] 'Unconscious knowledge' is what is there already, out of which 'true opinions' and then knowledge proper are recovered. What happens in the learning process – in 'recollection' – is that 'true opinions [are] aroused by questioning and turned into knowledge' (86A). The distinction between 'true opinion' and 'full-blown knowledge' might be deemed enough on its own to solve the dilemma as presented. Socrates remarks that 'a man who does not know has in himself true opinions on a subject without having knowledge' (85C), and these 'true opinions' could be taken as sufficient for embarking on the search for knowledge. But Socrates presumably feels that a similar dilemma arises in the case of 'true opinion', and that the regress that then threatens can only be halted by appeal to 'unconscious knowledge'. However, he is less explicit about this than he is about the distinction between 'true opinion' and 'full-blown knowledge'; and it is this that is of interest here.[2]

The key to the distinction is suggested towards the end of the dialogue. Socrates says:

> True opinions are a fine thing and do all sorts of good so long as they stay in their place; but they will not stay long. They run away from a man's mind, so they are not worth much until you tether them by working out the reason. That process, my dear Meno, is recollection, as we agreed earlier. Once they are tied down, they become knowledge, and are stable. That is why knowledge is something more valuable than right opinion. What distinguishes one from the other is the tether. (97E-98A.)

It is this idea that we might regard as the starting-point of Aristotle's philosophy, for what characterizes Aristotle's work is the systematic 'tethering' of all the 'true opinions' that had then been aroused, syllogistic theory being developed to provide the framework for this 'tethering'. As we saw in §1.3, Aristotle opens the *Posterior Analytics* with the remark that 'All teaching and all intellectual learning comes about from already existing knowledge' (71a1-2), and goes on to distinguish between 'ordinary knowledge' and 'scientific knowledge'; and the puzzle in the *Meno* is specifically mentioned in this connection (71a30-1). What Aristotle does, in other words, is provide content to the Socratic distinction between 'true opinion' and 'full-blown knowledge'; and logic can then be seen as having value to the extent that it plays a 'tethering' role.

In the *Posterior Analytics* (I 13) Aristotle distinguishes two elements in the 'tethering' process, understanding 'the fact' (*to oti*) and understanding 'the reason why' (*to dioti*). Aristotle's own example can be used to illustrate the distinction. Consider the following two syllogisms:

(PN)	The planets do not twinkle	(PT)	The planets are near
	What does not twinkle is near		What is near does not twinkle
	The planets are near		The planets do not twinkle

Both are valid arguments, but whilst the first is merely a 'deduction of the fact', the second constitutes a 'demonstrative syllogism' or 'scientific deduction', providing an *explanation* of the conclusion. That the planets do not twinkle is hardly an explanation of why they are near; rather, that they are near is (part of) an explanation of why they do not twinkle (making allowances for Aristotle's cosmology). (Cf. 78a23-b3.) Only in the latter case have we 'tethered' the propositions in the right way, generating *scientific knowledge*.

In the first case, then, we start with an effect (the planets not twinkling) and identify its cause (the planets being near), and in the second case, having identified the cause, we display the movement from cause to effect; and it is this that developed into the distinction between *analysis* (which literally meant 'untying'), which involved the uncovering of truths that were epistemically or metaphysically more primitive, and *synthesis*, which involved the organization of truths in a deductive system. As mentioned in §1.5, synthesis was regarded, in the Aristotelian/Euclidean tradition, as the more important, since it was here that we had *scientific deduction*.[3]

In the 17th century, as part of his repudiation of the Aristotelian tradition, Descartes was highly critical of this emphasis on synthesis, and even accused the Greeks of deliberately withholding the secret of their analytic methods.[4] Given that Aristotelian science was increasingly seen as flawed, this was an understandable reaction; but it was Descartes' own work on *analytic* geometry that lent weight to his criticisms, for it was the development of powerful new problem-solving techniques that made the mere presentation of results seem trivial.[5] It is not surprising, then, that

Descartes should have wished to develop an alternative analytic method, for use in 'first philosophy' or metaphysics, to uncover the 'real' primitive truths. This was Descartes' 'Method of Doubt', which advocated the (temporary) repudiation of all things about which there was the remotest doubt. Anything that was merely *deducible* could not survive the process, since, according to Descartes, whilst each deductive step could be grasped at the time of doing so in a way that was immune to scepticism, doubt could creep in as soon as an attempt was made to recall previous steps and put the steps together (cf. *RDM*, Rules 3, 7, 11). For Descartes, the truth of a proposition was apprehended in a primitive act of *intuition*, not by deduction; and the task was to attain 'clear and distinct ideas' of the fundamental truths.

What lay at the heart of Descartes' strategy, then, was a form of epistemological atomism: something was only certain if it could be grasped in a single act of intuition, by the attainment of a 'clear and distinct idea'. It was this feature of Cartesianism that Locke so uncritically inherited and so influentially incorporated into his new 'way of ideas', and that became a fundamental presupposition of British Empiricism. In Book I of the *Essay*, as part of his attack on innatism, Locke argued that knowledge of particular instances of general principles is acquired long before knowledge of the principles themselves (I ii 12, 25); and in Book IV he drew the obvious conclusion, that knowledge of particulars is not therefore arrived at by *deduction* from such principles:

> Is it impossible to know that *One* and *Two* are equal to *Three*, but by virtue of this, or some such Axiom, *viz. the Whole is equal to all its Parts taken together*? Many a one knows that *One* and *Two* are equal to *Three*, without having heard, or thought on that, or any other Axiom, by which it might be proved; and knows it as certainly, as any other Man knows, that the *Whole is equal to all its Parts*, or any other Maxim; and all from the same Reason of self-evidence; the Equality of those *Ideas*, being as visible and certain to him without that, or any other Axiom, as with it, it needing no proof to make it perceived. Nor after the Knowledge, *That the Whole is equal to all its parts*, does he know that *one and two are equal to three*, better, or more certainly than he did before. (IV vii 10.)

The rejection of the Socratic/Aristotelian conception is explicit: if something is self-evident, then no 'tethering' is necessary. If someone has the ideas of *one*, *two* and *three* at all, Locke goes on, mere inspection will yield the equality. 'For a Man cannot confound the *Ideas* in his Mind, which he has distinct: That would be to have them confused and distinct at the same time, which is a contradiction: And to have none distinct, is to have no use of our Faculties, to have no Knowledge at all.' (Ibid.) According to Locke, then, self-evidence, and not proof, is what secures an item of knowledge.

Leibniz, in responding to both Descartes and Locke, sought to reinstate the traditional belief in the need for proof; and in his own account of

analysis and synthesis, showed how the two could be seen as complementing and reinforcing one other (see Appendix 2). One of Leibniz's main
criticisms of Descartes concerned his appeal to clear and distinct ideas.
Descartes' own criteria for 'clarity' and 'distinctness' were too subjective,
and as Leibniz rightly remarked, what seems clear and distinct to someone who judges rashly may actually be obscure and confused.[6] Instead,
Leibniz offered his own *objective* criteria: I have a *clear* concept if I can
recognize any object that falls under it, and a *distinct* concept if I can
enumerate its component marks.[7] Since the enumeration of 'marks' was
the purpose of analysis, the basic belief in the importance of analysis was
maintained.

It is worth noting here how Leibniz reshaped and developed certain
elements of Cartesian thought even whilst attacking other aspects. For it
was Descartes' use of algebra in geometry that impressed him the most
and that he sought to generalize. According to Leibniz, the great value of
algebra lay in the way it 'unburdens the imagination', and his aim was to
develop a symbolic system to encompass all areas of reasoning.[8] Within
such a system, the proof of a proposition would be generated purely
mechanically, thereby freeing it from the vagaries of our own mental
processes. For Leibniz, the status of a proposition – its truth or falsity,
necessity or contingency – was dependent not on its *mode of apprehension*
(as it was for Descartes and Locke), but on its *method of proof*.

In his response to Locke, in the *New Essays*, Leibniz remarks (through
his spokesman Theophilus): 'I would like no limits to be set to our analysis,
definitions to be given of all terms which admit of them, and demonstra-
tions – or the means for them – to be provided for all axioms which are not
primary, *without reference to men's opinions about them and without
caring whether they agree to them or not*' (I i 1; p. 75; my emphasis).
Although self-evidence is indeed the characteristic of what Leibniz calls
'primary truths' – those explicit 'identities' to which all other truths can
be reduced – the point about these is that their self-evidence depends on
their *form*, not their content (see Appendix 2). Locke's view, as given in the
passage cited above, is thus rejected. In a comment that is quoted with
approval by Frege (*GL*, §17), Leibniz notes: 'we are not concerned here
with the sequence of our discoveries, which differs from one man to
another, but with the connection and natural order of truths, which is
always the same' (*NE*, IV vii 9; p. 412). Leibniz then proceeds to provide
his proof that $2 + 2 = 4$ (IV vii 10). Although he remarks that this 'is not
quite an immediate truth', which the Lockean might presumably deny, it
is clear that the real point concerns the *objective interdependence* of truths,
not the way in which truths strike the human mind. As Leibniz makes
Philalethes, the Lockean, admit, 'The demonstration of such a thoroughly
known conclusion is hardly necessary, but it does show how truths depend
on axioms and definitions' (ibid., p. 414). Once again, it is the method of
proof, the process of 'tethering', that determines the real status of a

proposition, not its mode of apprehension, which may vary from person to person.

In suggesting how analysis and synthesis could be seen as complementing each other, Leibniz hoped to show how a 'logic of proof' could at the same time be a 'logic of discovery' (again, for details, see Appendix 2). But although in operating a logical system one might legitimately talk of 'discovering' the *connections* between truths, there remains the traditional problem of how one can be regarded as acquiring knowledge of *new* truths. Indeed, on Leibniz's account, the problem now seems even more acute. For whilst the Cartesians and Lockeans had merely questioned *synthesis*, if analysis and synthesis simply reflect the two directions of movement along the same deductive chain, then the same problem arises with analysis. Leibniz's own answer was essentially the Platonic one: we already have within us an infinity of 'confused perceptions', which when sufficiently 'distinguished and heightened' constitute 'sensations', and only become 'reflective knowledge' when noticed in an act of 'apperception'.[9]

In his 'Preface' to the *New Essays*, Leibniz compares his own system to Plato's, and Locke's system to Aristotle's. Both Aristotle and Locke, Leibniz remarks, believe that the soul in itself is a *tabula rasa*, whilst both he and Plato believe that the soul contains innate knowledge (*NE*, pp. 47-8). In his attempt to combine the best in the two traditions (as he saw it), Kant, in the *Critique of Pure Reason*, set out to show how 'reflective knowledge' requires a contribution from *both* experience *and* our innate conceptual framework. As he tendentiously remarked, 'Leibniz *intellectualised* appearances, just as Locke ... *sensualised* all concepts of the understanding'.[10] Kant opens the *Critique* with the words: 'There can be no doubt that all our knowledge begins with experience', but goes on: 'it does not follow that it all arises out of experience. For it may well be that even our empirical knowledge is made up of what we receive through impressions and of what our own faculty of knowledge ... supplies from itself' (B1). Knowledge, he later makes clear, arises from the union of both sensibility and understanding: 'Without sensibility no object would be given to us, without understanding no object would be thought. Thoughts without content are empty, intuitions without concepts are blind.' (A51/B75.)

The details of Kant's system need not concern us. All we need note is yet a further transformation of the notions of 'analysis' and 'synthesis'. Kant retains the Leibnizian conception of analysis as the explication of concepts, but treats it, as Descartes and Locke before him had treated 'synthesis', as of little epistemological value. 'Synthesis', on the other hand, as Kant understands it, becomes the most central conception of all, for it is in 'synthesis' that 'intuitions' and 'concepts' are united in yielding knowledge. 'By *synthesis*, in its most general sense, I understand the act of putting different representations together, and of grasping what is manifold in them in one [act of] knowledge' (A77/B103). All that analysis does, in revealing the 'marks' of a concept, is exhibit the logical *form* of a judgement (cf. A78-9/B104-5); it is synthesis that supplies the *content*.

Kant's reconstrual of the notions of 'analysis' and 'synthesis' is reflected in the criteria that he provides for what he entitles *analytic* and *synthetic* judgements. His 'official' criterion for analyticity, as given in the *Critique*, may be formulated as follows:

(AN$_O$) A (true) judgement of the form '*A* is *B*' is *analytic* if the predicate *B* is contained in the subject *A*. (Cf. A6-7/B10.)

It is clear that Kant understands the notion of 'containment' here in something like the Leibnizian sense. As he goes on to say, analytic judgements are *explicative*, 'adding nothing through the predicate to the concept of the subject, but merely breaking it up into those constituent concepts that have all along been thought in it, although confusedly'. Synthetic judgements, on the other hand, are *ampliative*, adding 'to the concept of the subject a predicate which has not been in any wise thought in it, and which no analysis could possibly extract from it'. (A7/B11.)

The problem with such a criterion is obvious. For who is to say whether a particular predicate is or is not *really* 'contained' in the concept of the subject? Kant himself allows that it may be 'covertly' contained, so who is the judge? Leibniz's own conception highlights the problem, since for him, *all* truths are 'analytic' in this Kantian sense, (AN$_O$) being a criterion not merely for analyticity, but for *truth*.[11] The difference between necessary and contingent truths, which was the distinction that Leibniz himself drew, lay rather in whether the relevant analysis was *finite*, and hence surveyable by us, or *infinite*, and only apprehended by God. According to Leibniz, as we have just noted, each of us starts out with 'confused' knowledge of everything; so that all supposedly 'synthetic' truths are covertly 'analytic'. But to close off this possibility, Kant must stress what is 'actually' thought; and this threatens to make what counts as 'analytic' a purely individual matter.[12]

What seems to be required, then, is a more objective criterion, a *logical* rather than merely *phenomenological* criterion. In fact, however, Kant himself supplies just such a criterion later on in the *Critique*. The 'highest principle of all analytic judgements', he writes, is the *principle of contradiction*: 'no predicate contradictory of a thing can belong to it' (A150-1/B189-91). This enables us to formulate the following alternative criterion for analyticity:

(AN$_L$) A (true) judgement of the form '*A* is *B*' is *analytic* if its negation '*A* is not *B*' is self-contradictory.

This criterion is clearly satisfactory in all those cases of what Leibniz termed 'identities', since the self-contradiction expressed by any proposition of the form '*A* is not *A*' is immediately seen. But in other cases we may need to provide some analysis of the concepts to ascertain the self-contradiction, and we are then back with the problem of relying on what is 'actually thought'.[13]

However, Kant's fundamental motivation in introducing the terms 'analytic' and 'synthetic' lay in distinguishing between what merely *explicates* our concepts and what actually *amplifies* our knowledge; and the criteria he offers must simply be read as attempts to express this distinction.[14] Since Kant *antecedently* believed that mathematics, for example, *extends* our knowledge,[15] we cannot conclude that Kant should really have held, on some interpretation of his criteria, that arithmetic is a body of analytic truths. If a particular criterion yields the analyticity of arithmetic, in other words, then so much the worse for the criterion, *not* for Kant's antecedent belief. However, this should not be taken as diminishing Frege's critique of Kant's arguments for the syntheticity of arithmetic (as discussed in §3.4 above), depending as they do on (AN$_0$); it merely puts them in perspective. As we shall see in the next section, both Kant and Frege agreed on the central issue – that in arithmetic we can indeed *advance* our knowledge. And Kant, after all, was perfectly right about one thing: neither arithmetic nor geometry is reducible to *Aristotelian* logic; and if this is what is meant by asserting the syntheticity of mathematics, then there can be no disagreement.

5.2 The 'Fruitfulness' of Definitions

If Kant's doctrine that arithmetic is a body of *synthetic* truths was an attempt to express his antecedent belief that arithmetic *extends* our knowledge, then Frege's doctrine that arithmetic is a body of *analytic* truths was equally an attempt to express his own antecedent belief in the purely *logical* nature of arithmetic. As we saw in chapter 3, Frege shared the fundamental Pythagorean belief that the realm of the thinkable is the realm of the enumerable. Since, for Frege, genuine thought involves the application of *sortal* concepts, each concept determining a precise number of objects falling under it, then every such concept has a number associated with it. According to Frege, in other words, whatever can be properly conceptualized can be enumerated. Given that the realm of the conceptual was traditionally seen as part of the realm of the logical, it was therefore natural for Frege to regard the realm of the enumerable as itself part of the realm of the logical. Furthermore, since Kant had himself treated logical truths as analytic, it was also plausible to suppose – *pace* Kant himself – that arithmetic was really a system of analytic truths.

Frege was well aware that he was widening the class of analytic truths; yet he insisted that he was not departing in any radical way from Kant's view. In offering his own characterizations in §3 of the *Grundlagen*, Frege remarks, 'By this I do not, of course, wish to introduce new senses, but only to capture what earlier writers, in particular *Kant*, have meant' (p. 3, n.;

cf. §88). To an extent, this is true, for we might regard Frege as endorsing Kant's *logical* as opposed to *phenomenological* criterion for analyticity (cf. *GL*, §88, p. 100, n. 1). If, on the supposition that the negation of a proposition is true, we can derive a contradiction, appealing only to logical laws, then we have thereby proved the original proposition, by purely logical means. Generalizing (AN$_L$), then, Frege's own criterion (AN) emerges naturally (cf. §3.4 above):

> (AN) A truth is *analytic* if its proof depends only on general logical laws and definitions.

However, Frege's reconstrual involved two deeper revisions of Kant's views. Firstly, as Frege himself explicitly remarks, Kant's own distinction between analytic and synthetic truths is not exhaustive. '[Kant] is thinking of the case of the universal affirmative judgement. Here one can speak of a subject concept and ask – according to the definition – whether the predicate concept is contained in it. But what if the subject is an individual object? What if the question concerns an existential judgement? Here there can be no talk at all of a subject concept in Kant's sense.' (§88.) On the Leibnizian account, this is not quite correct, since proper names are indeed terms for subject concepts.[16] But Frege's essential point is right. For Kant's own criterion (AN$_O$) assumes that every proposition is fundamentally of subject-predicate form; yet as Frege's development of function-argument analysis showed, this is far too restrictive an assumption. Clearly, a more widely serviceable criterion is needed, and (AN$_L$) provides the obvious basis.

The second revision also relates to the difference between (AN$_O$) and (AN$_L$). For the utility of (AN$_O$) seems to depend on a grasp of the *content* of a proposition of the form '*A* is *B*'; whereas all that (AN$_L$) seems to rely upon is the possibility of deriving a contradiction on the supposition of the falsity of the proposition. As we have already suggested, the problem with (AN$_O$) lies in the notion of 'containment'. Stressing what is 'actually thought' threatens to make the criterion too psychologistic. Just as Leibniz sought to provide a more objective criterion for 'clarity' and 'distinctness', which both Descartes and Locke understood in too subjectivist a manner, so too we can regard Frege as 'depsychologizing' Kant's criterion for analyticity. We noted in the last section Frege's endorsement of Leibniz's remark that 'we are not concerned here with the sequence of our discoveries, which differs from one man to another, but with the connection and natural order of truths, which is always the same'; and the point is also made in the context of Frege's alternative characterizations:

> It frequently happens that we first discover the content of a proposition and then provide a rigorous proof in another, more difficult way, by means of which the conditions of its validity can often also be discerned more precisely. Thus in general the question as to how we arrive at the content of a

judgement has to be distinguished from the question as to how we provide the justification for our assertion.

Now these distinctions between *a priori* and *a posteriori*, synthetic and analytic, in my opinion, concern not the content of the judgement but the justification for making the judgement. Where there is no such justification, there is no possibility of drawing the distinctions either. An *a priori* error is thus just as much an absurdity as, say, a blue concept. If a proposition is called *a posteriori* or analytic in my sense, then this is a judgement not about the psychological, physiological and physical conditions that have made it possible to form the content of the proposition in our mind, nor about how someone else, perhaps erroneously, has come to hold it to be true, but rather about the ultimate ground on which the justification for holding it to be true rests. (*GL*, §3.)

According to Frege, whether a proposition is analytic or not depends on the best possible proof. If that proof depends only on logical laws and definitions, then the proposition is analytic; and this does seem to provide a more general and objective criterion for analyticity.

However, as we noted at the end of §3.4, Frege's own criterion is not itself exhaustive, since it fails to cover the logical laws and definitions themselves.[17] As far as the logical laws are concerned, Frege simply inherited the fundamental Kantian assumption that these were the paradigm examples of analytic truths.[18] But what about definitions? From very early on, and throughout his life, Frege emphasized the legitimacy and unproblematic status of what we might call *stipulative* definitions – introducing a new and simple sign to abbreviate an already understood but more complex sign (e.g. defining '4' as '3 + 1'). In §24 of the *Begriffsschrift*, he wrote: 'Such definitions merely serve to effect a superficial simplification by fixing an abbreviation'; and once 'converted' into judgements (i.e. viewed as statements rather than stipulations), exhibiting what he termed their 'dual role' ('Doppelseitigkeit'), they can be regarded as *analytic*, 'since all that can come out again is what was put into the new symbols'. The notion of analyticity suggested here appears to allude to the original Kantian criterion (AN$_O$). In later papers, Frege not only stressed the stipulative character of such definitions, and their consequent lack of epistemic value, but also clearly saw them as the only *proper* kind of definition.[19]

But this conception raises an obvious problem. For it does not seem to be this kind of definition that forms the core of the argument sketched in the *Grundlagen*. Frege remarks at several points in the *Grundlagen* that definitions must be *fruitful* (cf. p. ix; §§70, 88). Yet on a Kantian view, this alone would be enough for treating them as *synthetic*. So there is a *prima facie* conflict between Frege's belief in the fruitfulness of definitions and their supposed analyticity. The problem is just one aspect of the general issue concerning the epistemic value of logic. Frege's position on this general issue, very fittingly, is fully in accord with the two great logicians who preceded him, Aristotle and Leibniz. 'The aim of proof is not only to place the truth of a proposition beyond all doubt, but also to afford insight into the dependence of truths on one another' (§2). Later on, in discussing deduction, he admits that whilst theorems can be derived from axioms without being contained in any one of those axioms by itself, they 'are in a way contained covertly in the whole set taken together'. But, Frege goes on, 'this does not absolve us from the labour of actually extracting them and setting them out in their own right'. Having done so, each arithmetical truth 'would contain concentrated within it a whole series of deductions for future use, and the use of it would be that we need no longer make the deductions one by one, but can express simultaneously the result of the whole series'. (*FA*, §17.)

This suggests one conception of fruitfulness that might remove the apparent conflict in Frege's views. In his 'Introduction' to the *Grundlagen*, Frege remarked: 'Even I think that definitions must show their worth by their fruitfulness, by their usefulness in constructing proofs' (p. IX). Perhaps all that Frege meant by the 'fruitfulness' of definitions was their usefulness in facilitating movement along chains of reasoning, enabling us to extend those chains and arrive at conclusions that might otherwise have been hard to reach. Arithmetical truths abbreviate chains of reasoning just as stipulative definitions abbreviate chains of signs. The fruitfulness lies in shortening the journey to the frontiers of reasoning, where new theorems are being found and consolidated. Quoting Frege's words, 'If this be so, then indeed the prodigious development of arithmetical studies, with their multitudinous applications, will suffice to put an end to the widespread contempt for analytic judgements and to the legend of the sterility of pure logic' (*FA*, §17; cf. §91).

However, there is a much more interesting conception of fruitfulness that surfaces in later parts of the *Grundlagen*. In §70 Frege repeats his earlier assertion that 'Definitions prove themselves by their fruitfulness', but goes on: 'Those that could just as well be omitted without opening a gap in the line of argument should be rejected as completely worthless.' This remark immediately follows those central sections of the *Grundlagen* in which Frege 'splits up contents' in new ways; but it seems in direct opposition to the conception of definitions as abbreviatory devices. Frege returns to the issue in the concluding Part of the *Grundlagen*. He rejects what he takes as the Kantian conception of definition: 'Kant seems to think of a concept as defined by a conjunction of marks [*Merkmale*; i.e. constituent concepts]; but this is one of the least fruitful ways of forming concepts' (§88). What he presumably has in mind here is the Leibnizian model of the analysis of concepts (as illustrated in Appendix 2). He goes on:

Looking back over the definitions given above, there is scarcely one of this kind to be found. The same holds too of the really fruitful definitions in mathematics, for example, of the continuity of a function. We do not have here a series of conjunctions of marks, but rather a more intimate, I would say more organic, connection of defining elements. The distinction can be clarified by means of a geometrical analogy. If the concepts (or their extensions) are represented by areas on a plane, then the concept defined by a conjunction of marks corresponds to the area that is common to all the areas representing the marks; it is enclosed by sections of their boundaries. With such a definition it is thus a matter – in terms of the analogy – of using the lines already given to demarcate an area in a new way. But nothing essentially new comes out of this. The more fruitful definitions of concepts draw boundary lines that were not there at all. What can be inferred from them cannot be seen from the start; what was put into the box is not simply being taken out again. These inferences extend our knowledge, and should therefore be taken as synthetic, according to Kant; yet they can be proved purely logically and are thus analytic. They are, in fact, contained in the definitions, but like the plant in the seed, not like the beam in the house. Often several definitions are needed for the proof of a proposition, which is not therefore contained in any single one and yet does follow purely logically from all of them together. (*GL*, §88.)

What this passage suggests is that there are *two* kinds of definition. The first kind are genuinely stipulative definitions, which do serve as abbreviatory devices, and which generate straightforwardly analytic judgements in Kant's original sense, as given by the criterion (AN_0). The second kind are Frege's 'fruitful' definitions, which start from a given proposition and yield not the concepts originally 'thought in it' but *new* concepts. Taking Frege's own geometrical analogy, let us represent the difference in the following way:

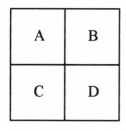

$$A + B + C + D = E$$

Diagram 1

$$A + B + C + D = P + Q + R + S$$

Diagram 2

The first kind of definition corresponds to the case of taking squares A, B, C and D and using them to construct square E, as represented in diagram

1. The second kind of definition corresponds to the case of taking the area composed of squares A, B, C and D (i.e. E) and drawing *new* boundary lines *within* that area, 'splitting it up' into P, Q, R and S, as represented in diagram 2. In both cases we have the same 'box', but whereas in the first case we are indeed simply taking out of the box again what we put into it, in the second case we are engaged in a creative activity, 'splitting up the contents of the box in a new way'.

What lies at the root of Frege's conception here is his use of function-argument analysis in logic. The idea was first explained in §9 of the *Begriffsschrift*. Consider the following proposition:

(HLC) Hydrogen is lighter than carbon dioxide.

As Frege remarks, in place of 'hydrogen' we can substitute 'oxygen' or 'nitrogen' and attain a proposition with a different sense. That part of the expression that is constant in this transformation represents the *function*, whilst that part that is variable represents the *argument*. Frege goes on:

> *This distinction has nothing to do with the conceptual content, but only with our way of grasping it.* Although as viewed in the way just indicated, 'hydrogen' was the argument and 'being lighter than carbon dioxide' the function, we can also grasp the same conceptual content in such a way that 'carbon dioxide' becomes the argument and 'being heavier than hydrogen' the function. (*BS*, §9; my emphasis.)

The same 'conceptual content' can thus be represented in different ways, depending on what are taken as the argument and function. Another example that Frege gives also illustrates the point:

(CKC) Cato killed Cato.

> Here, if we think of 'Cato' as replaceable at its first occurrence, then 'killing Cato' is the function; if we think of 'Cato' as replaceable at its second occurrence, then 'being killed by Cato' is the function; finally, if we think of 'Cato' as replaceable at both occurrences, then 'killing oneself' is the function. (*BS*, §9.)

As we saw in chapter 2, in his critique of Aristotelian and Boolean logic, Frege emphasized that he proceeds from judgements and their contents, not from concepts. In 'Boole's logical Calculus and the Concept-script', he writes: 'instead of putting a judgement together out of an individual as subject and an already previously formed concept as predicate, we do the opposite and arrive at a concept by splitting up the content of possible judgement' (p. 17). Later in that same paper, he stresses the importance of such 'concept formation' (p. 32), and remarks that 'fruitfulness is the acid test of concepts' (p. 33). He then uses precisely that analogy that we have just considered from the *Grundlagen* in suggesting that the truly fruitful definitions are those in which 'totally new boundary lines are drawn' (p. 34).[20]

The origin of Frege's thought in §88 of the *Grundlagen* is thus clear: it is function-argument analysis that permits 'splitting up the content' of a proposition in different ways. Since it is the *same* content that gets split up differently, the process is logically legitimate, and 'analytic'; but since *new* concepts are thereby formed, the process is at the same time fruitful. The resolution of the apparent conflict in Frege's account that this suggests is highly attractive; but it still leaves us with a number of problems. Conclusions may indeed be 'contained' in the premises as plants are 'contained' in their seeds, but since 'nutrition' is also essential in a generative process, questions remain as to the nature of 'logical nutrition'. And in any case, Frege's own use of 'fruitful' definitions is far from clear. For, as we saw in §4.2, Frege ends up *rejecting* those contextual definitions that involve 'splitting up contents' in different ways, and opts instead for what seem to be *stipulative* definitions. To assess this properly, however, we need to look more closely at Frege's central argument.

5.3 Frege's *Grundgedanke*

§§62-9 unquestionably form the basis of Frege's constructive argument in the *Grundlagen*, and they are also pivotal in the development of his philosophy; yet their interpretation is by no means straightforward. As we remarked in §4.2, the crucial move that is sprung on us in §68 is mystifying. How was it that Frege was led to identify certain *abstract objects*, such as numbers and directions, with *extensions of concepts*? Not only is such an identification counterintuitive, but it is also hard to reconcile with Frege's apparent initial contextualism. I shall call his fundamental thought here – that abstract objects can be identified with extensions of concepts – Frege's *Grundgedanke*;[21] and the aim of the present section is to explore its possible motivations and rationale.

I shall postpone for the moment the obvious question as to how Frege's alternative definition is meant to avoid the objection raised to the contextual one (the Caesar problem), and focus first on the assumption that underlies Frege's argument in this central core of the *Grundlagen*. Let us recall the four propositions, in the geometrical case, that Frege formulates:

(Da) Line a is parallel to line b.

(Db) The direction of line a is identical with the direction of line b.

(Dd) The extension of the concept 'line parallel to line a' is identical with the extension of the concept 'line parallel to line b'.

(De) The direction of line a is the extension of the concept 'parallel to line a'.

According to Frege, (Db) is attained by 'splitting up the content' of (Da) in a new way, but since this fails to yield an adequate definition of 'direction', one that enables us to distinguish directions from all other possible objects, (Dd) is then offered, from which (De) is suggested as an explicit definition. In the case of the transition from (Da) to (Dd), Frege does not actually talk of 'splitting up the content' in a further new way, but he presumably takes it that the two propositions do indeed have the same 'content' – the relationship between (Da) and (Dd) being viewed as the same as that between (Da) and (Db). In §65, in considering the definition of (Db) by means of (Da), Frege uses the word 'gleichbedeutend', and it is clear from an earlier remark in §44 that he understands this in terms of logical equivalence, in the sense that one member of the pair is true iff the other is true;[22] and it is logical equivalence to which Frege appeals in moving from (Da) to (Dd). It does appear, then, that it is his early notion of 'conceptual content' that is operative here, with its attendant criterion: two propositions have the same 'conceptual content' iff they are logically equivalent.

As we remarked at the end of §2.5, however, this early notion is ambiguous; and one way of appreciating the problem is to consider whether (De) could be *derived* from the equivalences between (Da) and (Db), and (Da) and (Dd). The suggestion might be that (De) results from 'splitting up' (Da) into (Db), 'splitting up' (Da) into (Dd), and then combining part of (Db) with part of (Dd). But could such reasoning be legitimate? As it stands, the argument looks fallacious, for it would appear to have the following (invalid) form:

(A) aRb, $aRb \to p = q$, $aRb \to r = s$ $\vdash$ $p = r$.
[(Da), (Da) $\to$ (Db), (Da) $\to$ (Dd) $\vdash$ (De).]

To turn this into a valid argument, '$p = q$' must express the *same* identity as '$r = s$' (this is the missing premiss); the mere logical equivalence of (Db) and (Dd) is insufficient to derive (De). To use the term introduced in §2.5, (Db) and (Dd) must be *cognitively equivalent*. The relation here has still to be characterized, but the essential difference, in the present case, can be illustrated by considering the following two arithmetical equivalences, symbolizing 'cognitive equivalence' by '$\equiv$' and logical equivalence by '$\leftrightarrow$':

(α) $(4 = 2 + 2) \equiv (3 + 1 = 2 + 2)$.
(β) $(4 = 2 + 2) \leftrightarrow (3 = 2 + 1)$.

(α) might represent a stage in a Leibnizian proof of '$4 = 2 + 2$', whereas (β) just shows that we still have a correct equation if we subtract 1 from both sides of an arithmetical equation. Only in the first case can we deduce '$p = r$' from '$p = q$' and '$r = s$'. The difference is not, of course, confined to arithmetic. Consider the following logical equivalence:

(γ) Dr Frege = The Great Gottlob iff the nose of Dr Frege = the nose of The Great Gottlob.

Such an equivalence clearly does not license identifying Frege with his nose (Gogolian worlds aside)!

So what exactly are the relationships in Frege's geometrical case? If (Da), (Db) and (Dd) are indeed all 'cognitively equivalent', then it would seem that we can *derive* (De), and Frege's *Grundgedanke* would be justified. But if they are not, did Frege nevertheless implicitly treat them as so, unconsciously trading on the ambiguity in his early notion of 'content', in proposing (De) as his explicit definition? Did Frege, in other words, *confuse* 'cognitive equivalence' with logical equivalence, and would this account for why he offered so little explanation in §68 of his crucial moves? Given that at the time of the *Grundlagen*, his notion of 'conceptual content' was still undifferentiated, this is a tempting suggestion. But before answering these questions, we must first expose an important omission in the 'derivation' as so far considered. For whilst (Db) is a *direct* result of 'splitting up the content' of (Da), (Dd) requires an intermediate step:

> (Dc) The concept 'line parallel to line *a*' is coextensive with the concept 'line parallel to line *b*'.

'Splitting up the content' of (Dc) results in (Dd) in exactly the same way as (Da) results in (Db); but what has now been revealed is a potentially different kind of transition – from (Da) to (Dc). The structure of the 'derivation' that is under consideration can now be represented as follows:

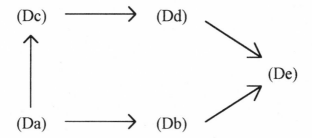

(Da) is 'split up' into (Db), but since this yields an inadequate definition, a further move is made from (Da) to (Dd), *via* (Dc), which was left implicit by Frege at the time. On the assumption that (Db) and (Dd) are 'cognitively equivalent', legitimizing 'cross-identifications', (De) can be derived.

Let us call a pair of propositions that are related in the way that (Da) and (Db) are, and (Dc) and (Dd) are, a 'horizontal Fregean pair'. The same 'content' is 'split up' differently, but the propositions remain on the same level. Contrastingly, let us call a pair of propositions that are related in the way that (Da) and (Dc) are, a 'vertical Fregean pair'. The transition here involves what we may term *conceptual ascent*: there is a shift from talking about the *objects* of geometry to talking about the *concepts* used in so talking.[23] So whilst the transitions from (Da) to (Db), and from (Dc) to

(Dd), occur on the same level, the object-level and concept-level (concept-level-one), respectively, the transition from (Da) to (Dc) involves a shift from one level to the other.

On this analysis, then, there are two ways in which the attempted 'derivation' might break down: if either horizontal Fregean pairs or vertical Fregean pairs fail to embody the necessary 'cognitive equivalence' (they could, of course, both so fail). Since Frege explicitly talks of (Da) and (Db) having the same 'content', it might be thought that he regards horizontal Fregean pairs as 'cognitively equivalent'. Yet, as we have seen, it is unclear whether Frege had in mind here 'cognitive content' or merely 'logical content'. But what of the case of vertical Fregean pairs? Although Frege did not formulate (Dc) in the *Grundlagen*, there can be little doubt that Frege would also have asserted that vertical Fregean pairs have the same 'content'; and furthermore, there seems good reason to attribute to him the view that such pairs possess the same *'cognitive* content'. Recall Frege's construal of syllogistic *A*-propositions, as defended, for example, in §47 of the *Grundlagen* (discussed in §§2.4 and 4.1 above). (Wa), Frege argues, should be analysed as (Wc):

(Wa)   All whales are mammals.

(Wc)   The concept *whale* is subordinate to the concept *mammal*.

Here we do indeed have a case of *conceptual ascent*; yet Frege's whole point is that (Wc) makes clearer what the 'real content' of (Wa) is. Consider also the following pair, the pattern of analysis involved being fundamental to Frege's logicist project (as we saw in the last chapter):

(Oa)   There are 0 *F's* .

(Oc)   The concept *F* is not instantiated.

These examples plainly show that Frege thinks that a 'content' can be 'split up' in such a way that a *concept* becomes the subject of the proposition ('content' being unaffected by how the subject/predicate distinction is drawn); and the legitimacy of the process seems to depend on the preservation of 'cognitive content'.

However, it remains the case that Frege was unclear at the time of the *Grundlagen* as to exactly what his notion of 'content' involved. Perhaps this unclarity itself accounts for the tentativeness with which Frege offers (De) as his explicit definition. More charitably, it might be suggested that Frege regarded the various propositions he formulated as indeed only *logically* equivalent, that he realized that (De) could not be *derived*, and that this was why (De) was offered as a *stipulative definition* – whose 'fruitfulness' was to be judged when actually employed in deriving the 'well-known properties of numbers' (cf. *GL*, §70). But in the light of what was said in the last section, the stipulative character of Frege's definition must not be overstressed, since the conception of 'fruitfulness' that emerges in §88 of the *Grundlagen* reinforces the idea, present in the initial pursuit of the contextual approach, that definitions involve 'splitting up contents' in new ways. (De) should not, then, be interpreted as a *mere* stipulation, but as something that itself depends on a 'content' already given. And whatever Frege's *later* views about stipulative definitions may have been (which we discuss in §5.5), there remains the lurking suspicion that Frege was not entirely clear about all this at the time of the *Grundlagen*, and that the ambiguity in his early notion of 'content' may, if only at an unconscious level, have helped motivate his *Grundgedanke*.

However, even if the attempt to read a 'derivation' of (De) into Frege's thought cannot in the end be sustained, the problem as to the relationships between the various propositions involved is nevertheless highlighted; and I shall consider this further in the next section. But before doing so, we must return to the Caesar problem. For, even if a 'derivation' were possible, how did Frege think that appealing to *extensions* satisfied his requirement on the adequacy of a definition? If (Dd) stands in the same relation to (Dc) as (Db) does to (Da), and we were to request an explicit definition of an *extension*, then are we not back in the original predicament – of not knowing what such objects are, having failed to provide for all cases? The analogous move would be to make a further conceptual ascent, shifting up from (Dc) to (Df), 'split up the content' of (Df) into (Dg), and use (Dg) to provide the explicit definition (Dh):

(Df) The concept 'concept coextensive with the concept "line parallel to line *a*" ' is coextensive with the concept 'concept coextensive with the concept "line parallel to line *b*" '.

(Dg) The extension of the concept 'concept coextensive with the concept "line parallel to line *a*" ' is identical with the extension of the concept 'concept coextensive with the concept "line parallel to line *b*" '.

(Dh) The extension of the concept 'line parallel to line *a*' is identical with the extension of the concept 'concept coextensive with the concept "line parallel to line *a*" '.

Clearly, an infinite regress threatens if we adopt Frege's own model in seeking to define *extensions*, and the only solution, as Frege himself realized, is to treat them as only implicitly definable. In the *Grundlagen*, Frege just assumed that we do know what the extension of a concept is;[24] what he later recognized was that this fundamental assumption required acknowledgement, capturing in its generality the essence of the move from (Dc) to (Dd). It was this that became Axiom V of the *Grundgesetze*, the controversial Axiom that Frege himself held responsible for the paradox that was later discovered to undermine his logical system.[25] What is worth highlighting here is its origin in the central argument of the *Grundlagen*, for it was precisely the transition from (Dc) to (Dd) that was left implicit at the time, but which rightly came to be seen as fundamental.

We can characterize Axiom V as asserting the legitimacy of the transition between the following two propositions:

(Va) The function F has the same value for each argument as the function G.

(Vb) The value-range [*Werthverlauf*] of the function F is identical with the value-range of the function G. (Cf. *GG*, I, §§ 3, 9.)[26]

Since concepts, on Frege's mature view, are functions whose values are truth-values, (Va) and (Vb) yield the following:

(Ca) The concept F applies to the same objects (generating the same true propositions) as the concept G.

(Cb) The extension of the concept F is identical with the extension of the concept G. (Cf. e.g. *FC*, pp. 30-1.)

(Dc) and (Dd) are clearly instances of (Ca) and (Cb), and hence of (Va) and (Vb); and in 'Function and Concept' (1891), where the first formulation of what becomes Axiom V can be found, Frege writes: 'The possibility of regarding the equality holding generally between values of functions as a [particular] equality, viz. an equality between [value-ranges] is, I think, indemonstrable; it must be taken as a fundamental law of logic' (*FC*, p. 26).

However, if Frege is now to be understood as admitting that *extensions*, unlike other objects, *are* contextually definable, encapsulating this in Axiom V, how is it that he thought that the Caesar problem could be solved? The answer is that Frege conceived extensions as *logical objects*, objects that are 'immediately given to reason'.[27] It is at this point that the significance of the conceptual ascent can be appreciated. For Frege's thought is that by moving up to the concept-level, we free ourselves from the obscurities of the ordinary world, and enter the pure world of logical entities. As Frege put it in one of the concluding sections of the *Grundlagen*:

> On this conception of numbers [as extensions of concepts], it seems to me, the attraction that work on arithmetic and analysis holds is easily explained. Adapting the familiar words [presumably 'the proper study of mankind is man'], it might well be said: the proper object of reason is reason itself. We are concerned in arithmetic not with objects that become known to us through the medium of the senses as something foreign from outside, but with objects that are immediately given to reason, which can fully comprehend them, as its own. (§105.)

As long as concepts are determinate,[28] then their extensions are also determinate, and criteria of identity for those extensions are readily available. For any two extensions are identical iff their respective concepts are coextensive – it was just this that was encoded in Axiom V.[29]

In §147 of Volume II of the *Grundgesetze*, Frege remarks that logicians and mathematicians, in talking of extensions of concepts, classes or sets, have already made use of the transformation encapsulated in Axiom V. He goes on:

> What we are doing by means of our transformation is thus not really anything novel; but we do it with full awareness, appealing to a fundamental law of logic. And what we thus do is quite different from the lawless, arbitrary construction of numbers by many mathematicians.
>
> If there are logical objects at all – and the objects of arithmetic are such objects – then there must also be a means of apprehending, of recognizing, them. This service is performed for us by the fundamental law of logic that permits the transformation of an equality holding generally into an equation. Without such a means a scientific foundation for arithmetic would be impossible. (*TPW*, p. 161.)

The importance of Axiom V for Frege is clear. Understood as a law of logic, it legitimated the appeal to extensions, so that taken with the central argument of the *Grundlagen*, it justified his definitions of mathematical objects, and underpinned his logicism.

One final comment may be made here, in relation to Frege's contextualism. There are two respects in which the context principle should not be seen as abandoned in his later work. Firstly, in rejecting his initial contextual definition, Frege does not deny the legitimacy of the move from (Da) to (Db); the definition is insufficient rather than incorrect. The move to (Dd) does not *restart* the argument, but *develops* it, since, whether or not (De) can be *derived*, without (Db) the definition (De) would be incomprehensible. Even if (De) is seen as a stipulation, in other words, its point can only be appreciated against the background of *both* (Db) and (Dd). Since definitions such as (De) are *retained* in Frege's later work, the general argument itself, which depends on his initial contextualism, can hardly be viewed as repudiated. The fact that the argument is not repeated need only show that Frege had convinced himself that his definitions were acceptable. In the *Grundgesetze* (I, §§38, 40-3, 45), for example, he just refers at the relevant points to his earlier *Grundlagen*, and provides no further justification for the definitions he gives. Secondly, as we have seen, extensions themselves are treated as only contextually definable; what happens is that the crucial move from (Dc) to (Dd) is recognized, and incorporated into Axiom V, which *is* explicitly stated. Contextualism is not abandoned, then, but remains as a presupposition of Frege's later work. It plays an essential role in setting up the logical system, in laying the foundations of axioms and definitions, but does not require formulation *within* that system.[30]

Frege was aware that his definitions and appeal to extensions were counterintuitive, and that there were problems concerning the status of Axiom V.[31] But, as we shall now see, his response was not so much to reassess the argument that motivated his *Grundgedanke*, as rather to forge his new distinction between 'Sinn' and 'Bedeutung', the wielding of which, he felt, would be enough to dispel the worries. Frege realized, in other words, that philosophical justification was still required, but it was the distinction between 'Sinn' and 'Bedeutung' that took over the leading role in this, pushing his contextualism into the background.

5.4 The Paradox of Analysis

The paradox of analysis is usually associated with the work of G.E. Moore; and the term 'paradox of analysis' does indeed seem to have been first used in connection with Moore's work.[32] Yet the fundamental problem strikes at the heart of analytic philosophy, and it would have been surprising if concern with the problem had not also surfaced in the thought of the other three founders of analytic philosophy. Both Russell and Wittgenstein certainly had much to say about their own programme of logical analysis.[33] Yet it is in the work of Frege that the problem is first seriously addressed, and an attempt made to resolve it.

This is not to say, however, that there were no historical precedents. As suggested in §5.1, the general issue that underlies the problem was raised in Plato's *Meno*. How can any explication of something be *informative*? As we shall see, the essential insight expressed in the Socratic idea of 'tethering' and developed by Aristotle, in answer to this question, was something that Frege himself came to endorse in response to the paradox of analysis. But even the paradox in its more specific form can be recognized in the work of pre-analytic philosophers, even of pre-modern philosophers. The 16th-century sceptic, Francisco Sanchez, for example, made use of the paradox in his critique of Aristotelianism. This is how Richard Popkin (1979: p. 37) reports the dilemma Sanchez expresses at the beginning of *Quod nihil scitur* (published in 1581):

> if the names assigned to an object such as man, like 'rational animal', all mean the same thing, then they are superfluous and do not help to explain what the object is. On the other hand, if the names mean something different from the object, then they are not the names of the object.

Definitions, such as 'Man is a rational animal', according to Sanchez, are merely nominal, and give no information about the nature of an object; and the dilemma posed was intended to support his nominalism. But the use of the phrase 'mean the same thing' here simply cries out for disambiguation: two expressions may *refer to the same object* but not necessarily *convey the same information*. As we shall see, this is essentially Frege's own response to the paradox of analysis.

The paradox itself can be stated very simply. Call the *analysandum* (what is analysed) '*A*', and the *analysans* (what is offered as the analysis) '*B*'. Then either '*A*' and '*B*' are equivalent in meaning, in which case the analysis ('A is B') merely expresses a trivial identity; or else they are not, in which case the analysis is incorrect. So there is no such thing as an analysis that is both correct and informative. If it is correct, it is uninformative; and if it is informative (in avoiding triviality), it can only be incorrect. The entire project of philosophical analysis would appear to be pointless.

The immediate response might be to suggest that an identity statement of the form 'A is B' *may* be informative to someone – if they do not already know the meaning of 'A', yet do understand that what is being offered is an explanation of that meaning, using terms the meaning of which they do grasp. (Here, if 'learning' is to take place, some knowledge must indeed be presupposed, as Socrates himself argued when the general problem was first formulated.) Such a situation corresponds to the case of *stipulative* definitions discussed in §5.2, but as we saw then, there is no difficulty about explication of stipulative definitions, since no *genuine* information is thereby imparted.

The real problem arises, however, when we do have some grasp of the meaning of 'A'. If the analysis is to be informative, must not 'B' possess a *different* meaning? It is precisely this problem that emerges from Frege's argument in the central sections of the *Grundlagen*. How can Frege's 'fruitful' definitions be both correct and of epistemic value? Merely suggesting, as Frege does in §70, that their 'fruitfulness' lies in deriving 'the well-known properties of numbers' only seems to impale us once again on the horns of the dilemma. Obviously, if we *cannot* derive these properties, then the definitions are incorrect, but if we *can* derive them, then how can the definitions be seen as *adding* to our knowledge? The answer that emerged in §5.2, however, can be expressed as follows. A definition is *correct* in so far as 'A' and 'B' have the same 'content', and *informative* to the extent that that 'content' is 'split up' differently. The solution to the paradox would seem to be immediate.

But do Frege's 'fruitful' definitions really embody sameness of 'content', and what exactly is meant by 'content' here? In his *Philosophie der Arithmetik*, published in 1891, Husserl objected to Frege's definitions, arguing that whilst the *definiendum* and *definiens* might be equivalent in 'extension', their 'contents' – construed as reflecting the *knowledge* involved – were in no way the same.[34] It might be pointed out, for example, in Frege's geometrical case, that whilst (Da) may be true whenever (Db) is true, and vice versa, someone can understand (Da) without understanding (Db), or the other way round, where that person possesses one but not the other of the two relevant concepts, that of parallelism and that of direction. So in some important sense, they are not 'epistemically equivalent' – they do not utilize the same conceptual resources.

But if sameness of 'content' is given by 'epistemic equivalence' in the sense just indicated, then the two members of a Fregean pair (whether 'horizontal' or 'vertical') do not, after all, possess the same 'content'. It would then be illegitimate to talk of 'splitting up *the* content' in a new way, and the whole analytic basis of Frege's project collapses. However, we are no better off, on this construal, if we found two propositions that *are* 'epistemically equivalent', since it would then be illegitimate to talk of 'splitting up the content' in a *new way*, two propositions being 'epistemically equivalent' only if the same concepts are utilized in their articulations. What we have here is a version of the paradox of analysis; and what it suggests is that the notion of 'content' should not be explicated in terms of 'epistemic equivalence', but that an alternative construal must be found that supports a viable distinction between 'content' and 'way of splitting up content'.

In his reply to Husserl's objections, in his 1894 review of Husserl's book, Frege provides the first clear statement of the paradox:

> If words and combinations of words mean ideas, then for any two of them there are only two possibilities: either they designate the same idea or they designate different ideas. In the former case it is pointless to equate them by means of a definition: this is 'an obvious circle'; in the latter case it is wrong. These are also the objections the author raises, one of them regularly. A definition is also incapable of analysing the sense, for the analysed sense just is not the original one. In using the word to be explained, I either think clearly everything I think when I use the defining expression: we then have the 'obvious circle'; or the defining expression has a more richly articulated sense, in which case I do not think the same thing in using it as I do in using the word to be explained: the definition is then wrong. (*RH*, p. 199.)

The first two sentences state the problem in terms of ideas,[35] and Frege then formulates the paradox in terms of sense. In his reply, he makes clear that 'coincidence in extension' is *all* that a definition need capture, the 'Bedeutung' of words being what matters to a mathematician. There is no requirement that either the 'senses' of the relevant expressions, or the 'ideas' evoked by them (which must be distinguished from the senses), be the same, this being of interest merely to the 'psychological logician'. (Ibid., p. 200.) Indeed, and this is the message that Frege takes from the paradox, were there to be such a requirement, definitions would involve the 'obvious circle', so that the requirement is not just unnecessary but is also to be repudiated.

Frege's answer here clearly utilizes his distinction between 'Sinn' and 'Bedeutung', and his review of Husserl's book was indeed published three years after the distinction first appeared in print.[36] It is also clear how he thought the distinction resolved the paradox. A definition can be both correct, in so far as the *definiens* and the *definiendum* have the same *Bedeutung*, and informative, to the extent that the *definiens* has 'a more richly articulated sense' than the *definiendum*. According to Frege, in other words, extensional equivalence is the criterion of correctness, and relative degree of conceptual articulation the measure of informativeness.

Mapped onto the resolution of the paradox that we extracted from Frege's earlier account, 'content' and 'way of splitting up content' have thus become 'Bedeutung' and 'Sinn', respectively.

Frege obviously recognized that the status of his *Grundlagen* definitions and his conception of 'splitting up content' in different ways required clarification; but his new distinction between 'Sinn' and 'Bedeutung', at least in its 'official' version, falls short of providing it, since the notion of 'Bedeutung' is too coarse-grained and the notion of 'Sinn' too fine-grained. Very simply, the problem is this. If arithmetic is a system of *analytic* truths, then the axioms and definitions must embody sameness of *sense* and not just sameness of *Bedeutung*. As we suggested in the last section, at the time of the *Grundlagen* Frege does seem to have had in mind a stronger notion of 'content' than that provided by a criterion based merely on extensional equivalence. In cases of *conceptual ascent*, Frege clearly assumes that 'cognitive content' is preserved; and as far as *horizontal Fregean pairs* are concerned, it would be hard to justify the supposition that Frege had all along only intended that they encapsulate sameness of *Bedeutung*.

Before elaborating on this, however, let us note one particular formulation that Frege uses in his statement of the paradox, which, suitably disambiguated, is worth retaining. For we surely do wish to endorse the view that the *definiens* must possess 'a more richly articulated sense' than the *definiendum*. What is presumably wanted, though, under the right construal, is for it to be the *same* sense, which is just 'more richly articulated'. Only then can we still talk of 'splitting up content in a new way' as the mark of a 'fruitful' definition, whilst taking 'content' to be more than merely 'Bedeutung'. The required notion of 'sense', in other words, capturing the conception of 'content' relied upon in the central argument of the *Grundlagen*, falls somewhere *between* Frege's own later 'official' notions of 'Bedeutung' and 'Sinn'.

To see just why Frege's definitions must embody more than mere sameness of *Bedeutung*, let us return to Frege's example and compare the following two propositions:

(De) The direction of line *a* is the extension of the concept 'parallel to line *a*'.

(Di) The direction of line *a* is the extension of the concept 'parallel to line *b*'.

Even on the assumption, as given by (Da), that lines *a* and *b* are parallel, (Di), unlike (De), is clearly inadequate as a definition, despite (according to Frege) the referring expressions having the same *Bedeutung* and that *Bedeutung* being specified as an extension (a logical object). So even on Frege's own terms, some notion of 'sense' is required such that (De), but not (Di), embodies sameness of 'sense' as well.[37]

The problem with Frege's 'official' notion of 'sense' can now be seen. For on a fine-grained epistemic conception, definitions such as (De) are regarded as involving singular terms with *different* 'senses'. But this conception does not allow us to discriminate identity statements that *can* function as definitions, e.g. (De), if we accept Frege's *Grundgedanke*, from those that *cannot*, e.g. (Di), since *both* would appear to embody difference of 'epistemic sense' (whilst retaining sameness of *Bedeutung*). The prongs of Frege's own 'official' distinction between 'Bedeutung' and 'epistemic sense', in other words, are set too widely apart, leaving out a middle prong of what we may term 'semantic sense' that is crucial if the conceptual ground is to be raked properly.[38]

Frege's unclarity as to exactly what notions are needed to justify his definitions and defuse the paradox of analysis is reflected in remarks he makes in other places. The distinction between *Sinn* and *Bedeutung* first appears in 'Function and Concept', a lecture delivered in January 1891. In clarifying the conception of a function, he points out that 'Difference of sign cannot by itself be a sufficient ground for difference of the thing signified' (*FC*, p. 22), since two different functions may yield the same value for given arguments; and he provides examples, such as '1 + 1' and '3 – 1', where 'different expressions correspond to different conceptions and aspects, but nevertheless always to the same thing' (*FC*, p. 23). Since the different expressions will be associated with different thoughts, they must be regarded as having different *senses*, whilst having the same *Bedeutung* (cf. *FC*, p. 29). The notion of sense involved here is clearly as fine-grained as the epistemic notion we extracted from Husserl's objections.

However, the same paper also contains a hint of a coarser-grained notion. Frege considers the two functions $x^2 - 4x$ and $x(x - 4)$, and writes that the statement that these two functions have the same value for each argument 'expresses the same sense, but in a different way' as the statement that the value-range of the one function is equal to that of the other (*FC*, p. 27). What we have here is an instance of what becomes Axiom V of the *Grundgesetze*, which, as we noted in the last section, Frege remarks 'must be taken to be a fundamental law of logic' (*FC*, p. 26). What Frege seems to be saying, then, is that the two sides of Axiom V, i.e. (Va) and (Vb), and by implication, the two members of any (horizontal) Fregean pair, do indeed have the *same sense*; they simply express that sense in a different way – the same 'content' is 'split up' differently.

In §3 of Volume I of the *Grundgesetze* (which was published in 1893), where Axiom V receives its first official formulation, however, Frege merely talks of both sides being *gleichbedeutend*, which again would seem to indicate that he has only extensional equivalence in mind. Given that both this work and his 1894 review of Husserl's book were published *after* 'Function and Concept', it might be suggested that the apparent tension in Frege's later thought can be easily smoothed away by treating 'Function and Concept' as a transitional paper: it was not until 1893 that Frege finally managed to eradicate all vestiges of his early notion of 'content', and could consistently advocate his 'mature' view. However, in §27 of Volume I of the *Grundgesetze*, where he discusses definitions, and also uses the word 'gleichbedeutend', he specifically states that the *definiendum* is stipulated as having the same 'Sinn' as well as the same 'Bedeutung' as the *definiens*. So the apparent tension remains.

Although we might suggest, then, that it was the problem concerning the status of Frege's definitions, and in particular, Axiom V, that prompted the bifurcation of his early notion of 'content', the distinction that emerged seems not to have been adequately thought through. However, in all three of the later works that we have mentioned (*FC*, *GG* and *RH*), Frege refers us to his essay 'Über Sinn und Bedeutung', where his official view is presented, so we must postpone further elucidation of the different possible notions involved until we have considered this essay in detail in the next chapter.

What implications does this have, though, on Frege's resolution of the paradox of analysis? The response we extracted from his earlier philosophy seemed promising: the correctness of an analysis depends on sameness of 'content', and its informativeness on that 'content' being 'split up' in different ways. But if Frege's later distinction between 'Bedeutung' and 'Sinn' inadequately captures this earlier distinction, where are we left? In a paper written towards the end of his life, Frege returns to the issue, and adopts a different approach, revealing deeper features of his mature philosophy, as we shall now see.

5.5 Constructive and Analytic Definitions

Let us return to the problem of Frege's *Grundgedanke*. As we have noted, Frege was aware of its counterintuitive character. After laying down his definition of number in §68 of the *Grundlagen*, Frege remarks: 'That this definition is correct will hardly, perhaps, be clear at first. For is an extension of a concept not thought to be something different [from a number]?' (§69.) We talk, for example, of an extension being 'wider' than another, but not a number. In response, Frege points out that the two propositions involved – (Na) and (Nd) – are *logically equivalent*, so that 'here there is complete agreement'. And in answer to the specific objection, Frege states that there is nothing to stop us extending talk of one thing being 'wider' than another to numbers, should we so wish. (Ibid.)

Nevertheless, in reviewing his argument later, Frege admits to a certain unease:

> We assumed here that the sense of the expression 'extension of a concept' was known. This way of overcoming the difficulty may well not meet with universal approval, and many will prefer removing the doubt [the Caesar problem] in another way. I too attach no great importance to the introduction of extensions of concepts. (§107.)

Frege clearly had qualms from the beginning about appealing to extensions; and it seems, in fact, that he went through a stage, immediately after the publication of the *Grundlagen*, of trying to do without them.[39] But the attempt failed, and he soon reverted to his original explicit definitions; and by the time of the *Grundgesetze*, the appeal to extensions had, after all, become of decisive importance. What had happened by then is that the central argument of the *Grundlagen* had been *generalized*, the equivalence between (Va) and (Vb) being formulated as a fundamental law of logic, legitimating *value-ranges*, in terms of which extensions could then be characterized as a special subclass (see §5.3 above). But simply encapsulating the crucial move (left implicit in the *Grundlagen*) in an axiom is hardly to justify it, and the problem remains as to the status of his definitions.

With the formulation of the distinction between *Sinn* and *Bedeutung*, however, a way is suggested of at least easing the qualms that Frege's *Grundgedanke* induces. For whilst an abstract object and an extension of a concept do not *appear* to be the same thing, it may actually be only the *senses* of the terms that are different (giving rise to different *thoughts*), not the objects themselves. Worries about (De) can be defused, in other words, by assimilating it to (Db), which would seem to have the same logical form:

(Db) The direction of line *a* is identical with the direction of line *b*.

(De) The direction of line *a* is identical with the extension of the concept 'parallel to line *a*'.

What (Db) tells us is that the same direction can be given in two different ways, as the direction of line *a*, and as the direction of line *b* (where *a* and *b* are parallel); and it is certainly this kind of example that is in Frege's mind at the beginning of 'Über Sinn und Bedeutung'.[40] If we accept Frege's *Grundgedanke*, then what (De) suggests is that it can also be given as the extension of the appropriate concept.

However, all this presupposes that (De) is a *correct* identity statement – that the two sides do indeed have the same *Bedeutung* (even if not the same *Sinn*) – and it is just this that is in dispute. As we argued in §5.3, (De) can only be *derived* from the 'equivalence' between (Db) and (Dd) if it is 'cognitive equivalence' and not merely logical equivalence that is involved; and it might well be thought that, from his later perspective, Frege would not have suggested that such a derivation was possible (I return to this shortly). Even in the *Grundlagen*, Frege never talks of *deriving* (De) or (Ne), and it is tempting to suppose that he already assumed that such talk was illegitimate. But did he nevertheless think that *something* could be established on the basis of mere logical equivalence? This does seem to be the message of §69, where the logical equivalence of (Na) and (Nd), and (Da) and (Dd), is implied. But, taking this latter case, all we are in fact entitled to infer is the following:

(Dj) Line a has a direction iff the concept 'parallel to line a' has an extension.

This does not equate a direction with an extension, but merely shows that whenever you have one, you have the other. Something can indeed be derived, then, but it is not (De) itself.

The point is worth elaborating. If (De) *were* seen as the result of a 'derivation' (as represented in the diagram of §5.3), then the objection might be that it trades on the ambiguity in Frege's early notion of 'content'. But since, in distinguishing between 'Sinn' and 'Bedeutung', Frege later recognized this ambiguity, the natural reply is that the material was later provided to repair the fault. The suggestion might then be that whilst (De) cannot be derived at the level of *Sinn*, it *can* be derived at the level of *Bedeutung*. But it should now be obvious just how confused such a suggestion would be. For the 'derivation' of (De) *as an identity statement* (equating *Bedeutungen*) depends on 'cognitive equivalence' and not just logical equivalence. At the level of *Bedeutung*, (Dj) is all that can be derived. Distinguishing between 'Sinn' and 'Bedeutung', then, does not dispel worries about a definition already derivable, but destroys the reasoning that would constitute that derivation. What we would have, in fact, is a case of shutting the stable door after the horse has bolted.

If anything, then, qualms about (De) are simply exacerbated by the awareness of Frege's later distinction between 'Sinn' and 'Bedeutung'; and the only remaining strategy is to treat it as a stipulation. As we suggested at the end of §5.3, this strategy too is problematic, for even a stipulation requires some rationale, and Frege never actually repudiates his central argument in the *Grundlagen*, which performs an essential motivating role. (De), after all, seems 'more correct' than the identification of a direction with Julius Caesar! But Frege did eventually recognize that even his 'fruitful definitions' had to be treated as stipulative, when he finally faced up to the problem in his 1914 paper, 'Logic in Mathematics' (published posthumously), a paper which not only clarifies his position but also contains his fullest and final answer to the paradox of analysis.

Frege distinguishes between 'constructive definitions' (*aufbauende Definitionen*) and 'analytic definitions' (*zerlegende Definitionen*).[41] The former, which he regards as the only proper form of definition, are what we have been calling 'stipulative definitions', serving merely as abbreviatory devices. Here it is simply *stipulated* that the new and simpler sign is to have the same *sense* as well as the same *Bedeutung* as the already understood but more complex expression. Such definitions therefore have no real value, and as before, Frege accepts this implication. But, as he puts it, 'To be without logical significance is still by no means to be without psychological significance', since we need abbreviations to help us think. (*LM*, pp. 208-10.) 'Analytic definitions', on the other hand, corresponding to Frege's 'fruitful definitions', involve the analysis of a sign 'with a long established use'. Here there may be genuine uncertainty as to whether the senses of the relevant expressions are the same or not. In so far as the senses do agree, Frege writes, this 'is not a matter for arbitrary stipulation, but can only be recognized by an immediate insight'. But in this case, Frege goes on, we should talk not of 'definitions' but of *axioms*, encapsulating what is thereby taken as self-evident. But where the senses do not unequivocally agree, we do indeed have a problem. How can logical analyses be provided in these cases? Frege writes:

> Let us assume that A is the long-established sign (expression) whose sense we have attempted to analyse logically by constructing a complex expression that gives the analysis. Since we are not certain whether the analysis is successful, we are not prepared to present the complex expression as one which can be replaced by the simple sign A. If it is our intention to put forward a definition proper, we are not entitled to choose the sign A, which already has a sense, but we must choose a fresh sign B, say, which has the sense of the complex expression only in virtue of the definition. The question now is whether A and B have the same sense. But we can bypass this question altogether if we are constructing a new system from the bottom up; in that case we shall make no further use of the sign A – we shall only use B. We have introduced the sign B to take the place of the complex expression in question by arbitrary fiat and in this way we have conferred a sense on it. This is a definition in the proper sense, namely a constructive definition.
>
> If we have managed in this way to construct a system for mathematics without any need for the sign A, we can leave the matter there; there is no need at all to answer the question concerning the sense in which – whatever it may be – this sign had been used earlier. In this way we court no objections. However it may be felt expedient to use sign A instead of sign B. But if we do this, we must treat it as an entirely new sign which had no sense prior to the definition. We must therefore explain that the sense in which this sign was used before the new system was constructed is no longer of any concern to us, that its sense is to be understood purely from the constructive definition that we have given. In constructing the new system we can take no account, logically speaking, of anything in mathematics that existed prior to the new system. Everything has to be made anew from the ground up. Even anything that we may have accomplished by our analytical activities is to be regarded only as preparatory work which does not itself make any appearance in the new system itself. (*LM*, pp. 210-11.)

Frege's final answer to the paradox of analysis, which these two paragraphs suggest, brings together a number of his most characteristic ideas. The most fundamental idea (operative from the time of the *Begriffsschrift*) is that of *replacing* our ordinary (mathematical) language with a more precise, logically perspicuous language. The question as to the *relationship* between the two systems is in effect pushed aside – we can be satisfied if we are simply able to *work* with the new system (do the same basic things, but more rigorously). In particular, the issue as to *how* that new system arose (out of the old) is dismissed as irrelevant – reflecting Frege's own repeated insistence that logical questions (concerning justification) be severed from historical questions (regarding the genesis of our under-standing).[42] All this lends support to the view that the original sense of a word (whatever its degree of clarity) can be discarded once the new system is in place.

The solution to the paradox of analysis now seems straightforward. For if the original sense drops out of consideration, then no problem can arise in attempting to analyse it. It only plays a role where the relevant signs can be immediately judged to have the *same* sense, but then what we have is an *axiom*. But if no such judgement can be made, either where the senses are not obviously the same, or where the established sign has no clear sense at all, then we simply *replace* the old sign with a new sign, defined in the way we want, and hence *bypass* the question as to whether the senses are the same, by treating what we have as a 'constructive definition'. Since the paradox is only acute in relation to 'analytic defini-tions', Frege's 'solution' is thus to eliminate this category. There are no real 'analytic definitions', only 'axioms' and 'constructive definitions', and with these there is no problem, since whilst they embody sameness of sense, they are also uninformative.

If this is Frege's most considered response, however, then it might seem, at best, to evade rather than answer the paradox (simply removing the offending category), and at worst, to impale us once again on the horns of the dilemma. For if there are now *no* informative 'axioms' or 'defini-tions', then how can any system erected on this basis itself have epistemic value? But let us look at Frege's response in more detail. Taking 'A' as the long-established sign and 'C' as the complex expression representing the *analysans*, then, on the assumption that the sense of 'C' is clearly grasped from the way it is constructed, there are three kinds of case to consider. In the first two cases, 'A' is also assumed to have a sense that is clearly grasped, and in these cases the paradox of analysis cannot be circum-vented. Either 'A' and 'C' have the same sense, or they do not. If they do, then the analysis, whilst correct, is uninformative; if they do not, then the analysis, however informative it might seem, is incorrect. The interesting case, however, occurs when there is *no* sense that is clearly grasped. But in this case, according to Frege, it is open to us to *stipulate* what that sense is to be, discarding whatever sense the established sign 'A' might (argu-ably) have had, yielding a straightforward 'constructive definition'. The paradox only arises, then, on the assumption that the established sign has a sense that is clearly grasped; where this assumption fails to hold, the paradox evaporates. What logical analysis thus does is not *explicate* an antecedently given sense, but *determine* what the sense of a sign is to be.[43] Frege goes on:

> The fact is that if we really do have a clear grasp of the sense of the simple sign, then it cannot be doubtful whether it agrees with the sense of the complex expression. If this is open to question although we can clearly

recognize the sense of the complex expression from the way it is put together, then the reason must lie in the fact that we do not have a clear grasp of the sense of the simple sign, but that its outlines are confused as if we saw it through a mist. The effect of the logical analysis of which we spoke will then be precisely this – to articulate the sense clearly. (*LM*, p. 211.)

This echoes a remark Frege made in the 'Introduction' to the *Grundlagen*. In criticizing the historical approach, Frege commented: 'Often it is only through enormous intellectual work, which can last for hundreds of years, that knowledge of a concept in its purity is achieved, by peeling off the alien clothing that conceals it from the mind's eye.' He continued: 'Instead of finding concepts in particular purity near to their imagined source, everything is seen blurred and undifferentiated as through a fog.' (*GL*, pp. VII-VIII.) Even in his earlier work, then, Frege clearly saw as his task the definitive specification of our fundamental (arithmetical) concepts – exhibiting the 'true sense' of our concept words.

However, there is a certain ambiguity here. Do the problematic concept words (e.g. 'number') have a sense already, which is just not clearly grasped, or do they have no sense at all? Obviously, if the latter, then we are indeed free to stipulate a sense. But if there are pre-existing senses, however partially grasped, then are we not responsible to them in offering an analysis? Are there not certain constraints on any stipulation? Frege's answer is not to deny that there are constraints, but to maintain that they only operate at the *pre-theoretical* level.

[Logical analysis] is very useful; it does not, however, form part of the construction of the system, but must take place beforehand. Before the work of construction is begun, the building stones have to be carefully prepared so as to be usable; i.e. the words, signs, expressions, which are to be used, must have a clear sense, so far as a sense is not to be conferred on them in the system itself by means of a constructive definition. (*LM*, p. 211.)

Obviously, in preparing the building stones, one has to work with the material already to hand; but the result may have a degree of solidity that was not there initially.

But can anything be said about how this process occurs? It might seem that Frege has reverted to that ancient conception of analysis as imagined by Descartes – analysis as that arcane process that goes on prior to the systematic construction of a theory. But in Frege's case, he already saw himself as having openly performed this analytical work: his argument in the *Grundlagen* was precisely conceived as the preliminary to the formal project of the *Grundgesetze*, carefully preparing the building stones by conferring clear senses on our fundamental arithmetical concept words.

In the light of Frege's later account, then, let us return to the problem of the status of his *Grundlagen* definitions and Axiom V. We can now see that Frege did indeed mean Axiom V to embody sameness of sense as well as sameness of *Bedeutung*. As a supposedly fundamental law of logic, taken as an axiom and not a mere (constructive) definition, it was intended to encapsulate an equivalence recognizable by an 'immediate insight'.[44] We can also see why Frege was nevertheless apprehensive about this. For at the pre-theoretical level, it is doubtful whether the two sides of Axiom V do have clear senses, so that talk of 'immediate insight' seems out of place. But in view of our discussion in §2.5 of the relationship between 'conceptual content' and logical equivalence, a defence of Frege can be offered here. It is neither correct to say that (Va) and (Vb) can be taken as equivalent *because* they have the same sense, nor correct to say that they have the same sense *because* their equivalence can be 'immediately intuited'. Rather, the sense they have in common is *crystallized* in the very process of equating them; binding (Va) and (Vb) in an axiom *shows what is meant by sameness of sense*.[45] The point applies equally to vertical Fregean pairs. In offering (Wc) as the analysis of (Wa), for example (see §5.3), Frege is also, for logical purposes, *crystallizing* the sense of (Wa). In general, we can say that formalization itself plays a role in the determination of sense: it makes more specific how the sense of a proposition is to be taken. In learning how to operate a logical system, then, we at the same time acquire the appropriate 'insights'.

But what then of the status of Frege's original definitions, (De) and (Ne)? If both horizontal and vertical Fregean pairs can indeed be seen as embodying sameness of sense, then (De) can, after all, be 'derived'. But this should not now come as a surprise. For, on the defence of Frege just offered, this is precisely the result of *crystallizing* the sense of 'direction' and 'number'. Of course, if these definitions are simply *stipulations*, then the equivalence between (Da) and (Db) can itself be derived from the equivalence between (Da) and (Dc), Axiom V, and the definitions (reversing the 'derivation' considered in §5.3).[46] But once again, the temptation to interpret Frege's argument as running in just one direction must be resisted. It is neither the case that (De) can be justified by 'deriving' it from the equivalences, nor the case that the initial equivalence can be justified with the aid of Axiom V and the stipulation that (De) encodes. Rather, it is in the 'tethering together' of the whole system of relationships that justifications are to be sought.[47]

But is Frege's own process of crystallization really acceptable? Does the paradox of analysis not re-emerge in some form at the pre-theoretical level? At this point Frege's answer can be given in the words of Spinoza, as quoted at the beginning of this chapter. Although there is no intention to depart too radically from common usage, in the end the analyses are answerable not to the meanings of words, but to *the nature of things*. I shall return to the *realism* that this implies in the final chapter; but it is worth noting here that after the *Grundlagen*, Frege no longer talks of the *analyticity* of arithmetic, but merely of its reducibility to logic.[48] To talk of analyticity might suggest that we are indeed attempting to explicate senses that are already clearly grasped, and Frege realizes that this is problematic. He retains, though, the Leibnizian and anti-Kantian view that what is important is not what has been 'actually thought' in understanding a proposition, but its most perfect method of proof. But in demonstrating (for the first time) how an arithmetical proposition can be derived purely logically, Frege recognizes that a (clearer) sense is thereby *conferred upon it*.

But if Frege's later account of analysis can still be rendered compatible with his project in the *Grundlagen*, what has happened to his earlier conception of definitions, and the response to the paradox that we extracted from the *Grundlagen*? Can something not be preserved of the idea of 'splitting up contents' in different ways? The realism we have just mentioned suggests a positive answer. If 'content' becomes 'Bedeutung', and the 'Bedeutung' of a singular term is the *object* referred to, then since the objects are there all along (on a realist view), any analysis remains answerable to things themselves. We can still maintain, in other words, that sameness of *Bedeutung* is a necessary condition for the correctness of an analysis. What we are doing in offering an analysis is specifying the *Bedeutung* of a term within a richer conceptual system, thereby crystallizing the *sense* of the term.

However, before we can fully assess Frege's position here, there are still two fundamental issues to clarify. Firstly, how exactly are Frege's notions of 'Sinn' and 'Bedeutung' to be characterized? We have seen how Frege utilized the distinction in his reply to Husserl; but we also suggested that there was a certain tension between a fine-grained and a coarser-grained conception of sense. His later response to the paradox of analysis seemed to bypass this problem by arguing that what he was doing was 'reconstructing' our ordinary notions. But this raises the second issue. How legitimate are such 'reconstructions'? And what, in general, is the relationship between ordinary language and 'logically correct' language? I discuss the first issue in the next chapter, and take up the second in chapter 7, before returning to the question as to how sense is crystallized in the final chapter.

6. *Sinn* and *Bedeutung*

Can we understand two names without knowing whether they signify the same thing or two different things? – Can we understand a proposition in which two names occur without knowing whether their meaning [*Bedeutung*] is the same or different? (Wittgenstein, *Tractatus*, 4.243.)

The distinction between *Sinn* and *Bedeutung* is undoubtedly the most widely known and influential element of Frege's philosophy, and, as we have seen, it was certainly viewed by Frege as playing a crucial role in the justification of his logicist project. Yet, even a century after its official articulation in his 1892 essay 'Über Sinn und Bedeutung', there is no settled consensus on its interpretation. In this chapter I examine in detail the main ideas of this essay, elucidating Frege's motivations and exploring the strengths and weaknesses of the arguments; but I shall leave an overall assessment until the final chapter, after further consideration, in the next chapter, of related topics.

Although the notions of 'Sinn' and 'Bedeutung' did not emerge until the 1890s, even at the time of the *Begriffsschrift* Frege had distinguished between 'content' and 'mode of determination of content'; and I clarify this earlier view, and his own later critique of it, in §6.1. In §6.2 I suggest what led Frege to adopt the rather bizarre thesis that the *Bedeutung* of a sentence is its truth-value, and show that his own arguments underdetermine the thesis. Frege is often seen as on stronger ground in relation to his conception of the *Sinn* and *Bedeutung* of names; but even here there is a major problem of interpretation, revolving around the question as to whether a name can properly be said to have a sense if there is no *Bedeutung*. As I suggest in §6.3, Frege's 'official' view seems to be that it can; but as I go on to argue in §6.4, this view is problematic in the case of 'simple' names. In the final section I explain Frege's further distinctions between customary and indirect *Sinn* and *Bedeutung*, and briefly respond to Russell's critique of Frege's conception of sense.

6.1 The Splitting of 'Content'

Although we have discussed Frege's early notion of 'conceptual content' in previous chapters, we have mainly focussed on sentences rather than subsentential expressions; yet, if the beginning of 'Über Sinn und Bedeutung' is anything to go by, the fundamental motivation behind the later distinction between 'Sinn' and 'Bedeutung' concerns what Frege calls *proper names* (*Eigennamen*), i.e. terms that uniquely refer to an object. Here too, though, the origins lie in his early work. In §8 of the *Begriffsschrift* Frege introduces his notion of 'identity of content' by stating that it differs 'from conditionality and negation by relating to names, not to contents', and he goes on:

> Whilst elsewhere symbols simply represent their contents, so that each combination into which they enter merely expresses a relation between their contents, they at once stand for themselves as soon as they are combined by the symbol for identity of content; for this signifies the circumstance that two names have the same content. Thus with the introduction of a symbol for identity of content a bifurcation in the meaning of every symbol is necessarily effected, the same symbols standing one moment for their content, the next moment for themselves. (*BS*, §8.)

In an ideal language (a 'language of pure thought', as the subtitle of the *Begriffsschrift* has it), one might have supposed that there should be no need for different symbols for the same content, and hence no need for a symbol for identity of content either. Frege responds by taking an example from geometry in which the same point is determined in two different ways.

> To each of these two modes of determination [*Bestimmungsweisen*] there corresponds a separate name. The need for a symbol for identity of content thus rests on the following: the same content can be fully determined in different ways; but that, in a particular case, *the same content* is actually given by *two modes of determination* is the content of a *judgement*. Before this judgement can be made, two different names corresponding to the two modes of determination must be provided for that that is thereby determined. But the judgement requires for its expression a symbol for identity of content to combine the two names. It follows from this that different names for the same content are not always merely a trivial matter of formulation, but touch the very heart of the matter if they are connected with different modes of determination. In this case the judgement as to identity of content is, in the Kantian sense, synthetic. (Ibid.)

That the same point can be determined in two different ways clearly expresses a *thought* (the judgement is 'synthetic'), and hence requires – in Frege's ideal language – proper representation, for which the symbol for identity of content is deemed essential.

The 'bifurcation' introduced into the meaning of every symbol that Frege talks about clearly anticipates the later distinction between *Sinn* and *Bedeutung* – the *Bedeutung* being what Frege here calls the 'content', and the *Sinn* being the 'mode of determination' of that content. Yet at the beginning of 'Über Sinn und Bedeutung' Frege criticizes his *Begriffsschrift* account. So how exactly was the distinction foreshadowed? Frege's criticism relies on the premiss that the name/bearer relationship is *arbitrary*

(*SR*, pp. 56-7); and it is this that leads Frege to reject the idea that 'identity' is a relation between *names* rather than contents. Were this the case, then identity statements 'would express no proper knowledge' (*SR*, p. 57) – in the same way, presumably, as arbitrarily giving a name to something 'expresses no proper knowledge'. Now we might well reject the view that the name/bearer relationship is always arbitrary, arguing that there is often a good reason why a particular name is chosen to represent something. But in a way, this is just Frege's point – what is important is the *sense* we attach to that name, not the mere sign itself. The critique of the *Begriffsschrift* account is not the *volte-face* that it might appear, then, since there too it was the 'mode of determination of a content' that was crucial. What was wrong was just Frege's characterization of 'identity of content' as a relation between names (which, anyway, made the term 'identity of content' inappropriate).

What led Frege to treat 'identity of content' as a relation between names was the perceived difficulty with the only envisaged alternative. For if what is symbolized is a relation between *contents*, that is, between the *objects* designated by the terms flanking the identity sign, then a statement of the form '*a* = *b*' would appear to say the same as one of the form '*a* = *a*'; yet the former may express genuine knowledge, whilst the latter is a mere analytic truth.[1] However, the distinction between 'Sinn' and 'Bedeutung' enables this difficulty to be overcome, and hence removes the motivation for the *Begriffsschrift* construal. Identity is indeed a relation between objects, or *Bedeutungen*, but the informativeness of identity statements is explained by difference in *Sinn*, or 'mode of presentation' of the *Bedeutung*. (Cf. *SR*, pp. 56-7.)

In 'Über Sinn und Bedeutung' Frege also uses a geometrical example to illustrate his distinction:

> Let *a*, *b*, *c* be the lines connecting the vertices of a triangle with the midpoints of the opposite sides. The point of intersection of *a* and *b* is then the same as the point of intersection of *b* and *c*. So we have different designations for the same point, and these names ('point of intersection of *a* and *b*', 'point of intersection of *b* and *c*') likewise indicate the mode of presentation; and hence the statement contains actual knowledge. (*SR*, p. 57.)

He goes on to note that whilst the names have the same *Bedeutung*, their *senses* are different, reflecting the different 'modes of presentation'. The diagram on the following page clarifies the idea. Here the point *X* can be determined in one of three different ways, as the point of intersection of *a* and *b*, as the point of intersection of *b* and *c*, and as the point of intersection of *a* and *c*. It comes as a geometrical discovery that the points so designated are indeed one and the same, the appropriate identity statements therefore expressing 'actual knowledge'.

To facilitate comparison with Frege's geometrical example in the *Grundlagen*, let us represent the situation as follows (two pairs of lines

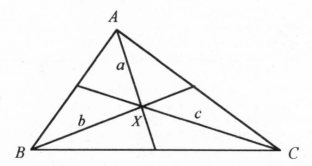

being 'equi-intersectant' if one pair intersects in the same point as the other):

(Pa) Lines *a* and *b* are equi-intersectant with lines *b* and *c*.

(Pb) The point of intersection of lines *a* and *b* is identical with the point of intersection of lines *b* and *c*.

As we have seen, it is the relationship between the two members of such a pair of propositions that is of central concern, and in particular, the focus is on identity statements of the form of (Pb) – statements, as Frege frequently puts it, that express our recognition of something as the same again. The implication of Frege's considerations in 'Über Sinn und Bedeutung' is thus clearly that each side of such an identity statement has a *different* sense.

Of course, in this particular case, the notion of 'equi-intersectance' has been defined in terms of two pairs of lines intersecting in the same point – (Pa), in other words, being defined in terms of (Pb), rather than the other way round; and this might seem to mirror the situation in the geometrical case that Frege takes in the central argument of the *Grundlagen*: the concept of direction is arguably prior to the concept of parallelism.[2] But in the example just considered, we might allow that the diagram itself provides the context in which the appropriate abstract objects (geometrical points) are defined. And in the numerical case, as we saw in chapter 4, Frege's thought is clearly that the first member of the relevant Fregean pair, i.e. (Na), is used to define the second, i.e. (Nb), by supplying the 'content' (characterizable purely logically) which is 'split up' in a new way.

But what now *is* this 'content' that is 'split up' differently? In the case of singular terms, the distinction between 'content' and 'mode of determination of content' evolves straightforwardly into the distinction between the object designated – the *Bedeutung* – and the 'mode of presentation' of that object – the *Sinn*; and it is hard to deny the legitimacy of such a distinction. But how does the distinction extend to the case of sentences? If the two sides of an identity statement such as (Pb) have *different* senses, then the two members of a Fregean pair such as (Pa) and (Pb) must surely also have different senses: something is clearly being grasped in a different way. This seems unproblematic: the notion of 'Sinn' is the direct descendant of the earlier notion of 'way of splitting up content'. This suggests that it is 'content' that gives way to 'Bedeutung'. But what then is the 'content' or 'Bedeutung' of a sentence? What is it that (Pa) and (Pb), for example, have in common? The natural answer is that they both refer to the same (objective) state of affairs, as represented in the diagram. The same geometrical figure – the same array of lines – can be described either in terms of 'equi-intersectance' or in terms of the identity of points, just as, in Frege's earlier example, two lines can be described either as being parallel or as possessing directions that are identical. The explanation of why Frege nevertheless rejected such an answer is provided in the next section.

6.2 Sentences and Identity Statements

According to Frege, the 'Bedeutung' of a sentence is a truth-value. Such a conception strikes most people as bizarre; and it does seem absurdly minimalist. There is undoubtedly a degree of unclarity in Frege's earlier notion of 'content' in both the *Begriffsschrift* and the *Grundlagen*, but in so far as a metaphysical gloss can be put on the notion, 'state of affairs' would probably be the best term to use in characterizing what Frege meant by the 'content' of a sentence.[3] The 'natural answer' given at the end of the last section to the question as to what propositions that have the same 'content' have in common is thus, arguably, indeed the answer that might be extracted from Frege's early philosophy. It is the task of the present section to explain why Frege abandoned such a plausible, even if at the time inchoate, conception.

The key to the issue lies in Leibniz's principle of substitutivity *salva veritate*, which, as we saw in §4.2, Frege himself endorses in §65 of the *Grundlagen*:

> (SV) *Eadem sunt, quorum unum potest substitui alteri salva veritate.*
> [Those things are identical of which one can be substituted for the other without loss of truth.]

As formulated, (SV) involves a confusion of use and mention, and the question as to Leibniz's own understanding of the principle is controversial.[4] But its import is clear: if two expressions can be substituted for one another without changing the truth-value of any sentence in which they appear, then the things that those expressions designate are one and the same. This principle was operative in Frege's thought right from the time of the *Begriffsschrift*. At the end of §8, where Frege introduces his symbol for 'identity of content', he states that '⊢ $(A \equiv B)$' means that 'the symbol A and the symbol B have the same conceptual content, so that A can always be replaced by B and vice versa'. And as we have already seen, Frege adopts Leibniz's principle as his own definition of identity in the *Grundlagen*: 'in universal substitutivity all the laws of identity are contained' (§65). We can therefore use this principle to formulate a general criterion for identity of 'content':

> (GC) Two expressions have the same 'content' iff they are everywhere intersubstitutable *salva veritate*.

On the assumption that it is 'content' that becomes 'Bedeutung', this would appear to provide us with a ready-made criterion for 'Bedeutung'. It certainly seems applicable in the case of names: two names have the same 'Bedeutung', that is, designate the same object, iff they can be substituted for one another *salva veritate*. In the case of *sentences*, the application of Leibniz's principle might be thought to be trivial. For replacing any one true sentence by any other true sentence clearly still leaves us with a true sentence: here what remains the same when any two true sentences are intersubstituted is the truth-value itself. If the principle therefore applies equally to both names and sentences, and supplies us with a criterion for 'Bedeutung', then it would seem that whilst the *Bedeutung* of a name is the object it stands for, the *Bedeutung* of a sentence is its truth-value. To use the terminology introduced at the end of §2.5, it is indeed 'veritable content' rather than any stronger form of 'content' that becomes 'Bedeutung'.

However, in its unqualified form, (GC) does not in fact provide us with a criterion for Frege's later conception of 'Bedeutung', for it is strictly incorrect to say *either* that any two co-referring names *or* that any two true sentences can always be intersubstituted *salva veritate* – the thesis must be restricted to *extensional* contexts. For, to use Frege's canonical example, consider the following:

> (GMM) Gottlob believes that the Morning Star is the Morning Star.
> (GME)　 Gottlob believes that the Morning Star is the Evening Star.

It was an astronomical discovery that 'the Morning Star' and 'the Evening Star' designate the same object, namely, Venus, so that both embedded identity statements are true; but (GMM) may clearly be true without (GME) being true, where Gottlob has not yet learnt of this astronomical discovery. Substituting 'the Evening Star' for the second occurrence of 'the Morning Star' in (GMM), or, equivalently, substituting 'the Morning Star is the Evening Star' for the embedded sentence 'the Morning Star is the Morning Star', may therefore result in a *change* of truth-value. What we have here is an *intensional* context, that is, a context involving the ascription of a propositional attitude ('X knows that P', 'X believes that P', etc.); and there are two possible responses to the problem that this creates. We may either revise our conception of the 'Bedeutung' of expressions, in order to preserve the universal applicability of Leibniz's principle, or else restrict the applicability of the principle, and provide a separate account of intensional contexts. Frege took the latter course, and I shall examine his own account of intensionality in §6.5. Here I shall focus on why he was so insistent that the *Bedeutung* of a sentence was its truth-value.

Let us call the argument that we have considered for Frege's view of the *Bedeutungen* of names and sentences the *argument from substitutivity*. Then the point we have just made is that this argument only yields the desired result if the application of Leibniz's principle is restricted to *extensional* contexts. The criterion for 'Bedeutung', in other words, requires a modification of (GC):

(CB) Two expressions have the same *Bedeutung* iff they are intersubstitutable *salva veritate* in all extensional contexts.

Of course, such a criterion presupposes an *independent* characterization of 'extensional contexts' – it would clearly be circular to define an extensional context as one in which *Bedeutungen* are preserved in substitutions; but for the moment we need only note that since Frege's primary interest was in strictly 'scientific' – in particular, arithmetical – contexts, where issues of intensionality are extruded, then the necessary restriction of Leibniz's principle would have been implicitly assumed.

However, even with this implicit restriction, there is still a circularity in the argument, at least as regards the *Bedeutung* of a sentence. For, as we have noted, all that the application of Leibniz's principle involves here is the tautology that what all true sentences have in common is their truth-value. To call this the *Bedeutung* simply begs the question. But it would be wrong to interpret Frege as relying on what we might call the *direct* argument from substitutivity – merely applying Leibniz's principle to the case of sentences. If we examine the arguments that Frege presents in 'Über Sinn und Bedeutung', what we are in fact offered is an *indirect* argument from substitutivity – ascertaining what remains constant when names with the same *Bedeutung* are intersubstituted *within* a sentence. Here is the passage in which Frege explicitly quotes Leibniz's principle:

> If our supposition that the *Bedeutung* of a sentence is its truth-value is correct, the latter must remain unchanged when a part of the sentence is replaced by an expression with the same *Bedeutung*. And this is in fact the case. Leibniz gives the definition: '*Eadem sunt, quae sibi mutuo substitui possunt, salva veritate.*' ['Those things are identical which can be intersubstituted without loss of truth.'] If we are dealing with sentences for which the *Bedeutung* of their component parts is at all relevant, then what feature except the truth-value can be found that belongs to such sentences quite generally and remains unchanged by substitutions of the kind just mentioned? (*SR*, pp. 64-5.)

What underlies the argument here is a general principle relating the *Bedeutung* of a sentence to the *Bedeutung* of its parts. Since this principle, and the corresponding principle in the case of *Sinn*, turn out to be crucial to Frege's 'mature' thought, let us formulate these two principles thus:

(PDB) The *Bedeutung* of a complex expression is determined by the *Bedeutung* of its parts.

(PDS) The sense of a complex expression is determined by the sense of its parts.

Both these principles appear to conflict with Frege's earlier context principle, which suggested that it was the meaning of *sentences* that determined the meaning of its parts, and I shall return to this in chapter 8. But the role of (PDB) here is clear. If, in substitutions, the *Bedeutung* of its parts does not change, then the *Bedeutung* of a sentence cannot change; and according to Frege, the only thing that does not change in this process is the *truth-value*, which must therefore be regarded as its *Bedeutung*.

But *is* truth-value the only thing that does not change? Our earlier remarks suggest an obvious alternative candidate – the 'state of affairs' that a sentence represents. This too remains unchanged by substituting different expressions for the same objects, and is a feature that belongs to sentences just as generally, at least in the sense that every sentence can be correlated with a 'state of affairs'.[5] Of course, not every true sentence can be correlated with the same state of affairs, whereas every true sentence does indeed have the same truth-value; but if this is what Frege means by 'belonging quite generally', then the suspicion must be that he is tacitly appealing to the *direct* argument from substitutivity, which we have already criticized as circular. Even if such an alternative candidate turns out to be ultimately unsuitable, it does at least deserve consideration; and it certainly shows that, on its own, the argument in the passage just quoted *underdetermines* what is to be regarded as the *Bedeutung* of a sentence.

However, as the opening sentence of the passage suggests, the use of Leibniz's principle was merely meant to *confirm* a supposition already put forward. (The next paragraph but one indicates that this was just offered as a 'test' for the supposition.) So is there a more convincing argument for the view that it is truth-value that constitutes the *Bedeutung* of a sentence? The preceding discussion is indeed concerned with truth rather than, say, states of affairs; but what we still find is an indirect argument from substitutivity. What is different is simply that the argument proceeds not by considering what remains constant when terms with the same *Bedeutung* are intersubstituted, but by considering what is missing when one of the parts of a sentence *lacks* a *Bedeutung*.

The argument is worth looking at in detail. By this point Frege takes himself to have established his views on the *Sinn* and *Bedeutung* of names (I say more about this in the next section), and he now turns to the question of sentences. Since a sentence expresses a thought, the question is whether this thought is to be regarded as its sense or its *Bedeutung* (*SR*, p. 62).

> Let us assume for the time being that the sentence does have a *Bedeutung*. If we now replace one word of the sentence by another having the same *Bedeutung*, but a different sense, this can have no effect upon the *Bedeutung* of the sentence. Yet we can see that in such a case the thought changes; since, e.g., the thought in the sentence 'The morning star is a body illuminated by the Sun' differs from that in the sentence 'The evening star is a body illuminated by the Sun'. Anybody who did not know that the evening star is the morning star might hold the one thought to be true, the other false. The thought, accordingly, cannot be the *Bedeutung* of the sentence, but must rather be considered as its sense. (*SR*, p. 62.)

The use of both (PDB) and (PDS) is clear; and I shall discuss in chapter 8 the criterion for sameness of sense revealed here. But for the moment we may allow that the *Bedeutung* of a sentence cannot be equated with the thought expressed. But what, then, is it? Frege asks whether a sentence can have a sense but *no Bedeutung*, and suggests that it can in those cases where sentences contain names that themselves lack a *Bedeutung*. He goes on:

> The sentence 'Odysseus was set ashore at Ithaca while sound asleep' obviously has a sense. But since it is doubtful whether the name 'Odysseus', occurring therein, has a *Bedeutung*, it is also doubtful whether the whole sentence does. Yet it is certain, nevertheless, that anyone who seriously took the sentence to be true or false would ascribe to the name 'Odysseus' a *Bedeutung*, not merely a sense; for it is of the *Bedeutung* of the name that the predicate is affirmed or denied. Whoever does not admit the name has a *Bedeutung* can neither apply nor withhold the predicate. But in that case it would be superfluous to advance to the *Bedeutung* of the name; one could be satisfied with the sense, if one wanted to go no further than the thought. If it were a question only of the sense of the sentence, the thought, it would be needless to bother with the *Bedeutung* of a part of the sentence; only the sense, not the *Bedeutung*, of the part is relevant to the sense of the whole sentence. The thought remains the same whether 'Odysseus' has a *Bedeutung* or not. The fact that we concern ourselves at all about the *Bedeutung* of a part of the sentence indicates that we generally recognize and expect a *Bedeutung* for the sentence itself. The thought loses value for us as soon as we recognize that the *Bedeutung* of one of its parts is missing. We are therefore justified in not being satisfied with the sense of a sentence, and inquiring also as to its *Bedeutung*. But now why do we want every proper name to have not only a sense, but also a *Bedeutung*? Why is the thought not enough for us? Because, and to the extent that, we are concerned with its truth-value. This is not always the case. In hearing an epic poem, for instance, apart from the euphony of the language we are interested only in the sense of the sentences and the images and feelings thereby aroused. The question of truth would cause us to abandon aesthetic delight for an attitude of scientific investigation. Hence it is a matter of no concern to us whether the name 'Odysseus', for instance, has a *Bedeutung*, so long as we accept the

poem as a work of art. It is the striving for truth that drives us always to advance from the sense to the *Bedeutung*.

We have seen that the *Bedeutung* of a sentence may always be sought, whenever the *Bedeutung* of its components is involved; and that this is the case when and only when we are inquiring after the truth-value.

We are therefore driven into accepting the *truth-value* of a sentence as constituting its *Bedeutung*. (*SR*, pp. 62-3.)

This passage raises a number of issues; and I shall discuss the problem of *bedeutungslos* names in the next section. But the drift of the argument is clear: if a name lacks a *Bedeutung*, then there is no point in asking after the truth-value of any sentence containing it; and if we are uninterested in the truth-value of a sentence, then we are not going to worry about whether any of its parts has a *Bedeutung*. But equally, making an implicit appeal to (PDB), if a name lacks a *Bedeutung*, then there is no point in asking after the *Bedeutung* of any sentence containing it; and if we are uninterested in the *Bedeutung* of a sentence, then we are not going to worry about whether any of its parts has a *Bedeutung*. So what could be more natural than to equate *Bedeutung* with truth-value? What we are offered, in other words, is two biconditionals:

(BBD) The parts of a sentence all have a *Bedeutung* iff the sentence has a *Bedeutung*.

(BTV) The parts of a sentence all have a *Bedeutung* iff the sentence has a truth-value.

(BBD) and (BTV) on their own do not establish Frege's conclusion, but presumably something like the following final step is implicit: since intersubstituting 'the truth-value of a sentence' and 'the *Bedeutung* of a sentence' preserves truth, then the objects they designate are one and the same (we might view this as a second-level argument from substitutivity). However, the most that is shown is that this intersubstitution preserves truth in the particular case of (BBD) and (BTV); to assume more is already to beg the question as to their identification. Once again, Frege's argument *underdetermines* what is to be regarded as the *Bedeutung* of a sentence: there are alternative biconditionals onto which (BBD) could equally be mapped. Our earlier suggestion provides one such example:

(BPS) The parts of a sentence all have a *Bedeutung* iff the sentence presents a possible state of affairs.[6]

All we are in fact entitled to infer from (BBD) and (BTV), then, is the following:

(TVB) A sentence has a truth-value iff it has a *Bedeutung*.

This does not equate the *Bedeutung* of a sentence with its truth value, but merely shows that whenever there is one, there is the other. The position is thus similar to the position with regard to Frege's 'argument' for the identification of abstract objects with extensions of concepts in the *Grundlagen*, where, as we suggested in §5.5, all that is actually established is this:

(Dj)   Line *a* has a direction iff the concept 'parallel to line *a*' has an extension.

What we have in 'Über Sinn und Bedeutung', then, is a familiar Fregean move: there is an *X* iff there is a *Y*; so let *X* be identified with *Y*. As we argued, however, this move is logically illegitimate, and the identification must therefore be treated as a *stipulation*, whose justification is to be sought in relation to the resulting theory as a whole.

The identification of the *Bedeutung* of a sentence with its truth-value did indeed yield a simplification of Frege's formal system. In particular, with truth-values admitted as *objects*, it allowed economy in his ontology: at the level of *Bedeutung*, there are only objects and functions – not, for example, 'conceptual contents', 'facts', or 'states of affairs'. It also permitted a neater definition of a concept: a concept is a function that maps objects onto one or other of two particular objects, the True and the False. I shall say more about these matters in the following chapter. But it remains the case that Frege's arguments in 'Über Sinn und Bedeutung' for the identification are inconclusive: we are simply left with a line of thought that bears a striking similarity to the reasoning in the central sections of the *Grundlagen*, which, as we saw in the last chapter, is highly problematic.

However, these resulting simplifications aside, can any other explanation be offered of Frege's minimalist conception of the *Bedeutung* of a sentence? It is at this point that we can suggest that it was Frege's concern with *identity statements* that made such a conception seem so natural. For in the case of identity statements, it is much harder to see how anything other than truth-value is preserved in substitutions. Not only does the beginning of 'Über Sinn und Bedeutung' indicate that it is the problem of identity statements that motivates the conceptions of *Sinn* and *Bedeutung*, but, as we have seen, it is the role and status of identity statements that is of crucial significance in Frege's logicist project.

Let us start with an identity statement of the form '*a = a*'. As Frege remarks, such a statement 'holds *a priori* and, according to Kant, is to be labelled analytic' (*SR*, p. 56). Since, as we suggested in §5.5, Frege had by this time (i.e. by the early 1890s) recognized that the notion of 'analyticity' was problematic and abandoned use of it himself, we might rephrase the point by saying that such a statement has *minimal content*. It certainly has no 'cognitive value' ('Erkenntniswert'), to use Frege's own term, and it would indeed seem that the only 'content' that might be ascribed to it is its truth-value, in this case, its truth. It has, in other words, mere 'veritable content': its only 'significance' – to use one of the suggested translations of 'Bedeutung' – is that it is true.[7] But now consider replacing the second occurrence of '*a*' by '*b*', where '*b*' designates the same object as '*a*'. If '*a*' and '*b*' have the same 'content' or 'Bedeutung', then replacing '*a*' by '*b*', yielding the identity statement '*a* = *b*', cannot change the 'content' or 'Bedeutung' of the statement itself – by (PDB). So if the *Bedeutung* of '*a* = *a*' is its truth-value, then so too must the *Bedeutung* of '*a* = *b*' be its truth-value.

If such a conception seems counterintuitive, the appearance is removed, according to Frege, by the distinction between 'Sinn' and 'Bedeutung'. For whilst '*a* = *a*' has no 'cognitive value', '*a* = *b*' may well do; but this is readily explicable on the assumption that '*a*' and '*b*' have *different senses*. For to say that identity statements have minimal 'content' in the sense of 'veritable content' is not necessarily to say that they have minimal 'cognitive content': the notion of 'content' does indeed need disambiguating. That this is so, and that this is crucial to an understanding of arithmetic, is made clear by Frege in a letter written to Peano in 1896:

> What stands in the way of a general acceptance of [my view of identity] is frequently the following objection: it is thought that the whole content of arithmetic would then reduce to the principle of identity, *a* = *a*, and that there would be nothing more than boring instances of this boring principle. If this were true, mathematics would indeed have a very meagre content. But the situation is surely somewhat different. When early astronomers recognized that the evening star (Hesperus) was identical with the morning star (Lucifer), or when an astronomer now brings out by calculation that a comet he observed is identical with one mentioned in ancient reports, this recognition is incomparably more valuable than a mere instance of the principle of identity – that every object is identical with itself – even though it too is no more than a recognition of an identity. (*PMC*, p. 126.)

This passage shows very well the ambiguity in the notion of 'content' (in the case of sentences), for the objection as Frege formulates it depends upon it: if identities are deducible from other identities, and so have the same ('veritable') content, how can they have different ('cognitive') contents? With the parentheses removed, however, the apparent paradox evaporates.

What is counterintuitive about Frege's notion of *Bedeutung*, then, is supposedly resolved by his conception of *Sinn*, which tidies up after it. But the question that needs to be asked is whether too much has been left to be picked up by just one notion of 'Sinn'. As we have suggested, it seems natural to regard the 'content' of a sentence as the 'state of affairs' it represents. But if the *Bedeutung* of a sentence is its truth-value, and its *Sinn* is the *thought* expressed by the sentence, then there is no longer any room for such a view. The view itself is by no means unproblematic, but what Frege has done is simply squeeze it out of consideration. However, if we are right that Frege's fundamental concern was with identity statements, then we do at least have an explanation of why this natural view was extruded. For in the case of identity statements, it is much more difficult to see what the relevant 'state of affairs' might be. If we start with a statement of the form '$a = a$' (as we did in the line of thought just sketched), then there is no obvious fact about the world for it to represent: its mere truth exhausts its 'content'. In the case of statements of the form '$a = b$', however, the situation may be very different, as Frege's own examples show. Statements such as (Pb) formulated in the last section, and in general, the second member of any horizontal Fregean pair, do provide us with information about a particular situation; and the very fact that they are seen as equivalent to the first member of such a pair, which is *not* an identity statement, suggests that they do have 'objective content'. As we remarked in the case of (Pa) and (Pb), we are characterizing a certain property of triangles, so what could be more plausible, on a realist view to which Frege is hardly antipathetic, than to take this feature as the *Bedeutung* of the sentences?

The idea could even be extended back to the case of identities of the form '$a = a$'. Given that Frege himself construes identity as a relation between objects – it is the relation that an object has to itself – why should this relation not be taken as the *Bedeutung* of identity statements? We could still allow that this relation could be thought of in different ways. The important advantage that this conception has is that it allows us to discriminate more effectively than Frege does between sets of identity statements that involve the same object. Adapting the example we used in §5.3, consider the following:

(φ) $4 = 3 + 1$.
(ψ) $2 + 2 = 1 + 1 + 1 + 1$.
(π) $3 = 2 + 1$.

According to Frege, all three identity statements have the same *Bedeutung* but different senses (each expression flanking the identity signs having a different sense), but as it stands, this obscures the fact that (φ) and (ψ) stand in a closer relation to one another than either (φ) and (π), or (ψ) and (π). Of course, one can state that the expressions flanking the identity signs in (φ) and (ψ) all have the same *Bedeutung*, unlike in the case of the other two pairs, but why should this fact not be reflected at the level of the *Bedeutung* of the statements themselves?[8]

However, the point here is not to argue for a particular view as to how the *Bedeutung* of a sentence should be construed, but merely to show that Frege's own view is not the only option, and that his arguments in 'Über Sinn und Bedeutung' underdetermine the issue. But there is one final argument to consider. Although we have so far concentrated on Frege's 'official' account, the distinction between 'Sinn' and 'Bedeutung' first appeared in 'Function and Concept', where it seems to be motivated by Frege's generalization of the notion of a *function*. After remarking that he has extended the field of mathematical operations (addition, multiplication, etc.) that serve for constructing functions, to include, most notably, identity, he asks what the values of, for example, the function $x^2 = 1$ are for different arguments.

> Now if we replace x successively by $-1, 0, 1, 2$, we get:
> $$(-1)^2 = 1,$$
> $$0^2 = 1,$$
> $$1^2 = 1,$$
> $$2^2 = 1.$$
> Of these equations the first and third are true, the others false. I now say: 'the value of our function is a truth-value', and distinguish between the truth-values of what is true and what is false. I call the first, for short, the True; and the second, the False. Consequently, e.g., what '$2^2 = 4$' *bedeutet* is the True as, say, '2^2' *bedeutet* 4. And '$2^2 = 1$' *bedeutet* the False. (*FC*, pp. 28-9.)

The implication is clear. If a statement can be analysed in function-argument terms, then it must have a value for any given argument. This value is the *Bedeutung* of the statement, and, so it turns out, is one of the two truth-values.

In his earlier work, the 'value' of a statement was its 'conceptual content': it was this that could be analysed into function and argument. A function could thus be understood as mapping objects onto 'conceptual contents'.[9] As we have suggested, it does seem natural to regard the 'content' of a statement as its *Bedeutung*; and we might express this by saying: the *Bedeutung* of a statement is the value that that statement has when construed in function-argument terms. The motivation for Frege's later conception is then straightforward: since the 'value' of a statement is now to be seen as a truth-value, it follows that its *Bedeutung* too is its truth-value.

Let us call this the *argument from functionalization*. Like the argument from substitutivity, it too is inconclusive, and for precisely the same reason. For even if we accept that the *Bedeutung* of a statement is the value that that statement has when construed functionally, it remains open exactly what that value is, as Frege's own earlier view highlights. According to Frege, the 'value' of an *identity statement* must be seen as a truth-value, but we have already shown that even here this is not the only option. What '$(-1)^2 = 1$' and '$1^2 = 1$', for example, have in common is not only their truth-value but also the fact that they express the *same identity*. On Frege's view, the difference between this pair and, to take another of his examples, the pair '$2^2 = 4$' and '$2 > 1$' is obscured, since all four propositions have the *same Bedeutung*. As we have seen, Frege's response is to appeal to their *senses*; but since each proposition has a *different* sense, this fails to effect the necessary discrimination.

This response is also given – in its embryonic form – in 'Function and Concept':

The objection here suggests itself that '$2^2 = 4$' and '$2 > 1$' nevertheless tell us quite different things, express quite different thoughts; but likewise '$2^4 = 4^2$' and '$4.4 = 4^2$' express different thoughts; and yet we can replace '2^4' by '4.4', since both signs have the same *Bedeutung*. Consequently, '$2^4 = 4^2$' and '$4.4 = 4^2$' likewise have the same *Bedeutung*. We see from this that from sameness of *Bedeutung* there does not follow sameness of the thought [expressed]. (*FC*, p. 29.)

The failure to provide a means of distinguishing the two pairs is manifest. (The second pair, unlike the first pair, involves the *same identity*.) But what we may also note is Frege's talk of 'replacement', indicating that it is the argument from substitutivity that takes over the central role in motivating his conception of *Bedeutung*. The rest of the paragraph makes this explicit: substituting 'the Morning Star' for 'the Evening Star' in a sentence, for example, does not change its truth-value. And in the footnote to the paragraph, Frege refers us to his essay 'Über Sinn und Bedeutung' for a fuller account of his views.[10]

The argument from functionalization, then, adds nothing further to the argument from substitutivity. Indeed, after its appearance, it simply gives way to his 'official' argument. But it does reinforce the suggestion developed above – that it was Frege's concern with identity statements that led him to regard the *Bedeutung* of a sentence as its truth-value. It also helps explain why Frege used the term 'Bedeutung', for the first step in the argument from functionalization is a natural one to take: the *Bedeutung* of a statement is the 'value' that that statement has when construed in function-argument terms. What his arguments leave underdetermined, however, is exactly what this 'value' is. Even if we understand his motivations, then, the conclusion can only be that Frege offers us no convincing argument for his doctrine that the *Bedeutung* of a sentence is its truth-value.[11]

6.3 Proper Names

In the last section, we considered two versions of the argument from substitutivity as it related to the *Bedeutung* of sentences. In its direct form, it was seen to beg the question; and in its indirect form, it was shown to underdetermine the issue. In its indirect form, it relied on the assumption that the *Bedeutung* of a name is the object it designates. This view is more plausible than Frege's view of the *Bedeutung* of a sentence, and as we suggested in §6.1, the distinction between the object designated and the way in which that object is designated is not only important but was also recognized in Frege's early thought. But, as we shall see, this is not to say that Frege's attempts to give expression to this distinction are unproblematic.

Leibniz's *salva veritate* principle seemed to afford us a straightforward proof of Frege's doctrine that the *Bedeutung* of a name is the object it designates: this was the direct argument from substitutivity offered at the beginning of the last section. Adapting the criterion that was formulated there, we can write down the following:

(CBS) Two names have the same *Bedeutung* iff they are intersubstitutable *salva veritate* in all extensional contexts.

(CBS) is certainly satisfied if the *Bedeutung* of a name is the object designated; but is this the only way in which it can be satisfied? All that (CBS) tells us is that the *Bedeutung* of a name is whatever it is that makes a difference to the truth-value of the sentences in which it appears. To adapt our previous neologism, let us call this feature of a name its 'veritable value'.[12] Then the question is why Frege was led to identify the veritable value of a name with the object designated. Here, as before, Frege's own view seems to be *underdetermined* by the argument offered. If a term designates an object, then it indeed has a veritable value, but why should these be one and the same?

It is at this point that we can remark on the policy, followed up to now, of leaving the term 'Bedeutung' untranslated. For the term as used by Frege, even in its 'official' sense, has a certain ambiguity, and exegetical prudence requires that we do not prejudge issues of interpretation. As a technical term in what we may broadly regard as Frege's semantic theory, it does indeed mean *veritable value*: that element in an expression's overall meaning that makes a difference to the truth-value of any sentence in which it appears. But at the ontological level, it also serves to signify the object designated: the *Bedeutung* of an expression, in other words, being its *referent*. Given Frege's preoccupation with 'scientific' contexts, where the concern is with *existent objects*, the conflation of *veritable value* and *referent* would have seemed natural, at least in the case of proper names; but it is nevertheless important to keep the two elements separate. If a term is to be chosen as the translation of 'Bedeutung', then 'reference' is probably the most appropriate, for it too has a certain ambiguity and need not necessarily be understood as 'referent'. A proper name such as 'Aristotle', for example, can have a *reference* (viz. *veritable value*) even if its *referent* no longer exists; and even in 'scientific' contexts, we can clearly say true things about objects that do not, at the present time, exist.[13]

The importance of keeping the two elements separate can also be brought out by considering the case of *fictional names*. Take Frege's own example:

(OI) Odysseus was set ashore at Ithaca while sound asleep.

According to Frege, (OI) lacks a truth-value since 'Odysseus' lacks a referent, both being *bedeutungslos*. However, as we argued in §2.4, there is no reason why truth-values should not be attributed to fictional sentences; and indeed there is good reason why they should, to effect the necessary discriminations *within* the realm of fictional discourse. Compare (OI) with the following:

(OC) Odysseus was dismembered and eaten by the Cyclops.

In Homer's epic, (OI) is true whilst (OC) is false: regarding them both as truth-valueless obscures this difference. But if fictional sentences can, and indeed should, be regarded as possessing a *Bedeutung*, then, if the principle (PDB) is also endorsed, 'Odysseus' too must possess a *Bedeutung*. But how can this be if there was never such a person as Odysseus? We can, of course, treat 'Odysseus' as referring to a fictional person; but the important point here is that such a treatment *presupposes* that 'Odysseus' has a veritable value – in this case determined by Homer's narrative. Whilst we may only be able to *learn* how proper names function by being acquainted with the appropriate referents, having done so, and hence having grasped what the veritable value is of certain kinds of names, we can then talk of deceased or fictional referents. Any plausible account of proper names requires that we distinguish between veritable value and referent.[14]

But it may now look as if by 'veritable value' we really mean what Frege called 'sense'; and in 'Über Sinn und Bedeutung' Frege did indeed allow that there could be senses without referents. However, even where there are veritable values but no (existing) referents, there may still be *different* senses corresponding to one and the same veritable value. 'The husband of Penelope' and 'the father of Telemachos', for example, both identify the same Homeric hero, but in different ways. So veritable value and sense are not to be equated. But can there, in fact, be senses without veritable values? The difficulty here is that Frege's account of sense appears inconsistent; and this, if anything, has proved to be the most controversial issue of all in Frege's thought. The basic problem can be stated very simply. The opening pages of 'Über Sinn und Bedeutung' introduce senses as *modes of presentation* of referents. Every name refers to something in a particular way, and its sense just is this mode of presentation. But if a name *lacks* a referent, how can there be a mode of presentation of it, and so how can it possess a sense at all? This is in obvious conflict with Frege's claim, and indeed insistence, that a name can have a sense without a referent. He writes, for example:

It may perhaps be granted that every grammatically well-formed expression figuring as a proper name always has a sense. But this is not to say that to the sense there also corresponds a *Bedeutung*. The words 'the celestial body most distant from the Earth' have a sense, but it is very doubtful if they also have a *Bedeutung*. The expression 'the least rapidly convergent series' has a sense, but demonstrably there is no *Bedeutung*, since for every given convergent series, another convergent, but less rapidly convergent, series can be found. In grasping a sense, one is not thereby assured of a *Bedeutung*. (*SR*, p. 58.)

As we saw in the last section, allowing that there can be senses without *Bedeutungen* played an important role in defusing worries about how sentences can express thoughts even though they lack truth-values and the terms within it lack referents.

The short answer to the problem might be to make use of the distinction just drawn between veritable value and referent: there can be senses without referents, but no senses without veritable values. But even if we interpret Frege's notion of 'Bedeutung' as having two strands, which only come together in certain paradigm cases, there remains a tension in Frege's conception of 'Sinn'. For the passage just quoted suggests that a name has a sense merely if it is 'grammatically well-formed', which clearly does allow that there may be no referent; whilst his initial – and more familiar – explanation in terms of 'mode of presentation' implies that there must be a referent and not just a veritable value. The first construal is semantic, whilst the second is epistemological. Of course, had Frege recognized the distinction between veritable value and referent, then the conflation of the semantic and epistemological construals might not have been made. It is one thing to understand the contribution that the use of a name makes to the truth-value of sentences in which it appears; it is quite another to apprehend the object, if any, that is designated. But equally clearly, if there *is* an object, then any way of apprehending it can be expressed by a suitable name, and the use of a name may well be conventionally correlated with a particular mode of presentation, its 'grammatical form' even reflecting this mode of presentation. 'The Morning Star' and 'the Evening Star' are obvious examples of names that wear their mode of presentation on their sleeve.[15] But if we allow that there *are* senses without referents, then we do need to distinguish the semantic from the epistemological construals.

If we want to make room for there being senses without referents, then we need to talk not of 'modes of presentation' but of 'modes of determination'. On this more liberal conception, senses are *routes* to referents, and it may well turn out that there is nothing – or at least not what was expected – at the end of the journey.[16] Travelling along the path set by 'the greatest Being', for example, may result in the realization that there can be no such thing; but (arguably) the term is not *senseless*. Modes of determination can then be regarded as the basic type of sense – modes of presentation being modes of determination plus something else – the object being appropriately present. Frege readily utilizes both conceptions, but does not distinguish them – just because of his assumption, which we have emphasized (and criticized) at various points, that names in a logical language *presuppose* the existence of objects. Certainly in mathematics, and on Frege's assumption that there are mathematical *objects*, the distinction seems unnecessary. Since mathematical objects are taken as 'independent' ('*selbständig*'), talk of 'modes of presentation' seems appropriate; but since we do not have access to these objects inde-

pendently of our powers of conceptualization (we cannot, for example, just
'see' them), modes of presentation are equally modes of determination.[17]

This can be illustrated with a simple example:

(7a) $6 + 1 = 8 - 1$.

What this expresses is that one and the same number – the number 7 –
can either be thought of as one more than 6 or as one less than 8. In this
case, to 'present' the number 7 *is* to 'determine' its position in the number
sequence relative to another number. However, even here, where the
analogy with Frege's paradigm example of the Morning Star and the
Evening Star might seem closest, there is an important difference. For it
is not at all clear that someone could be said to 'understand' either '6 + 1'
or '8 – 1' without knowing *which* object was referred to, namely, the
number 7, and hence that they could be said to grasp the *sense* of the
identity statement without knowing that the two terms had the same
referent. If (7a) nevertheless has 'cognitive value', then this is so *not* in
virtue of the possibility of 'understanding' both terms without knowing
that they refer to the same object (as in Frege's paradigm example), but
simply in virtue of representing that referent in two different ways. It can
never come as a genuine discovery, in other words, that 6 + 1 is the same
as 8 – 1, but (7a) does express the fact that there is one and only one
natural number between 6 and 8.[18]

Of course, (7a) is, in many ways, *too* simple; and it is important to
appreciate just how differently identity statements function. One of
Frege's own arithmetical examples only highlights the need for finer
discriminations than he himself effected:

(7b) $$\frac{5^2.211 - 4}{753} = 7. \quad (\text{Cf. } PMC, \text{ p. 164.})$$

Frege makes clear that whilst both sides of the identity sign have the same
Bedeutung, they differ in sense. Yet do they have sense in the same sense?
I cannot, of course, understand the term '7' without knowing *which*
number it stands for (I return to this shortly). But can I grasp the sense of
the left-hand side without knowing which number it stands for? If I can,
then the identity statement can be used to inform me that an object with
which I am acquainted (the number 7) is the 'value' of a particular *mode
of determination*. What Frege goes on to say in the letter from where the
example is taken shows that he does indeed have *modes of determination*
in mind. For I can understand the sense of the complex sign without
knowing which number it stands for, i.e. without knowing its *Bedeutung*,
iff I can understand the identity statement without knowing whether it is
true, i.e. without knowing its own *Bedeutung*; and Frege admits both
possibilities. Sense, he states explicitly, is 'independent of whether there
is a *Bedeutung*'; and we are interested in the *Bedeutung* of a component

sign iff we are concerned with the *truth-value* of the sentence of which it is part (*PMC*, p. 165).

In reply it might be suggested that since Frege's remarks occur in the context of talk about 'legend and poetry', he should only be interpreted as admitting that senses should be construed as modes of determination in *fictional discourse*; in normal discourse, senses are modes of presentation. But this suggestion is hard to sustain when the context itself is placed in (wider) context, since 'legend and poetry' are mentioned precisely to motivate the independence claim – that sense is independent of *Bedeutung*. This is reinforced by the opening paragraph of the section on '*Sinn* and *Bedeutung*' in Frege's 1906 notes, 'Introduction to Logic'. In asking whether it is necessary that a component name designate an object for a sentence as a whole to express a thought, Frege writes:

> People certainly say that Odysseus is not an historical person, and mean by this contradictory expression that the name 'Odysseus' designates nothing, has no *Bedeutung*. But if we accept this, we do not on that account deny a thought-content to all sentences of the *Odyssey* in which the name 'Odysseus' occurs. Let us just imagine that we have convinced ourselves, contrary to our former opinion, that the name 'Odysseus', as it occurs in the *Odyssey*, does designate a man after all. Would this mean that the sentences containing the name 'Odysseus' expressed different thoughts? I think not. The thoughts would strictly remain the same; they would only be transposed from the realm of fiction to that of truth. So the object designated by a proper name seems to be quite inessential to the thought-content of a sentence which contains it. (*IL*, p. 191.)

This is as explicit as one could want; and elaborates on Frege's remark in 'Über Sinn und Bedeutung' that 'The thought remains the same whether "Odysseus" has a *Bedeutung* or not' (*SR*, p. 63; quoted in §6.2). The appeal to fictional discourse is clearly intended to *substantiate* the independence claim, and does not merely serve to circumscribe the area to which its applicability is restricted.

Nevertheless, it must still be emphasized that, on Frege's view, expressions that have sense in the 'realm of truth', i.e. in logic or science, must also have *Bedeutung*. But the crucial point is that such expressions have *Bedeutung not* in virtue of their having sense but in virtue of their being 'logical' or 'scientific'. Despite his paradigm example of the Morning Star and the Evening Star, and the associated talk of 'modes of presentation', then, Frege's 'official' view must be characterized as the view that senses are modes of determination.[19]

However, this is not to say that even here there are not important differences. Consider the following alternatives to (7b), replacing the right-hand side by more complex terms:

$$(7\text{c}) \quad \frac{5^2.211 - 4}{753} = \frac{16^3 - 302}{23^2 + 13} \, . \qquad (7\text{d}) \quad \frac{5^2.211 - 4}{753} = \frac{5275 - 2^2}{27^2 + 24} \, .$$

Determining that (7c) is true might indeed require working out the numerical value of each side; but in the case of (7d), one can determine that the statement is true, i.e. what its *Bedeutung* is, *without* knowing exactly what the numerical value – the *Bedeutung* – of each side is (since the two sides have the same numerical value as numerator, and the same numerical value as denominator). In the latter case, the modes of determination themselves bear a structural similarity, and do not merely have in common the same *Bedeutung*. Frege has a tendency to treat any two terms that are typographically distinct as having different senses; yet some senses are more different than others.[20]

However, it is still open to us, in all these cases, to say that the fundamental type of sense is a mode of determination, and that any finer discriminations presuppose this foundation. In arithmetic, one grasps the sense of an expression if one knows how to *work out* its numerical value – to *determine* its *Bedeutung*; and this idea is simply extended by Frege to all other expressions. One grasps the sense of a proper name if one can 'work out' what object (if any) is referred to; and one grasps the sense of a sentence if one can 'work out' what its truth-value (if any) is – if one knows what needs to obtain for that sentence to be true.[21] The problem, though, is that this conception of sense does not so readily apply to *simple* names such as '7' or 'Aristotle'. For, returning to (7b), whilst Frege's 'official' view implies that it is possible to understand the left-hand side without knowing *which* object is referred to, this cannot also hold in the case of the right-hand side. It seems absurd to talk of 'working out' that the referent of '7' is indeed the number 7. Frege appears to have overlooked the peculiarities of simple names. How *is* their sense to be characterized? Is even appeal to *modes of presentation* appropriate? I take up these questions in the next section.

6.4 Deeper into *Sinn*

The dilemma that confronts Frege with regard to simple names such as '7' or 'Aristotle' can be easily stated. Either such names have no sense at all, but purely *refer*; or else they are to be treated as abbreviations of more complex expressions which do reveal the appropriate mode of presentation or mode of determination.[22] It is quite clear that Frege rejects the first horn: since the sense of a sentence is determined by the senses of its parts, if a sentence has a sense, then any component name, however simple, must itself have a sense.[23] So does he equate the sense of a proper name with the sense of some corresponding *definite description*? This is certainly what is suggested by Frege's notorious 'Aristotle' footnote at the beginning of 'Über Sinn und Bedeutung':

> In the case of an actual proper name such as 'Aristotle' opinions as to the sense may differ. It might, for instance, be taken to be the following: the pupil of Plato and teacher of Alexander the Great. Anybody who does this will attach another sense to the sentence 'Aristotle was born in Stagira' than will a man who takes as the sense of the name: the teacher of Alexander the Great who was born in Stagira. So long as the *Bedeutung* remains the same, such variations of sense may be tolerated, although they are to be avoided in the theoretical structure of a demonstrative science and ought not to occur in a perfect language. (*SR*, p. 58, n.)

Clearly, for the first person, 'Aristotle was born in Stagira' will be informative; whereas for the second person, it will count as a trivial 'analytic' truth.[24] In both cases, the sense of 'Aristotle' is understood as given by some definite description.

However, it might be suggested that Frege's use of this example was not so much to illustrate a 'description theory' of proper names, as merely to highlight how far short ordinary language falls of the ideal logical language that Frege was primarily concerned to develop. The fact that there might be disagreement over what statements about Aristotle count as 'analytic' shows that ordinary proper names cannot be simply incorporated into a logical system without having their sense uniquely defined. But Frege's criticism of ordinary language here does not in itself rule out interpreting him as a description theorist. As in the case of fictional names, it may be that the appeal to ordinary proper names is intended to reinforce his conception of sense, not merely to circumscribe the limits of its applicability. The point of the footnote is to make clear that in the case of an ordinary proper name, there is typically no *unique* definite description that supplies *the* sense of the name. Only in an ideal language can the demand for uniqueness be satisfied.

But if, in an ideal language, every proper name is uniquely defined by means of some definite description, is this not in conflict with Frege's stress in the *Grundlagen* on the *fruitfulness* of definitions? Definitions of terms for objects are inadequate, according to Frege, if they fail to enable us to recognize the object again in any other guise than that initially involved (cf. *GL*, §66). In §67 of the *Grundlagen* (quoted and discussed in §4.2), Frege distinguishes between introducing an object (specifying the *Bedeutung* of a term) and saying something about that object (expressing a *Sinn*, as it can now be put). Only with this distinction can a stipulative definition be regarded as transformable into a synthetic judgement (which is what was involved in Frege's conception of the *Doppelseitigkeit* of definitions). The particular way in which the object is introduced in a definition (the *Sinn* of the relevant term) is deemed of no logical significance; all that is important is that we come to know the *Bedeutung* in such a way that we can recognize it again under other modes of presentation.[25]

We can see from this how the distinction between *Bedeutung* and *Sinn* is waiting to emerge. But once Frege's conception of sense is in place, his requirement on the adequacy of a definition looks unsatisfiable. The idea that, despite introducing an object in a particular way, it might be possible to recognize the object in other ways is undermined, since from one mode of presentation of an object, it is not in general possible to extract information about other modes of presentation. Frege himself suggests as much in the passage to which the 'Aristotle' footnote is appended (at the point asterisked):

> The sense of a proper name is grasped by everybody who is sufficiently familiar with the language or totality of designations to which it belongs;* but this serves to illuminate only a single aspect of the *Bedeutung*, supposing it to have one. Comprehensive knowledge of the *Bedeutung* would require us to be able to say immediately whether any given sense attaches to it. To such knowledge we never attain. (*SR*, pp. 57-8.)

If every term has a sense, which exhibits just one facet of a thing, then how indeed can we recognize the object again in other guises?

The dilemma formulated above simply re-emerges more insistently. It seems that either we have to say that understanding a proper name refers us directly to the object concerned, in such a way that we 'fully know' the object; or else we have to allow that there is some 'privileged' definite description, the understanding of which supplies us with the necessary recognitional capacities. Neither position seems at all plausible.[26] The dilemma, then, does not just have implications for a theory of proper names, but is critical to Frege's logicist project.

What is Frege's response? We have seen how, in his logicist work, Frege defines numbers as *extensions of concepts*, and more generally, construes abstract objects as *value-ranges*; and this might be understood in either of two ways, reflecting the problem discussed in the last chapter as to how to interpret Frege's central argument in the *Grundlagen*. On the one hand, he appears to end up simply *stipulating* what the reference is of an abstract object name. '0', for example, refers to the extension of the concept 'equinumerous to the concept *not identical with itself*'; and we are assumed to 'fully know' what extensions are (at least of logical concepts). On the other hand, he might be thought to grasp the dilemma by the second horn, and offer a 'privileged' definite description, characterizing all relevant objects as value-ranges. Let us consider the second possibility first. This characterization is offered not only in the *Grundlagen*, where numbers are so defined, but also in the *Grundgesetze*, where, in §10 of Volume I, the two truth-values are so defined.[27] Since Axiom V lays down when two value-ranges are identical, then the means are provided of recognizing objects as the same or different – as long as they are given as value-ranges.

But, of course, this latter qualification gives the game away. We still have no guarantee of recognizing an object if it is *not* given as a value-range. The immediate response might be to suggest that since everything can be given as a value-range, the necessary transformations must simply be made as part of the recognitional process. For if Frege's *Grundgedanke* (as discussed in §5.3) is legitimate, then the following transition can be effected *for any X*:[28]

(Xa) X is identical with Y.

(Xd) The extension of the concept *is identical with X* is identical with the extension of the concept *is identical with Y*.

(Xe) X is the extension of the concept *is identical with X*.

According to Frege, we must be able to determine the truth-value of every statement of the form of (Xa), but if (Xa) is taken as the same identity statement as (Xd) through the explicit definition (Xe), then, via Axiom V, this is indeed achieved. As long as everything can be introduced as a value-range, of which an extension is a special case, then the necessary discriminatory powers are enabled.

An analogy might help clarify the idea. Imagine being at a masked ball, and not only not knowing who is behind each mask, but also not even knowing if it is the same person each time, since everyone is continually swopping masks. But suppose that you are given each person's (uniquely identifying) *fingerprints*. It would now be possible – in principle – to work out who everyone is, by taking their fingerprints as you encountered them. As long as everyone who turned up at the ball was fingerprinted as they arrived, they could be 'recognized' again whatever their guise.

However, this procedure only works in an artificially controlled set-up; and we can, of course, only recognize the objects to the extent that they are 'presented' in the appropriate way. In §10 of Volume I of the *Grundgesetze*, Frege himself rejects the possibility of generalizing the essential move – characterizing every object as a value-range. In showing that the generalization does not hold if the object is already given as a value-range, he writes that 'it is intolerable to allow it to hold only for such objects as are not given us as value-ranges; the way in which an object is given must not be regarded as an immutable property of it, since the same object can be given in a different way'.[29] This is precisely the point that Frege had earlier made in §67 of the *Grundlagen*, in objecting to contextual definitions (see §4.2 above). So how can his own definitions nevertheless be justified? The answer (as discussed in the last chapter) returns us to the first horn of the dilemma. They are simply to be treated as *stipulations*, assigning to each term a logical object with which we are assumed to be fully familiar. It is not that numbers, taken as already given, can be characterized – in a 'privileged' way – *as* extensions of concepts; they are stipulated to *be* extensions of concepts, where it is these that are taken as already given.

Returning to the analogy, the Fregean move here would be to *identify* each person with their unique set of fingerprints, eliminating at one go the worry about how they might be recognized otherwise than by their fingerprints. In this case, of course, the Fregean move looks absurd; and as we suggested in the last chapter, the distinction between *Sinn* and *Bedeutung* may well have prevented Frege from appreciating the problem. For it is tempting to see what is going on as simply providing a *sense* to numerical terms (a 'privileged' definite description), numbers being assumed as the same objects with which we have all along been familiar. Yet what Frege is in fact doing is providing a *Bedeutung* to numerical terms, specifying *which* objects (from the domain of extensions) numerals are to be taken as referring to.[30]

We have already indicated the problem with such a radically reconstructive project. For it is only if we have some prior grasp of what numbers are that we can recognize the 'legitimacy' of the identifications with the appropriate extensions. Returning to our analogy, we can only engage in the fingerprinting exercise if the people are already there in all their embodied glory. The problem is highlighted if we consider any attempted stipulation of the form of (Xe) above. For we only grasp the concept *is identical with X* if we already know what *X* is. Of course, in Frege's logicist project, the appropriate concepts are defined purely logically, so that the overt circularity is removed. But even here, we must have some understanding of arithmetic if the 'right' stipulations are to be made.[31]

What Frege's confusion here also reflects is an unclarity in his conception of the domain of objects to which his theory applies. For his aim is to develop a logical language to encompass all objects; yet in the formal system of the *Grundgesetze*, the domain seems merely to comprise value-ranges, and in particular, the value-ranges of concepts regarded as purely logical. The tension can be removed by allowing that the formal system is only the logical heart of the ideal language, which can be progressively expanded to include all the areas of science in just the way Frege had envisaged in the 'Preface' to the *Begriffsschrift* (see §2.1 above). But even in the *Grundgesetze* Frege emphasizes that functions have to be defined, i.e. their values determined, for *all* objects as arguments; and the underlying assumption does seem to be of a universal, homogeneous domain, any object of which is a legitimate argument for any function.[32]

It is this assumption that made Frege's objection to contextual definition seem unanswerable. For the problem arose from requiring, from any adequate definition of a term '*X*', that it be possible to determine the truth-value of '*X* is identical with *Y*' (i.e. (Xa) above) *for any Y*. A criterion of identity, in other words, had to be specified to distinguish the object from every other object in the universal domain; and a mere contextual definition, confined to a particular sub-domain, seemed incapable of doing this. But what Frege ended up doing was restricting his attention to the sub-domain of value-ranges, Axiom V in effect functioning as the relevant contextual definition. But if this is legitimate here, then why not allow it from the beginning? If we divide up the universal domain into a number of sub-domains, each of which contains objects of a certain kind, then 'X is identical with Y' is automatically *false* if X and Y are objects of different categories, and the relevant contextual definition provides us with the means of determining the truth-value of (Xa) if X and Y are objects within the *same* sub-domain.

Developing this idea not only allows us to answer Frege's objection but also suggests a way of dissolving the dilemma that has been threatening to destroy the coherence of a Fregean conception of *Sinn* and *Bedeutung*. For with the underlying assumption of a universal, homogeneous domain of objects, and Frege's requirement on the adequacy of a definition, it does seem that we are forced to decide between two extreme positions regarding the sense of simple names. Either we adopt a *minimalist* conception, whereby the specification of the sense of a name merely consists in the assignment of an object from the universal domain, sense apparently reducing to reference; and then, to satisfy the requirement, we have to ensure that the object assigned is a *logical* object with which we are already familiar. Or else we endorse a *maximalist* conception, whereby the sense is so richly articulated as to afford us a means, by grasping it, of recognizing the object designated in other guises and of distinguishing it from every other object of the domain. But in abandoning the underlying assumption, by allowing that the universal domain can be partitioned into sub-domains, we loosen the requirement on the adequacy of a definition, legitimizing contextual definitions, and thereby open up the possibility of a more satisfying account of sense.

The strategy involves expanding slightly on the minimalist conception, whilst resisting any major concession to the maximalist conception. We can allow that what occurs in the specification of the sense of a simple name is the assignment to that name of an object from some particular sub-domain (e.g. the sub-domain of persons, geometrical objects, or value-ranges). But sense does not *reduce* to reference, since in grasping the sense of the name, we must know what *kind of object* is referred to. If it is a condition of understanding the sense of 'X' and 'Y' that we know what *kind of object* is referred to, then if 'X' and 'Y' refer to *different* kinds of objects, and we grasp the sense of the statement at all, then we immediately know that 'X is identical with Y' is *false*. We would immediately know that an abstract object such as a direction or a number was not Julius Caesar or England, to use Frege's own examples once more.

On this conception, then, I grasp the sense of 'Aristotle' if I know *which person* is referred to, and I grasp the sense of '7' if I know *which number* is referred to.[33] But is this not to abandon one of Frege's insights – that the referent of a name can only be apprehended through some particular means of identification? As Frege himself put it, 'it is *via* a sense, and only *via* a sense that a proper name is related to an object' (*CSR*, p. 124). We have granted that we can only know something *as* a certain *kind* of thing (we can only understand who Aristotle is if we know that he is a person); but this clearly does not uniquely determine the relevant object. In the 'Aristotle' footnote, Frege suggests that different people may attach *different* senses to the name 'Aristotle', since they may have different means of identifying him; but there is no need to take this line to respect the insight just mentioned. So long as each person has *some* means of identification, it does not matter *which* means it is. In the case of simple names there is no *one way* of identifying the referent which a person must possess in order to be attributed a grasp of the sense of the name. An elementary scope distinction serves to clarify the point:

(SMI) Anyone who grasps the sense of a name possesses some particular means of identifying the referent.

(MIS) There is some particular means of identifying the referent of a name that is possessed by anyone who grasps its sense.

Although (MIS) – where the existential quantifier has wider scope than the universal quantifier – might be appropriate for complex names, (SMI) – where the universal quantifier has wider scope – is all that is required in the case of simple names. To utilize a distinction that has become familiar, the sense of 'Aristotle' can be *shown* by *saying* what its referent is in any number of different ways: which person is referred to may be indicated by stating that he is the pupil of Plato and teacher of Alexander the Great, the teacher of Alexander the Great who was born in Stagira, the author of the *Prior Analytics*, or with the help of any other uniquely identifying description, which at least preserves something of Frege's idea in the 'Aristotle' footnote.[34]

However, it remains the case that what is being suggested here amounts to a *modification* or *reconstruction* of Frege's conception of the sense of proper names, since Frege himself seems to have been insensitive to the distinction between simple and complex names. In the 'Aristotle' footnote, Frege is still wedded to the picture of senses as modes of presentation; and he imagines that the problem of variability lies in the inadequacies of ordinary language. It is true that in the controlled environment of a formal system, where each primitive name is uniquely assigned to one particular object of a clearly specified domain, the problem of variability is avoided; but this is only achieved by invalidating the identification of senses with modes of presentation.

In any case, there is an obvious problem with taking the sense of each proper name as identical with the sense of some definite description. For, on the assumption that a definite description is a *complex* expression, the senses of its component parts must be known, and an infinite regress threatens if we treat these too as given by definite descriptions. So at some point we must allow that knowledge of the sense of a (primitive) name simply consists in knowing *which object* is referred to. Indeed, since Frege himself was insistent that not everything can be defined, and that at the very primitive level we must rely on 'hints' and 'illustrative examples', it is surprising that he did not explicitly relate this to the issue of the sense of simple names.[35]

In the case of a simple name, then, knowledge of its sense consists in knowing *which object* in the appropriate (sub-)domain is referred to; and this requires a modification to Frege's 'official' conception of sense. However, in a formal system, once the initial assignments have been made, Frege's 'official' conception yields a plausible account of the sense of complex expressions, for since the sense of a complex expression is determined by the senses of its parts, its *Bedeutung* can be regarded as 'presented' in a way that reflects this determination. In the case of (7c) and (7d) of the last section, for example, the sense of each side of the identity statement can be taken to reflect the way in which the number 7 is determined – as the value of a certain arithmetical formula.

But where does this now leave us on the issue of Frege's *Grundlagen* requirement on the adequacy of a definition? Can we ever define a name in such a way that we can recognize its referent in other guises? It is obviously absurd to expect that in understanding, say, what '7' stands for, we must have 'comprehensive knowledge' of the number 7 – that we must know, for example, that it can be represented as the fraction on the right-hand side of (7c). Such a requirement is absurd even in the case of 'logical objects'. But it is not at all unreasonable to suggest that to properly understand what '7' stands for, I must be able to *work out* that 7 is the number referred to when designated by more complex expressions. But there is no straightforward answer as to exactly what complex expressions need to be mastered in any particular case. Someone might be credited with an understanding of the natural numbers iff they know how to add and subtract, so that it may not be required that they grasp formulations such as (7c) and (7d) above. However, merely knowing that 7 is the successor of 6 might well be deemed *insufficient* for an understanding of what '7' stands for. If this is so, then it is hard to see how any single definition could possibly acquaint us with the object in an adequate way. But what this then suggests is the need to move to a *holistic* rather than *atomistic* conception of what it is to grasp the meaning of words. I am properly acquainted with a natural number if I understand the whole set of axioms governing the natural numbers, and the criterion for this is whether I can operate the system correctly, that is, whether I can derive the appropriate theorems, even if only a selection of those theorems are immediately accessible.

However, this should not be taken to imply that our rules may never, in practice, lead to anomalies. In particular, our rules may well allow us to construct expressions that, as it turns out, have no referent. That '1 – 2' has no *Bedeutung* within the system of natural numbers may induce us to extend our system to the signed integers; but even in the relatively 'complete' system of the real numbers, '0/0' remains an undefined expression.[36] When we turn to ordinary language, the problem is pervasive. We may have a perfectly good understanding of terms for relations such as 'the son of *X*' or 'the present King of *Y*', but under certain substitutions, valid to the extent that the names that are substituted are from the right category, such as 'the son of Kant' or 'the present King of France', there may be no referent. Since such phrases are legitimately constructed, we are inclined to grant them sense, but, as it happens, they are without a *Bedeutung*.[37]

It may have been this general line of thought that induced Frege to treat senses as fundamentally modes of determination rather than modes of presentation – precisely to leave open the possibility that expressions may lack a referent.[38] Here all that is necessary to grasp the sense of a name is to understand how to 'work out' or 'determine' what its referent (if any) is; we do not need to know *which object* is thereby designated. However, as we have argued in this section, Frege's 'official' conception of sense fails to yield a plausible account of the sense of simple names, an issue that Frege himself seems not to have appreciated. Here to grasp the sense of a name is indeed to know *which object* is referred to. Such a conception clearly *presupposes* that the names have referents, so that at this primitive level there is no option but to appeal to modes of presentation, even if senses are not to be *identified* with modes of presentation. If the objects did not exist, then the whole conception of sense would break down. Although Frege was explicit about the need for this presupposition in logic, he seems not to have thought through the consequences for his conception of sense.

6.5 Extensional and Intensional Contexts

In §6.2 we used Leibniz's Law to formulate a general criterion for identity of 'content':

(GC) Two expressions have the same 'content' iff they are everywhere intersubstitutable *salva veritate*.

As we argued, however, if this is to be adapted as a criterion for sameness of *Bedeutung*, the intersubstitutability must be restricted to *extensional* contexts. Consider, for example, the following two propositions, where an identity statement occurs in an *intensional* context:

(GAA) Gottlob believes that Aristotle is Aristotle.
(GAP) Gottlob believes that Aristotle is the author of the *Prior Analytics*.

(GAA) may clearly be true without (GAP) being true, despite the fact that 'Aristotle' and 'the author of the *Prior Analytics*', considered in normal contexts, possess the same *Bedeutung*. It looks as if what we have here is a counterexample to Frege's principle of the determination of *Bedeutung*:

(PDB)   The *Bedeutung* of a complex expression is determined by the
        Bedeutung of its parts.

If the component parts have the same *Bedeutung*, then (GAA) and (GAP),
by (PDB), must also have the same *Bedeutung*, i.e. have the same truth-
value; but this will not always be the case.

The obvious response is to repudiate (PDB), or at least to restrict its
applicability to extensional contexts. However, Frege's own response,
preserving (PDB) in all its generality, is to deny that in intensional
contexts the *Bedeutung* of an expression remains the same as it is in
extensional contexts; rather, its intensional or *indirect Bedeutung* becomes its *customary* sense (cf. *SR*, p. 59). In other words, in (GAP), for
example, the *Bedeutung* of 'Aristotle is the author of the *Prior Analytics*'
is the sense or *thought* that this identity statement expresses in normal,
extensional contexts; and this is clearly different from the thought expressed by 'Aristotle is Aristotle'. Frege's strategy here seems reasonable,
for we surely do want to say that the truth-value of statements such as
(GAA) or (GAP) depends on what *thought* is expressed (in extensional
contexts) by the embedded sentence. To make this explicit, (GAA) and
(GAP) might be rephrased as follows:

(GAA') Gottlob holds as true the thought expressed by 'Aristotle is Aris-
        totle'.
(GAP') Gottlob holds as true the thought expressed by 'Aristotle is the
        author of the *Prior Analytics*'.

In stating what someone believes, I refer to the *thoughts* that they hold as
true; and these thoughts just are, according to Frege, the senses of the
appropriate sentences.

However, as well as distinguishing between indirect and customary
Bedeutung, Frege also distinguishes between indirect and customary
sense; and this raises the possibility of an infinite hierarchy of *Bedeutungen* and senses. Consider the following proposition:

(BGAA) Bertrand knows that Gottlob believes that Aristotle is Aris-
        totle.

In 'Gottlob believes that Aristotle is Aristotle', as we have just noted,
'Aristotle' has its indirect *Bedeutung*, that is, its customary sense; and its
sense, according to Frege, is its *indirect* sense. But when doubly embedded
in (BGAA) the *Bedeutung* of 'Aristotle' becomes this indirect sense. In
other words, the doubly indirect *Bedeutung* of an expression is its (singly)
indirect sense; and so on *ad infinitum*. Frege may well have countenanced
the possibility of such an infinite hierarchy of *Bedeutungen* and senses, in
the same way as he countenanced an infinite hierarchy of functions, each
with a corresponding extension; but it has been suggested that Frege's

conception of indirect sense, in particular, is open to a fundamental objection.[39]

The issue can be approached by considering the critique of Frege's conception of sense that Russell offered, albeit in a confused form, in his seminal 1905 paper 'On Denoting' (*OD*). The basic problem concerns how the sense of a name is to be specified. In the case of a complex name, this might seem straightforward: its customary sense can be explained in terms of the senses of its parts; and even in the case of apparently simple names such as 'Hesperus' or 'Phosphorus', two of the traditional terms used for 'the Evening Star' and 'the Morning Star', respectively, which are really disguised definite descriptions, their sense too can be readily specified. But as we saw in the last section, the case of genuinely simple names such as 'Aristotle' is different; and on pain of regress, one cannot specify the sense of such a name by equating that sense with the sense of some corresponding or representative definite description. It might seem that the only way we have of identifying such a sense is by use of the denoting phrase 'The sense of "Aristotle" '. In these cases, to quote Russell's words, 'the [sense] cannot be got at except by means of denoting phrases' (*OD*, p. 49).[40] But what now is the sense of this denoting phrase, which must clearly be grasped if its referent is to be apprehended? To specify this as 'The sense of "The sense of Aristotle" ' would involve us in another infinite regress. On Frege's own view, whilst sense determines reference, reference does not determine sense, so that the sense of 'Aristotle' cannot itself tell us how to understand the expression 'The sense of "Aristotle" '. Again, as Russell put it, 'there is no backward road from denotations to [senses], because every object can be denoted by an infinite number of different denoting phrases' (*OD*, p. 50). Ultimately, then, there would appear to be no way of specifying what the sense of a name is, suggesting that the whole notion of sense is incoherent.

However, from what was said in the last section, it should be clear that to request a *specification* of the sense of a simple name is to misconstrue what is involved. I understand the sense of a simple name if I know *which object* is referred to; and my grasp of this sense is *shown* in my use of the name: there may be no definitive way of exhibiting that grasp. So we cannot conclude that there is no such thing as the sense of 'Aristotle', for it is just this that I grasp when I correctly use the name 'Aristotle'. But if this is so, then 'The sense of "Aristotle" ' must surely possess a referent, in which case the denoting phrase 'The sense of "Aristotle" ' itself must surely possess a sense; and why should *this* sense not be taken as the *indirect* sense of 'Aristotle'? I understand this indirect sense if I can use the denoting phrase 'The sense of "Aristotle" ' to convey a thought successfully; and since, if the account just given is correct, I have just done so, then there is no reason to suppose that the notion of indirect sense is incoherent.

Now Dummett has suggested that Russell's argument is indeed effective against Frege's notion of indirect sense, although not against the notion of customary sense. This might appear surprising, since it is Dummett who has most strongly defended Frege's notion of sense (at least as he interprets it), and who first proposed that the (customary) sense of a word is *shown* by saying, in an appropriate way, what its referent is. Why should such a conception not equally apply to indirect sense? The idea would be this: I grasp the indirect sense of 'Aristotle' in knowing that the denoting phrase 'The sense of "Aristotle" ' refers to the (customary) sense of 'Aristotle', the (customary) sense of 'Aristotle' being what I grasp when I know which object 'Aristotle' refers to. Since I can know the customary sense of 'Aristotle', I can also know its indirect sense. However, Russell's objection to this, which Dummett endorses, is that when it comes to referring to the sense of 'Aristotle', all I can do is use the denoting phrase 'the sense of "Aristotle" ': there is no other way of knowing which object is referred to; and then we are back with the infinite regress.

Dummett does not make his own position on this entirely clear;[41] but it is, I think, possible to identify the source of the worry. For the underlying issue concerns the construal of senses as *objects*. The coherence of the notion of sense depends on the possibility of knowing *which object* a term refers to. In the case of proper names of objects such as persons, this is unproblematic. I have everyday acquaintance of the people who live around me; and I have a variety of well-established ways of identifying people who live elsewhere or who lived in the past.[42] But in the case of *senses*, there is a genuine difficulty in suggesting that I can know *which object* is referred to. It presupposes that senses are indeed objects, but even allowing that they could be regarded as a type of abstract object, their criteria of identity must clearly be laid down. Merely being in possession of a denoting phrase is no guarantee that I know which object is denoted. I must also, at least, know the sense of that phrase; but it is just this that is in dispute.

However, there is, in Frege's work, an obvious answer to the question as to how we apprehend senses – through contextual definitions. Let us consider how an account of this might run. Adapting (GC) above, we have already offered the following criterion for sameness of *Bedeutung* (§6.2):

(CB)   Two expressions have the same *Bedeutung* iff they are intersubstitutable *salva veritate* in all extensional contexts.

It should now be clear what corresponding criteria for sameness of sense might be specified:

(CCS) Two expressions have the same customary sense iff they are intersubstitutable *salva veritate* in all singly intensional contexts (i.e. contexts in which they are singly embedded).

(CIS) Two expressions have the same indirect sense iff they are intersubstitutable *salva veritate* in all doubly intensional contexts.

It goes without saying that if two expressions satisfy (CIS), then they satisfy (CCS), and if they satisfy (CCS), then they satisfy (CB). The criteria for doubly indirect sense, triply indirect sense, and so on, can be readily formulated from (CCS) and (CIS).

(CCS) can then be used to provide a contextual definition of the customary sense of a term in the standard form (compare this with the other examples of Fregean pairs discussed in §5.3):

(Sa) Expression 'A' is intersubstitutable *salva veritate* in all singly intensional contexts with expression 'B'.

(Sb) The (customary) sense of 'A' is identical with the (customary) sense of 'B'.

But now we are faced with Frege's own objection to contextual definition – that whilst (Sa) allows us to distinguish one sense from another, it does not allow us to distinguish a sense from any other type of object. For all we know, Alexander of Aphrodisias might turn out to be the sense of 'Aristotle'! It does not, in other words, tell us *which* object from the universal domain a sense is.

However, at this point, we might appeal to the considerations advanced in the last section. If we allow that the universal domain can be divided into sub-domains, then we can rule out in advance any 'cross-identifications'. But in this case, to distinguish a sub-domain of *senses* would already be seen as begging the question as to whether there are such things as senses. So as far as Russell's argument is concerned, we appear to have reached stalemate: if we accept senses as legitimate (abstract) objects, then we can formulate a criterion, but if we do not, then Russell is right that there is a problem of specification.[43] I shall return to this in the final chapter; but in the light of what has just been said, we can at least identify a tension in Dummett's intermediate position. For if we allow that there are customary senses, as Dummett does, then Russell's argument can no longer be endorsed in rejecting indirect senses.

However, Dummett's considered response to the issue of indirect senses is to reject not their possibility, but merely their explanatory utility: whilst the existence of intensional contexts requires the notion of indirect *Bedeutung*, it does not require the notion of indirect sense.[44] It was Frege's conception that sense determines reference that induced him to posit indirect senses, by means of which indirect referents could be apprehended. But on Dummett's amended account, *ordinary* (i.e. customary) senses are treated as determining indirect referents in the appropriate contexts. As Dummett puts it, on his view 'there is no such thing as the indirect sense of a word: there is just its sense, which determines it to have in transparent [extensional] contexts a reference distinct from this sense, and in opaque [intensional] contexts a referent which coincides with its sense' (1981a: p. 268). An infinite hierarchy of *Bedeutungen* and senses is thereby avoided. However, such an account does involve a modification to

Frege's general conception of sense. For the sense of an expression is now only seen as determining a reference *together with a context*. The importance of context to semantic questions has been stressed before, particularly in §2.4; but since the issue is thrown into sharpest relief in the case of demonstratives, I shall postpone further discussion of this until §7.4.

7. Language, Logic and Paradox

A logical theory may be tested by its capacity for dealing with puzzles, and it is a wholesome plan, in thinking about logic, to stock the mind with as many puzzles as possible, since these serve much the same purpose as is served by experiments in physical science. (Russell, 'On Denoting', p. 47.)

In this chapter I shall be concerned with the relationship between ordinary language and the 'logically correct' language that Frege strove to develop. A logical language was seen as superior to ordinary language, firstly, by avoiding the various inadequacies of ordinary language, and secondly, by reflecting more accurately the real nature of thoughts. Here I shall focus primarily on the first, more negative aspect, and only turn to the positive aspect in §7.5. In the first three sections, I discuss three paradoxes that touch the heart of Frege's logical system – the paradox of the concept *horse*, Russell's paradox, and the Sorites paradox – all of which reveal features of Frege's understanding of concepts and their extensions. The fourth problem, explored in §7.4, concerns the use of demonstratives, expressions whose sense and reference vary from context to context. According to Frege, such expressions are to be avoided in an ideal language, but as we have already suggested (§2.4), the project of *decontextualism* is ultimately incoherent. The use of the demonstrative 'I' to express thoughts is particularly problematic. Frege has often been taken to hold that *I-thoughts* are in principle unshareable; but this seems in direct conflict with his assumption that senses are objective. I discuss Frege's Platonist conception of thoughts in the final section.

7.1 Concepts and Objects

We discussed in the last chapter the issues of the *Sinn* and *Bedeutung* of names and of sentences, which Frege addressed in 'Über Sinn und Bedeutung'. No mention was made in this paper, however, of the *Sinn* and *Bedeutung* of concept words and other functional expressions; and in the early days of Fregean scholarship, this question was controversial. Some commentators thought that Frege had never intended to extend the distinction to functional expressions, and others offered suggestions as to how it did apply.[1] At the time not all of Frege's writings had been published; and it was only later that three particular pieces revealed Frege's position.

The earliest piece is a letter Frege wrote to Husserl in May 1891, just before the publication of 'Über Sinn und Bedeutung'. Frege comments on the disagreement between them on how concept words relate to objects, and states that the following schema should clarify his position:

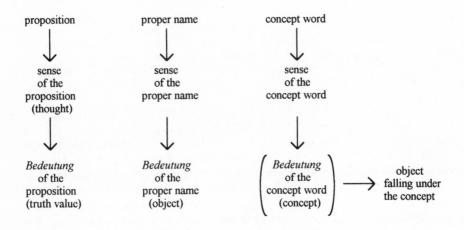

With a concept word it takes one more step to reach the object than with a proper name, and the last step may be missing – i.e. the concept may be empty – without the concept word's ceasing to be scientifically useful. I have drawn the last step from concept to object horizontally in order to indicate that it takes place on the same level, that objects and concepts have the same objectivity (see my *Grundlagen*, §47). In literary use it is sufficient if everything has a sense; in scientific use there must also be *Bedeutungen*. (*PMC*, p. 63.)

For Husserl, on the other hand, Frege suggests that the schema would be this:

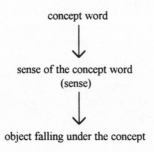

On this view, Frege goes on:

> it would take the same number of steps to get from proper names to objects as from concept words. The only difference between proper names and concept words would then be that the former could refer to only one object and the latter to more than one. A concept word whose concept was empty would then have to be excluded from science just like a proper name without a corresponding object. (*PMC*, p. 64.)

But, according to Frege, whilst empty proper names are illegitimate in science, empty concept words are not (as the need for the concept *is not identical with itself* in Frege's logicist project shows). So it must be possible for a concept word to have a *Bedeutung* independently of whether there are – or even could be – any objects that fall under the concept.

What underlies Frege's objection to Husserl's view here is his assumption that in science we are concerned with *truths* – that scientific propositions must possess a truth-value, i.e. a *Bedeutung*. By the principle (PDB), a proposition has a truth-value iff each logically significant part itself has a *Bedeutung* (see §6.2 above); and this principle applied as much to predicates as to names. This is made clear in the section on 'Sinn und Bedeutung' in Frege's 1906 notes 'Introduction to Logic'. According to Frege, the thought expressed by a proposition of the form '*a* is *F*' can be analysed into two components, a 'saturated' part, corresponding to the proper name '*a*', and an 'unsaturated' part, corresponding to the predicate expression '( ) is *F*'. A thought is formed when the unsaturated part is 'completed' by a saturated part. Frege writes:

> Now the question arises whether to the unsaturated part of the thought, which is to be regarded as the sense of the corresponding part of the sentence, there does not also correspond something which is to be construed as the *Bedeutung* of this part. As far as the mere thought-content is concerned it is indeed a matter of indifference whether a proper name has a *Bedeutung*, but in any other regard it is of the greatest importance; at least it is so if we are concerned with the acquisition of knowledge. It is this which determines whether we are in the realm of fiction or truth. Now it is surely unlikely that a proper name should behave so differently from the rest of a singular sentence that it is only in its case that the existence of a *Bedeutung* should be of importance. If the thought as a whole is to belong to the realm of truth, we must rather assume that something in the realm of *Bedeutung* must correspond to the rest of the sentence, which has the unsaturated part of the thought for its sense. (*IL*, p. 192.)

The involvement here of the two principles (PDB) and (PDS) is clear: if a sentence both expresses a thought and possesses a truth-value, then *all* of its components must themselves have both a *Sinn* and a *Bedeutung*. As Frege goes on to remark, 'It is inconceivable that it is only for the proper names that there can be a question of *Bedeutung* and not for the other parts of the sentence which connect them' (*IL*, p. 193). Since a statement such as 'Venus is not identical with itself' clearly has a truth-value, namely, the False, the predicate expression '( ) is not identical with itself' must itself have a *Bedeutung* – despite the fact that there is no possible 'completion' of this expression by a proper name that could yield a true proposition. The *Bedeutung* of a concept word is therefore distinct from the objects, if any, that fall under the concept.

Frege's fullest discussion of concept words is contained in a piece (*CSR*) written shortly after 'Über Sinn und Bedeutung', and presumably intended to resolve just those issues left untouched by the published paper. The piece opens with a clear statement of Frege's position:

> In an article ('Über Sinn und Bedeutung') I distinguished between sense and *Bedeutung* in the first instance only for the case of proper names (or, if one prefers, singular terms). The same distinction can also be drawn for concept-words. Now it is easy to become unclear about this by confounding the division into concepts and objects with the distinction between sense and *Bedeutung*, so that we run together sense and concept on the one hand and *Bedeutung* and object on the other. To every concept-word or proper name, there corresponds as a rule a sense and a *Bedeutung*, as I use these words. Of course in fiction words only have a sense, but in science and wherever we are concerned about truth, we are not prepared to rest content with the sense, we also attach a *Bedeutung* to proper names and concept-words; and if through some oversight, say, we fail to do this, then we are making a mistake that can easily vitiate our thinking. The *Bedeutung* of a proper name is the object it designates or names. A concept-word refers to [*bedeutet*] a concept, if the word is used as is appropriate for logic. (*CSR*, p. 118.)

On an undifferentiated notion of 'content', it would be tempting to regard the 'content' of a proper name as the object referred to, and the 'content' of a concept word as its sense.[2] But in holding that both names and predicates have both *Sinn* and *Bedeutung*, Frege makes clear that the object/concept distinction does not line up with the *Bedeutung*/*Sinn* distinction. Frege goes on to contrast his own position with both intensionalism and extensionalism. For the intensionalist, the 'content' of a concept word is its *intension* – what is understood in understanding the expression; whilst for the extensionalist, the 'content' of a concept word is its *extension* – the set of objects that fall under the concept. In distinguishing between the *Sinn* and *Bedeutung* of a concept word, Frege equates the sense with the intension (cf. *CSR*, p. 122), but he does not regard the *Bedeutung* as the extension; rather, the *Bedeutung* of a concept word is the concept itself.

One of Frege's deepest convictions was that concepts are quite distinct from objects, and this was why the *Bedeutung* of a concept word could not be identified with its extension, since extensions, according to Frege, are objects (*CSR*, pp. 118-19; cf. *FC*, p. 32). As we have seen, the distinction between concept and object arose from Frege's use of function-argument analysis in logic; and adherence to it constituted the third of his 'fundamental principles' in the *Grundlagen*. Its root lay in the idea that any functional expression contains 'gaps' where the names of the arguments are inserted. As Frege put it in his 1891 paper 'Function and Concept', which contains the clearest account of his notion of a function, 'a function by itself must be called incomplete, in need of supplementation, or "unsaturated" ' (*FC*, p. 24). A concept is simply a special kind of function – 'a function whose value is always a truth-value' (*FC*, p. 30). Objects are then seen as whatever are legitimate candidates as arguments and values of functions. But, Frege goes on: 'I regard a regular definition as impossible, since we have here something too simple to admit of logical analysis. It is only possible to indicate what is meant. Here I can only say briefly: An object is anything that is not a function, so that an expression for it does not contain any empty place.' (*FC*, p. 32.)

The circularity in these characterizations is obvious: functional expressions are formed by removing proper names from sentences, creating 'gaps'; and proper names are whatever do not contain 'gaps'. Given Frege's view of the logical priority of judgements over concepts – that concepts are generated by 'splitting up' the contents of propositions (see §5.2 above), the only way of breaking into this circle is by providing some independent characterization of a proper name. As we saw in §4.1, in the case of number terms, Frege offers two reasons for believing that they stand for objects, i.e. that they are proper names: firstly, that the definite article is used in constructions of the form 'the number *x*'; and secondly, that such terms do not admit of plurals. Generalizing from this, we might suggest that any phrase of the form 'the *F* ', when used correctly, represents an object; but even here we still need to add the qualification that the phrase must be 'saturated' – 'the author of *φ*', for example, requiring 'completion' to yield a unique definite description.

However, whether or not a non-circular characterization could be provided here, Frege's insistence on the distinction between concept and object faces an obvious difficulty, one which he confronted in 'On Concept and Object' (1892), the paper that immediately followed 'Function and Concept'. For the natural way of referring to concepts is by use of such phrases as 'the concept *horse*'; yet, according to Frege, in utilizing the definite article, such phrases designate *objects*, not concepts. But if names of concepts designate objects, then the absolute distinction between concept and object is eroded. Even if there are some objects that cannot be concepts, the two categories are not mutually exclusive, since it is possible for one and the same thing to be both a concept and an object.[3] Yet if concepts are essentially 'unsaturated' and objects 'saturated', then there is no way that one and the same thing could be both 'saturated' and 'unsaturated'.

Frege's response is to deny that 'the concept *horse*' does designate a concept; but he admits that there is an 'awkwardness' in therefore saying that the concept *horse* is not a concept (*CO*, p. 46). He blames the paradox that arises here on the limitations of ordinary language, which fails to provide us with any direct means of referring to concepts. 'By a kind of necessity of language, my expressions, taken literally, sometimes miss my thought; I mention an object, when what I intend is a concept. I fully realize that in such cases I was relying upon a reader who would be ready to meet me half-way – who does not begrudge a pinch of salt.' (*CO*, p. 54.) The reason that we cannot directly refer to a concept lies in its 'predicative' or 'unsaturated' nature. But to give up the idea of the 'unsaturatedness' of concepts, according to Frege, would leave us unable to account for the unity of a proposition. For if concepts as well as objects were 'complete', then there would need to be some way of linking them in order to express a thought: an appropriate *relation* would have to obtain to bind them together. But if this relation in turn were 'saturated', then there would need to be some further way of linking the object, concept and relation, and an infinite regress threatens. So at some point there must be something 'unsaturated', which can effect the necessary connections without itself requiring connection; and as soon as we accept this, we are back with the problem of not being able to refer to such a thing, on pain of picking out an object instead. Since the appeal to something 'unsaturated' is indispensable, we simply have to face up to the difficulty that results. (Cf. *CO*, pp. 54-5.) As Frege concludes, 'on thorough investigation it will be found that the obstacle is essential, and founded on the nature of our language; that we cannot avoid a certain inappropriateness of linguistic expression; and that there is nothing for it but to realize this and always take it into account' (*CO*, p. 55).

However, even if we accept that Frege has a right to use the words 'concept' and 'object' in his own way (cf. *CO*, p. 54), and that there is an extent to which this use can only be indicated by means of hints rather than definitions (cf. *CO*, pp. 43, 45), Frege's discussion remains unclear on one crucial issue. For if a phrase such as 'the concept *horse*' refers to an object rather than a concept, *which* object does it pick out? Nowhere in Frege's writings is there any suggestion as to what such an object might be or how it might be apprehended. All we are told is that it stands proxy for the corresponding concept. In order to talk about a concept, Frege remarks, 'it must first be converted into an object, or, more precisely, an object must go proxy for it. We designate this object by prefixing the words "the concept" ' (*CO*, pp. 46-7); and he gives the following example:

(CM) The concept *man* is not empty.

Here he simply says that 'the first three words are to be regarded as a proper name', adding in a footnote that 'I call anything a proper name if it is a sign for an object' (*CO*, p. 47).

What is leading Frege astray here is his doctrine that the definite article always indicates an object (cf. *GL*, §§38, 51; *CO*, p. 45). Presumably his thought is this. Since propositions about concepts can be true, i.e. possess a *Bedeutung*, then any (logically significant) constituent phrase must itself have a *Bedeutung*. For example, since (CM) is true, then the subject term 'the concept *man*' must have a *Bedeutung*, which its linguistic form, according to Frege, reveals to be an object. However, given that Frege himself, in replacing traditional subject-predicate analysis by function-argument analysis (see §2.2 above), had shown that the linguistic form of a sentence need not exhibit its logical form, it is perhaps surprising that he did not apply this idea to the present problem. For (CM) can be readily formalized as follows, '*Ma*' symbolizing '*a* is a man':

(CM*) $(\exists x)\, Mx$.

Represented like this ('There is something which is a man'), there is no longer a temptation to construe 'The concept *man*' as designating an object, since the phrase is *eliminated* when sentences in which it appears are correctly analysed. Such an eliminative strategy should indeed have appealed to Frege, since he himself pursued such a strategy in the *Grundlagen* in 'reducing' the adjectival use of number terms to the substantival: we do not need to provide any separate account of adjectival constructions but merely show how they can be transformed into equivalent substantival ones.[4]

But of course, the fact that it is the substantival form that is seen as fundamental already indicates a realist predilection (*objectivity* being assumed to require *objects*); and it might be suggested that Frege does indeed have a way of legitimately introducing those objects that function as his 'concept-correlates', by means of contextual definition.[5] Using Frege's geometrical example once again, recall the two members of what we termed a *vertical* Fregean pair (see §5.3):

(Da) Line *a* is parallel to line *b*.
(Dc) The concept *line parallel to line a* is coextensive with the concept *line parallel to line b*.

It might well be suggested that 'splitting up' in a new way the 'content' of (Da), taken as already given, and presupposing an understanding of the relation of coextensiveness, introduces us to the two objects – the concept-correlates – designated by 'the concept *line parallel to line a*' and 'the concept *line parallel to line b*'. However, since Frege himself came to reject contextual definitions – precisely because they do not adequately determine the relevant objects, Frege could not have adopted this suggestion himself. The only plausible strategy, then, is the eliminative one. Phrases of the form 'the concept *F*' only appear to designate objects: when sentences containing them are correctly analysed, such phrases are eliminated. For example, (Dc) would be formalized as follows, '*Ap*' symbolizing '*p* is a line parallel to line *a*' and '*Bp*' symbolizing '*p* is a line parallel to line *b*':

(Dc*) $(\forall x)\,(Ax \leftrightarrow Bx)$.

Once again, in any natural language reading of (Dc*), such as 'All lines parallel to line a are parallel to line b, and vice versa', phrases of the form 'the concept F' make no appearance; and so the worry about what their *Bedeutungen* might be evaporates. There are no such objects as concept-correlates.

It may well have been the problem of specifying criteria of identity for concept-correlates that made Frege avoid saying anything about such objects.[6] But if he was hesitant about even committing himself to the existence of concept-correlates, understood as the referents of phrases of the form 'The concept F', he nevertheless did believe that there were certain objects that were uniquely correlated with concepts, namely, their *extensions*; and these objects were indeed introduced by contextual definition, albeit one elevated to the status of a fundamental axiom, Frege's notorious Axiom V. We have discussed some of the problems surrounding Axiom V in previous sections, but since the issue is explored further in the next section, I shall return to it then.

Without anticipating any of what follows, however, let us conclude the present section by noting a further problem about Frege's understanding of concepts to which the introduction of extensions offers a solution. For if concepts are not objects, and cannot be referred to by any denoting phrase, and there are no such things as concept-correlates to stand proxy for them, then how can their criteria of identity be given? Any identity statement of the form 'The concept F is ...' is regarded as logically defective. Frege's answer is to appeal to their extensions. Two concept words designate the same concept iff their extensions are the same. As Frege remarks, this constitutes an important concession to the extensionalist (*CSR*, pp. 118, 122). But he nevertheless rejects the further (extensionalist) suggestion that the *Bedeutung* of a concept word be *identified* with the extension – precisely because extensions are objects (*CSR*, pp. 118-19). So Frege's position is clear: concepts are neither extensions nor any other kind of object, but their criteria of identity can be given in terms of their extensions.

Such a conception, however, only raises problems of its own. One obvious problem is that since all concepts under which no objects fall have the same extension, namely, the null set, they turn out to be the *same concept*. According to Frege's criterion, then, '( ) is a prime number between 13 and 17', '( ) is the greatest number' and '( ) is not identical with itself', for example, all refer to the same concept. The absurdity of this view is only partially mitigated by the distinction between *Sinn* and *Bedeutung*: whilst the concept expressions may have the same *Bedeutung*, they do not possess the same *Sinn*. But as in the cases considered in the last chapter, such a distinction is too crude to do justice to all the relationships involved here.[7] There is also the assumption, without which Frege's criterion would be useless, that all genuine concepts have definite extensions; but this raises issues that are discussed further in §7.3.

7.2 Russell's Paradox

Frege spent more than two decades attempting to show that arithmetic is reducible to logic; and it was only as the end appeared finally to be in sight, with Volume I of the *Grundgesetze* already published and Volume II in press, that Russell wrote to him, on 16 June 1902, informing him of the paradox that was to prevent him from ever completing the task. After expressing his agreement with Frege on all substantial issues, Russell writes that 'I have encountered a difficulty only on one point' and proceeds to formulate his contradiction:

> Let *w* be the predicate of being a predicate which cannot be predicated of itself. Can *w* be predicated of itself? From either answer follows its contradictory. We must therefore conclude that *w* is not a predicate. Likewise, there is no class (as a whole) of those classes which, as wholes, are not members of themselves. From this I conclude that under certain circumstances a definable set does not form a whole. (*PMC*, pp. 130-1.)

In the light of what was said in the last section, it should be clear that Frege's own theory is not open to the specific objection formulated in the first half of this passage, as Frege himself notes in the reply he wrote to Russell six days later. For a predicate, according to Frege, is a function requiring 'saturation' by an object, and hence cannot have itself as argument, since a 'gap' for an object would still remain. (Cf. *PMC*, p. 132.) But Russell's alternative formulation in terms of classes indicates the general nature of the paradox, and Frege immediately recognized that his own system fell prey to an analogous contradiction. For whilst, on Frege's view, a predicate cannot be predicated of itself, a concept can be predicated of its own extension; and it was from this assumption that the problem arose. Frege wrote back:

> Your discovery of the contradiction has surprised me beyond words and, I should almost like to say, left me thunderstruck, because it has rocked the ground on which I meant to build arithmetic. It seems accordingly that the transformation of the generality of an identity into an identity of value-ranges (§9 of my *Grundgesetze*) is not always permissible, that my law V (§20, p. 36) is false, and that my explanations in §31 do not suffice to secure a *Bedeutung* for my combinations of signs in all cases. I must give some further thought to the matter. It is all the more serious as the collapse of my law V seems to undermine not only the foundations of my arithmetic but the only possible foundations of arithmetic as such. And yet, I should think, it must be possible to set up conditions for the transformation of the generality of an identity into an identity of value-ranges so as to retain the essentials of my proofs. Your discovery is at any rate a very remarkable one, and it may

perhaps lead to a great advance in logic, undesirable as it may seem at first sight. (*PMC*, p. 132.)[8]

As we saw in §5.3, Axiom V asserts the equivalence between the following two propositions:

(Va) The function *F* has the same value for each argument as the function *G*.

(Vb) The value-range of the function *F* is identical with the value-range of the function *G*.

(Va) and (Vb) embody precisely the same relationship as that involved in those contextual definitions that Frege considers, and rejects, in the *Grundlagen*; and the only reason that Axiom V is regarded as acceptable is that it lays down identity-conditions for objects that are taken as *logical* (i.e. value-ranges). As we have seen, what we have here is a generalization of one of the moves made in the central argument of the *Grundlagen*; in the intervening period, Frege provides no further justification for this move, but merely encapsulates it as a fundamental logical law.[9] As his letter to Russell suggests, Frege thought that only with this assumption could the foundations of arithmetic be secured (cf. *GG*, II, §147; quoted in §5.3 above). But to Frege's credit, he never hid his unease as to the status of Axiom V. In his preface to the *Grundgesetze*, he admitted:

A dispute can break out here, so far as I can see, only with regard to my Axiom concerning value-ranges (V), which has not yet perhaps been expressly formulated by logicians, although one has it in mind, for example, when speaking of extensions of concepts. I hold it to be purely logical. At any rate the place is hereby indicated where the decision must be made. (*GG*, I, p. vii.)

When the contradiction was eventually made known to Frege, a decade later, it was Axiom V that he immediately blamed, as his initial response to Russell indicates.[10]

But before examining exactly what was wrong with Axiom V, we need to spell out two further assumptions that are also involved. In his second letter, in reply to Russell's suggestion that formulae expressing the attribution of a concept to its own extension be simply prohibited, Frege writes:

But if you admit a sign for the extension of a concept (a class) as a *bedeutungsvoll* proper name and hence recognize a class as an object, then the class itself must either fall under the concept or not; *tertium non datur*. (*PMC*, p. 135.)

The two assumptions here may be formulated as follows:

(ECO) Extensions of concepts (classes) are objects.

(CDO) Every genuine concept must be defined for all objects.

These assumptions themselves can be used to generate the paradox. For what (CDO) says is that every concept divides up all objects into those that do, and those that do not, fall under it (there is no third possibility); taken with (ECO) it implies that extensions themselves can be divided into those that fall under the concept whose extension they are (e.g. the extension of '( ) is an extension'), and those that do not (e.g. the extension of '( ) is a horse').[11] But now consider the concept '( ) is the extension of a concept under which it does not fall'. Does the extension of *this* concept fall under the concept or not? If it does, then it does not, and if it does not, then it does. A contradiction emerges that threatens the basis of Frege's philosophy.[12]

But what exactly is the relationship between these two assumptions and Axiom V, and what is really responsible for the contradiction? The suppressed premiss in the above argument is the assumption that every genuine concept does indeed have an extension; and it is just this that Axiom V encodes, in laying down a criterion of identity for extensions. Axiom V, as it relates to concepts (functions that map objects onto one of the two truth-values), asserts the equivalence between the following two propositions:

(Ca)   The concept F applies to the same objects as the concept G.

(Cb)   The extension of the concept F is identical with the extension of the concept G.

Putting these together, the Axiom may be formulated as follows:

(V_c)   Whatever falls under concept F falls under concept G, and vice versa, iff the concepts F and G have the same extension.

Formally, adapting Frege's notation for extensions, '$\dot{x}\,Fx$' representing 'the extension of the concept F', this may be formalized thus:

(V^*) $(\forall x)\,(Fx \leftrightarrow Gx) \leftrightarrow \dot{x}\,Fx = \dot{x}\,Gx.$

As Frege understands this, 'Fx' and 'Gx' must possess a *Bedeutung* (a truth-value) for all values of x, which is to say that the two concepts F and G must be defined for all objects, and '$\dot{x}\,Fx$' and '$\dot{x}\,Gx$' are proper names, and hence the objects to which they refer, i.e. extensions, are legitimate arguments for the concepts of which they are the extensions. Indeed, since Axiom V has just the form of those contextual definitions that Frege considers in the *Grundlagen*, its purpose is clearly to legitimize the introduction of extensions as logical objects. The two assumptions involved here are precisely (CDO) and (ECO). It is not surprising, then, that Frege himself should have laid the blame for the contradiction on Axiom V, which for him embodies just those assumptions.

But can Axiom V be interpreted, in its bare schematic form, in such a way as to preserve it whilst repudiating one or both of the underlying assumptions? To answer this, let us consider how the paradox itself can be avoided. One response is to reject, or at least qualify, (ECO). Abandoning it altogether is clearly incompatible with Frege's objectivism. As we have seen, numbers are regarded as objects, and are defined as extensions of concepts. If extensions were not themselves objects, then Frege's logicist project would collapse.[13] However, in his Appendix (*Nachwort*) to Volume II of the *Grundgesetze*, hastily written whilst the book was in press, where he attempts to respond to Russell's paradox, Frege does consider the possibility that extensions are *improper objects*, objects to which the law of excluded middle does not apply (i.e. objects for which '*Fa* ∨ ¬*Fa*' is not a universal truth). But he quickly dismisses this suggestion because of the complexity of the system that would result – for every first-level function, it would have to be specified whether proper objects, improper objects or both were admissible as either argument or value. There would thus be nine types (*Arten*) of first-level functions, to which there would correspond nine types of value-ranges, that is, of improper objects, between which logical distinctions would have to be drawn:

> Classes of proper objects would have to be distinguished from classes of classes of proper objects; extensions of relations holding between proper objects would have to be distinguished from classes of proper objects, and from classes of extensions of relations holding between proper objects; and so on. We should thus get an incalculable multiplicity of types; and in general objects belonging to different types could not occur as arguments of the same function. But it appears extraordinarily difficult to set up a complete system of rules for deciding which objects are allowable arguments of which functions. (*FRP*, p. 216.)

What Frege is rejecting here is just such a theory of types as Russell was to develop in response to the paradox, and it did indeed prove complex and in the end only workable with the addition of axioms whose status as logical truths was no less problematic than that of Axiom V.[14]

Frege's own response was to modify (CDO):

> (CDO′) Every genuine concept must be defined for all objects except the extension of that concept.

Given that the contradiction arose from considering extensions that fall under the concept whose extension they are, simply outlawing the applicability of concepts to their own extensions is the obvious move to make. The resulting restriction of (V_c) may be formulated thus:

> (V_c') Whatever falls under concept F, except its own extension, falls under concept G, and vice versa, iff the concepts F and G have the same extension. (Cf. *FRP*, p. 223; *PMC*, p. 150.)

To examine this response in more detail, let us split (V_c') up into its two component conditionals:

(V$_c$'α) If whatever falls under concept *F*, except its own extension, falls under concept *G*, and vice versa, then the concepts *F* and *G* have the same extension.

(V$_c$'β) If two concepts *F* and *G* have the same extension, then whatever falls under one, except its own extension, falls under the other.

Now as far as (V$_c$'α) is concerned, it is not, in fact, necessary to make the qualification that it embodies. For, taking the limiting case in which the concept *F* and the concept *G* are one and the same, and considering the concept that generates the paradox, it is not true that if the extension of the concept '( )' is the extension of a concept under which it does not fall' falls under the concept (viz. *F*), then it falls under the concept (viz. *G*). The antecedent of the original conditional – as expressed by (V$_c$'α) without the qualification – is therefore false, so that the whole conditional has not itself been rendered false (and if *F* and *G* are the very same concept, then the consequent is in any case true). So (V$_c$'α) can be returned to its original form:

(V$_c$α) If whatever falls under concept *F* falls under concept *G*, and vice versa, then the concepts *F* and *G* have the same extension.

All that (V$_c$α) states is a *sufficient* condition for the identity of extensions: it leaves open the possibility that two concepts may have the same extension even if there is some object that falls under one but not the other. In the paradoxical case, the antecedent of (V$_c$α) is simply false; there is no situation in which there is a true antecedent and a false consequent, so that (V$_c$α) remains valid. (Cf. *FRP*, pp. 219, 223; *PMC*, p. 150.)

As far as (V$_c$'β) is concerned, however, the qualification is crucial. For compare it with the original conditional:

(V$_c$β) If two concepts *F* and *G* have the same extension, then whatever falls under one falls under the other.

Russell's paradox precisely shows that two concepts *F* and *G* can have the same extension, as they clearly do in the limiting case where *F* and *G* are one and the same, without it being true that anything that falls under the concept *F* falls under the concept *G* – where the concept that is taken is the concept '( )' is the extension of a concept under which it does not fall'. In the paradoxical case, in other words, the antecedent of (V$_c$β) is true, and the consequent false, so that the conditional itself is invalidated. At the very least, then, (V$_c$β) requires modification to (V$_c$'β).

Unfortunately, however, Frege's modified axiom too has been found to generate a contradiction; and I shall indicate just why this was inevitable shortly. But aside from the inconsistency, it is clear that the modification violates Frege's own requirement on definitions, as Frege himself recognizes (*FRP*, p. 223). For, as we have already noted, the main purpose of Axiom V was to legitimize the introduction of extensions, by laying down a criterion of identity. But, returning to ($V_c{}'$), to say that two concepts have the same extension iff whatever falls under one, *except its own extension*, falls under the other, is to presuppose on the latter side of the biconditional precisely what it was the aim of the axiom to define. Regardless of whether, at the technical level, Frege ever realized that a new contradiction was derivable, then, it is not surprising that he should have abandoned further work on his logicist project. Value-ranges, of which extensions of concepts were a special category, could no longer be introduced in a logically impeccable way.

Of course, it would still have been possible for Frege to go back to his original contextual definition of number; but for him, this would have entailed solving the Caesar problem, which the appeal to Axiom V had been intended to circumvent. According to Frege, a contextual definition only provides us with a way of distinguishing an object given to us as of a certain kind from another object given to us as of the same kind: it provides a merely local rather than global criterion of identity. But as we saw in §6.4, the underlying assumption here is of an homogeneous universal domain, a domain of all objects, neither partitioned into sub-domains nor arranged in any kind of hierarchy. Since, for Frege, numbers were already conceived as objects, and hence as members of the universal domain, any adequate definition must serve to distinguish them from all other members of the domain.

But the assumption that there is a universal domain, the domain of *all objects* (concrete as well as abstract), can be shown, very simply, to be incoherent. We mentioned in §3.1 Cantor's proof that the set of all subsets of a given set is larger than the original set, since a set of n members has 2^n subsets (taken as including both itself and the null set) and $2^n > n$, for all n (including where n is infinite). A set of two objects a and b, for example, has $2^2 = 4$ subsets: $\emptyset$, $\{a\}$, $\{b\}$, $\{a, b\}$; and a set of three objects a, b and c has $2^3 = 8$ subsets: $\emptyset$, $\{a\}$, $\{b\}$, $\{c\}$, $\{a, b\}$, $\{a, c\}$, $\{b, c\}$, $\{a, b, c\}$. But now consider the set of *all objects*. There are more subsets of this set than there are members of the set itself; so that if sets are themselves regarded as objects, then we clearly arrive at the contradiction that there are more objects (viz. subsets) than there are objects (viz. members).

This contradiction led Russell to deny that sets (classes) were proper objects at all; though it was only when his theory of descriptions had been developed that he felt justified in pursuing this line, removing the major motivation for construing them realistically.[15] As Russell himself remarked, the central point of his theory of descriptions was that 'a phrase may contribute to the meaning of a sentence without having any meaning at all in isolation' (*MPD*, p. 64). What this suggested was that class names, like definite descriptions, might also contribute to the meaning of sentences without necessarily denoting anything themselves. Classes, he came to believe, were 'logical fictions'.[16] Such a view entails a modification of (ECO) along just the lines that Frege repudiated – regarding extensions, or classes, as *improper objects*. The result was as Frege feared – a complex theory, involving a multiplicity of stratifications – but it was a result that Russell accepted, and attempted to work out in full, with Whitehead, in *Principia Mathematica*.

The first sketch of Russell's 'theory of types' was made very shortly after his discovery of the paradox, in Appendix B of *The Principles of Mathematics*, which was completed in late 1902. The two essential points were, firstly, that every propositional function $\varphi(x)$ possesses a 'range of significance, i.e. a range within which x must lie if $\varphi(x)$ is to be a proposition at all, whether true or false'; and secondly, that 'ranges of significance form *types*, i.e. if x belongs to the range of significance of $\varphi(x)$, then there is a class of objects, the *type* of x, all of which must also belong to the range of significance of $\varphi(x)$, however φ may be varied' (*POM*, p. 523). The result is a *hierarchy of types* – individuals (objects which are not themselves 'ranges'; this is the lowest type), classes (or 'ranges') of individuals, classes of classes of individuals, and so on – such that anything that can be meaningfully asserted of any member of one type cannot, in general, be meaningfully asserted of that type itself, or of any member of any higher type (cf. *POM*, pp. 523-4). Talk of classes which are members of themselves is thus ruled out, thereby blocking the formation of Russell's paradox.

Although the key elements of Russell's 'simple theory of types' were already present in *The Principles of Mathematics*, however, his early version failed to prevent related contradictions arising, as he recognized at the time (*POM*, pp. 527-8); and it eventually proved necessary to introduce not only a hierarchy of *types*, but also a hierarchy of *orders*, producing further stratification *within* types. But the details of what became Russell's 'ramified theory of types' need not concern us here.[17] The two crucial points are those we have just noted, the first of which involves a modification of (CDO) and the second of which involves a modification of (ECO). Cantor's paradox showed the naivety of assuming that extensions of concepts (sets or classes) could be unproblematically regarded as on the same level as the objects that fall under the concepts (the members of the sets or classes). It is not surprising, then, that even Frege's revised version of Axiom V should still have generated a contradiction; and in fact it has been shown that Frege's amended theory is inconsistent in any domain of two or more objects.[18] Since at the very beginning of the *Grundgesetze*, the True and the False are introduced as objects of the domain, Frege's system is undermined at a fundamental level.[19]

(ECO) can only be maintained, in a modified form, within some kind of type theory. Extensions can only be regarded as objects, albeit 'improper' objects, if they are distinguished from the 'proper' objects that fall under them. There is no such thing as the domain of *all objects* ('proper' as well as 'improper'): the objects that fall under a given concept should be seen as comprising a domain distinct from the domain that includes the extension of that concept. Axiom V, since it has the form of a contextual definition that in normal situations is legitimate (e.g. defining the direction of a line in terms of parallelism), can also be regarded as legitimate so long as it is understood that the contextual definition is introducing us to a *new* set of abstract objects, not objects that are already there in the domain comprising the referents of the terms utilized in the *definiens*. But to say, along with Russell, that there are distinct *types* of objects is to admit that concepts do not need to be defined for all objects, and this implies the abandonment of (CDO) too in its unqualified form. I explore further the issues involved here in the next section.

7.3 Vagueness

The assumption that every genuine concept must be defined for all objects – (CDO) – was fundamental to Frege's thought. As we saw in §3.4, it underlay Frege's Pythagorean belief that the realm of arithmetic is as wide as that of conceptual thought. If genuine thought requires sharply defined (sortal) concepts, implying a determinate number of objects falling under each concept, then it seems natural to suppose that enumerability is part of the essence of conceptual thought and hence is a purely logical matter. Every concept has a definite extension, in other words, to which a number is assigned. As Frege wrote in the letter from which we quoted, 'The only barrier to enumerability is to be found in the imperfection of concepts. Bald people for example cannot be enumerated as long as the concept of baldness is not defined so precisely that for any individual there can be no doubt whether he falls under it.' (*PMC*, p. 100.) The concept *bald* is a paradigm case of a *vague* concept; so that Frege's assumption amounts to a repudiation of vagueness. Whatever the deficiencies of ordinary language, vagueness is to be avoided in a logical language, a language that faithfully reflects objective thought.

If (CDO) is accepted, then not only do we have a motivation for Frege's logicism and a crucial element in his vision of an ideal language, but we also have an immediate solution to the paradox discussed in §7.1. The following proposition might seem to us to be an obvious tautology:

(CHC) The concept *horse* is a concept.

According to Frege, however, 'The concept *horse*' picks out an *object*, not a concept, so that (CHC) is strictly speaking *false*. But given (CDO), what we are trying to say can now be better expressed thus:

(CHC′) Everything is either a horse or not a horse.

This has a precise formalization (making clear its tautological nature):

(CHC*) $(\forall x)\,(Hx \vee \neg Hx)$.

If the essence of a concept is to divide up all objects in the domain into those that do and those that do not fall under it, then to say (illegitimately, by Frege's lights) that a certain concept is a concept is just to say that such a division is effected. Even if we admit that Russell's paradox shows that (CDO) cannot be maintained as it stands, the requirement that a concept be defined merely for a certain *type* of object is enough to retain the essential solution to the paradox of the concept *horse* – as long as the relevant restrictions are made.[20]

But do all concepts – concepts, at any rate, that we would normally regard as contributing to the formation of genuine thoughts – divide up the members of some appropriate domain exhaustively into two classes, comprising those that fall under the concept and those that do not? The phenomenon of *vagueness* suggests otherwise. A concept F is *vague* if there is some value of 'x', in the domain over which 'x' ranges, for which 'Fx' lacks a truth-value. There are some objects, in other words, which seem neither to fall nor not to fall under a vague concept. Of course, one could simply deny that such concepts are genuine concepts at all. But not only is vagueness pervasive, and continually re-emerges when any particular vague concept is made more precise, threatening to shrink the realm of genuine thought to nothing; but there also seem to be cases where the use of a vague concept expresses something that clearly does have a truth-value, and hence, according to Frege, should be seen as expressing a *thought* (which *refers to* the truth-value). Saying of a man X with no hair at all that he is bald, for example, is surely true, regardless of whether there are other men for whom it is neither obviously true nor obviously false. However, with regard to this last point, a Fregean could insist that the statement 'X is bald' is still vague, since it does not specify *how bald X* is. If it expresses a thought, then the thought that is expressed (in this context) is more accurately expressed by 'X has no hair at all', which is far less vague, and only reinforces the point that the concept of baldness is vague, and that any thought involving it requires a more precise formulation.

There is a deeper problem here, though, which lends firmer support to the Fregean view that vague concepts should be banned from logic. For there is a familiar argument that starts from such an apparently obvious truth as that an absolutely hairless man is bald, but ends up with such an obvious non-truth as that a man with a full head of hair is also bald. What is involved here is the so-called *Sorites paradox* – named after its traditional formulation as the paradox of the heap. We start by agreeing on what *definitely* constitutes, say, a heap of beans:

(1,000) 1,000 beans (piled up together) constitute a heap of beans.[21]

We then endorse what has been called the *principle of tolerance*, which we might roughly characterize as the (apparent) tautology that insignificant differences are indeed insignificant.[22] In this case it could be expressed in the form of a conditional:

(NB) If n beans constitute a heap of beans, then $n - 1$ beans constitute a heap of beans.

From (1,000) and (NB) we can then infer the following:

(999) 999 beans constitute a heap of beans.

But if 999 beans constitute a heap, then so too do 998 beans, and so on, all the way down to 1 bean and even 0 beans; which is clearly absurd.

It was just this paradox that Frege recognized in the *Begriffsschrift*, in offering his logical analysis of mathematical induction. As he put it there, what this shows is that if f is the procedure of removing one bean, then the property of being a heap cannot be hereditary in the f-series.[23] Frege drew from this the conclusion that logic (understood as concerned with the movement from truths to truths) cannot apply to vague concepts – or rather, since logic was seen as the general science of conceptual thought, and in stricter accordance with his mature doctrines, vague concepts cannot really be regarded as concepts at all. But is such a conclusion inevitable, and if there are other options in response to the paradox, why did Frege himself not take them?

Since the whole argument involved agreeing on a starting point (we could have taken a million beans as definitely constituting a heap, if we had found that more unobjectionable), we cannot reject the initial premiss. Nor, for a similar reason, can we accept the conclusion – one bean is patently not a heap of beans. As for the reasoning involved, this simply uses (in successive applications) the fundamental logical rule of *modus ponens*, i.e. the rule that entitles us to infer 'Q' from 'P' and 'If P, then Q'. Since to reject this would be to abandon logic altogether, this too is an unacceptable response – and it is certainly not one that Frege himself would have endorsed.[24] So we are simply left with rejecting the principle of tolerance.

Now it is certainly true that (NB) would be invalidated if the concept of a heap were to be *sharpened*, i.e. specified in such a way that there is a sharp dividing line between being a heap and not being a heap.[25] We might, for example, introduce a new concept defined thus:

(13PH) A collection of beans is a *thirteenplusheap* if it contains 13 or more beans.

Interpreting 'heap' in (NB) as 'thirteenplusheap' clearly *falsifies* the conditional – where n is 13, we have a true antecedent and a false consequent; and (NB) will be invalidated whatever sharpening we effect, i.e. whatever new *nplusheap* concept we define. But whilst it is always open to us to *replace* a vague concept by a sharply defined one, this only evades rather than solves the paradox. It makes (NB) false *by fiat*, and whatever dividing line is specified seems arbitrary.

The Fregean response is subtly different. (NB) is not taken to be *false* –

which would indeed imply that there is some number n such that n beans constitute a heap, but $n - 1$ beans do not. The concept of a heap is vague just because there are some collections of beans for which it is neither true that they constitute a heap, nor true that they do not: for some values of n, 'n beans constitute a heap' *lacks* a truth-value, which means that (NB) as a whole lacks a truth-value. The very fact that a concept is vague means that the principle of tolerance in its relevant form cannot itself be specified.

As to the plausibility of the principle, this rests on its legitimacy in all those *non-penumbral* contexts in which there is no reasonable doubt as to whether the relevant concept applies or not.[26] But should we regard the principle as *true* in non-penumbral contexts? This brings us back to the question as to whether there are some cases where 'X is bald', say, can be taken as definitely true – for example, in the case where X has no hair at all. What is wrong with allowing that propositions involving the use of vague concepts do have truth-values in certain contexts? Indeed, the message of the last section seemed to be that concepts are only applicable within a 'range of significance': to suppose that they must be defined for all objects generates contradiction. We have seen that Frege was adamant that the domain of logic was the domain of *all* objects, without pre-partitioning into sorts. But does he provide any justification for this?

The issue is confronted most explicitly in §§56-65 of Volume II of the *Grundgesetze*, where Frege discusses the first of the two principles of definition which he feels mathematicians violate most frequently – the *principle of completeness* (*Grundsatz der Vollständigkeit*).[27]

A definition of a concept (of a possible predicate) must be complete; it must unambiguously determine, as regards any object, whether or not it falls under the concept (whether or not the predicate is truly ascribable to it). Thus there must not be any object as regards which the definition leaves in doubt whether it falls under the concept; though for us men, with our defective knowledge, the question may not always be decidable. We may express this metaphorically as follows: the concept must have a sharp boundary .... [Just as an area without a sharp boundary is not really an area,] a concept that is not sharply defined is wrongly termed a concept. Such quasi-conceptual constructions cannot be recognized as concepts by logic; it is impossible to lay down precise laws for them. The law of excluded middle is really just another form of the requirement that the concept should have a sharp boundary. Any object Δ that you choose to take either falls under the concept Φ or does not fall under it; *tertium non datur*. (*GG*, II, §56/ *FDI*, p. 139.)

The next few sections make clear Frege's main target – *piecemeal definition*, which he refers to as 'the mathematicians' favourite procedure' (§57). One starts, for example, by defining addition for the integers, and then redefines it for the rational numbers, the real numbers, and so on. This might be acceptable if every extended system is set up from scratch each time, but, according to Frege, most mathematicians do not appreciate the need for this, and use the original definitions in formulating the redefinitions in the wider domain (cf. §58). Frege writes: 'if the first definition is already complete and has drawn sharp boundaries, then either the second definition draws the same boundaries – and then it must be rejected, because its content ought to be proved as a theorem [i.e. it must be shown that it does draw the same boundaries] – or it draws different ones – and then it contradicts the first one'. And if the second definition is not ruled out in either of these ways, then 'that is possible only because the first one is incomplete and has left the concept unfinished, i.e. in a condition in which it may not be employed at all – in particular, not for definitions'. (§58/ *FDI*, p. 142.)

What we have here is less an argument than an assertion made twice. If a definition is complete, then there is no need for any subsequent redefinition; and (contrapositively) if there *is* such a need, then the original definition is incomplete.[28] But why is a definition of a concept incomplete if its application is explicitly restricted? Frege thinks that this leaves theorems themselves incomplete:

> Piecemeal definition likewise makes the status of theorems uncertain. If, e.g., the words 'square root of 9' have been defined with a restriction to the domain of positive integers, then we can prove, e.g., the proposition that there is only one square root of 9; but this is at once overthrown when we extend our treatment to negative numbers and supplement the definition accordingly. But who can tell if we have now reached a definitive proposition? Who can tell but that we may see ourselves driven to recognize four square roots of 9? How are we really going to tell that there are no more than two square roots of –1? So long as we have no final and complete definitions, it is impossible .... If we have no final definitions we likewise have no final theorems. We never emerge from incompleteness and vagueness. (*GG*, II, §61/ *FDI*, pp. 144-5.)

This is an extraordinary argument. For surely, if the relevant restrictions are stated, then there may be nothing at all incomplete or vague about a proposition. Take Frege's example:

($\sqrt{9}$) There is only one square root of 9.

Without specifying the domain, this does indeed lack a truth-value. But, appropriately indexed, the following proposition seems definitively true:

($\sqrt{9}_n$) Within the natural number system, there is only one square root of 9.

As Frege understands this, however, such a proposition involves implicit quantification over the universal domain; and this means, he thinks, that the concept 'square root of 9' needs to be defined for the whole domain. If ($\sqrt{9}_n$) is read as 'There is one and only one natural number that is the square root of 9', then a possible formalization of it would be as follows, 'Nx' representing 'x is a natural number' and 'Sx' representing 'x is a square root of 9':

$$(\sqrt{9}_n{}^*) \quad (\exists x)\,[(Nx \,\&\, Sx) \,\&\, (\forall y)\,((Ny \,\&\, Sy) \to x = y)].$$

The quantifiers here range over more than just the domain of natural numbers. To say 'For all y, *if* y is a natural number ...' presupposes that y could be something *other* than a natural number. Both 'Ny' and 'Sy' must therefore be defined for all objects.

But why can we not simply take as our domain the domain of natural numbers? This would yield a simpler formalization:

$$(\sqrt{9}^*) \quad (\exists x)\,[Sx \,\&\, (\forall y)\,(Sy \to x = y)].$$

At the root of Frege's dissatisfaction with this lies what we called in §2.4 his *decontextualism*. In logic, nothing must be left to guessing, and any restriction to a subdomain is a presupposition that requires representation. $(\sqrt{9}_n{}^*)$, then, is the preferable formalization; and this forces us to quantify over the whole domain. This comes out clearly in the final argument that Frege offers:

> Let us suppose for once that the concept *number* has been sharply defined; let it be laid down that italic letters are to indicate only numbers; and let the sign of addition be defined only for numbers. Then in the proposition '$a + b = b + a$' we must mentally add the conditions that a and b are numbers; and these conditions, not being expressed, are easily forgotten. But let us deliberately not forget them for once! By a well-known law of logic, the proposition
> 'if a is a number and b is a number then $a + b = b + a$'
> can be transformed into the proposition
> 'if $a + b$ is not equal to $b + a$, and a is a number, then b is not a number'
> and here it is impossible to maintain the restriction to the domain of numbers. The force of the situation works irresistibly towards the breaking down of such restrictions. But in this case our antecedent clause
> 'if $a + b$ is not equal to $b + a$'
> is senseless, assuming that the sign of addition has not been completely defined. (*GG*, II, §65/ *FDI*, pp. 149-50.)

To see what is wrong with this, consider how a similar argument might be run in relation to existential presuppositions. Take the following proposition:

(MIE) Moses led the Israelites out of Egypt.

According to Frege, this can only be true if Moses actually existed. So, presumably, the proposition ought really to be expressed as follows:

(MIE') If Moses existed, then he led the Israelites out of Egypt.

But, by a well-known law of logic, we can transform this into its contrapositive:

(MIE") If Moses did not lead the Israelites out of Egypt, then he did not exist.

But now it appears impossible to restrict the domain to *actual existents* (past or present): we seem forced to widen it to include *possible existents* too (fictional as well as real objects).[29]

Frege himself would clearly have rejected this particular version of the argument. As we saw in §2.4, he was adamant that 'The rules of logic always presuppose that the words we use are not empty' (*DPE*, p. 60). But if we can allow that *existential presuppositions* do not need to be formulated within the logical system itself, then there seems to be nothing intrinsically wrong with admitting *sortal presuppositions*. Indeed, since Frege's assumption of a universal domain, without sortal partitioning, led him into contradiction, there is good reason to restrict the application of a concept to a certain 'range of significance'.

Returning to the problem of vagueness, then, we might take this idea one step further. The fact that there are some values of 'X' for which 'X is bald' lacks a truth-value does not imply that no true statement can be made using this sentence in *non-penumbral* cases. 'X is bald', said of a man with no hair at all, for example, is quite definitely true. The sentence uttered on its own may not tell us *how bald* the man is; but then nor does 'X has between 0 and 100 hairs on his head' tell us *how many hairs X has*, although it nonetheless has a truth-value on any given occasion.[30] The Sorites paradox itself can be blocked if the principle of tolerance in its general form is rejected as truth-valueless; but it can still be maintained that any particular statement ascribing a vague concept to an object in a non-penumbral context is either true or false, so that the law of excluded middle is still taken as governing the domain of thoughts.

Of course, this strategy only works if an assurance can be given that a non-penumbral case is indeed non-penumbral. But this too can be allowed to be gleaned from the context. The fact that we cannot say exactly where the line between the penumbral and non-penumbral cases should be drawn is no reason to deny that we may be perfectly clear, on a particular occasion, as to what kind of case it is.[31] What goes wrong in Sorites arguments is that the arguments are run in a completely decontextualized form – in a form that is oblivious to all those presuppositions that condition the meaning of any individual statement. However, whilst it is essential to recognize the importance of context in determining what thought is expressed on a given occasion and hence what truth-value the relevant proposition possesses, this is not to say that the relationship between the context and any thought expressed is readily amenable to theoretical explanation, as we shall see in the next section.

7.4 Demonstratives and Indexicality

The problem that *demonstratives* pose for Frege's theory of *Sinn* and *Bedeutung* appears at first sight to be rather different from the problem raised by proper names that we discussed in the last chapter. Here the focus seems to be not so much on expressions that arguably have senses without referents as on expressions that arguably have referents without senses. But as we shall see, the underlying issue turns out to be the same – the problem of specifying just what the senses of such expressions are. Demonstratives – or *indexicals* as they are also called – are expressions such as 'I', 'you', 'here', 'there', 'now', 'then', 'this' or 'that', whose reference depends systematically on the context. 'Gottlob Frege' or 'The author of the *Begriffsschrift*' as used by me today is likely to refer to the same person as 'Gottlob Frege' or 'The author of the *Begriffsschrift*' as used by you tomorrow, but the referent of 'I' depends on *who* is using the word, and the referent of 'today' depends on *when* the word is used.[32] An understanding of the *context* of utterance is thus essential in determining the truth-value of any sentence using a demonstrative; and it is this context-dependence that constitutes the phenomenon of indexicality. But if the *referent* of a demonstrative varies according to the context, then must not its *sense* vary also? Indeed, if senses are *modes of presentation* of referents, then not only will they vary whenever the referents vary, but since any referent may have indefinitely many senses associated with it, they may also vary even when the referent remains constant – in the extreme case, a different sense being associated with a demonstrative on each occasion of use. 'There', for example, might be used on two different occasions to refer to the same place, but since the place may well be 'presented' in two different ways (perceived, say, from two different directions), however slight this difference might be, the senses attached to the term will arguably themselves be different. The problem of variability which Frege raised in relation to the senses of proper names seems even more pervasive in the case of demonstratives. If our use of proper names reveals a defect in ordinary language, then the phenomenon of indexicality indicates an even greater deficiency, since in vast areas of our discourse, our linguistic expressions are spatially and temporally indexed.

Consider a simple sentence involving the demonstrative 'today':

(TS)   Today is sunny.

Imagine uttering this sentence first on Monday and then on Tuesday – expressing, on Frege's view, two different *thoughts*. Whether the thought expressed on one of these days is *true* will depend on whether it is sunny on that particular day, and this is clearly consistent with Frege's principle (PDB). The truth-value (*Bedeutung*) of the sentence as uttered on a particular occasion is dependent on *which day* 'today' refers to (and also, of course, on whether that object falls under the concept *sunny*). But as we saw in the last chapter, Frege adopted an analogous principle concerning sense. The sense of (TS) as uttered on a particular day – the *thought* expressed – is dependent on the senses of its two components, 'today' and '( ) is sunny'. So 'today' must clearly *have* a sense on each occasion, since otherwise the whole sentence would lack a sense, but since we can assume that the sense of '( ) is sunny' remains the same (the same concept being applied in the same way), the sense of 'today' as used on Monday and the sense of 'today' as used on Tuesday must differ.

Yet at the purely *linguistic* level, what I understand in uttering 'Today is sunny' is the same on both days: there is clearly some element of the meaning of 'today' that remains constant. This constant feature in our use of a demonstrative has been termed its *character* or *role*;[33] and to make explicit the level at which this operates, I shall call this its *linguistic role*. I understand the linguistic role of a demonstrative if I understand the *rule* that takes me from the context of utterance to the object denoted. I understand the linguistic role of 'today', for example, if I understand that the correct use of the term refers to the day on which it is uttered, and I understand the linguistic role of 'I' if I understand that it refers to whoever utters it. Now it is clearly not possible for a Fregean to identify the sense of a demonstrative with its linguistic role – as we have just seen, if the thoughts expressed by a sentence involving a demonstrative are different on different occasions, then the demonstrative itself must have a different sense on each occasion; yet its linguistic role remains the same. So what *is* the sense of 'today' as uttered on a particular occasion?

For a Fregean, the answer must lie in finding a suitable way of conceiving of the day to which one refers when using the word 'today'. Just as in the case of names, the natural suggestion is to offer some definite description by means of which to 'present' the referent in the appropriate way. One way of conceiving of today, for example, might be in terms of its *date*. When I utter (TS) today, what I might mean might be expressed as follows:

(DS) Tuesday 14 June 1994 is sunny.

But it is clearly possible to think that today is sunny without knowing what date it is or even what day of the week it is. And, on the assumption that the 'is' in (DS) is understood in a 'timeless' sense, it is clearly possible to grasp the thought expressed by (DS) without knowing that that day happens to be today.[34] One might go further here. Not only can (TS) be held to be true without (DS) being held to be true, by the same person on the day in question, but it is also possible to imagine (DS) being held to be true without (TS) being held to be true, by the same person on the day in question.[35] Suppose that on Sunday 12 June I am informed by a reliable weather forecaster that the next three days will be sunny; but that on Monday 13 June I get beaten unconscious by some students who hated the examination questions I set them on Frege, and that I wake up on Tuesday 14 June in a darkened room in hospital. I remember the weather forecast, so still believe the (timeless) truth expressed by (DS), but since my black eyes and the darkened room impair my sight, I do not hold that the thought expressed by (TS) is true, wrongly concluding, say, that I must have been unconscious for several days. If such cases are possible, then even if today *is* Tuesday 14 June 1994, the sense of 'today' cannot be identified with the sense of 'Tuesday 14 June 1994'. Since the same will apply to any such attempt to explain the sense of 'today' by means of a definite description, it might seem that there is no mode of presentation to which we can appeal in specifying that sense.

What we have here is just an instance of a general dilemma concerning indexicals. Consider any attempt to explicate the sense of an indexical, as used on a particular occasion, by means of a definite description that 'cashes out' that indexical (in the way that 'Tuesday 14 June 1994' cashes out 'today'). As we have just illustrated, it is possible to hold that a sentence involving the indexical is true whilst not holding that the corresponding sentence involving the definite description is true, and vice versa. In other words, I can believe that the referent of a definite description has a certain property, without believing that it is *this* object – *this* person (me), *this* place (here), or *this* day (today), say – that has that property; and I can conceive of *this* object having a certain property without, for any given definite description, conceiving of the object under that description.[36] Whatever description is offered as a way of conceiving of today, then, I still need to know that it applies to *today*, and we are no further forward in understanding what it is to grasp the sense of 'today'. It is this dilemma that John Perry (1979) has called *the problem of the essential indexical*. To take Perry's example, I may follow a trail of sugar round one of the aisles of a supermarket trying to stop the shopper whose bag has split; but it is only when I realize that *I* am causing the mess, as the trail gets thicker each time round, that I actually check the bag in my own trolley. There is no way of expressing that realization – the belief that explains my action (checking my own bag) – in any 'cashed out' form. I do, of course, believe at the start that the referent of the definite description 'shopper with a split bag of sugar' is responsible for the mess, but it is only when I realize that that referent is *me* that I stop my own trolley. The use of the indexical here is *essential* in characterizing that realization.[37]

But if all this is right, then it would seem that we have no option, unless we are going to deny that indexicals have senses at all (which, for Frege, would be to deny that sentences involving them express thoughts), but to treat the sense of any indexical, as used on a particular occasion, as primitive and irreducible. On this view, grasping the sense of 'today' simply consists in thinking of today *as* today, and no further explanation is possible. But if we take this line, we are in danger of a proliferation of *once-only senses*. Let us call the way of thinking of today *as* today a *today-sense*, which contributes to the formation of *today-thoughts* such as that expressed by (TS). Is the today-sense grasped today, in uttering (TS), the same as the today-sense grasped yesterday, in uttering (TS), i.e. do we think the same thing in using the term 'today' on each day? Since, according to Frege, wherever there is a different referent, there must be a different sense, the today-senses (as grasped on each day) must all be *different*. If this is so, and any today-sense is primitive and irreducible, then once I have thought of today as today, there is no way that I can ever, on any subsequent day, have *that* thought again. Not only are such thoughts primitive and irreducible, therefore, they are also *temporally isolated*: we have no access to them at any other time.

Just how acute the problem becomes can be seen if we consider not (TS) but the following:

(NS) It is sunny now. (Now is sunny.)

When I utter (NS) now I express a different thought from that expressed when I uttered (NS) a few moments ago. If the sense of 'now', as used on a particular occasion, is primitive and irreducible, then there are as many different thoughts expressible by means of (NS) as there are moments in time, and each thought can only be grasped at its corresponding moment. If, in thinking that it is sunny now, I am presented with this moment in a unique way, then that thought is lost for ever as the next moment arrives. As a final example, consider a sentence involving all three primary indexicals:

(IHN) I am here now.

If the argument just given applies equally to other indexicals, then (IHN) will express different thoughts for every different person at every different point in space at every different moment in time, i.e. it will express a different thought on each occasion of use.

That this argument was definitely not endorsed by Frege, at least in the case of spatial and temporal indexicals, is made clear in his late paper 'Der Gedanke' ('Thoughts'), which contains his only discussion of the problem of indexicality. Frege writes:

> If someone wants to say today what he expressed yesterday using the word 'today', he will replace this word with 'yesterday'. Although the thought is the same its verbal expression must be different in order that the change of sense which would otherwise be effected by the differing times of utterance may be cancelled out. The case is the same with words like 'here' and 'there'. In all such cases the mere wording, as it can be preserved in writing, is not the complete expression of the thought; the knowledge of certain conditions accompanying the utterance, which are used as means of expressing the thought, is needed for us to grasp the thought correctly. Pointing the finger, hand gestures, glances may belong here too. (*T*, p. 358.)

Just as in his early work Frege argued that the same 'content' can be represented by more than one sentence, so too in his mature and late work he emphasized that the same thought can be expressed in many different ways. According to Frege, then, I can indeed grasp, on a different day, just that thought I express today in saying 'Today is sunny'. The point is simply that I will need to change the indexical I use, as well as the tense of the verb, in order to do so. Tomorrow, for example, I will have to utter the following sentence:

(Y₁S)   Yesterday was sunny.

Clearly, in rejecting the conception of *once-only senses*, (Y₁S) is the obvious sentence to use for re-expressing tomorrow the thought grasped today in uttering (TS).

But is this strategy not also ruled out by the argument given above in repudiating the attempt to identify the sense of an indexical with the sense of some definite description? Surely it is possible to hold today that today is sunny without believing tomorrow the thought expressed by uttering (Y₁S) tomorrow? I may simply forget what the weather was like, or, after a night spent dreaming of thunderstorms, be under the misapprehension that it rained all day. However, the argument as originally presented was based on the possibility of holding true one but not the other of the two relevant sentences (the sentence involving the indexical and the sentence involving the definite description) *at one and the same time*. This condition is clearly not met in the present case, so the argument is inapplicable. To appreciate the relevance of this condition, we need only note that the fact that 'Gottlob Frege was a great philosopher' could be held to be false today but true tomorrow (someone goes away and reads some of his work) does not show that the sense of 'Gottlob Frege' is not the same as the sense of 'Gottlob Frege'! I shall, however, return to the issue of the criterion for sameness of thought in §8.1.

The difference between the two cases is that in the original case the indexical is replaced by a definite description, which is envisaged as 'cashing out' the indexical, whilst in the present case the indexical is replaced by *another* indexical, which is simply seen as the minimum that is required if there is to be continued access to the thought involved. As Gareth Evans has put it, in commenting on the passage from 'Der Gedanke' just quoted, 'Frege's idea is that being in the same epistemic state may require different things of us at different times; the changing circumstances force us to change in order to keep hold of a constant reference and a constant thought – we must run to keep still' (1981: p. 85). Evans refers to the indexical thoughts here as *dynamic* thoughts, and writes: 'the *way of thinking of an object* to which the general Fregean conception of sense directs us is, in the case of a dynamic Fregean thought, a *way of keeping track of an object*' (1981: p. 87). Just as our ability to think about a moving object depends on our ability to *keep track* of the object through space, so too our ability to think about today depends on our ability to keep track of it through time.[38] The key thing about this tracking process, we can then add, is that it need never leave the indexical realm. The thought I express today by saying 'Today is sunny' is expressed tomorrow by saying 'Yesterday was sunny', the day after tomorrow by saying 'The day before yesterday was sunny', and so on.

But does the 'and so on' here not hide the real problem? What am I to say next Tuesday? Taking the 'and so on' literally, I might use the following:

(Y₇S)   The day before the day before the day before the day before the day before the day before yesterday was sunny.

But there is obviously a better sentence, which abbreviates this:

(LTS)   Last Tuesday was sunny.

Admittedly, this introduces the concept of *day of the week*, but it still remains within the realm of the indexical (I need to know when (LTS) is uttered in order to determine the reference of 'last Tuesday'). But what about in a few years' time? Surely at some point, to express the thought that today is sunny as succinctly as possible, I am going to have to help myself to the concept of a *date* and say 'Tuesday 14 June 1994 was sunny' (or utter (DS) understood in the timeless sense). But now we seem to have 'cashed out' the indexical after all, and are impaled once again on the horns of the dilemma.

It is tempting to think that indexicals come in tidy semantic sets, such as the set of personal pronouns or the set of 'pure' temporal indexicals:

(PP)   {I, you (singular), he, she, it, we, you (plural), they}.
(TI)   {... the day before yesterday, yesterday, today, tomorrow, the day after tomorrow ...}.

Since a proper understanding of one member presupposes an understanding of other members of its set, each set being in some sense 'complete' (even if infinite), it might seem plausible to suppose that any tracking process need only draw from the resources of one such set. But linguistic life is not that simple. Cases of indexicals from within the same set being intersubstituted, in keeping track of the relevant object, are comparatively rare. Far more often, the use of one indexical will be explained in terms of, or used alongside, indexicals from other sets (e.g. 'you' meaning 'the person now reading this book'), and ultimately, it would seem, we may need to break out of the realm of the indexical altogether to express ourselves more effectively (e.g. using dates or proper names).

But can we really break out of the realm of the indexical? Even saying 'Tuesday 14 June 1994 was sunny' presupposes the Christian (Gregorian) calendar, so that dates too are implicitly indexed – in our culture, relative to the supposed day of Christ's birth. On closer examination, the boundary line between indexicals and definite descriptions fades away, and if this is so, then the dilemma we formulated earlier does indeed need to be confronted. However, it is at this point that we can bring in the considerations of §6.4. As we argued, to deny that the sense of a simple name is to be equated with the sense of any definite description is not to suggest that the sense cannot be explained at all by utilizing definite descriptions. Grasping the sense of such a name consists in knowing *which object* is referred to, and this can be *shown* in any number of different ways. The same response can be given in the case of indexicals. What it is to grasp the sense of 'today', as used on a particular occasion, is to know *which day* is being referred to, and this too may be variably manifested. We can preserve the idea that some way of *tracking* the day is required, and we might agree that at the very least I must be able to use 'tomorrow' and 'yesterday' correctly in order to grasp today-thoughts. But there is no reason to require that there be some particular way of tracking the day that everyone must possess in order to grasp these thoughts (e.g. understanding the members of the set (TI) above). Once again, what we need to recognize here is a simple scope distinction:

(SWT) Anyone who grasps the sense of 'today', as used on a given occasion, possesses some particular way of tracking the day referred to.

(WTS) There is some particular way of tracking the day referred to by 'today', as used on a given occasion, that is possessed by anyone who grasps its sense.

As a condition for the grasp of the sense of 'today', we need only insist on (SWT). To know *which day* is referred to when using the indexical 'today', I must indeed have some way of tracking the day, but as long as someone else can track that same day, not necessarily in exactly the same way, then we can both be considered to grasp the same today-thoughts.

But can this approach really be attributed to Frege? We have already sounded a word of caution here in the case of names, and since Frege's discussion of indexicals is far less developed, we are moving even further away from what can justifiably be ascribed on the basis of his texts. But I shall return to this issue in §8.3. In the final section of this chapter I shall consider further the impulse to break out of the indexical realm in the specification of thoughts.

7.5 Frege's Semainomenalism

As we have just seen, one response to the dilemma concerning indexicals is to treat the sense of an indexical, as used on a given occasion, as primitive and irreducible. Quoting a passage from 'Der Gedanke', we made clear that this was not Frege's own response, at least in the case of spatial and temporal indexicals. But the qualification here is important. Immediately after the passage quoted, Frege writes: 'The same utterance containing the word "I" in the mouths of different men will express different thoughts of which some may be true, others false' (*T*, p. 358). This acknowledgement of the indexicality of 'I', in the very same paragraph as his remarks about 'today' and 'yesterday', 'here' and 'there', might suggest that Frege believed that *I-thoughts* were to be treated in the same way as today-thoughts and here-thoughts. But, he goes on: 'The occurrence of the word "I" in a sentence gives rise to some further questions' (ibid.); and he imagines the following case. Dr. Gustav Lauben says, 'I was wounded', and Leo Peter, who hears this, remarks a few days later, 'Dr. Gustav Lauben was wounded'. Do these two utterances (of different sentences) express the same thought? Frege argues that since a third person (Rudolph Lingens) could hear both utterances, yet not realize that it was the same incident involved (not knowing that it was Gustav Lauben who had uttered the first sentence), they do not express the same thought. So does this suggest that the sense of 'I', as used on a given occasion, *is* primitive and irreducible?

Frege makes some further remarks concerning the sense of proper names, which I shall discuss in detail in §8.3; but for present purposes, the crucial paragraph is the following:

> Now everyone is presented to himself in a special and primitive way, in which he is presented to no one else. So, when Dr. Lauben has the thought that he was wounded, he will probably be basing it on this primitive way in which he is presented to himself. And only Dr. Lauben himself can grasp thoughts specified in this way. But now he may want to communicate with others. He cannot communicate a thought he alone can grasp. Therefore, if he now says 'I was wounded', he must use 'I' in a sense which can be grasped by others, perhaps in the sense of 'he who is speaking to you at this moment'; by doing this he makes the conditions accompanying his utterance serve towards the expression of a thought. (*T*, pp. 359-60.)

The first three sentences have often been taken to show that Frege holds that I-thoughts are private and incommunicable.[39] But the passage as a whole indicates that Frege's position is actually more complex than this. Certainly, he implies that there *is* a sense of 'I' – a *mode of presentation* – that is primitive and irreducible for each person, but he also suggests that 'I' can be used in a sense that *can* be grasped by others, and indeed, he offers an explicit definition in terms of other indexicals ('he who is speaking to you at this moment'). In the light of what was said in the last section, we might then regard him as recognizing that for someone else to *track* my I-thoughts, they have to make some appropriate substitution for the 'I' that I use to express those thoughts.

What this suggests, then, is that on any given occasion of use, 'I' has both a *subjective sense*, a sense which, necessarily, no one but the speaker can grasp, and an *objective sense*, which someone else can grasp by making an appropriate substitution for the indexical. But does this mean that there are two kinds of thought involved here, a thought that only I can grasp and a thought that I can communicate, or merely that any I-thought has both a subjective and an objective 'specification'? If the former, then is this not in conflict with Frege's insistence that thoughts are objective? If the latter, then we surely need some account of what constitutes a 'specification'. Do we not have to abandon the assumption that thoughts are determined by their 'constituent' senses? And are we then to repudiate the essential indexicality of certain thoughts?

The key sentence of the passage is this: 'And only Dr. Lauben himself can grasp thoughts specified in this way' ('Und den so bestimmten Gedanken kann nur Dr. Lauben selbst fassen'; more literally, 'And the so determined thought only Dr. Lauben himself can grasp'). As it stands, this sentence is ambiguous: it could mean either that only Dr. Lauben can grasp the specific kind of thought that is based on the 'special and primitive' way in which he is presented to himself, or else that only Dr. Lauben can grasp the I-thought *as* specified in this way. The first possibility legitimizes *necessarily private* thoughts, whilst the second possibility allows that other people can grasp my I-thoughts, merely admitting that they cannot grasp them *as* (their own) I-thoughts.

Gareth Evans has suggested that Frege did hold that there are unshareable thoughts, but that this should not be seen as impugning their objectivity, which only requires that thoughts be *independent* of their being grasped by anyone.[40] But as an interpretation of Frege, this is untenable. Frege is indeed insistent, throughout his life, on the objectivity of thoughts, but for him, objectivity and shareability are inextricably connected, since it is the shareability of thoughts that their independence guarantees. In 'Der Gedanke' itself, for example, in stating that 'I can ... acknowledge thoughts as independent of me', he immediately goes on: 'other men can grasp them just as much as I' (*T*, p. 368).[41] A thought is by its very nature capable of being grasped by more than one person; according to Frege, it is just this that distinguishes thoughts from ideas.

That Frege admits the communicability of I-thoughts is implicit even in the three sentences of the passage that are often taken to suggest otherwise. For when Frege says 'when Dr. Lauben has the thought that he was wounded, he will probably be basing it on this primitive way in which he is presented to himself', he is precisely expressing Dr. Lauben's I-thought from a third person perspective – 'the thought that he was wounded' – making the appropriate indexical substitution. Admittedly, I cannot myself grasp this thought *as* an I-thought, but I do reflect its indexicality when I say 'Dr. Lauben has the thought that *he* was wounded' – no substitution for 'he' by any definite description will capture the structure of the thought. However, we are still left with the implication that there *is* a sense of 'I' that is primitive and irreducible, even if it does not contribute to the formation of primitive and irreducible I-thoughts, and the problem of characterizing 'specifications' remains. But I shall return to these issues shortly.

The question that Frege asks immediately after the passage quoted might suggest that, despite what we have just said, Frege does not take himself at this stage to have established the communicability of I-thoughts: 'Yet there is a doubt. Is it at all the same thought which first that man expresses and then this one?' (*T*, p. 360.) The point of this question, though, is not to raise the specific worry that Gustav Lauben and Leo Peter do not express the same thought, i.e. that a thought expressed from a first person point of view and a thought expressed from a third person point of view cannot be identical. Rather, it is to raise the general worry that *no thought* can be shared. If thoughts are the contents of consciousness, and, like ideas, these contents are essentially private, then the communicability of thoughts is ruled out from the start. So more precisely, what Frege presumably regards himself as having established at this stage is the conditional claim: *if* thoughts (in general) are communicable, then there is no reason to deny that I-thoughts are communicable.

It is at this point that Frege launches into a long discussion about the nature of ideas, and the distinction between ideas and thoughts, the main purpose of which is to defuse the general worry that *no* thoughts are communicable; and this occupies him for the rest of 'Der Gedanke'. No more is said specifically about the communicability of I-thoughts, only reinforcing the suggestion that Frege did take this as settled, at least in the form of the conditional claim just stated. But it is, I think, possible to find in his general remarks further support for the thesis that I-thoughts are communicable.

Frege begins by arguing that ideas, as constituents of the inner world, are distinct from the things of the outer world (physical objects) in four ways.[42] Firstly, they cannot be sensed: they are not themselves apprehended through any of the five senses. Secondly, they are something we *have*: an idea belongs to the content of someone's consciousness. Thirdly, they need an owner: they cannot exist independently. Fourthly, each idea has only one owner: no two people have the same idea. Frege then considers whether thoughts are ideas. They too cannot be sensed, but, according to Frege, they do not possess the other three characteristics of ideas. Taking the example of the thought I express in stating the Pythagorean theorem, Frege argues that if this were the content of my consciousness, then I should not really speak of *the* Pythagorean theorem, but of *my* Pythagorean theorem, and other people would have *different* Pythagorean theorems. Truth itself would be relativized to individuals, and there could be no genuine disputes about what thoughts were true.[43]

The conclusion Frege draws is that 'thoughts are neither things in the external world nor ideas' (*T*, p. 363), and he goes on:

A third realm must be recognized. Anything belonging to this realm has it in common with ideas that it cannot be perceived by the senses, but has it in common with things that it does not need an owner so as to belong to the contents of his consciousness. Thus for example the thought we have expressed in the Pythagorean theorem is timelessly true, true independently of whether anyone takes it to be true. It needs no owner. It is not true only from the time when it is discovered; just as a planet, even before anyone saw it, was in interaction with other planets. (*T*, p. 363.)

In seeking to secure the objectivity of thoughts, Frege has come a long way from the objectivism of the *Begriffsschrift*. Neither citizenship of a 'third realm' nor timelessness had been seen as features of 'conceptual contents', which, as we suggested in §6.2, would probably best be characterized, at the metaphysical level, as 'states of affairs', constituents of the temporal 'first realm'.[44]

Before elucidating these two features, however, we must highlight an obvious circularity in Frege's argument. Frege's aim, we have just seen, is to show that thoughts are communicable, and the strategy is to distinguish thoughts from ideas. But the basis of this distinction, it turns out, lies in the communicability of thoughts and the non-communicability of ideas. Since it is absurd to suppose that we cannot communicate with one another about *the* Pythagorean theorem, Frege argues, the thoughts we express in doing so cannot be ideas. But surely this is just what the idealist sceptic would deny? In response, it might be suggested that what Frege is in fact offering is a *transcendental deduction* of the objectivity of thoughts, answering the Kantian question 'How is logic and science possible?'. It is a fundamental condition of scientific investigation, construed as the discovery of true thoughts (cf. *T*, p. 368), and indeed, of conceptual discourse in general, at least in so far as it involves the application of determinate sortal concepts, as governed by logic, that thoughts be independent and publicly accessible, that is, objective. Since the possibility of logic and science is not seriously in question, thoughts cannot but be objective and communicable.

Frege does in fact offer a Kantian argument in the case of demonstrating the existence of a subject that *has* the ideas. Every idea must have an owner, but if this owner is itself an idea, then that too must have an owner, and so on *ad infinitum*, which is absurd. He concludes:

I am not my own idea; and when I assert something about myself, e.g. that I am not feeling any pain at the moment, then my judgement concerns something which is not a content of my consciousness, is not an idea, namely myself. Therefore that about which I state something is not necessarily my idea. But someone perhaps objects: if I think I have no pain at the moment, does not the word 'I' answer to something in the content of my consciousness? and is that not an idea? That may be so. A certain idea in my consciousness may be associated with the idea of the word 'I'. But then this is one idea among other ideas, and I am its owner as I am the owner of the other ideas. I have an idea of myself, but I am not identical with this idea. What is a content of my consciousness, my idea, should be sharply distinguished from what is an object of my thought. Therefore the thesis that only what belongs to the content of my consciousness can be the object of my awareness, of my thought, is false. (*T*, p. 366.)

There are several points to make about this passage. Frege is following Kant in his critique of Hume in arguing that ideas presuppose an owner, which cannot itself be an idea. But the complexities and tensions of Kant's own theory of the self are bypassed by Frege in simply claiming that the self is an object of thought. If the self is not a mental object, an inhabitant of the 'second realm', i.e. an idea, is it a physical object? Since Frege allows that I can have ideas *of* myself, and ideas provide our sensory access to the external world, then it would seem natural to suppose that he believes that the self is an empirical object. The only other possibility is to see the self as an inhabitant of some 'third realm', but since, for Frege, this is the realm of *thoughts*, this cannot be Frege's view. Whilst the self can be an *object of thought*, it is not itself a thought – although, as we shall see, it was the failure to properly appreciate this distinction that was responsible for Frege's mythic conception of thoughts as inhabiting a 'third realm'. But at least in this case he is quite explicit that the self is a possible *object of thought* (*Gegenstand des Denkens*).[45]

If the self *is* an empirical object, and ideas and thoughts can be distinguished, then the communicability of I-thoughts is no longer problematic. For someone else can grasp the thought that I express when I say 'I am in pain' when they see me writhing about in agony. Of course, no one else can *have* my pain, but what is called for here is just that distinction between object of thought and content of consciousness that Frege was so concerned to draw.[46] Furthermore, when Frege talks of being presented to oneself in a 'special and primitive way', he can now be interpreted as referring to the *ideas* that one has in thinking about oneself, which he has admitted exist and which are indeed private and incommunicable. Perhaps we can deny that there is a *subjective sense* of 'I', after all; what there is instead is a 'special and primitive' *idea* of oneself, which is no barrier to the communication of I-thoughts. But since Frege himself does not explicitly draw this conclusion, nor return to the communicability of I-thoughts, this can only be offered as a speculation.[47]

The role of Frege's claim that the self is an object of thought, however, is clear. Having argued that he himself is the owner of his ideas, and not one of those ideas, he goes on:

> Nothing now stops me from acknowledging other men to be owners of ideas, just as I am myself .... Not everything is an idea. Thus I can also acknowledge thoughts as independent of me; other men can grasp them just as much as I; I can acknowledge a science in which many can be engaged in research. We are not owners of thoughts as we are owners of our ideas. (*T*, pp. 367-8.)

However, it is at this point that the distinction between *thoughts* and *objects of thoughts* appears to have been eroded. What Frege seems to be arguing is that since there are objects of thought of which no one is the owner, the thoughts of those objects must themselves be independent. Spelled out more, the argument runs as follows. Since I, as owner of my ideas, am not myself an idea, not every object of my thought is an idea. But other people also exist as owners of their ideas, so there are other objects of my thought that are not the contents of my consciousness. Since I can think about something that is not an idea and hence is not owned by me, thoughts are independent of me, and hence can be grasped by other people too.

Accepting that other people do exist as independent owners of their ideas,[48] the crucial move in the argument is from the obvious truth that I can think about something that is not owned by me to the tendentious conclusion that thoughts themselves are independent. If all this means is that thoughts are shareable, then we might well accept it; but Frege's talk of a 'third realm' suggests that he has a stronger conception in mind. For him, thoughts are independent of all thinkers and not just of any particular thinker. But someone may well wish to endorse only the latter claim: the existence of a thought does require a thinker, although there is no one thinker upon whom the thought depends.[49] If Frege fails to appreciate this, then it is because he fails to distinguish between the independence enjoyed by objects of thought, which may indeed be 'self-subsistent',[50] from the independence enjoyed by thoughts themselves, which may simply mean that they are shareable.

Frege's confusion about the distinction between thoughts and objects of thoughts is reflected in the difficulties he encounters in understanding what thinking involves.

> We do not *have* a thought as we have, say, a sense-impression, but we also do not see a thought as we *see*, say, a star. So it is advisable to choose a special expression; the word 'grasp' suggests itself for the purpose. To the grasping of thoughts there must then correspond a special mental capacity, the power of thinking. In thinking we do not produce thoughts, we grasp them. (*T*, p. 368.)

Frege recognizes that talk of 'grasping' is metaphorical, but he is still misled into treating it as a relation that one has to a thought.[51] If it *is* such a relation, then a subject is required as well as an object, and it is here that there is a dependence on a thinker. Frege writes:

> The grasp of a thought presupposes someone who grasps it, who thinks. He is the owner of the thinking, not of the thought. Although the thought does not belong with the contents of the thinker's consciousness, there must be something in his consciousness that is aimed at the thought. But this should not be confused with the thought itself. Similarly Algol itself is different from the idea someone has of Algol. (*T*, p. 369.)

Presumably, as the contents of consciousness, it is *ideas* that are directed towards thoughts (as perhaps the last sentence is meant to suggest). So Frege's position seems to be that thinking involves ideas, which, in being owned, are distinct from the thoughts at which they are aimed. We might note in passing that this provides further support for the speculation offered above concerning the communicability of I-thoughts. I may *think* about myself in a 'special and primitive' way, using my private ideas, but the I-thoughts themselves are shareable.[52]

If thinking does involve ideas, then this might be taken to justify Frege in not saying anything more about how such a mysterious process occurs, for it would presumably be a matter for the psychologist and not the philosopher. The philosopher can concentrate on limning the structure of thoughts, whilst the psychologist does the empirical work of investigating how those thoughts are actually 'grasped'.[53] But the attraction of Frege's theory of sense and reference, as it was originally articulated, has often been felt to lie in its avoiding positing senses as independent objects which we must somehow 'grasp'. Senses are *modes of presentation* of referents, and modes of presentation are not themselves objects to which we must in turn be related. At the most basic level, to grasp a thought (e.g. that the pencil in front of me is red) is simply to think about an object – an object from the 'first realm' – in a certain way (the object presented to me as a pencil is conceived as red). What I am intentionally directed towards is the ordinary empirical world, not an object in some other world.[54] However, as we saw in the last chapter, Frege himself did feel compelled to construe senses as objects – partly because he felt that senses could exist independently of their referents (see §6.3) and partly because of the demands of intensional contexts (see §6.5). What Frege's later conception of thoughts thus indicates is a further pull away from the construal of senses as modes of presentation that had seemed so attractive about his original formulation.

As in the case of numbers, Frege clearly felt that the *objectivity* of senses required that senses be *objects*. Since these could be neither physical objects (because senses cannot themselves be perceived) nor mental objects (since thoughts had to be distinguished from ideas to combat psychologism), they had to be housed in a 'third realm'. I shall call this metaphysical thesis – that thoughts inhabit a 'third realm' of their own – Frege's *semainomenalism*. If *phenomenalism* is the view that the world of phenomena (ideas, sense-impressions, sensations, etc.) is the primary reality, and *noumenalism* is the view that the noumenal world (the realm of things in themselves) is the ultimate reality, then *semainomenalism* can be defined as the view that it is the world of meanings or senses that has a fundamental status. Typically, the noumenalist will believe in the existence of a world of phenomena as well, but will hold that such a world is ontologically secondary; and so too the semainomenalist may believe in the existence of other worlds – in Frege's case, both the physical and mental worlds (the 'first' and 'second' realms) – but will still regard the semainomenal world, just as Plato conceived his Forms, as intellectually purer and more basic.[55]

The particular characteristic of the semainomenal world that grants it its privileged status is the *timelessness* of its inhabitants. What this means for Frege is that thoughts are understood as the senses of 'complete' sentences, sentences in which all indexicality – whether explicit or implicit – has been 'cashed out'; and it is this that allows Frege to treat such 'naturally timeless' truths as the propositions of arithmetic in the same way as what are normally regarded as *contingent* truths – which, we might say, are *made necessary* by the process of decontextualization.[56] Frege writes:

> Now is a thought changeable or is it timeless? The thought we express by the Pythagorean theorem is surely timeless, eternal, unvarying. But are there not thoughts which are true today but false in six months' time? The thought, for example, that the tree there is covered with green leaves, will surely be false in six months' time. No, for it is not the same thought at all. The words 'This tree is covered with green leaves' are not sufficient by themselves to constitute the expression of thought, for the time of utterance is involved as well. Without the time-specification thus given we have not a complete thought, i.e. we have no thought at all. Only a sentence with the time-specification filled out, a sentence complete in every respect, expresses a thought. But this thought, if it is true, is true not only today or tomorrow but timelessly. Thus the present tense in 'is true' does not refer to the speaker's present; it is, if the expression be permitted, a tense of timelessness. (*T*, p. 370.)

Rather than using Frege's own example (which actually requires the tree to be specified as well as the time), let us illustrate the idea by taking the sentence briefly considered in the last section:

(IHN) I am here now.

Supposing that I utter (IHN) now, then the following might be offered as the 'complete' sentence that fully cashes out the indexicality:

(MBL) Mike Beaney is in Room G05 in the Department of Philosophy, University of Leeds, England, at 11.00 am on 21 June 1994.

Of course, if this is to work, then the 'is' here must itself be understood timelessly, since taken as a verb in the present tense, it must be replaced by 'was' when someone wants to express the thought later or by 'will be' had someone had the knowledge to express the thought earlier. This might be raised as an objection to Frege: here at least we have some essential indexicality – we can only ever express contingent propositions in a way that reflects our own temporal perspective. But the reply will be that the reason we do replace 'is' by 'was' or 'will be' is precisely to express the *same* thought, and if we are going to allow that that thought can be given any linguistic expression at all that cashes out temporality, then (MBL) is the best that can be offered, 'is' being understood timelessly – in exactly the same way as the 'is' in '3 is a prime number' is understood timelessly.[57]

What this example brings out, though, Frege would say, is just that need to distinguish *grasp* of a thought from the thought itself. It may well be that (MBL) represents the best attempt at expressing the relevant thought, but even here, as we argued in the last section, there is implicit indexicality (e.g. the time is specified relative to the Christian calendar, and my name is assumed to be uniquely individuating). In expressing such a thought in everyday life, we are bound to use indexicals that reflect our own personal and spatio-temporal perspective. But whilst *grasp of a thought* may reflect the idiosyncrasies of the thinker, the thought itself remains independent of the linguistic forms used in expressing it. The process of *grasping* may be temporal, but the thought itself is timeless. As Frege puts it, 'The time-specification that may be contained in the sentence belongs only to the expression of the thought; the truth ... is timeless' (*T*, p.370).

But can thoughts really be regarded as having no temporal properties at all, and would this not render them useless? Frege recognizes the problem: 'Even the timeless, if it is to be anything for us, must somehow be implicated with the temporal. What would a thought be for me if it were never grasped by me? But by grasping a thought I come into a relation to it, and it to me.' (*T*, pp. 370-1.) And if this is so, then the thought itself must be regarded as having the (temporal) property of being grasped by me at a certain time. In response, Frege distinguishes between essential and inessential properties of a thought: 'A property of a thought will be called inessential if it consists in, or follows from, the fact that this thought is grasped by a thinker' (*T*, p. 371). So being grasped by a thinker is not seen as affecting the essential timelessness of a thought. The problem remains as to how such timeless truths can indeed be 'grasped', but as already suggested, Frege's response here is to pass the problem over to the psychologist.

On this view, then, it would be perfectly consistent to deny that there can be any linguistic expression that fully cashes out indexicality – that adequately reflects the timelessness of a thought; and in fact, this is really Frege's own position. Not only does he not himself offer examples of 'complete' sentences cashing out contingent propositions (in the way that (MBL) attempted to provide), but, as we have seen, he was also insistent throughout his life that ordinary language is inadequate for logical purposes. In a footnote to the key passage concerning I-thoughts that we quoted at the beginning of this section, Frege writes:

> I am not here in the happy position of a mineralogist who shows his audience a rock-crystal: I cannot put a thought in the hands of my readers with the request that they should examine it from all sides. Something in itself not

perceptible by sense, the thought, is presented to the reader – and I must be content with that – wrapped up in a perceptible linguistic form .... So one fights against language, and I am compelled to occupy myself with language although it is not my proper concern here. I hope I have succeeded in making clear to my readers what I mean by 'a thought'. (*T*, p. 360.)

These remarks are appended to Frege's suggestion that Dr. Lauben, in seeking to communicate with others, 'makes the conditions accompanying his utterance serve towards the expression of a thought'. It is these conditions that someone else has to appreciate in order themselves to grasp the thought that Dr. Lauben expresses in saying 'I am wounded'. Frege's point can be readily generalized: whenever someone communicates a thought, they rely on certain conditions being recognized to obtain. On Frege's view, all thoughts are clothed in some form, and need to be undressed by the mind to be apprehended in their pure state (to use a well-worn pun, this might be called Frege's doctrine of original *Sinn*).

However, in distinguishing between grasp of a thought and the thought itself, and locating thoughts in some timeless realm – in being pushed to such an ethereal conception of thoughts – Frege appears to have abandoned some of his key earlier ideas. To see this, we need only return to the case of my uttering (IHN). According to Frege, this is to be taken as expressing the same thought as (MBL). But it is clearly possible for me to use (IHN) to say something true without holding that (MBL) is true. In the most extreme situation, I might suffer from severe amnesia, and not know who or where I am, or what time it is; and it frequently happens that one can express truths using the indexical 'now' without knowing exactly what time it is. As we argued in a similar case in the last section, the two sentences cannot therefore be regarded as having the same sense. But this is in direct conflict with the position that Frege seems to have been driven to in 'Der Gedanke'. In trying to maintain that thoughts are communicable in the face of the problem of indexicality, Frege appears to have abandoned his own criterion for sameness of sense. It is this conflict that I discuss in the first section of the next chapter.

But there is a further tension revealed by Frege's account of indexicality. If (MBL), for example, is to be seen as offering at least a 'more complete' characterization of the thought I express in uttering (IHN), then what now of the role of the principle (PDS)? If I can indeed express a thought using an indexical without being able to cash it out in its fullest possible form, then is that thought not determined by constituents that I do not myself grasp (e.g. the precise time when I use the indexical 'now'). The thought seems to be determined not just by what I understand in using the words I use but also by the *context*. If knowing exactly how the sense is determined is the condition for properly grasping the thought, then do we not need to draw a more subtle distinction here between *expressing* and *grasping* a thought? If I can truly say 'I am here now' without holding (MBL) as true, for example, have I not *expressed* the thought without having *grasped* it? But if I can express thoughts without really grasping them, then have we not further distanced ourselves from Frege's original conception of sense? If *context* is allowed as a determinant of sense, then do principles of compositionality not need to be modified? I take up these questions in §8.2.

One obvious way out of the problem is to deny that I do express a complete thought when I utter (IHN), say, without being able to fully cash out its indexicality. But if all sentences involve some kind of indexicality, and there is no such thing as a genuinely 'timeless' linguistic expression of a thought, then the result would seem to be that *no* thoughts can ever be fully expressed or grasped. In fact, however, Frege's own later conception of 'grasping' thoughts seems to point in the other direction. According to Frege, anyone can in principle grasp the thought that someone else expresses, but will do so in a different way, since 'grasping' involves ideas, and ideas are essentially private. But the obvious objection to this is hardly less devastating. For, even if someone else does grasp the thought I express, I can never *know* that they do so, since I do not myself have access to their ideas.[58] In the end, then, this seems a high price to pay for the objectivity of thoughts. Thoughts have become so ethereal that either grasp of them is no longer possible at all or else I can never know whether anyone else grasps them. Like locking up one's money in a chest, burying it on some remote island, and then throwing away the key, to prevent anyone from stealing it, what we aimed to protect has been rendered valueless. This is the ultimate paradox of Frege's semainomenalism: the logical realm has become so sublimated that it is hard to see how ordinary linguistic life can go on at all.

8. The Crystallization of Sense

The more narrowly we examine actual language, the sharper becomes the conflict between it and our requirement. (For the crystalline purity of logic was, of course, not a *result of investigation*: it was a requirement.) The conflict becomes intolerable; the requirement is now in danger of becoming empty. – We have got on to slippery ice where there is no friction and so in a certain sense the conditions are ideal, but also, just because of that, we are unable to walk. We want to walk: so we need *friction*. Back to the rough ground! (Wittgenstein, *Philosophical Investigations*, §107.)

In the preceding chapters, we have traced the development of Frege's philosophy, focussing on his conception of 'sense', from the emergence of his early notion of 'conceptual content', through the bifurcation of that notion into 'Sinn' and 'Bedeutung' in response to the problem of the status of his logicist definitions, to his late account of 'timeless thoughts'. In this final chapter, I want to draw together some of the threads of the discussion, and consider a number of outstanding problems. At various points we have suggested that there is a certain tension in Frege's conception of sense, and in the first section I elucidate this further by considering the criteria for sameness of sense that Frege himself offers and that might be formulated on his behalf. In §8.2 I explore the relationship between Frege's context principle and his principles of compositionality, all of which we have seen playing key roles in his thought; and in the following two sections, I consider what conclusions can be drawn concerning the coherence of Frege's conception of sense. In the final section, I return to the central theme of this book, highlighting the way that 'sense' is *made* or *crystallized* in our attempts to deepen our understanding in a given area through the process of analysis.

8.1 Criteria for Sameness of Sense

In §2.5 we formulated the following criterion for Frege's early notion of 'conceptual content':

(CC) Two propositions have the same *conceptual content* iff they are logically equivalent.

Intuitively, the idea seems simple. If P implies Q, and Q implies P, then P and Q have the same 'conceptual content', however else they may differ. But as we also noted, the 'logical equivalence' here must be interpreted as more than mere 'material equivalence'; and even 'provable material equivalence' fails to do justice to all of our intuitions about sameness of 'content'. Frege's logicism shows the need for an additional, finer-grained conception: it is just because the propositions of arithmetic have different 'cognitive contents' that their sameness of 'logical content' requires demonstration. This led us to distinguish the following three versions of (CC):

(CC#) Two propositions have the same *veritable content* iff they are materially equivalent.

(CC*) Two propositions have the same *logical content* iff they are logically equivalent (provably materially equivalent).[1]

(CC†) Two propositions have the same *cognitive content* iff they are cognitively equivalent.

(CC#) provides us with the criterion for Frege's later notion of *Bedeutung*, whilst (CC†) was intended as a place-holder for the elucidation of *Sinn* that it has been our subsequent task to provide. We also noted that (CC*) is offered in one place as the criterion for *Sinn*, but that this cannot be considered as Frege's 'official' view.

Nevertheless, it remains the case that there is a certain tension in Frege's conception of *Sinn*, and this was highlighted in chapter 5. The paradox of analysis shows that the notion of 'content' requires disambiguation. In analysing anything, the *analysans* and the *analysandum* must, at the very least, be logically equivalent; yet if the analysis is to be 'fruitful', it would seem that they must also have different 'cognitive contents'. Frege's distinction between 'Bedeutung' and 'Sinn' was offered as a response to the paradox, but as we argued, it is inadequate as it stands. For sameness of *Bedeutung* is too weak a relation to act as the only constraint on the adequacy of an analysis; and whilst the notion of *Sinn* does indeed accommodate informativeness, since the *analysans* and *analysandum* are regarded as having *different* senses, there is no longer any way of making out the notion of 'logical content' to act as the required constraint. As we suggested in §5.4, Frege's conception of *Sinn* appears to be *epistemic* rather than semantic, yet the paradox of analysis demands a *semantic* conception of sense as well. Certainly, Frege's 'official' conception, as presented in 'Über Sinn und Bedeutung', is epistemic; although, as we also hinted, a more semantic conception does seem to surface in the *Grundgesetze*. The position is summarized in the diagram on the page opposite.

Although Frege operated with an undifferentiated notion of 'content' in his early work, he did distinguish between 'content' and 'way of splitting up content', which anticipated to some extent his later distinction between 'Bedeutung' and 'Sinn'. As we saw in §5.2, Frege held that the same 'content' can be 'split up' in different ways, a conception that was grounded in the idea of alternative function-argument analyses. This early distinction appeared to offer an attractive resolution of the paradox of analysis, 'content' being understood as 'logical content' and 'way of splitting up

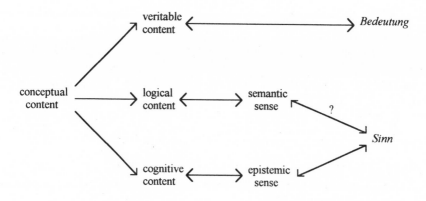

content' as 'cognitive content'. But as we showed in §5.3, the legitimacy of certain kinds of argument (where 'cross-identifications' are involved) seems to depend on 'cognitive content' and not just 'logical content'; and Frege was by no means clear about this at the time. In any case, it is implausible to maintain that the relationship between the two members of what we termed a 'Fregean pair' (Fregean pairs being fundamental to Frege's logicist project, as we saw in chapter 4) is simply one of alternative function-argument analyses: introducing terms for abstract objects, or engaging in conceptual ascent, seems to generate an arguably *different* (albeit logically equivalent) proposition. Recall, for example, (Da), (Db) and (Dc):

(Da) Line a is parallel to line b.
(Db) The direction of line a is identical with the direction of line b.
(Dc) The concept 'line parallel to line a' is coextensive with the concept 'line parallel to line b'.

Compare these with one of Frege's paradigm examples of alternative function-argument analyses of the same 'conceptual content' (see §5.2 above), with parentheses highlighting the argument place:

(HLC) (Hydrogen) is lighter than carbon dioxide.
(CHH) (Carbon dioxide) is heavier than hydrogen.

Although the concept *lighter than carbon dioxide* is different from the concept *heavier than hydrogen*, it does seem that it is the same relation between the same two objects with which (HLC) and (CHH) are concerned, so that the same 'content' is involved.[2] But it is hard to see how (Da), (Db) and (Dc) fit the same model: despite their logical equivalence, it is not just that different concepts are used, but that different relations are being stated to obtain between things of different kinds (parallelism of lines, identity of directions, coextensiveness of concepts).

One way of expressing the difference between these two cases is to say that whilst it is impossible to hold that (HLC) is true without holding that (CHH) is true, and vice versa, it *is* possible to hold that (Da) is true without holding that (Db) is true, and vice versa. To use the distinction discussed in §6.5, whilst (Da) and (Db) are *extensionally equivalent*, they are not *intensionally equivalent*: substituting one for the other in intensional contexts does not necessarily preserve truth-value. If this is right, and Frege's own account of intensionality in 'Über Sinn und Bedeutung' gives an essential clue to his conception of sense, then the implication must be that (Da) and (Db) possess *different senses* – they express *different thoughts*. This suggests the following criterion:

> (SIE) Two propositions have the same *sense* iff they are *intensionally equivalent*, i.e. iff they can be intersubstituted *salva veritate* in all intensional contexts.[3]

But did Frege really want to hold that members of Fregean pairs possess different senses? As we have seen, Frege's primary concern in drawing the distinction between *Sinn* and *Bedeutung* was with the status of the 'analytic definitions' of the *Grundlagen* and Axiom V of the *Grundgesetze*; but this suggests that he wants at least the two members of that fundamental Fregean pair, (Va) and (Vb), to possess the *same sense*. It was just this that was indicated by his remark in 'Function and Concept' that each side of Axiom V 'expresses the same sense, but in a different way' (*FC*, p. 27; see §5.4 above). Frege's logicism thus clearly demands a notion of sense that is finer-grained than the notion of *Bedeutung*, yet coarser-grained than his 'official' notion of epistemic sense.

It was no doubt the tension between the requirements of his logicism and his desire to nevertheless uphold the informativeness of identity statements that contributed to Frege's uncharacteristic reluctance to specify exactly what he meant by 'Sinn'. There are just two passages, both written around the same time, 1906, where he offers what seem to be his most careful formulations; but the two criteria he suggests appear to be in marked conflict. In a letter written to Husserl, after stating that 'an objective criterion is necessary for recognizing a thought again as the same, for without it logical analysis is impossible', Frege provides the following criterion:

> (SLE) Two propositions *A* and *B* possess the same *sense* (express the same *thought*) iff '*both* the assumption that the content of *A* is false and that of *B* true *and* the assumption that the content of *A* is true and that of *B* false lead to a logical contradiction, and ... this can be established without knowing whether the content of *A* or *B* is true or false, and without requiring other than purely logical laws for this purpose'. (*PMC*, p. 70.)

In a posthumously published piece (*BSLD*), however, Frege offers a rather different criterion:

(SEE) Two propositions *A* and *B* possess the same *sense* (express the same *thought*) iff 'anyone who recognizes the content of *A* as true must straight away [*ohne weiteres*] also recognize that of *B* as true, and conversely, anyone who recognizes the content of *B* must immediately [*unmittelbar*] also recognize that of *A* (*equipollence*)'. (*NS*, p. 213.)

Whilst (SLE) bases sameness of sense on *logical equivalence* (provable material equivalence), (SEE) grounds it on what can be called *epistemic equipollence*. Once more, the conflict seems to be between a fairly coarse-grained notion of sense, echoing the central strand in Frege's earlier notion of 'conceptual content', and a much finer-grained one.[4]

In other places, Frege's notion of sense is left to be gleaned from the examples he gives, or else, where he does offer some characterization, he simply talks loosely of two propositions having different senses if one can be taken as true but not the other.[5] So how are we to offer a criterion that best captures Frege's intentions, and how are we to explain the conflict between the two criteria just stated? The difference between the two criteria can be seen by considering their application to Fregean pairs. According to (SLE), the two members of a Fregean pair, such as (Da) and (Db), or (Va) and Vb), would possess the *same* sense, since they are certainly logically equivalent, whereas according to (SEE), they would presumably possess *different* senses, since it does seem possible to recognize one as true without immediately recognizing the other as true.

The conflict becomes even sharper if we apply the criteria to arithmetical propositions. If Frege's logicism is right, then, by (SLE), all arithmetical truths turn out to possess the same sense, since they are all provably materially equivalent; yet in the vast majority of cases, someone can take one as true without immediately recognizing another as true (some kind of reasoning will typically be needed), so that, by (SEE), they would possess different senses. However, in his formulation of the first criterion, Frege makes a qualification that arguably rules out its application in just these cases: 'I assume that neither of the two propositions contains a logically self-evident component part in its sense' (*PMC*, p. 70). Despite his talk of 'a logically self-evident component part', Frege's intention here was presumably to exclude the application of the criterion to any pair of propositions whose negations in themselves lead to a logical contradiction, to avoid what would certainly be for Frege an absurdity – that all logical truths (taken as including arithmetical truths) possess the same sense.[6]

A similar qualification is made in his formulation of the second criterion. Frege writes: 'I assume there is nothing in the content of either of the two equipollent sentences *A* and *B* that would have to be immediately accepted as true by anyone who had grasped it properly' (*BSLD*, p. 197). *Self-evident* propositions are excluded for an equally obvious reason. If it is taken as a mark of a self-evident truth that it is not possible to grasp its content without immediately recognizing it as true, then (SEE) – interpreted literally – would imply that all self-evident truths have the same sense, and this too cannot have been Frege's intention.[7]

Of course, in the case of self-evident logical truths, both criteria yield the result that they all possess the same sense, so that here at least the conflict is removed. But it is clear not only that the conflict would remain in the case of non-self-evident logical truths, but also that such a result is inconsistent with the many illustrations that Frege gives of his conception of sense. '2 + 2 = 4' and '2^2 = 4', for example, would by both criteria possess the same sense (assuming that they are indeed self-evident truths, to anyone with a reasonable knowledge of arithmetic); yet Frege himself explicitly states that they possess *different* senses (see e.g. *GG*, I, §2). Since it is hardly likely that Frege failed to recognize the obvious implications of the use of the two criteria in just that area with which he was most concerned, namely, arithmetic, one can only conclude that the qualifications he made were precisely intended to rule out in advance the inconsistencies we have just considered.[8] If this is appreciated, then perhaps the seriousness of the conflict between the two criteria can be played down.

However, neither member of a Fregean pair need in itself be a self-evident logical truth. In the case of (Va) and (Vb), it is the proposition that asserts their equivalence that is meant to be a self-evident logical truth. Within Frege's system, of course, (SLE) yields the sameness of sense of (Va) and (Vb) very trivially, since Axiom V is precisely one of the logical laws. But what of the application of (SEE)? To claim that Axiom V is a self-evident logical truth would indeed be to claim that anyone who recognizes (Va) as true must immediately recognize (Vb) as true, and vice versa; but it is just this that is problematic. As we saw in §7.2, Frege admitted in the preface to the *Grundgesetze* that a dispute might arise as to the status of Axiom V, although he held it to be purely logical. But in the Appendix to Volume II, where he attempted to face up to Russell's paradox, he remarked that 'I have never disguised from myself its lack of the self-evidence that belongs to the other axioms and that must properly be demanded of a logical law' (*FRP*, p. 214). This suggests that whilst Frege *wanted* Axiom V to be self-evident, he had doubts that it really was, doubts only confirmed by the appearance of Russell's paradox.[9] If Frege had these doubts all along, then this would have been reflected in doubts about whether (Va) and (Vb) possessed the same sense, which would certainly explain his vacillation over what criterion to offer. To have insisted that they do possess the same sense would have meant rejecting (SEE) and offering something much more like (SLE), which is what he does do in his letter to Husserl.

It remains the case, then, that (SLE) and (SEE) yield different results, a tension that was reflected in, if not generated by, Frege's uncertainty about the status of Axiom V. According to the first criterion, two (contingent) propositions have the same sense if one cannot be true without the other being true, whilst according to the second criterion, two (non-self-evident) propositions have the same sense if one cannot be recognized to be true without the other being recognized to be true. The first encapsulates a *semantic* conception of sense, and the second an *epistemic* conception.[10] Of the two, however, (SLE) is the anomaly. Most of the illustrations that Frege gives of his conception of sense are more consistent with adherence to (SEE). But as we have suggested, this implies that (Va) and (Vb) – and presumably other members of Fregean pairs – possess *different* senses, which is not what Frege wanted. Indeed, as we argued in §5.4, if Frege's notion of 'Bedeutung' is the only other notion available to us, then the epistemic conception of sense encapsulated in (SEE) would render us unable to satisfactorily respond to the paradox of analysis. For whilst a fine-grained conception of sense allows us to account for the informativeness of analyses, sameness of *Bedeutung* provides an insufficient constraint on their correctness.

So can a criterion be found that would provide the right constraint on the correctness of analyses, encapsulating a coarser-grained conception of sense than (SEE) but a finer-grained conception of sense than (SLE)? The best that can be offered, I think, is the following, which can be taken as filling out the required notion of 'cognitive equivalence' mentioned above:

> (SCE) Two propositions *A* and *B* possess the same *sense* (express the same *thought*) iff anyone who understands both propositions at a given time can immediately recognize that *A* is true (or false) if they recognize *B* as true (or false), and vice versa.[11]

At first glance, this might seem no different to (SEE), and it is, indeed, as close as one can get to (SEE) whilst leaving room to assert the equivalence in sense of members of Fregean pairs. The crucial difference is that (SCE) contains the qualification that both propositions must be understood at a given time before the test of immediate recognition can be applied.

To appreciate the difference between (SEE) and (SCE), let us return to Frege's original contextual definition of *direction* in terms of the parallelism of lines. Applying (SEE) implies that (Da) and (Db) *differ* in sense: it is perfectly possible to recognize that (Da) is true without immediately recognizing that (Db) is true – where, for example, someone simply lacks the concept of direction. However, since this is just what we are attempting to specify through contextual definition, to appeal to this possibility in repudiating the view that they possess the same sense would appear to rule out such definitions from the start. Frege's own objection to contextual definitions was only that they were *insufficient* for fully determining the relevant abstract *objects*, not that they cannot legitimately yield new *concepts*.[12] We certainly want (Da) and (Db) to possess the same sense ('content', to use Frege's original term) under some appropriate conception of sense; and it is just such a conception of sense that (SCE) encapsulates. For if we *do* understand (Db), then we *will* possess the concept of direction, and we ought then to immediately recognize that (Db) is true if we recognize that (Da) is true. If someone cannot do this, then we will say that they cannot *really* have understood (Db) after all. So the extra condition that (SCE) embodies does seem to yield the desired result that members of Fregean pairs possess the same sense.

To see that such a criterion still leaves *differences* of sense where Frege typically locates them, let us consider Frege's paradigm example:

(MSB)　The Morning Star is a body illuminated by the Sun.
(ESB)　The Evening Star is a body illuminated by the Sun. (Cf. *SR*, p. 62.)

It is clearly possible to *understand* both propositions without immediately inferring that (ESB) is true in recognizing that (MSB) is true. I may know what is meant by 'the Evening Star' – it refers to the bright heavenly body that I see in the evening, but I may not realize that the Evening Star *is* the Morning Star. In holding (MSB) as true, for example, I may know that the Morning Star is actually one of the planets in our solar system (and hence is a body illuminated by the Sun), but in not thereby recognizing that (ESB) is true, I may well lack the belief that the Evening Star is a planet. By (SCE), therefore, (MSB) and (ESB) have different senses.

The use of (SCE) also yields the results that Frege wants in at least the vast majority of arithmetical cases. Consider the following two propositions:

(28PN)　28 is an even perfect number [where a perfect number is a number whose proper divisors add up to the number itself].
(28EN)　28 is a Euclid number [where a Euclid number is a number that can be represented in the form 2^{k-1} $(2^k\text{-}1)$, where $2^k\text{-}1$ is prime].

It has been proved that all and only even perfect numbers are Euclid numbers (and it is conjectured that all perfect numbers are even, in which case all and only perfect numbers are Euclid numbers), so that by (SLE), (28PN) and (28EN) possess the same sense, which is certainly not what Frege wished. (SEE), on the other hand, yields the result that they possess different senses, since someone can clearly recognize that (28PN) is true without recognizing that (28EN) is true. But (SCE) also yields the desired result, since even if someone does grasp both the concept of an even perfect number and the concept of a Euclid number, they need not immediately recognize (28EN) as true if they recognize (28PN) as true: unless they know the proof, they will typically need to *work out* that (28EN) is true. Only in the case of very elementary propositions such as '2 + 2 = 4' and '2 + 3 = 5' might it be possible to use (SCE) to argue that both propositions possess the same sense; and here we can simply introduce the qualification that Frege made in formulating (SEE) – ruling out its application to such self-evident propositions.[13]

(SCE) does, then, provide a criterion for sameness of sense that best captures Frege's intentions – having, in particular, the desired result that members of Fregean pairs can have the same sense. However, as formulated, (SCE) is open to an obvious objection. For what exactly is involved in 'understanding' the relevant propositions, which is the precondition of applying the test of immediate recognition? If we return to Frege's own specification of the criterion given by (SEE), we might suggest that to 'understand' a proposition is to grasp its 'content'; but this threatens to undermine any criterion incorporating a requirement of 'understanding'. For if the 'content' of a proposition is precisely the 'thought' expressed (and we are indeed trying to capture that notion of 'content' that Frege used in the *Grundlagen* in discussing contextual definitions), then, if two propositions do express the same thought, to grasp the 'content' of one is *ipso facto* to grasp the 'content' of the other, and if it is the 'content' that we recognize as true or false, then we automatically recognize the 'content' of one as true if we recognize the 'content' of the other as true.[14] Not only does this make the criterion useless, but it also violates the constraints on an adequate criterion: it is unacceptable to presuppose on the right hand side of the biconditional precisely that notion that we are attempting to specify. However, it is absurd to suggest that in understanding one proposition – by grasping its 'content' – I thereby 'understand' (in having grasped that 'content') any other proposition that has the same 'content' (I can grasp a thought in English, for example, without understanding its expression in any other language). Clearly, in making (SCE) a workable criterion, there must be a way of 'understanding' a proposition that does not simply consist in grasping its 'content'.

The obvious suggestion, which we have, in fact, been assuming in discussing (SCE), is that we 'understand' a proposition if we understand the concepts involved in its articulation. What is needed here is something along the lines of Frege's earlier distinction between 'content' and 'way of splitting up content', where it is the latter notion that exploits the idea of conceptual articulation. The difficulty for Frege, as we have seen, is that the distinction between 'Bedeutung' and 'Sinn' which replaced this distinction did not inherit the virtues of the earlier one. In restricting 'Bedeutung' purely to truth-value, the notion of 'Sinn' was given too much work to do: it had to capture both our 'understanding' of a proposition as well as the 'content' of that understanding; so that it is not surprising that a definitive criterion could not be laid down.

The problem was only exacerbated by his later adoption of principles of compositionality, which might at first sight appear to fill out the necessary notion of conceptual articulation. According to Frege, the thought expressed by a proposition is determined by the senses of its parts; and it seems natural to then suggest that to understand a proposition is to appreciate the way in which the senses of its parts do determine the sense of the whole. But such a suggestion only generates two further difficulties.

Firstly, it still leaves an ambiguity concerning the individuation of thoughts. Does every 'determination' yield a different thought, or is it possible for the same thought to be 'determined' in different ways? If the former, then thoughts are individuated as finely as 'conceptual articulations', but this seems incompatible with Frege's insistence that the same thought can be expressed in different linguistic forms. If the latter, then how exactly is this to be explained? On the face of it, this might seem no more problematic than Frege's earlier conception of the 'content' of a proposition being 'split up' in different ways. But that earlier conception had been embedded in a contextualism that had granted sentences logical priority over their parts, whereas his later compositionalism reverses the priority. I shall take up the issue of the tension between his earlier contextualism and his compositionalism in the next section.

Secondly, our discussion of indexicality and Frege's later conception of thoughts in §§7.4 and 7.5 suggested that there is a *gap* between our understanding of sentences and our grasp of the thoughts expressed by sentences. The thought I express by using a sentence involving an indexical seems to be determined not just by what I understand by the words I use but also by the *context*. So understanding a sentence seems to be neither a necessary condition for grasping the thought expressed, since that thought can be expressed in a different linguistic form, nor a sufficient condition, since an appreciation of the context also plays a role. I shall return to this in §8.3.

8.2 Contextualism and Compositionality

As we saw in §§2.2 and 5.2, in distinguishing his 'Begriffsschrift' from the systems of previous logicians, Frege emphasized that he proceeds not from concepts but from judgements: 'instead of putting a judgement together out of an individual as subject and an already previously formed concept as predicate, we do the opposite and arrive at a concept by splitting up the content of possible judgement' (*BLC*, p. 17). It was Frege's use of function-argument analysis that was crucial here. The removal of a proper name from a sentence that represents a 'content' (that can be used to make a judgement) yields an incomplete expression that represents a concept; and with a complex sentence there will be more than one way of doing this. Since different concepts thus result, definitions and analyses can be fruitful in revealing new concepts from a given content.

This process was accorded fundamental significance in the central argument of the *Grundlagen*, which formed the basis of Frege's logicist programme (see §§4.2 and 5.3 above). Through contextual definition the concepts of *direction* and *number* can be yielded from contents initially specified in terms of equivalence relations – parallelism and equinumerosity – holding between lines and concepts, respectively. It is therefore clear that judgements or 'conceptual contents' were seen as having logical priority over concepts; and we might capture this in the following principle:

> (PDC) The concepts that can be yielded from the content of a judgement are determined by (function-argument) analysis of that judgement, each concept corresponding to a distinct analysis.

Such a principle, however, seems in direct conflict with the two principles that were formulated in §6.2 as underlying Frege's arguments concerning the *Sinn* and *Bedeutung* of expressions:

> (PDB) The *Bedeutung* of a complex expression is determined by the *Bedeutung* of its parts.
>
> (PDS) The sense of a complex expression is determined by the sense of its parts.

(PDC) seems to accord *sentences* logical priority, whilst (PDB) and (PDS) seem to accord the elementary *parts* of a sentence logical priority.

The apparent conflict here is only sharpened if we bring in Frege's context principle. The context principle is first used in the *Grundlagen* in combatting psychologism about numbers. That we can form no *idea* of the content of a number word, Frege argues, is no reason for denying all meaning to the word. As long as propositions involving number terms have a sense as a whole, then their parts also must have a content. 'Only in a proposition do the words really have a meaning [*Bedeutung*].' (*GL*, §60; see §4.1 above.) But the principle is formulated again, almost immediately, in §62, where the constructive part of Frege's project gets under way. Its role is clear. We can define the meaning of number terms by defining the sense of sentences in which such terms appear, in particular, identity statements of the form of (Nb). (Nb) is defined contextually by means of (Na), which in turn is definable purely logically. (See §§4.2 and 4.3 above.) The context principle can thus be seen as a generalization of (PDC), according sentences logical priority not only over concept expressions but also over names; and we might formulate it as follows:

> (CP) The contents of parts of a sentence are determined by the content of the whole.[15]

Once again, what we have here seems in direct conflict with (PDB) and (PDS).

Now the obvious response is simply to suggest that Frege changed his mind – that his earlier contextualism gave way to compositionalism. Two points might be made in support of this. Firstly, Frege himself came to reject contextual definitions in the *Grundlagen*, and opted instead for explicit definitions. Secondly, despite its emphatic endorsement as one of the three fundamental principles of the *Grundlagen* (p. X), the context principle was never again even mentioned.[16] However, with regard to the first point, we have already replied that contextual definitions were only seen as *insufficient*, not as incorrect, and that in any case, a contextual definition of *value-ranges* was in fact embodied in Axiom V of the *Grundgesetze* (see §5.3 above). With regard to the second point, we can reply that the context principle was not explicitly repudiated either, and that there was a perfectly good reason why it could not have been formulated again, namely, that it depended on just that undifferentiated notion of 'content' that was later replaced by the notions of 'Sinn' and 'Bedeutung'.

Of course, it would have been simple to have formulated two corresponding versions of (CP), one in relation to *Bedeutung* and the other in relation to sense:

(CPB) The *Bedeutungen* of parts of a sentence are determined by the *Bedeutung* of the whole.

(CPS) The senses of parts of a sentence are determined by the sense of the whole.

However, on Frege's conception of *Bedeutung*, (CPB) would be implausible: the referent of a name hardly seems dependent on the truth-value of the sentence in which the name appears. Here it does seem that it is the *Bedeutung* of the whole that is determined by the *Bedeutungen* of its parts; and as we saw in §6.2, Frege uses precisely (PDB) in motivating his conception of the *Bedeutung* of a sentence.[17] (CPS), on the other hand, might be felt to remain valid, at least to the extent that Frege continues to allow alternative function-argument analyses in yielding different concepts.

That Frege did insist on the logical priority of judgements over concepts throughout his life is made clear in notes that Frege wrote in 1919 for the historian of science Ludwig Darmstaedter:

> I do not begin with concepts and put them together to form a thought or judgement; I come by the parts of a thought by analysing the thought. This marks off my concept-script from the similar inventions of Leibniz and his successors, despite what the name suggests; perhaps it was not a very happy choice on my part. (*NLD*, p. 253.)

This is a firm endorsement of his earlier position. Indeed, in suggesting that the name of his logical notation, 'Begriffsschrift', was misleading, the priority thesis is only underlined.[18] Yet the semantic theory of the *Grundgesetze* seems to be based on the idea that the *Sinn* and *Bedeutung* of complex expressions are determined by the *Sinn* and *Bedeutung* of their parts (see esp. *GG*, I, §§28-32); and his last paper 'Compound Thoughts', published in 1923, opens with a ringing statement of the compositionalist view:

> It is astonishing what language can do. With a few syllables it can express an incalculable number of thoughts, so that even if a thought has been grasped by an inhabitant of the Earth for the very first time, a form of words

can be found in which it will be understood by someone else to whom it is entirely new. This would not be possible, if we could not distinguish parts in the thought corresponding to the parts of a sentence, so that the structure of the sentence can serve as a picture of the structure of the thought ...

If, then, we look upon thoughts as composed of simple parts, and take these, in turn, to correspond to the simple parts of sentences, we can understand how a few parts of sentences can go to make up a great multitude of sentences, to which, in turn, there correspond a great multitude of thoughts. (*CT*, p. 390.)[19]

This is a frequently quoted passage. An adequate explanation of what is now called *linguistic creativity* – the ability to use and understand new linguistic constructions – requires just that compositionalism that Frege is here articulating; and indeed, it was Frege's attempt to develop such a compositional theory in the *Grundgesetze* that has entitled him to be regarded as the founder of modern semantic theory.[20] But the question remains: how is this compatible with his earlier contextualism?

At least with respect to concepts, an answer can be readily given; and indeed, was provided by Frege himself in one of his earliest works. Immediately after the remark quoted at the beginning of this section, concerning the formation of concepts by 'splitting up' contents, Frege goes on:

Of course, if the expression of the content of possible judgement is to be analysable in this way, it must already be itself articulated. We may infer from this that at least the properties and relations which are not further analysable must have their own simple designations. But it doesn't follow from this that the ideas of these properties and relations are formed apart from objects: on the contrary they arise simultaneously with the first judgement in which they are ascribed to things. Hence in the concept-script their designations never occur on their own, but always in combinations which express contents of possible judgement. I could compare this with the behaviour of the atom: we suppose an atom never to be found on its own, but only combined with others, moving out of one combination only in order to enter immediately into another. (*BLC*, p. 17.)

The possibility of alternative function-argument analyses *presupposes* that the judgement is already articulated, and this requires that the judgement has elementary parts. What Frege nevertheless maintains is that even these elementary parts are incapable of existing independently.[21]

The idea can be illustrated by taking Frege's *Begriffsschrift* example once again:

(HLC)   Hydrogen is lighter than carbon dioxide.

This can be analysed either as saying of hydrogen that it has the property of being lighter than carbon dioxide or as saying of carbon dioxide that it has the property of being heavier than hydrogen. Of course, if we wished to express these by respecting subject/predicate position (regarded by Frege as of no *logical* significance), then the latter might more accurately be stated as follows:

(CHH) Carbon dioxide is heavier than hydrogen.

But, as we have seen, there is a clear sense in which (HLC) and (CHH) possess the same 'content', since it does seem that it is the same relation between the same two objects that is involved. But this suggests that there is a fuller analysis that would bring this out – that would elucidate the essential structure of the 'content'. Whilst (HLC) and (CHH) can be represented in the form 'Fa', then, the 'real' logical form that makes the alternative function-argument analyses possible must be represented as 'Rab' (or 'aRb') – saying of object a that it stands in relation R to object b. But since the relation involved here cannot be conceived except as relating objects in the relevant way, even the compositionalism that the idea of a complete analysis legitimizes is not incompatible with continued adherence to the principle (PDC). Indeed, the logical priority of judgements over concepts is simply a presupposition of Frege's doctrine of the unsaturatedness of functions: expressions for concepts or relations are formed by removing names from sentences; and this doctrine Frege continued to hold to the end of his life.[22]

Michael Dummett has suggested that what is required in reconciling Frege's views here is a distinction between *decomposition* and *analysis*, taken with a corresponding distinction between *component* and *constituent* concepts.[23] Decomposition is what is involved in yielding *component* concepts – extracting the concept *lighter than carbon dioxide* from the 'content' of (HLC), for example. It is with the process of decomposition that the contextualist principle (PDC) is concerned; and judgements do indeed have logical priority over *component* concepts. Analysis, on the other hand, is what is involved in uncovering the 'real' logical form of a judgement, revealing its *constituent* concepts or relations. To grasp a thought we must understand those elementary parts that *constitute* it, and it is with this process, which analysis elucidates, that Frege's principles of compositionality are concerned. To understand (HLC), for example, I must grasp the relation *lighter than* and know which objects hydrogen and carbon dioxide are. Having done so, I can then form the concept *lighter than carbon dioxide*, but such a decomposition presupposes that I have already grasped the thought in the way revealed by the correct analysis. So contextualism and compositionalism, at least with regard to concepts, are not in conflict: properly understood, contextualism presupposes compositionalism; and it was just this compositionalism that came to the fore in Frege's philosophy as he thought things through more fully.

However, whilst the distinction between decomposition and analysis is undoubtedly useful, the issue is more complex than the account just given might imply. Dummett maintains that whilst there can be alternative function-argument *decompositions* of a given thought, there is only one correct *analysis* of it. But if we look more carefully at Frege's *Begriffsschrift* example, we can see that this cannot be accepted without qualification. (HLC) and (CHH), we suggested, are both concerned with the same relation between the same two objects – it is this that underpins their sameness of 'content'. But are there not two *different* relations involved here? For if we represent the relation *lighter than* by 'R', then the relation *heavier than* is its *inverse*, R'; so that if a is hydrogen and b is carbon dioxide, then the judgement can be represented either as 'Rab' ('aRb') or as '$R'ba$' ('$bR'a$'). So even at the deepest level, there seems to be room for alternative analyses.

An obvious response is to make use of Frege's distinction between sense and reference and to say that whilst at the level of *reference*, it is the same relation that is involved, there are two different *modes of presentation* of that relation: we can conceive of it either as the referent of the expression 'ξ is lighter than ζ' or as the referent of the expression 'ζ is heavier than ξ'.[24] However, in admitting that these two expressions have different senses, we would be admitting – if (PDS) were still to be endorsed – that (HLC) and (CHH) themselves have different senses, i.e. express different thoughts; and this would certainly not have been Frege's view. Now it would be possible to deny that we do have two different senses here: once the order of the place-holders for the relata is appreciated, the two expressions can be seen to have the same sense. But at least without the place-holders, what we understand by the expression 'is lighter than' is different from what we understand by the expression 'is heavier than', and if place-holders *are* to enter into the expression for a relation, then we would now be working *back* from the sense of the sentence as a whole to the sense of the part that designates the relation. Indeed, this was just what was involved in Frege's conception of the *unsaturatedness* of functions. Either way, then, (PDS) cannot be endorsed as it stands. If the two relational expressions in (HLC) and (CHH) have different senses, then there can be alternative analyses of one and the same thought; and if the two expressions have the same sense, then this can only be apprehended by working back from the sense of the whole.[25]

However, we can agree with Dummett that there is only one correct analysis of the thought expressed by (HLC) *as expressed by* (HLC). For I do need to understand the expression 'is lighter than' to understand (HLC) itself. But it is not necessary to understand this expression to grasp the thought itself, since if that thought can also be expressed by (CHH), then it can also be grasped by understanding the expression 'is heavier than' – together, of course, with an understanding of the names 'hydrogen' and 'carbon dioxide' and an appreciation of their order in the sentence.

The distinction just drawn here between the thought expressed by a sentence and the thought *as* expressed by the sentence may seem unnecessarily subtle, but it is essential to respect it if we are to preserve Frege's fundamental conception that the same thought can be expressed in different linguistic forms. Indeed, it really amounts to no more than Frege's original distinction between 'content' and 'way of splitting up content'. Dummett himself was led to underestimate the importance of retaining such a distinction by the emphasis he places on the following thesis:

(TIS) A thought is isomorphic with the sentence whose sense it is.[26]

Now it is true that this thesis is a presupposition of the compositional principle (PDS), and it is also explicitly endorsed in the statement of the compositionalist view that we quoted above. But what was omitted (at the place indicated) from the passage quoted is the following admission:

> To be sure, we really talk figuratively when we transfer the relation of whole and part to thoughts; yet the analogy is so ready to hand and so generally appropriate that we are hardly even bothered by the hitches which occur from time to time. (*CT*, p. 390.)

Although Frege suggests that 'hitches' only occur occasionally, he is clearly aware that (TIS) is only *generally* applicable; and a similar qualification is implicit in his notes for Ludwig Darmstaedter: 'We can regard a sentence as a mapping of a thought: corresponding to the whole-part relation of a thought and its parts we have, *by and large*, the same relation for the sentence and its parts' (*NLD*, p. 255; my emphasis). So we cannot treat Frege as having ruled out entirely the possibility of different sentences of quite different linguistic forms expressing the same thought.

As far as the example from the *Begriffsschrift* is concerned, however, (TIS) is not in any case incompatible with the possibility of alternative analyses of the relevant thought, for (HLC) and (CHH) are presumably isomorphic with each other, and hence if one is isomorphic with the thought it expresses, then so too is the other. Whether or not we say that the two relational expressions possess the same sense, in other words, the two sentences have the structural similarity that justifies regarding them as isomorphic: they both involve a relational expression and two proper names. So whilst (PDS) may imply (TIS), (TIS) does not on its own imply (PDS).

However, what does threaten (TIS) are examples of *Fregean pairs* – not only *horizontal* ones such as (Da) and (Db) but also *vertical* ones such as (Da) and (Dc):

(Da) Line *a* is parallel to line *b*.
(Db) The direction of line *a* is identical with the direction of line *b*.
(Dc) The concept 'line parallel to line *a*' is coextensive with the concept 'line parallel to line *b*'.

Members of Fregean pairs are not isomorphic with one another, since, as we remarked in the last section, they are concerned with different relations between objects of different kinds. But before we conclude that Fregean pairs cannot, after all, embody sameness of sense, let us note that such a conclusion would wreck Frege's logicist programme of analysis. For if we recall our discussions in §§4.1 and 5.3, we can see that the relationships between members of Fregean pairs are essentially no different from the relationships between propositions involving the adjectival use of number terms, propositions involving the substantival use of number terms, and propositions that more explicitly attribute properties to concepts. Compare (Da), (Db) and (Dc), for example, with the following:

(Oa) There are 0 F's.
(Ob) The number of F's is 0.
(Oc) The concept F is not instantiated.

As we saw, Frege clearly held that a 'content' can be 'split up' in such a way that the resulting propositions have different subjects (the subject/predicate distinction being regarded as of no logical significance); and even with the bifurcation of 'content' into sense and reference, the basic idea – at the level of sense – was still endorsed. In 'On Concept and Object', Frege is explicit that the following two sentences express the same thought:

($\sqrt{4}$a) There is at least one square root of 4.
($\sqrt{4}$c) The concept *square root of 4* is realized.

Prescinding from Frege's worries about referring to concepts by use of phrases of the form 'the concept F',[27] we can take his point to be that, as he puts it, 'a thought can be split up in many ways, so that now one thing, now another, appears as subject or predicate' (*CO*, p. 49). He writes:

> The thought itself does not yet determine what is to be regarded as the subject. If we say 'the subject of this judgment', we do not designate anything definite unless at the same time we indicate a definite kind of analysis; as a rule, we do this in connexion with a definite wording. But we must never forget that different sentences may express the same thought. For example, the thought we are considering could also be taken as saying something about the number 4:
> [($\sqrt{4}$b)] 'The number 4 has the property that there is something of which it is the square.'
> Language has means of presenting now one, now another, part of the thought as the subject; one of the most familiar is the distinction of active and passive forms. It is thus not impossible that one way of analysing a given thought should make it appear as a singular judgment; another, as a particular judgment; and a third, as a universal judgment. It need not then surprise us that the same sentence may be conceived as saying something about a concept and also as saying something about an object; only we must observe that what is being said is different. (*CO*, p. 49.)

All three propositions here, ($\sqrt{4}$a), ($\sqrt{4}$b) and ($\sqrt{4}$c), are not isomorphic with one another, yet Frege is insistent that they all express the same thought. So Frege cannot be taken to have held (TIS) in its unqualified form.

However, with regard to vertical Fregean pairs, such as (Da) and (Dc), (Oa) and (Oc), or ($\sqrt{4}$a) and ($\sqrt{4}$c), what we arguably have here are cases of *degenerate analyses*, or more accurately, *degenerate decompositions*.[28] There is an obvious sense in which the first of the two propositions is the more fundamental, and the second is dependent upon it. In these cases we have what was called in §5.3 *conceptual ascent*, involving a shift from talking about things of a certain kind to talking about the concepts used in so talking; and there is in principle no limit to how high such conceptual ascent can go. From (Dc), for example, we can in turn generate the following proposition:

(Df)   The concept 'concept coextensive with the concept "line parallel to line *a*" is coextensive with the concept 'concept coextensive with the concept "line parallel to line *b*" '.

A whole hierarchy of such propositions can be constructed, each spun out of the previous one, and each expressing, in an ever more complicated form, the same thought.[29]

The possibility of such conceptual ascent clearly suggests that only the first member of the series generated should be taken as fundamental, and this is obviously compatible with there being just one correct *analysis* of a thought. Only of the first member would it be reasonable to demand that it reflect the essential structure of the thought; all other sentences represent *decompositions* of the thought, becoming increasingly degenerate the further up the hierarchy they go. A simple modification of (TIS) thus readily suggests itself:

(TIS')   A thought is isomorphic with the sentence that expresses that thought in its most fundamental form.

But this now reduces the thesis of isomorphism to a tautology, for if a sentence is not isomorphic with the thought it expresses, then it would not be regarded as expressing it in its most fundamental form; and nothing has been said here about what does count as a thought's most fundamental form.

Whilst it is easy to determine which of the two members of a vertical Fregean pair is the more fundamental, there may be no obvious answer as to which member of a horizontal Fregean pair is fundamental. In the case of (Da) and (Db), Frege thought that (Da) was fundamental, since 'everything geometrical must surely originate in intuition', and lines are intuited before directions (cf. *GL*, §64). But in his central numerical case, the issue is more complex:

(Na)   The concept *F* is equinumerous to the concept *G*.
(Nb)   The number of *F*'s is identical with the number of *G*'s.

Frege's use of the context principle suggests that here too the first of the two propositions is regarded as more fundamental: (Na), which can itself be characterized purely logically, is to be used to define the 'content' of the number terms in (Nb). But of course Frege comes to reject such contextual definitions, and the reason might be put by saying that the number terms are already taken as referring to objects in the domain, i.e. they are already assumed to have an independent 'meaning'. As we saw in §4.1, this assumption first surfaces in §57 of the *Grundlagen*, where Frege shows that he treats *substantival* constructions such as (Ob) as more fundamental than *adjectival* constructions such as (Oa). And it is this underlying assumption that drives the Caesar problem, Frege's response to which we outlined in §4.2 and discussed in more detail in §§5.3 and 6.4.

Frege's use of the context principle in the *Grundlagen* is thus disingenuous. Although he writes in §60 that 'Only in a proposition do the words really have a meaning', using the word 'Bedeutung' for what is here translated as 'meaning', and talks of the proposition as a whole determining the 'content' ('Inhalt') of its parts, he does not really mean that the *referents* of the number terms, i.e. the numbers themselves, are dependent on the 'content' of the proposition, for he has already taken himself to have shown that numbers are independent objects (*GL*, §57; see §4.1 above). His use of the context principle is *epistemological* rather than ontological. Numbers are not abstract objects parasitic upon something else – our use of sortal concepts in classifying the ordinary objects of the world – but objects that are already there in the universal domain in their own right. But since we cannot apprehend such objects by either our senses (which would make our knowledge of arithmetic synthetic *a posteriori*) or our intuition (which would yield synthetic *a priori* knowledge), we must be taken to apprehend them by pure reason, by understanding the senses of propositions – definable purely logically – in which names for the objects appear.

The obvious strategy for dealing with horizontal Fregean pairs – treating (Nb) as contextually dependent on (Na), for example – was not therefore one that Frege himself felt able to adopt, at least in his central case. So should (Na) be treated instead as dependent on (Nb)? This would preserve both Frege's realism about numbers and also the idea that there is only one ultimate analysis of a thought – once its fundamental form is determined. This would also enable us to cut down on our ontological commitments: referents need only be required for the constituents of a sentence that expresses a thought in its most fundamental form. Given that there is in any case a problem with (Na), on Frege's view, since phrases of the form 'the concept *F*' do not in fact succeed in referring to what they are intended to refer, this is clearly attractive. It is also consistent with the account just given of vertical Fregean pairs, since in conceptual ascent too we make use of such misfiring phrases. But as we saw in §7.1, where the eliminative strategy was suggested as the obvious way of dealing with the paradox of the concept *horse*, it does not appear to have even crossed Frege's mind. This is significant, for it shows just how little ontological work – in the sense of reducing our ontological commitments – the context principle was regarded as doing. Even when contextual definitions cry out to be used as a way of eliminating the need to treat concepts as any kind of object – and the absoluteness of the distinction between concept and object was as deeply held as anything in Frege's philosophy – Frege fails to make the obvious move. Even phrases of the form 'the concept *F*' are seen as referring; they are just taken to refer not to concepts but to 'concept-correlates' – special objects that go proxy for concepts. It is worth noting that the passage quoted above concerning the different possible analyses of a thought comes from the very paper – 'On Concept and Object' – where Frege confronts most directly the problems raised by the paradox of the concept *horse*.

What could possibly have prevented Frege from making the obvious move? It is true that eliminativism as a strategy in philosophical logic was only first pursued by Russell in his theory of descriptions,[30] but what prevented Frege from pursuing this himself was his *compositionalism*, *implicit* in his thought even at the time when the context principle appeared on the surface to be dominant. For according to Frege, if a proposition is true, then all the names within it must refer. As we have seen, Frege regarded logic as a system of *truths*, and in his very early work had asserted that 'The rules of logic always presuppose that the words we use are not empty' (*DPE*, p. 60; quoted in §2.4 above). Since (Nb) is true if (Na) is true (they are, at least, *logically* equivalent), then regardless of the epistemological question as to which is prior in the order of explanation, the number terms contained in (Nb) must refer to pre-existing objects, as a condition of the truth of the proposition. Even in his early thought, then, some form of compositionalism was operative.

What we are therefore left with is the view that (Na) and (Nb) are *equally* fundamental, in the sense that they both involve reference to things that are viewed as ontologically independent ('*selbständig*'); and this means that there can after all be alternative *analyses* (and not just decompositions) of one and the same thought. For the thesis that there is just one correct analysis of a thought can only be maintained if there is some fundamental form that each thought takes. But definitional strategy aside, Frege saw no difference in ontological status between the members of a Fregean pair.[31] So even in its modified form, (TIS'), the thesis of isomorphism cannot be attributed to Frege as his considered view. But since, as we have already remarked, (PDS) implies (TIS), does this then not mean that (PDS) too cannot be attributed to Frege, and does this not blatantly contradict the claim that compositionalism was fundamental to Frege's philosophy?

However, just before we introduced (TIS), we drew a distinction that we can now use to suggest a modification of (PDS):

(PDS′) The sense *as* expressed by a sentence is determined by the sense of its parts.

This arguably preserves the essence of Frege's compositionalism, whilst leaving room for alternative analyses of thoughts, the possibility of which is intimately connected with Frege's central thesis that the same thought can be expressed in different linguistic forms.[32]

What, then, can we conclude about the relationship between Frege's contextualism and his compositionalism? At the beginning of this section we suggested that the context principle (CP) could be seen as a generalization of (PDC), the principle concerning the logical priority of judgements over concepts. Frege's doctrine of the unsaturatedness of concepts, and indeed the fundamental role that function-argument analysis plays in his logic, implies that this latter principle was central throughout his work.[33] But as we have seen, it had never been Frege's belief that the *referents* of proper names, i.e. the objects themselves, depended on anything else. The use of the context principle was *epistemological* rather than ontological: it was introduced – though no doubt inspired by (PDC) – to explain how analytic *a priori* knowledge of numbers is possible.

It is not surprising, then, that once the distinction between sense and reference had been drawn, which was a response to the problems that §§62-9 of the *Grundlagen* raised, the context principle could no longer be endorsed. For at the ontological level – the level of *Bedeutung* – there is certainly no dependence of the referents of terms on the truth-values of sentences.[34] Rather, the truth-value of a proposition is dependent on the reference of its parts. But at the epistemological level – the level of *Sinn* – the issue is more complex. Thoughts may be logically prior to concepts, in so far as they permit alternative analyses, but for any given expression of a thought, there is indeed only one correct analysis that explains how that particular expression is understood. It was the subtle complexity of Frege's position here, requiring further distinctions to be drawn of which Frege himself was not fully aware, that resulted in the context principle being neither explicitly endorsed (because contextualism at the level of *Bedeutung* was rejected) nor explicitly repudiated (because contextualism at the level of *Sinn* was in one respect retained).

8.3 The Varieties of Sense

A distinction was drawn in the last section between the thought expressed by a sentence and the thought *as* expressed by a sentence. The idea here is simple: what grasping the thought *as* expressed by a sentence involves is *understanding* the sentence; and it is entirely plausible to suppose that there is a unique analysis of what constitutes our *understanding* of a given sentence, which we might capture in the following principle:

(PDU) The understanding of a complex expression is determined by the understanding of its parts.

But the question that now needs to be addressed is whether this principle is the same as (PDS'), the modification offered of the compositional principle concerning sense, and whether (PDS') is in fact true. Our discussion of indexicality in §§7.4 and 7.5 suggests otherwise. For there appears to be a *gap* between our understanding of sentences and our grasp of the thoughts even *as* expressed by sentences, since *context* too is a determinant of sense.

I understand the *linguistic role* of an indexical if I understand the *rule* that takes me from the context of utterance to the object denoted. But this is not enough to grasp the *sense* of the indexical, as used on a particular occasion, since its linguistic role is the same from context to context, whilst its sense and reference varies. What is needed is some way of 'cashing out' the indexical which 'presents' the referent in an appropriate way. But on the assumption that the sense of the indexical, as used on a particular occasion, is to be identified with the sense of some definite description, we arrive at an inconsistency in the Fregean position. For as we argued, I can hold that a sentence involving the indexical is true without holding that the corresponding sentence involving the definite description is true, and vice versa – even where I 'understand' all the relevant words. What is operative here is just that criterion of identity for thoughts that we discussed in §8.1, together with the compositional principle concerning sense. Since the two sentences express different thoughts, the sense of the indexical must be different from the sense of the corresponding definite description.

Rather than concluding that the sense of an indexical, as used on a particular occasion, is primitive and irreducible, however, we suggested that we grasp that sense simply if we know *which object* is referred to, something that can be *shown* in any number of different ways, and that typically involves the ability to *track* the relevant object. The suggestion here drew on the analogy with simple names, the sense of which, we argued in §6.4, should also not be identified with the sense of any corresponding definite description. But as we remarked, this represents something of a departure from Frege's own ideas; and we can appreciate this if we return to the example that Frege discusses in 'Der Gedanke', which we considered in §7.5 in relation to the question of *I-thoughts*. This is the passage that we only summarized at the time:

> Consider the following case. Dr. Gustav Lauben says, 'I was wounded', Leo Peter hears this and remarks some days later, 'Dr. Gustav Lauben was wounded'. Does this sentence express the same thought as the one Dr. Lauben uttered himself? Suppose that Rudolph Lingens was present when Dr. Lauben spoke and now hears what is related by Leo Peter. If the same thought was uttered by Dr. Lauben and Leo Peter, then Rudolph Lingens,

who is fully master of the language and remembers what Dr. Lauben said in his presence, must now know at once from Leo Peter's report that he is speaking of the same thing. But knowledge of the language is a special thing when proper names are involved. It may well be the case that only a few people associate a definite thought with the sentence 'Dr. Lauben was wounded'. For complete understanding one needs in this case to know the expression 'Dr. Gustav Lauben'. Now if both Leo Peter and Rudolph Lingens mean by 'Dr. Gustav Lauben', the doctor who is the only doctor living in a house known to both of them, then they both understand the sentence 'Dr. Gustav Lauben was wounded' in the same way; they associate the same thought with it. But it is also possible that Rudolph Lingens does not know Dr. Lauben personally and does not know that it was Dr. Lauben who recently said 'I was wounded'. In this case Rudolph Lingens cannot know that the same affair is in question. I say, therefore, in this case: the thought which Leo Peter expresses is not the same as that which Dr. Lauben uttered. (*T*, pp. 358-9.)

The main point here is clear: even when Leo Peter and Rudolph Lingens both associate the same mode of presentation with the proper name 'Dr. Gustav Lauben', Dr. Lauben saying 'I was wounded' and Leo Peter later saying 'Dr. Gustav Lauben was wounded' do not express the same thought since Rudolph Lingens can hear and understand both utterances but not realize that it is the same incident involved. The key assumption of Frege's argument here is that a 'definite thought' is only expressed by a sentence if a unique mode of presentation is associated with every constituent singular term (indexical or proper name). Presumably the thought that Rudolph Lingens grasps when he hears Dr. Lauben saying 'I was wounded' would be expressed by Rudolph Lingens himself saying 'The man now speaking was wounded',[35] and the thought that he grasps when he hears Leo Peter saying 'Dr. Gustav Lauben was wounded' would be expressed by 'The only doctor living in house *H* [the house known to both Leo Peter and Rudolph Lingens] was wounded'. Clearly, these two thoughts *are* different. But are Leo Peter's corresponding thoughts different? If when he hears Dr. Lauben saying 'I was wounded', Leo Peter already knows that the man speaking *is* Dr. Gustav Lauben, then surely the thought that he himself grasps is better expressed by 'Dr. Gustav Lauben was wounded', in which case Leo Peter's two thoughts are the same. But for Frege, this would still raise the question as to what is actually understood by 'Dr. Gustav Lauben'; and it would indeed seem implausible to suggest that Leo Peter has the thought expressed by 'The only doctor living in house *H* was wounded' when he hears Dr. Lauben saying 'I was wounded'.

Of course, if thoughts are determined by their constituent modes of presentation, then there are many other possibilities as to what thoughts are involved here. Perhaps in saying 'I was wounded', Dr. Lauben thinks of *himself* under just that mode of presentation that Leo Peter and Rudolph Lingens associate with the name 'Dr. Gustav Lauben', in which case we might again have the same thought expressed both times. (They might all think of him as the man named 'Dr. Gustav Lauben', for example.) And why should Leo Peter not have a *compound thought* made up of *several* 'definite thoughts' when he hears Dr. Lauben saying 'I was wounded' – 'The man now speaking, who is called 'Dr. Lauben' and who is the only doctor living in house *H*, was wounded'? All that would then be needed to secure communication would be one particular component 'definite thought' that is common to all thinkers. Nevertheless, it is quite clear that the assumption isolated above plays a critical role, and this is only confirmed in the two paragraphs that immediately follow:

> Suppose further that Herbert Garner knows that Dr. Gustav Lauben was born on 13 September, 1875 in N.N. and this is not true of anyone else; suppose, however, that he does not know where Dr. Lauben now lives nor indeed anything else about him. On the other hand, suppose Leo Peter does not know that Dr. Lauben was born on 13 September 1875, in N.N. Then as far as the proper name 'Dr. Gustav Lauben' is concerned, Herbert Garner and Leo Peter do not speak the same language, although they do in fact refer to the same man with this name; for they do not know that they are doing so. Therefore Herbert Garner does not associate the same thought with the sentence 'Dr. Gustav Lauben was wounded' as Leo Peter wants to express with it. To avoid the awkwardness that Herbert Garner and Leo Peter are not speaking the same language, I shall suppose that Leo Peter uses the proper name 'Dr. Lauben' and Herbert Garner uses the proper name 'Gustav Lauben'. Then it is possible that Herbert Garner takes the sense of the sentence 'Dr. Lauben was wounded' to be true but is misled by false information into taking the sense of the sentence 'Gustav Lauben was wounded' to be false. So given our assumptions these thoughts are different.
>
> Accordingly, with a proper name, it is a matter of the way that the object so designated is presented. This may happen in different ways, and to every such way there corresponds a special sense of a sentence containing the proper name. The different thoughts thus obtained from the same sentences correspond in truth-value, of course; that is to say, if one is true then all are true, and if one is false then all are false. Nevertheless the difference must be recognized. So we must really stipulate that for every proper name there shall be just one associated manner of presentation of the object so designated. It is often unimportant that this stipulation should be fulfilled, but not always. (*T*, p. 359.)

As we remarked in §6.4, in relation to Frege's notorious 'Aristotle' footnote in 'Über Sinn und Bedeutung', Frege regarded the multiplicity of senses typically associated with a proper name as a defect of ordinary language. Only in a formal language such as that developed by Frege for arithmetic could the problem of variability be avoided. As we outlined in §4.3, we can start by defining the number 0, for example, as the extension of the concept 'equinumerous to the concept *not identical with itself*', and then proceed to define each subsequent number in terms of its predecessors. What we have in each case is a 'constructive definition', where the *definiendum* is stipulated to have both the same sense and the same reference as the *definiens* (cf. §5.5). Each numeral is indeed then associated with a unique mode of presentation – or what might be better called here a *mode of construction* – which 'determines' the relevant number. This clearly provides the model for the revision of ordinary language that Frege proposes in the above passage.

However, what the passage also suggests is that, strictly speaking, there may be nothing wrong with any *individual* person's language, as long as they consistently associate one particular mode of presentation with each singular term; the problem lies rather in individuals not being able to *communicate* with one another properly, since they may well associate *different* senses with the same name. This seems to be the point of Frege's remark that Herbert Garner and Leo Peter do not speak the same language in the case imagined: they may use the same words, but their understanding of those words is quite different. The defect of ordinary language that Frege is highlighting, then, is located at the *epistemological* rather than semantic level. It is thus unlike what is wrong, according to Frege, with our use of terms for *vague* concepts. As we saw in §7.3, sentences involving these terms were regarded as *lacking* a truth-value (a *Bedeutung*) and hence as not expressing a genuine thought at all. By his compositional principles, therefore, the terms themselves lack a reference and a sense. An ordinary proper name, as used by someone on a particular occasion, on the other hand, may well have both; it is just that someone else may not realize exactly what they are. The typical problem is not that such a name *lacks* a sense, which would be a semantic deficiency, as that there are *too many* senses with which it might be associated, which raises the epistemological question as to which sense is intended.

This only reinforces the point that we have emphasized throughout this book – that our understanding of the various elements involved in the use of an expression on a particular occasion requires an appreciation of the *context*. Indeed, if Frege is right here, then context-dependence is even more pervasive at the level of sense than it is at the level of reference. For whilst an awareness of the *immediate* context may be all that is needed to recognize the *referent* of a singular term as used by someone on a particular occasion, to grasp its *sense* I may well need to understand something of that person's *cognitive history* – to ascertain the mode of presentation which they associate with the term.

Carried to their logical conclusion, Frege's views seem absurd. For when I write 'Gottlob Frege was the most important influence on Wittgenstein', for example, the exact way in which I think of Frege (e.g. as the philosopher I am currently writing about) may well be irrelevant to the thought that I intend to convey. As long as you know *to whom* I am referring, and understand the property that is being ascribed, then you can be said to have grasped the thought I express. This can be compared with my saying 'The author of the *Grundgesetze* was the most important influence on Wittgenstein', where a grasp of one particular mode of presentation *is* necessary to grasp the thought I express (I might be implying, for example, that it was the *Grundgesetze* that most influenced Wittgenstein). What this points to is the need to draw just that distinction between simple names and definite descriptions for which we argued in §6.4. Only in the case of a definite description is it reasonable to identify its sense with one particular mode of presentation. In the case of simple singular terms (including simple indexicals as well as proper names), a different account is required.

Although the texts show that Frege was unaware of the need to draw this distinction, the suggestion that to grasp the sense of a simple singular term is to know *which object* is referred to is a *refinement* rather than a repudiation of Frege's views, since modes of presentation are still taken as playing a crucial role. Frege's central thesis that the referent of an expression can only be apprehended via some mode of presentation is retained. As we have seen, what is needed here is an elementary scope distinction. I can be said to grasp the sense of a simple singular term if I have *some* means of identifying its referent; it is not necessary that there be one particular mode of presentation with which everyone who grasps its sense associates the term.

The scope distinction revealed here is important, for a similar distinction can be utilized to elucidate Frege's argument in 'Der Gedanke'. The main argument in the first passage quoted above initially seems straightforward. Since Rudolph Lingens can understand Dr. Lauben saying 'I was wounded' and Leo Peter later saying 'Dr. Gustav Lauben was wounded', but not realize that it is the same incident involved, the two utterances do not express the same thought. According to Frege, I understand an expression by associating a mode of presentation with it; but this is ambiguous between the following two readings:

(UMP) Anyone who understands an expression associates some particular mode of presentation of its referent with it.

(MPU) There is some particular mode of presentation of the referent of an expression that is associated with that expression by anyone who understands it.

On the first reading, Rudolph Lingens can certainly be taken to understand Dr. Lauben saying 'I was wounded' – he apprehends Dr. Lauben under *some* mode of presentation (e.g. as the man who is speaking). Yet as we have just seen, Frege's conception of proper names suggests that it is the second reading that he has in mind. But if Dr. Lauben may associate quite a different mode of presentation with the indexical 'I', and if this is the mode of presentation that someone else must grasp in order to understand – on the second reading – what Dr. Lauben himself has said, then Rudolph Lingens does not in fact grasp the thought that Dr. Lauben expresses. So nothing can then be concluded about whether Dr. Lauben and Leo Peter do express the same thought. But if Rudolph Lingens *is* assumed to grasp the thought that Dr. Lauben expresses, then how would he himself express it? Obviously, if he said 'Dr. Gustav Lauben was wounded', then we are back with the original question; but presumably a similar question would arise with regard to any attempt to express Dr. Lauben's thought. If the problem here is not, perhaps, immediately recognized, then it may be due to our unconsciously having in mind that weaker conception of 'understanding' embodied in (UMP).

We can now see why it was so essential for Frege to allow that there *is* a way of understanding someone else's I-thoughts – or else we could never even judge that someone's I-thought was *different* from the thought expressed in some other form. As Frege goes on to suggest, Dr. Lauben saying 'I was wounded' might be expressed by Rudolph Lingens as 'He who is speaking to me at this moment was wounded' (cf. *T*, pp. 359-60; quoted in §7.5). But of course, if we then ask what justifies treating these two sentences as expressing the same thought, and appeal to how some third party might understand them, then we are faced with an infinite regress.

The issue is important in view of our attempt to find a useful role for the criterion for sameness of sense, (SCE), discussed in §8.1. The criterion is implicit in the first passage quoted (and more explicitly operative in the paragraph that follows, concerning Herbert Garner's thoughts). Since Rudolph Lingens can 'understand' both utterances, yet take up different cognitive attitudes towards them, then they cannot express the same thought. Now at the end of §8.1, an objection was raised to (SCE), namely, that on the assumption that 'understanding' a sentence involves grasping the thought expressed, if two sentences do express the same thought, then 'understanding' one sentence is *ipso facto* to grasp the thought expressed by the other. In the light of our discussion in the previous section, however, this is easily answered. One should say, more precisely, that I 'understand' a sentence if I grasp the thought *as* expressed by that sentence, which clearly does not entail that I grasp the thought *as* expressed by any other sentence, even if that sentence does in fact express the same thought. But as the case of I-thoughts reveals, there remains a problem. For even if 'understanding' a sentence involves grasping the thought *as* expressed by the sentence, we are still entitled to ask how we are to tell whether someone *has* grasped the thought as expressed by the sentence; and we cannot then appeal to the criterion itself, on pain of regress.

The problem is only exacerbated if we set Frege's denial that Dr. Lauben saying 'I was wounded' and Leo Peter saying 'Dr. Gustav Lauben was wounded' express the same thought against the conception of the 'timelessness' of thoughts that it was one of the main tasks of 'Der Gedanke' to establish – the 'timelessness' of thoughts being captured by 'complete' sentences in which all indexicality is cashed out. Since the first shot at decontextualizing Dr. Lauben's original utterance is to say 'Dr. Gustav Lauben was wounded', the conflict is obvious. (Fully decontextualized, of course, the implicit spatial and temporal indexicality would also need to be cashed out.) Now as we suggested at the end of §7.5, one response is to distinguish between expressing and grasping a thought. Dr. Lauben saying 'I was wounded' *expresses* the thought cashed out more fully as 'Dr. Gustav Lauben was wounded', even if he himself does not grasp that thought in its 'completeness' (he may not remember, for example, exactly when it was that he was wounded, or how he came to be wounded). The way is then open to hold that Rudolph Lingens also expresses that thought by saying, at the time of Dr. Lauben's original utterance, 'The man speaking to me at this moment was wounded', even if he too cannot fully grasp that thought by cashing out all indexicality. But equally we must allow that Leo Peter later expresses that same thought by saying 'Dr. Gustav Lauben was wounded', exhibiting in doing so a fuller grasp of that thought.

On this conception, the explanation of how Rudolph Lingens can take up different cognitive attitudes towards the thought as expressed by Dr. Lauben and the thought as expressed by Leo Peter is that he has not fully grasped at least the former, and hence does not know that they do in fact express the same thought. If Rudolph Lingens *were* to properly grasp both, then he would indeed immediately recognize that it is the same thought expressed. But this really does threaten to make the criterion (SCE) useless. For if 'understanding' a sentence as used on a given occasion involves fully grasping the thought as expressed by that sentence, then since, as we remarked at the end of §7.4, no one can break out of the realm of the indexical altogether, the criterion can never actually be applied. The criterion may not be invalidated, but its utility is certainly undermined. I shall, however, consider what conclusions might be drawn from this in the next section.

But before doing so, let us return to the question raised at the beginning of this section, since the answer should now be clear. For Frege, there is *no* gap between (PDU) and (PDS'), properly construed, since, as the passages from 'Der Gedanke' reveal, 'understanding' a sentence as used on a particular occasion precisely involves grasping the sense as expressed by that sentence, and a 'full understanding' involves grasping that sense *on the basis of* an appreciation of the context. Where the gap comes out is between *incomplete* and *complete* 'understanding', with corresponding distinctions to be drawn between incomplete and complete senses and incomplete and complete sentences. Any incomplete sense is determined by the sense of the parts of the corresponding incomplete sentence, and any complete sense is determined by the sense of the parts of the corresponding complete sentence. But what is false is the following thesis:

(PDS#) The *complete* sense expressed by the use of an *incomplete* sentence in a particular context is determined by the sense of the parts of that sentence.

A complete sense can still be *expressed* by the use of an incomplete sentence in a particular context, but the incompleteness of the sentence used does not show that the user of the sentence has fully *grasped* that sense.

Nevertheless, it remains the case that on Frege's conception of 'timeless' thoughts, Dr. Lauben saying 'I was wounded' and Leo Peter saying 'Dr. Gustav Lauben was wounded' express the same thought, however incomplete the sentences themselves may be, and however incompletely the thought may be grasped. But in view of the problems with that conception discussed in §7.5, where are we left? It seems clear that Frege did want some notion of thought such that someone else could at least express, if not grasp, just that thought that Dr. Lauben expresses in saying 'I was wounded'. What is needed, in fact, is to resurrect Frege's earlier notion of the 'content' of a proposition, where this is understood as something like the *state of affairs* (possible as well as actual) involved. Extending the refinement offered of Frege's conception of the sense of simple singular terms, it might be proposed that what it is to grasp the sense expressed by a sentence all of whose constituent singular terms are simple is to know *which state of affairs* is being referred to. This construal would not have been open to Frege, of course, because of his conception of the reference of a sentence as its truth-value; but as we suggested in §6.2, states of affairs are in many ways more plausible candidates.

However, such a proposal would have as a consequence that someone could grasp the thought as expressed by a sentence and grasp that same thought as expressed by another sentence but not realize that they were the same thought; and this does seem counterintuitive. But we could still argue that the 'content' of that person's two thoughts is the same, making use of the distinction between *thoughts* and *objects of thought* that Frege himself failed to appreciate (cf. §7.5 above), and here taking 'content' as the *object of thought*.[36] To return to Frege's example, we could maintain that the *content* of Dr. Lauben's, Leo Peter's and Rudolph Lingen's thoughts is the same; they just express or 'split up' that content differently. Thoughts would indeed then be construed epistemically, reflecting what would earlier have been regarded as ways of 'splitting up' content, rather than 'contents' themselves.

The obvious move would have been to take the *Bedeutung* of a sentence as its 'content' and the sense it expresses as the way of thinking of that content. But since Frege later conceived of the *Bedeutung* of a sentence as its truth-value, there remained a need for a notion of 'content', a need revealed not only in Frege's insistence that the same thought can be analysed in different ways (it would have been less controversial to have said that the same 'content' can be articulated in different ways) but also in his response to the problem of indexicality. Frege's conception of timeless thoughts can be seen as an attempt to restore something of his earlier notion of 'content', though with a less attractive metaphysical gloss. States of affairs may not be ontologically innocuous, but they are not so obviously bizarre as timeless thoughts.

The dilemma for Frege, though, is clear: either thoughts are discriminated so finely that no two different sentences can be regarded as expressing the same thought, or else they are distinguished so coarsely that someone can express the same thought in two different forms without knowing it. The formulation of the criterion (SCE) was an attempt to find a stable intermediate position. But in view of the tension in Frege's account, and the problems with this criterion, can it genuinely be said that Frege's conception of sense is ultimately coherent? I take up this question in the next section.

8.4 Sense and Substitutability

The criterion (SCE) was offered in §8.1 as the best attempt at capturing a notion of sense that is adequate for Frege's logicist purposes – allowing, in particular, the two members of a Fregean pair to possess the same sense. The idea was simple. Someone cannot *really* 'understand' (grasp the thought as expressed by) both (Da) and (Db), or (Na) and (Nb), for example, without immediately recognizing that one is true if they recognize that the other is true. But this seems in conflict with the criterion that emerged from Frege's discussion of intensionality in 'Über Sinn und Bedeutung':

(SIE)   Two propositions have the same sense iff they are intensionally equivalent, i.e. iff they can be intersubstituted *salva veritate* in all intensional contexts. (See §8.1 above.)

Take the following two propositions:

(LDa)   Ludwig believes that line a is parallel to line b.
(LDb)   Ludwig believes that the direction of line a is identical with the direction of line b.

Since (LDa) can be true without (LDb) being true, it might be argued, the two embedded sentences – (Da) and (Db) – cannot possess the same sense.

But the issue is not as straightforward as this might imply. For it is not absurd to maintain that if (LDa) is true, then (LDb) is true too, even if Ludwig himself lacks the concept of direction. As suggested in §6.5, (LDa) and (LDb) might be glossed as follows:

(LDa') Ludwig holds as true the thought expressed by 'Line a is parallel to line b'.
(LDb') Ludwig holds as true the thought expressed by 'The direction of line a is identical with the direction of line b'.

If (Da) and (Db) do express the same thought, then (LDb') will be true iff (LDa') is true. Compare the inference from (LDa') to (LDb') with the inference from (LDa') to the following proposition:

(LDa†) Ludwig holds as true the thought expressed by 'Die Gerade a ist parallel der Gerade b'.

If (LDa') is true, then (LDa†) is arguably also true, even if Ludwig does not speak German. Certainly, the fact that Ludwig does speak German and only German, say, does not mean that (LDa') could not be used to report one of Ludwig's beliefs.[37]

In view of the distinction drawn in §8.2, however, the obvious response is to point out that (LDa') and (LDb') have missed out the key little word 'as'. (LDa) and (LDb) should be glossed, more precisely, as follows:

(LDa″) Ludwig holds as true the thought *as* expressed by 'Line a is parallel to line b'.

(LDb″) Ludwig holds as true the thought *as* expressed by 'The direction of line a is identical with the direction of line b'.

There would still be room here to dispute whether (LDa″) could be regarded as true if Ludwig only spoke German; but the essential point is clear: (LDb″) does not necessarily follow from (LDa″). However, even if we reject the inference from (LDa″) to (LDb″), this does not mean that the thought expressed by (Da) is *not* the same as the thought expressed by (Db); it just means that the thought *as* expressed by (Da) is not the same as the thought *as* expressed by (Db). It is the *ways* in which the thought is expressed that are different; and this may or may not be relevant in our specification of someone's beliefs.

As it stands, then, (LDa) is ambiguous. It can be glossed either as (LDa') or as (LDa″), depending on whether we want to report just the belief or the belief as Ludwig himself would express it. But as well as (LDa') and (LDb'), there is another way of interpreting (LDa) and (LDb) that enables us to regard them as logically equivalent. To appreciate this, let us consider another pair of propositions:

(L00) Ludwig believes that 0 is 0.

(L0E) Ludwig believes that 0 is the extension of the concept 'equinumerous to the concept *not identical with itself*'.

It might seem indisputable that (L00) can be true without (L0E) being true; yet this is just what Frege's own views lead us to deny. For what is embedded in (L0E) is precisely that definition of the number 0 that forms the basis of his construction of the natural numbers, and definitions, according to Frege, must embody sameness of sense as well as sameness of reference. So if a belief can only properly be ascribed to someone if they fully grasp the senses of the terms used to express that belief, and if we accept, with Frege, that his logicist definitions do explicate the senses of our number terms, then (L0E) must indeed follow from (L00).

But if we can allow this ploy here, then we can allow it anywhere else. Frege's definition of the number 0, after all, is one of the most unlikely things that someone could be expected to know. Returning to Frege's paradigm example, what would it be to fully grasp the senses of 'the Morning Star' and 'the Evening Star'? We might think that all that is really required is knowledge of the following definitions:

(MSA) The Morning Star is the bright heavenly body that appears in the morning.

(ESA) The Evening Star is the bright heavenly body that appears in the evening.

It would indeed then be possible for one of the following to be true and the other false:

(LMSB) Ludwig believes that the Morning Star is a body illuminated by the sun.

(LESB) Ludwig believes that the Evening Star is a body illuminated by the sun.

But if we take the Caesar problem seriously, then these definitions are inadequate since they do not enable us to recognize the object defined under any other guise than that involved in the definition. And even if we find Frege's own demands on definitions excessive, we might still feel that within astronomical theory, an adequate definition must say more about what the object actually is. Better definitions might be the following:

(MSV) The Morning Star is Venus as it appears in the morning.

(ESV) The Evening Star is Venus as it appears in the evening.

Clearly, such definitions presuppose knowledge of what Venus is; but this is no different from Frege presupposing what the extension of a concept is in defining the natural numbers. (Venus might be specified, say, as the second planet in our solar system.) If these are the definitions that must be known to be attributed any proper beliefs about the Morning Star or Evening Star, then (LMSB) and (LESB) are logically equivalent. Anyone who understands at least that portion of astronomical theory that concerns our own solar system – and hence fully grasps the senses of the terms – must know that the Morning Star is the Evening Star.

Even in Frege's own paradigm case, then, considerations of substitutability are by no means straightforward, and there is at least room to pull the two criteria (SCE) and (SIE) into line. In much the same way as (SCE) incorporated a requirement of 'understanding' the relevant propositions, what we have done here is to restrict the application of (SIE) to contexts in which the senses of the propositions (those to which an attitude is being ascribed to someone) are fully grasped: we might call them *fully intensional* contexts. Anyone who fully understands (Euclidean) geometry, for example, must believe that line a is parallel to line b iff they believe that the direction of line a is identical with the direction of line b.

This might seem a mere fiddle; but there is an important moral here.

For any criterion of the form 'Two propositions have the same sense iff ...' will contain on the right hand side notions that can always be 'adjusted' to deliver the required conception of sense. This obviously threatens to make any specification of a conception of sense circular; but we have already dealt with this problem in discussing, in relation to Frege's earlier notion of 'conceptual content', what was called the 'Fregean circle' in §2.5. It is neither the case that our semantic intuitions underpin our logical inferences, nor that our assessments of logical equivalence underpin our judgements about sameness of 'conceptual content'. What we have instead is a delicate dialectical interplay, each reinforcing the other as our use and understanding of language develops. Exactly the same thing can be said here, since to substitute one word for another (*salva veritate*) just is to make a logical inference, and we have precisely been trying to refine a conception of sense to capture that notion of 'content' that Frege utilized in the central argument of the *Grundlagen*. Our judgements about sense and our practices of substituting words are mutually dependent.

Frege was thus absolutely right in seeing the fundamental connection between sense and substitutability. But what he failed to appreciate was the dialectical interplay between the various notions involved here. The fundamental connection is obvious in the extreme case of what might be called 'perfect synonymy'. Two expressions are *perfectly synonymous* iff they are intersubstitutable in every possible context. But of course, no two words can ever be perfectly synonymous. For they are bound to resonate slightly differently in somebody's ear, making the use of one more appropriate in some particular context. In Fregean terminology, they would thus have different *tones*.[38] But in crystallizing out from the cauldron of linguistic life the notions of *Sinn* and *Bedeutung*, Frege has to specify the kinds of substitutability that are relevant, specifications that can only be made in 'theory-laden' terms. According to Frege, two expressions have the same *Bedeutung* iff they are intersubstitutable *salva veritate* in all extensional contexts. But as we remarked in §6.2, we are not really given any independent characterization of 'extensional contexts'. All we have is Frege's repeated insistence that he is only concerned with *scientific* contexts, where the goal is *truth*, which begs the question as to whether 'non-scientific' propositions can have a truth-value. So here too what we have is an 'adjustment' of our notion of truth to deliver the requisite notion of *Bedeutung*. And as we saw, Frege's own arguments *underdetermine* what is to be regarded as the *Bedeutung* of an expression. The same problem arises with the criterion for sameness of sense: talk of intensional contexts presupposes an interpretation of statements ascribing a propositional attitude to someone, which already assumes some kind of conception of sense.

This is not in itself to deny the legitimacy of Frege's notions of *Sinn* and *Bedeutung*. It is simply to stress that their rationale cannot be given from any 'neutral' standpoint entirely outside the scope of his logical theory;

and it has, of course, precisely been the aim of this book to provide an account of his logical theory that makes those notions at least explicable. But there are, in fact, as many different notions of 'meaning' – whether called 'content', 'Bedeutung', 'sense', 'role' or whatever – as there are distinguishable types of context in which substitutions of linguistic expressions occur. At the opposite end of the spectrum to the case of perfect synonymy mentioned above is the case of two expressions that are only intersubstitutable on one particular occasion. Here it might be said that on this particular occasion they have the same 'sense'. Between these two extremes there is a whole range of cases. Frege himself only officially recognized two; having isolated a fairly clear-cut notion of 'Bedeutung' (whatever other possibilities we ourselves might contemplate), he assumed that every other notion could be swept up under the heading of 'Sinn', an assumption, as we have seen, that is questionable even for Frege's own philosophy.

Nevertheless, the connection between sense and substitutability remains, and in its general schematic form, the 'sense' of an expression can be contextually defined in the familiar way (cf. §6.5):

(Sa) Expression '*A*' is intersubstitutable *salva veritate* in all contexts of type *C* with expression '*B*'.

(Sb) The sense of '*A*' is identical with the sense of '*B*'.

But this threatens to raise an even more insidious problem. For the legitimacy of such contextual definitions seems to depend on (Sa) and (Sb) having the same sense, but the contextual definition is precisely an attempt to specify what it is to have the same sense. So do we not go round in an even tighter circle? However, the problem here is only serious on the assumption that the abstract objects defined by means of a contextual definition are independently existing objects; and there is every reason to reject this assumption.

The problem essentially concerns the status of Fregean pairs. If the abstract objects referred to in the second member of a Fregean pair were indeed 'independent' objects, then it would certainly be questionable whether the two members of a Fregean pair do possess the same sense. For the second member would appear to involve an ontological commitment not made by the first. On any reasonable conception of belief, someone could surely legitimately believe that two expressions are intersubstitutable in the relevant contexts without taking themselves to be referring to independent objects called 'senses'. Of course, we could argue that (Sa) makes *implicit* reference to senses, and that anyone who *fully* 'understands' (Sa) must know that senses are being referred to as independent objects; but then this really does seem to beg the question, building into our understanding of (Sa) exactly what we wish to extract.

In any case, our discussion of Russell's paradox in §7.2 should already have convinced us of the need to reject the assumption that objects contextually defined are 'independent'. For Axiom V, asserting the equivalence between (Va) and (Vb), has the form of a contextual definition, legitimizing the introduction of *value-ranges*, of which *extensions of concepts* were a special kind; and it was the assumption that extensions were objects already existing in the domain, and hence objects for which even the concepts of which they were the extensions had to be defined, that generated the contradiction. But as long as the objects contextually defined are seen as *dependent* entities, of a different *type* from that of the objects on which they are dependent, then the status of Axiom V, and contextual definitions in general, is unproblematic. In a genuine contextual definition, the two members of the relevant Fregean pair have the same sense *by stipulation*, since its purpose is not to capture a pre-existing equivalence (which would assume that both members had an independent meaning), but simply to specify how terms for abstract objects are to be understood.

As contextually defined by (Sa) and (Sb), then, senses too must be regarded as dependent entities, dependent on our practices of substituting expressions in certain contexts. That senses are dependent on our use of language might seem obvious. But if we accept Frege's thesis that the sense of a sentence is the thought it expresses, then thoughts too are dependent on our use of language, and this is by no means an uncontroversial claim.[39] It certainly conflicts with Frege's own conception of thoughts as timeless entities inhabiting a 'third realm' of their own, although as we argued in §7.5, this is a view that is fraught with difficulty. But unless senses are treated as dependent entities, then there is no way of responding to the Caesar problem – that the relevant objects have not been adequately distinguished from every other object of the universal domain. And as we shall see in the next section, even Frege did not attempt to provide explicit definitions of senses.

8.5 Analysis and Crystallization

In §6.4 we remarked that if the senses of names are construed as modes of presentation, and these are characterized by means of definite descriptions, then we face an infinite regress, since the sense of any definite description can only be grasped by grasping the senses of its components. So a different account is needed at least of simple names; and we suggested that the sense of such names should be seen as *shown* by saying, in one of any number of appropriate ways, what its referent is. Now although Frege failed to recognize the scope distinction that we drew in explaining the sense of simple names, he was well aware that not everything can be defined, and that there comes a point at which we must rely not on definition but on what he calls *elucidation* (*Erläuterung*), which makes clear the sense of an expression by example.[40] Elucidations, we can say, do indeed *show* the sense of an expression by *using* the expression in an appropriate way.

According to Frege, however, the crucial feature of elucidations is that they occur at the *pre-theoretical* stage, and at this stage there is always the possibility of misunderstanding. All we can then do is to 'count on a meeting of minds, on others guessing what we have in mind' (*LM*, p. 207). But, Frege emphasizes, 'all this precedes the construction of a system and does not belong within a system. In constructing a system it must be assumed that the words have precise meanings and that we know what they are.' (Ibid.) Once again, the possibility of misunderstanding is pushed aside as revealing the inevitable deficiencies of ordinary language.

To explore this further, however, let us return to Frege's definition of the number 0 that forms the basis of his logicist project:

(E0) The number 0 is the extension of the concept 'equinumerous to the concept *not identical with itself*. (Cf. §4.3 above.)

This is a definition *within* Frege's theory. But it clearly presupposes knowledge of what the extension of a concept is, the relation of equinumerosity and the concept *not identical with itself*. Frege takes the concept to be purely logical and the relation to be definable in terms of one-one correlation, which can in turn be defined purely logically. At the time of the *Grundlagen*, Frege just assumed that it was known what the extension of a concept was (cf. §5.5 above), but in the *Grundgesetze* extensions were in effect contextually defined in Axiom V. As we have seen, Frege understood extensions as objects, and objects were categorically distinct from concepts; so that even if we allow that all the elements of (E0) can be logically defined, it must still be assumed that the notions of object and concept are understood. Here indeed, as Frege admitted in 'On Concept and Object', we have reached the point at which 'hints' rather than definitions must be appealed to, where Frege has to rely 'upon a reader who would be ready to meet me half-way – who does not begrudge a pinch of salt' (*CO*, p. 54).

But if we put the remarks from 'Logic in Mathematics' and 'On Concept and Object' together, it would be misleading to suggest that this reliance on a meeting of minds occurs purely at the *pre-theoretical* stage, for the concept/object distinction arises from Frege's use of function-argument analysis in developing his logical *theory*. A relatively high degree of sophistication is required to understand this: we need to see how Frege's logical system works before we can grasp the concept/object distinction sufficiently well to even meet him half-way. This is no less so if we consider the other assumptions that Frege makes in offering his definition (E0). Frege clearly assumed that there were no problems in appealing to *logic*, regarded as governing all conceptual thought, and our knowledge of which was taken to be *a priori*. But as we are now more aware, the idea that there is such a thing as *the* logic of conceptual thought is highly problematic, and it is certainly not the case that Frege's own logical theory offers us *the* logic.

None of this *invalidates* Frege's definitions; it just suggests that we need to appreciate the whole working of his logical system to 'guess what he has in mind'. If, as in the *Grundgesetze*, (E0) is taken as laying down both the sense and reference of 'the number 0', then there is more to understanding it than simply what can be appealed to prior to the construction of a theory. Indeed, it is not just that we need to understand Frege's logical theory to understand his attempted reduction of arithmetic to logic; we also need to see what he does with his axioms and definitions to appreciate that it is *arithmetic* that he has reduced. Frege recognized as much at the time of the *Grundlagen*. Definitions, he wrote, 'prove themselves by their fruitfulness', where this was understood as enabling us to derive 'the well-known properties of numbers' (*GL*, §70); and this idea was endorsed in his 1914 paper 'Logic in Mathematics': 'a definition must prove itself in the construction of a scientific system' (*LM*, p. 228).

It was this latter idea that ended up taking centre stage in his final answer to the paradox of analysis. As we saw in §5.4, according to his initial response, as revealed, for example, in his reply to Husserl's objections to his *Grundlagen* definitions, the paradox can be solved by distinguishing between *Sinn* and *Bedeutung*. An identity statement is correct if the relevant two terms have the same *Bedeutung*, and informative if the two terms have different senses. Whilst numbers might not seem to us to be extensions of concepts, the difference lies only at the level of sense, not of *Bedeutung*. But as we argued, Frege soon realized that the identity statements that lie at the base of a theory, i.e. the axioms and definitions, require sameness of sense as well as sameness of *Bedeutung* (since otherwise their status would be problematic). But what we ordinarily understand by number terms is clearly not the same as what we understand by the terms as defined by Frege. Frege found himself forced to reject altogether our ordinary understanding. According to his final answer to the problem, as given in 'Logic in Mathematics', the paradox only arises on the assumption that there are clearly grasped senses to begin with, which our analyses are trying to capture. But it is just this assumption that needs to be discharged. The task of the theorist is to associate clearly grasped senses to the relevant terms where there were no such senses associated before. Talk of *reconstruction*, then, seems appropriate, since the aim is to build up again from scratch, and *replace* our ordinary discourse.

Yet this talk of reconstruction from scratch or replacement is highly problematic, for there must surely be *some* constraints on the adequacy of a reconstruction, and these can only have their source in our ordinary discourse. However poor our philosophical understanding of arithmetic might be, it is still *arithmetic* that we are trying to reconstruct. Frege is right that an analysis should not be regarded as simply trying to capture our pre-existing conceptions (correct analyses would indeed then be uninformative). But it is wrong to conclude that those pre-existing conceptions must be altogether ignored. The aim of analysis is to *extend* or *refine* those conceptions, for particular purposes. What led Frege to his later position was his *semainomenalism* – his view that senses, in all their determinate fullness, already exist in some 'third realm' waiting to be definitively associated with the appropriate terms. Since this association is not made in ordinary discourse, there is obvious work for the theorist to do. But if senses are contextually dependent on our linguistic practices, and those practices evolve over time, then so too will senses evolve. We can indeed offer reconstructions of our notions, but it is a condition of offering or understanding these that we start *from* the position of our everyday conceptions; and it is wrong to suggest that these can ever be replaced overnight.

Let us illustrate this by taking a simple example from chemistry, an area of science that Frege himself sometimes mentions for comparison. Consider the following two propositions:

(SW)   Salt dissolves in water.

(NH) $2H_2O + NaCl \rightarrow H_3O^+ + Cl^- + Na^+ + OH^-$.

(SW) represents a familiar, everyday process, and (NH), we could say, provides its 'chemical analysis'. There is also a sense in which, for the purposes of chemistry, (NH) does 'replace' (SW), in that it is this equation that represents the reaction and that plays its part in more complex analyses of chemical processes. Nevertheless, in no sense does a chemist *discard* its informal characterization, as captured in (SW). Whatever manipulation of chemical formulae a chemist may perform, the informal characterizations always stand in the background, being something that is *presupposed*. In offering (NH) as the analysis of (SW), then, the chemist is *refining* rather than *replacing* ordinary language.

This is not to suggest that there no cases where talk of 'replacement' is appropriate. Remaining with chemistry, the notion of phlogiston – the supposed 'principle' underlying the properties of combustible substances – is an obvious example of a notion that was abandoned once a better understanding of combustion was attained, as a result of the 'chemical revolution' of the late 18th century. However, it should be noted, firstly, that this revolution took place over a period of two decades, and in its initial stages did *not* involve the repudiation of the notion of phlogiston, and secondly, that what was radically transformed was the *theoretical* understanding of combustion. Although new experiments were done, there was a substantial body of empirical data that could be characterized, and hence agreed upon, using 'ordinary' notions (e.g. that sulphur produces sulphuric acid on combustion).[41] So this does not conflict with the claim that theoretical analysis offers a refinement rather than a replacement of our ordinary understanding. The 'paradigm shifts' that occur from time to time are located at the *theoretical* level, and although theory inevitably filters down and permeates our ordinary discourse, any transformation of our ordinary understanding takes a much longer time, and makes talk of 'paradigm shifts' at the ordinary level inappropriate.[42] So the general point remains: our ordinary understanding is *presupposed* (however vague it may be in certain areas) in the theoretical attempts that are made to *deepen* that understanding.

But does this not return us to Frege's original response to the paradox of analysis – that a correct analysis must preserve *Bedeutung* whilst allowing 'a more richly articulated sense' (see §5.4 above)? But if the *Bedeutung* of a sentence is merely construed as its truth-value, then this is inadequate as the required constraint. What is needed is something more like Frege's original notion of 'content', suitably understood (as referring, say, to the state of affairs involved). Correct and informative analyses 'split up' the same 'content' differently. What makes (NH) a correct analysis of (SW), for example, is that they both refer to the same 'content' – in this case, the same chemical process. However, even this requires qualification. For 'water' as we ordinarily understand it – the 'water' that we drink and wash in – is not just H_2O, but also contains various 'impurities'; and 'salt' too can refer to more than just NaCl. So the 'content' of (NH) is itself an idealized refinement of the 'content' of (SW). But what tends to happen in such cases is adjustment of our ordinary notions to reinforce the analysis. (NH) makes us interpret (SW) as 'Sodium chloride dissolves in "pure" water'; and once the adjustment is made, then we do have sameness of 'content'. As in the case of (Va) and (Vb) discussed at the end of §5.5, the sense that (SW) and (NH) have in common is *crystallized* in the process of offering the analysis. By taking (NH) as the correct analysis, the appropriate sense of (SW) is precipitated out. Senses are themselves like salts dissolved in the fluid of ordinary linguistic life, which are crystallized out with the help of the seeds of our theoretical notions. In answer to the paradox of analysis, then, what is needed is a synthesis of Frege's earlier and later responses. Sameness of 'content' is indeed a constraint on the adequacy of an analysis, but this is not to say that the 'real' content of the sentence of ordinary language is properly grasped prior to the theory in which the analysis is offered. In the end, what makes an analysis a good one is its success, as part of some overall theory, in convincing us that our ordinary discourse is indeed imprecise, and requires refinement for scientific purposes.

But such a strategy presupposes a *realist* view of the relevant 'contents'. The paradox of analysis seems easily solved in the case of chemistry, since chemical compounds are indeed taken to have a real essence (water is H_2O, salt is NaCl). But is arithmetic analogous to chemistry? What we are now forced to confront is the problem raised at the end of chapter 4. In setting up his logicist system – in *reconstructing* arithmetic – has Frege revealed for the first time the *real essence* of numbers, or merely introduced *analogues* of them? It is clear that, at the time of the *Grundlagen*, Frege saw himself as doing the former. As we noted in §0.3, Frege regarded himself as the culminator of centuries of intellectual effort, as the philosopher who had finally managed to achieve knowledge of the concept of number 'in its purity' (cf. *GL*, p. VII). That the ordinary person might not recognize numbers as extensions of concepts was not seen as an objection. 'To those who might want to declare my definitions unnatural, I would suggest that the question here is not whether they are natural, but whether they go to the heart of the matter and are logically unobjectionable' (*GL*, p. XI).

What motivated Frege's logicist project was the combination of his realism and his Pythagoreanism. For the reasons given in §4.1, Frege was in no doubt that numbers were objects; and as we saw in §3.4, he also regarded enumerability as part of the essence of conceptual thought and hence as purely logical. So the task simply became one of finding a logical characterization of numbers, of showing that numbers were *logical objects*. But in identifying numbers with extensions of concepts, regarded as objects already there in the universal domain, Frege ran into contradiction. And as we noted in §4.5, the subsequent development of mathematical logic has shown that there are alternative set-theoretic characterizations of the natural numbers, so that talk of having discovered *the* logical essence of number now seems misplaced.

The issue should already have struck Frege, even before the emergence of Russell's paradox, since he himself had insisted that the real numbers must be defined quite separately from the natural numbers (see §§4.4 and 4.5). According to Frege, whilst the natural numbers are to be identified with extensions of concepts, the real numbers are to be identified with extensions of relations. But this means that *the natural number 7*, for example, is not identical with *the real number 7*. Even in Frege's own system, then, the members of the corresponding subset of the real numbers, {1, 2, 3, ...}, are only *analogues* of the natural numbers. But if this is allowed here, then why should Frege's definitions of the natural numbers not also be regarded as only providing analogues?

But if, at best, Frege's own system could only have specified *analogues* of the natural numbers, and there is no such thing as *the* logical or set-theoretic reduction of the natural numbers, then how are we now to solve the paradox of analysis? No analysis would seem to be correct. In response, it might be argued that the only 'content' that needs to be preserved in a theoretical account is the *structure* of arithmetic.[43] Exactly what objects are specified is irrelevant, as long as, to use Frege's words, all the 'well-known properties of numbers' can be derived (cf. *GL*, §72). But would this mean that we should abandon talk of numbers as objects at all? However, if preservation of *structure* provides the constraint on adequate analyses, and we allow the legitimacy of contextual definition, then a familiar way of specifying numbers as abstract objects is open to us:

(NSa)   Number system S1 is isomorphic to number system S2.

(NSb)   The numbers defined by S1 are identical with the numbers defined by S2.

S1 and S2 could either both be ordinary number systems (e.g. the natural number system and the relevant part of the real number system), or both be set theories, or one be an ordinary number system and the other the relevant part of a set theory. Clearly, what is required to judge the relevant isomorphism is a detailed comparison of the two systems, which in turn requires an appreciation of the workings of both. But if such isomorphism could be appealed to, then there would no longer be any essential difference between the cases of arithmetic and of chemistry.

So would this mean that 'the natural number 7' and 'the real number 7' do, after all, have the same referent? Frege's theory of real numbers may suggest that they have different referents, and this may well be compatible with his final response to the paradox of analysis – that new systems are to be set up from scratch. But this leaves him with no way of explaining the relationship between the two. On the traditional account, however, whereby the real number system is generated by successive expansion of the natural number system, they would be regarded as having the same referent (which would be compatible with Frege's original response to the paradox of analysis). But the interesting question here concerns whether they have a different *sense*. However, in the light of what we have just been saying, the question can be seen to hide a confusion. For our understanding of the term 'the natural number 7' itself varies according to which stage in the development of number theory we have reached. If we have only learnt the system of natural numbers, then the question will have no meaning for us. If, on the other hand, we are familiar with the system of real numbers, then as part of our learning of this, we will have come to see that the real number 7 *is* the natural number 7. Once again, what we would have here is a case of the sameness of sense being crystallized as the new theory is developed. The real number system is not set up from scratch; but in moving to it from the system of natural numbers, the latter is *incorporated* into the former. The natural numbers *become* a subset of the real numbers. Our understanding of the natural numbers is *presupposed* in the development of the real number system, and becomes refined in the process.

Contextual definitions themselves provide a good illustration of the subtle transformations involved in developing a theory. Take Frege's central definition of sameness of number in terms of one-one correlation. We might intuitively think that the set of rational numbers has more members than the set of natural numbers, or the set of natural numbers more members than the set of even natural numbers; but once we are persuaded that one-one correlation underlies attributions of sameness of number, as it certainly does in the case of finite sets, then we are prepared to accept that the infinite sets just mentioned have the same number. Our concept of number has been *refined* in the process, allowing us, in particular, to understand the development of the theory of transfinite numbers.[44]

But if all this is right, then what it suggests is that the paradox of analysis cannot ultimately be 'solved' without taking an historical approach. For if what analysis involves is the crystallization of sense, then since this is a process that occurs over time, there is no ahistorically positioned answer as to whether it is both correct and informative. Before the theory is developed in which the analysis is offered, the analysis, if it is understood at all, will seem incorrect; and after it is developed, with the necessary transformation in our understanding effected, it will be correct but uninformative. To talk of 'correctness' is to make a move *within* a system; yet informativeness is located in the process of developing, learning and using a system. The paradox of analysis arises from trying to account for both features through 'logical justification', and in the end Frege's lack of success in dealing with the paradox results from his denigration of historical considerations. To see how an analysis is both informative, and comes to seem correct, we need to retrace the path by which that analysis was offered.

The point applies as much to logical theory as it does to chemical or mathematical theories. As we argued in chapter 2, understanding Frege's logic is itself to crystallize those semantic intuitions that are taken to lie at the base of the theory. 'All *A*'s are *B*' becomes *regimented* as 'If anything is an *A*, then it is a *B*', for example (which is not to say that we cannot represent cases in which there *is* existential import). 'There are 0 *F*'s' is interpreted, at the conceptual level, as 'The concept *F* is not instantiated' (cf. §5.3). Does Frege's logic offer a good analysis of our linguistic life? This cannot be straightforwardly answered since that linguistic life is itself refined by learning Frege's logic. To properly answer this question, we must carefully trace the development of that logic historically; and it has been one of the central aims of this book to do just that.

But as we noted in the introduction, such a conception of logic was not Frege's. Frege himself regarded the logical realm as lying entirely outside the domain of ordinary language, a view that found its ultimate expression in the semainomenalism of 'Der Gedanke'. The failure of his logicist project only reinforced him in his belief that there was something inherently deficient about ordinary language, since it tempts us into thinking that proper names such as 'the extension of the concept *F*' denote objects. 'So a great part of the work of a philosopher consists – or at least ought to consist – in a struggle against language.' (*SKM*, p. 270; cf. *DECN*, p. 263; *PWN*, pp. 265-6.) This idea became a guiding theme of analytic philosophy. As Wittgenstein was to put it, 'Philosophy is a battle against the bewitchment of our intelligence by means of language' (*PI*, §109). But although in his earlier work, Wittgenstein had shared Frege's belief in an absolute logic, one of the major motivations of his later work was to repudiate this conception.[45] As the passage quoted at the beginning of this chapter shows, he realized that whilst the frictionless environment of a perfect logic might seem ideal, we soon find that we are unable to walk. However, as Wittgenstein goes on to remark in the paragraph that follows, this was not to be understood as bargaining the rigour out of logic. 'The *preconceived idea* of crystalline purity can only be removed by turning our whole examination round.' (*PI*, §108.) For Wittgenstein, this meant returning to the 'rough ground' of our ordinary discourse, and 'describing' rather than 'explaining' our linguistic practices. But as I hope I have shown in the present book, adopting an historical approach not only removes the idea that the crystalline purity was there to begin with, but at the same time offers an *explanation* of the process of crystallization.[46]

Such an approach is also needed to explain Frege's conception of sense, which lay at the heart of his philosophy. We are tempted to think – seduced, perhaps, by Frege's semainomenalism – that if that conception is legitimate, then it must have been there all along, fully crystallized, in Frege's thought. But that conception too has a history, which extends indeed into the work of later philosophers, and different demands have been made upon it. I have concentrated in this book on Frege's notion of sense as it developed in his own thought; but this is clearly only one part of the much longer story that reaches to the present. However, in telling just this part of the story, in explaining the role Frege played in *making sense*, ideas have been used that are themselves refinements of Frege's own ideas (e.g. the distinction between semantic and epistemic sense, the deeper apprehension of the roles of context and presupposition, or the historicized synthesis of Frege's earlier and later responses to the paradox of analysis). In making sense of Frege's philosophy, in appreciating how his conceptions were crystallized and can be further crystallized, we too are *making sense*.

APPENDIX 1

Syllogistic Theory

Syllogistic theory is concerned with the systematic elucidation of the logical relations between the four types of proposition – of *quantity* either universal or particular and of *quality* either affirmative or negative – contained in the traditional square of opposition (as first described by Aristotle in *De Interpretatione*, 7, 10):

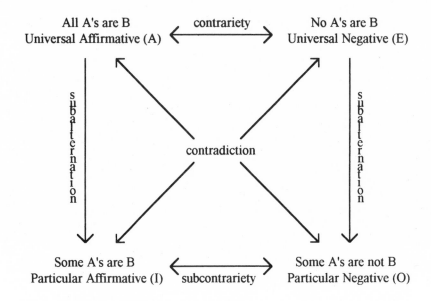

Following Smiley (1973) and Lear (1980), I formalize 'All *A's* are *B*' as '*Aab*', 'No *A's* are *B*' as '*Eab*', 'Some *A's* are *B*' as '*Iab*' and 'Some *A's* are not *B*' as '*Oab*'. (The most common alternative formalization in the literature is '*AaB*', '*AeB*', '*AiB*' and '*AoB*', respectively, the first four vowels of the alphabet traditionally being used to distinguish the four forms.) The relationships embodied in the square of opposition may be defined as follows:

(CD) Two propositions stand in the relation of *contradiction* if they can neither both be true nor both be false. The following are thus implicit rules of syllogistic theory: (a) 'From *Aab* infer not *Oab*'; (b) 'From not *Aab* infer *Oab*'; (c) 'From *Eab* infer not *Iab*'; (d) 'From not *Eab* infer *Iab*'.

(CR) Two propositions stand in the relation of *contrariety* if they cannot both be true but may both be false. This results in the following implicit rule: 'From *Aab* infer not *Eab*'.

(SC) Two propositions stand in the relation of *subcontrariety* if they cannot both be false but may both be true. The implicit rule derived here is thus: 'From not *Iab* infer *Oab*'.

(SA) Two propositions stand in the relation of *subalternation* if one proposition cannot be true without the other being true, but the latter may be true without the former being true. The latter is termed the *subaltern* of the former. In this case we arrive at the two traditional rules of subalternation: (a) 'From *Aab* infer *Iab*'; (b) 'From *Eab* infer *Oab*'.

In addition to these two rules of subalternation, and the rules of conversion discussed in §1.4, the following rules of *obversion* – relating propositions of the same *quantity* – were also recognized:

(OB) Two propositions stand in the relation of *obversion* if they have the same subject and quantity, but differ in quality, and possess predicates that are the negations of one another. Formalizing the predicate 'not-*b*' as '*b**', we thus have the following four rules: (a) 'From *Aab* infer *Eab**'; (b) 'From *Eab* infer *Aab**'; (c) 'From *Iab* infer *Oab**'; (d) 'From *Oab* infer *Iab**'.

A *syllogism* may be defined as an argument with two premises and a conclusion, each proposition taking one of the above four forms. In addition, as noted in §1.1, for the conclusion to establish that a predicate term ('*P*') applies to a subject term ('*S*'), the two premises must be linked by a 'middle term' ('*M*'), which can occupy either the subject or the predicate position in each premiss. Using the traditional formalization, then, with the conclusion expressed as '*SxP*' (where '*x*' stands for either '*a*', '*e*', '*i*' or '*o*'), the first premiss will take the form of either '*MxP*' or '*PxM*' and the second premiss the form of either '*SxM*' or '*MxS*'. This means that syllogisms fall into one of four *figures*, representing the four possible arrangements of the premises:

Figures

I		II		III		IV	
	MxP		*PxM*		*MxP*		*PxM*
	SxM		*SxM*		*MxS*		*MxS*
	SxP		*SxP*		*SxP*		*SxP*

Aristotle himself, however, recognized only *three* figures, and this has generated much controversy. The most convincing explanation has been provided by Patzig (1968: §25). If one appreciates that Aristotle's main concern in distinguishing the figures is with the *distribution* of the middle term, then it does seem plausible to suppose that there are only three possibilities: either the middle term in the two premises occupies both subject positions, or both predicate positions, or one of each (cf. *Prior Analytics*, I 4-6). Aristotle recognized the validity of the syllogisms of the fourth figure, but treated them as derivatives of the first figure syllogisms, in effect collapsing together the first and fourth figures. However, he failed to realize that this conflicts with the other criteria he provides for first figure syllogisms (as given in I 4), so that Aristotle cannot be totally absolved of confusion on this issue.

Accepting that there are four figures, then, and that each of the three propositions in each figure takes one of four forms, there are 4 x 4³, or 256, possible arrangements. Of these, only 24 are valid syllogisms, and these have traditionally been classified into *moods* and ingeniously given names that reflect their structure and method of proof. 19 of these moods constitute the heart of the syllogistic system, the other 5 being the 'weakened' or 'subalternated' derivatives of one of the main moods (in accordance with one of the two rules of subalternation). The moods are arranged in their figures, and the five subaltern moods italicized, as follows:

Moods

(I)	**Barbara**	*Barbari*	**Celarent**	*Celaront*	**Darii**	**Ferio**
$\begin{bmatrix} MxP \\ SxM \\ SxP \end{bmatrix}$	Abc <u>Aab</u> Aac	Abc <u>Aab</u> Iac	Ebc <u>Aab</u> Eac	Ebc <u>Aab</u> Oac	Abc <u>Iab</u> Iac	Ebc <u>Iab</u> Oac

(II)	**Cesare**	*Cesaro*	**Camestres**	*Camestrop*	**Festino**	**Baroco**
$\begin{bmatrix} PxM \\ SxM \\ SxP \end{bmatrix}$	Ecb <u>Aab</u> Eac	Ecb <u>Aab</u> Oac	Acb <u>Eab</u> Eac	Acb <u>Eab</u> Oac	Ecb <u>Iab</u> Oac	Acb <u>Oab</u> Oac

(III)	**Darapti**	**Felapton**	**Disamis**	**Datisi**	**Bocardo**	**Ferison**
$\begin{bmatrix} MxP \\ MxS \\ SxP \end{bmatrix}$	Abc <u>Aba</u> Iac	Ebc <u>Aba</u> Oac	Ibc <u>Aba</u> Iac	Abc <u>Iba</u> Iac	Obc <u>Aba</u> Oac	Ebc <u>Iba</u> Oac

(IV)	**Bamalip**	**Calemes**	*Calemop*	**Dimatis**	**Fesapo**	**Fresison**
$\begin{bmatrix} PxM \\ MxS \\ SxP \end{bmatrix}$	Acb <u>Aba</u> Iac	Acb <u>Eba</u> Eac	Acb <u>Eba</u> Oac	Icb <u>Aba</u> Iac	Ecb <u>Aba</u> Oac	Ecb <u>Iba</u> Oac

272 *Frege: Making Sense*

Traditionally, the 19 main moods were learnt with the help of a mnemonic verse, the following being one of the more familiar:

Barbara, Celarent primae, *Darii Ferioque;*
Cesare, Camestres, Festino, Baroco secundae;
tertia grande sonans recitat *Darapti, Felapton,*
Disamis, Datisi, Bocardo, Ferison; quartae
sunt *Bamalip, Calemes, Dimatis, Fesapo, Fresison.*

(The most common alternative has *Bramantip, Camenes* and *Dimaris* for *Bamalip, Calemes* and *Dimatis*, but the names are otherwise the same; cf. Keynes, 1906: §258). In addition, the names themselves cleverly revealed the formulation and proof of each syllogism. The three vowels represented the basic form of each of the two premisses and conclusion (i.e. whether it was an A, E, I or O proposition; *Ferio* standing for *Ebc, Iab ⊢ Oac*, for example); and the consonants indicated how the syllogism, in either the second, third or fourth figures, was to be 'reduced' to a first figure syllogism. The first letter showed to what first figure syllogism it was to be reduced (*Cesare* being reduced to *Celarent*, for example), and the letters immediately following the vowels suggested the precise method of proof, in accordance with the following instructions:

c   (*conversio*): suppose that the conclusion does *not* hold (i.e. take its negation) and proceed by *reductio ad absurdum*, showing how it contradicts the premiss denoted by the preceding vowel on the basis of the syllogism reached with the other premiss ('changing round' the syllogism).

m   (*muta*): transpose the premisses.

p   (*per accidens*): 'convert' the premiss denoted by the preceding vowel into its subaltern ('conversion by weakening').

s   (*simpliciter*): 'convert' the premiss denoted by the preceding vowel in accordance with one of the two rules of conversion 'From *Eab* infer *Eba*' and 'From *Iab* infer *Iba*' ('simple conversion').

Three examples may help clarify these instructions:

(BC)   Proof of *Bocardo* (*Obc, Aba ⊢ Oac*), illustrating *conversio*: Suppose not *Oac*, then *Aac* (its negation), in which case, with *Aba, Abc* can be reached (by *Barbara*); but not *Abc*, since *Obc* (its contradictory), so the initial supposition is false; hence *Oac*.

(CM)   Proof of *Camestres* (*Acb, Eab ⊢ Eac*), illustrating transposition and conversion *simpliciter*: If *Acb* and *Eab* imply *Eac*, then *Eab* and *Acb* imply *Eac* (by transposition). But if *Eab*, then *Eba*, and if *Eac*, then *Eca*, so *Eba* and *Acb* imply *Eca*, which is just the form of *Celarent*.

(FL)   Proof of *Felapton* (*Ebc, Aba ⊢ Oac*), illustrating conversion *per accidens*: If *Aba*, then *Iab* (its subaltern); so with *Ebc, Oac* (by *Ferio*).

How coherent is the syllogistic system that emerges from this account? As noted in §1.4, one of the main objections concerns the *existential import* of syllogistic propositions. There appears to be *no* plausible assignment of existential import that preserves *all* the relationships embodied in the traditional square of opposition – whether explicit, as formulated in (CD) to (SA) above, or implicit, as captured in (OB) above. By 'plausible assignment' I mean one which meets the following intuitive constraint (which effectively underlies all treatments of the issue):

(PA) If any syllogistic proposition *possesses* existential import, then (at the very least) it is the I form; and if any syllogistic proposition *lacks* existential import, then (at the very least) it is the E form.

If this constraint is met (which rules out ten of the sixteen possible sets of assignments), and we ignore all cases where only one of the four forms of syllogistic proposition either possesses or lacks existential import (which rules out another two possible sets – there are eight such cases altogether, all of which, at the minimum, invalidate one of the two relations of contradiction), then there are just four sets of assignments of existential import to syllogistic propositions that require consideration:

(A) *All four types of proposition – A, E, I and O – carry existential import.* This runs into the problem that whenever the subject term fails to refer, all four propositions are *false*, invalidating the rules of *contradiction* and *subcontrariety* – see (CD) and (SC) above.

(B) *No syllogistic proposition carries existential import.* This results in the breakdown of the rules of *contradiction* and *contrariety* – see (CD) and (CR) above – since, whenever the subject term fails to refer, all four propositions are *true*.

(C) *The I and O forms, but not A and E forms, carry existential import.* In this case, whenever the subject term fails to refer, '*Aab*' and '*Eab*' are *true*, and '*Iab*' and '*Oab*' *false*, invalidating the rules of *contrariety*, *subcontrariety* and *subalternation*. (Surprisingly, on the *reverse* assignment – the A and E forms, but not I and O forms, possessing existential import – *all* the relationships are preserved, but this fails to meet the intuitive constraint expressed in (PA).)

(D) *The A and I forms, but not E and O forms, carry existential import.* This assignment preserves all four relations *explicitly* captured in the traditional square of opposition, but at the cost of destroying the *implicit* relation that intuitively holds between propositions of the same quantity, as reflected in the rules of *obversion* – see (OB) above. In particular, it is implausible that 'Some *A*'s are *B*' should carry existential import, but not 'Some *A*'s are not *B*'. (The reverse assignment also preserves all relations except obversion, but fails to meet the intuitive constraint.)

What possibilities are there for restoring coherence to syllogistic theory? The two most promising strategies (conserving at least the *explicit* relations) consist in modifying (A) and (D):

(A*) *Syllogistic theory as a whole presupposes that all terms have reference.* The strategy here is to assign existential import not to each syllogistic proposition individually, as in (A), but to the system as a whole. In a sense, this constitutes a synthesis of (A) and (B), the point being that the existential import is *presupposed* rather than *entailed* by each proposition. If reference-failure is ruled out from the start, then *all* the traditional rules are valid. The only drawback is that syllogistic theory now appears to be even more limited, applying only to non-empty terms.

(D*) *Existential import is assigned only to the A and I forms, but the O form is construed as 'Not all A's are B' rather than 'Some A's are not B'.* This strategy still invalidates the rules of *obversion*, but it removes their intuitive appeal, and preserves the relations explicitly captured in the square of opposition.

(A*) accords better with Aristotle's *scientific* intentions (see §1.3 above), though the issue as to which strategy Aristotle himself favoured will remain controversial, since he seems not to have appreciated the problem and the texts themselves appear inconsistent (for the alternative view, that (D*) best captures Aristotle's position, see Thompson, 1953, and Wedin, 1978). However, (A*) represents the most familiar contemporary strategy (see e.g. Strawson, 1952: ch. 6, §7; Lukasiewicz, 1957: p. 4; Kneale, 1962: pp. 58-60; Smiley, 1962: §4; Lemmon, 1965: pp. 175-7; Patzig, 1968: §3; Corcoran, 1974a: §3; Ackrill, 1981: pp. 92-3). It was Strawson who first presented this strategy as based on the notion of *presupposition* (though it was anticipated by certain previous writers – see e.g. Johnson, 1892: pp. 24, 28; 1921: p. 139; Nelson, 1946), but Strawson himself only initially proposed that all *subject* terms had to refer. Thinking through the rules of conversion, however, should quickly convince us of the need for *all* terms to refer. It is this strategy that is pursued in §2.4, with the additional suggestion that syllogistic theory *can* be successfully applied in fictional contexts – providing the 'domain of discourse' is specified.

(D*) also represents a coherent strategy, and was familiar in medieval times, but has suffered relative neglect in recent years. (For details of the history of the question of existential import, see Church (1965) and Wu (1969). The strategy is noted by Prior (1962: p. 169; 1976: p. 123), who reports finding it in Keynes' extensive examination of the issue (1906: Part II, ch. 8). But Keynes, in fact, only mentions the strategy very briefly in a footnote (p. 226, n. 1), where it is immediately ruled out because of its invalidation of obversion. More recently, however, the strategy has been adopted by Clark (1980), who raises objections to (A*) (see esp. chs. 5-6), though they are not, I think, insuperable. Thom (1981: §§18 and 30) also discusses both strategies, but bases his full system on (A*).) There is nothing *incoherent* about construing O-propositions as 'Not all *A's* are *B*', nor in thereby dispensing with the rules of *obversion* (since their intuitive appeal does only depend on a specific interpretation of negative propositions), but if the strategy is seen as *more* plausible than (A*), because it does not make *any* presuppositions, then this is mistaken. This strategy too *presupposes* that we understand the various syllogistic propositions in a certain way; and if this is allowed, then (A*) might still seem preferable, for the reasons stated (preserving not only the explicit relations, but also obversion; and lending itself, in any case, to application in fictional contexts).

How does syllogistic theory fare when 'translated' into Fregean logic? Although all four strategies can be formalized, it is (C) that represents the construal that Frege himself implicitly adopted. This results in the destruction of all but the relation of contradiction within the traditional square of opposition. (It is worth noting that when Frege reproduced the square at the end of Part I of the *Begriffsschrift* (which has been excised from the translation in *TPW*), revealing his own formalizations of the four types of syllogistic proposition, he misleadingly *retained* the invalidated relations of contrariety, subcontrariety and subalternation. This suggests that at the time he had failed to think through the semantic implications of his new logical system, providing further support for the view that Frege developed that system for other reasons than any perceived difficulties in syllogistic theory, and only *later* sought to justify it – cf. ch. 2, n. 14.) However, as suggested in §2.3, this was not the only effect of the Fregean formalizations. The failure of subalternation invalidates all five subaltern moods as well as *Darapti*, *Felapton*, *Bamalip* and *Fesapo*, leaving a residue of fifteen moods. Given the equivalences between *Ebc* and *Ecb* (reflecting what we may call the *E rule of conversion*), and between *Iab* and *Iba* (reflecting the *I rule of conversion*), however, the number can be reduced further, since several of the moods then collapse into each other. This results in just eight 'moods' – *Barbara*, *Celarent/Cesare*, *Darii/ Datisi*, *Ferio/Festino/Ferison/Fresison*, *Camestres/Calemes*, *Baroco*, *Disamis/Dimatis*, and *Bocardo* – as is shown by the diagram on the following page (arrows indicating equivalences in accordance with the E and I rules of conversion).

But even these eight 'moods' can be reduced further, by using the simple rules of *substitution* and *transposition of premisses* (both were taken for granted by Aristotle, and the latter was codified in medieval times). For example, '*Icb, Aba* ⊢ *Iac*' (*Dimatis*) is equivalent to '*Aba, Icb* ⊢ *Iac*' (by tranposition), which is of the same logical form as '*Abc, Iab* ⊢ *Ica*' (substituting '*c*' for '*a*' and '*a*' for '*c*'), which is equivalent to '*Abc, Iab* ⊢ *Iac*' (by the I rule of conversion), which is *Darii*. With these additional rules, we arrive at just six 'moods': *Barbara*, *Celarent/Cesare/Camestres/Calemes*, *Darii/Datisi/Disamis/Dimatis*, *Ferio/Festino/Ferison/Fresison*, *Baroco* and *Bocardo*. This result is interesting, because it shows what is meant by

Residual Moods

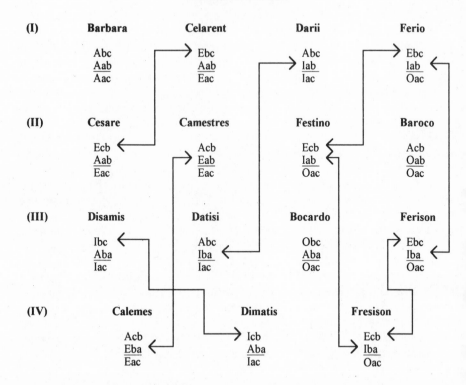

(I)   **Barbara**   **Celarent**   **Darii**   **Ferio**

    Abc   Ebc   Abc   Ebc
    Aab   Aab   Iab   Iab
    Aac   Eac   Iac   Oac

(II)   **Cesare**   **Camestres**   **Festino**   **Baroco**

    Ecb   Acb   Ecb   Acb
    Aab   Eab   Iab   Oab
    Eac   Eac   Oac   Oac

(III)   **Disamis**   **Datisi**   **Bocardo**   **Ferison**

    Ibc   Abc   Obc   Ebc
    Aba   Iba   Aba   Iba
    Iac   Iac   Oac   Oac

(IV)   **Calemes**   **Dimatis**   **Fresison**

    Acb   Icb   Ecb
    Eba   Aba   Iba
    Eac   Iac   Oac

the 'reduction' of the *C-moods* to *Celarent*, the *D-moods* to *Darii*, and the *F-moods* to *Ferio* – they all end up as logically equivalent, where this can be proved using only the E and I rules of conversion, and the rules of substitution and transposition. *Baroco* and *Bocardo*, however, cannot be so reduced to *Barbara* – they require a *reductio ad absurdum* argument (proceeding by *conversio*; see (BR) of §1.2, where *Baroco* is proved, and (BC) above, where *Bocardo* is proved). However, if we also admit the rules of *obversion* (see (OB) above), equally legitimate within Fregean logic, then these two moods too can be 'reduced away'. *Baroco* ($Acb, Oab \vdash Oac$), for example, is equivalent to '$Ecb^*, Iab^* \vdash Oac$' (by two of the rules of obversion – (a) and (d) of (OB) above), which is of the form '$Ecb, Iab \vdash Oac$' (substituting 'b' for 'b^*'), which is equivalent to '$Ebc, Iab \vdash Oac$' (by the E rule of conversion), which is *Ferio*. Likewise, *Bocardo* can be 'reduced' to *Darii* (by transposition, obversion of the O-propositions, substitution, and conversion). So does this then mean that the two moods were wrongly named? It remains the case that they cannot be 'directly reduced' (by merely conversion, substitution and transposition), but they do turn out to be logically equivalent to *Ferio* and *Darii*, rather than *Barbara*, which does indicate a certain confusion.

So have we then shown that there are just four basic 'moods', as Aristotle himself suggested – the four moods of the first figure? Unfortunately, however, if we allow ourselves the use of obversion, further reductions can be made. For *Ferio* can be 'reduced' to *Darii* (by obversion of the E- and O-propositions, and substitution), and *Celarent* can be 'reduced' to *Barbara* (by obversion of the E-propositions, and substitution). In the end, then, there are just *two* logically distinguishable 'moods' – *Barbara* (with the *C-moods*) and *Darii* (with the rest). But from a Fregean perspective, this need hardly surprise us. For what these correspond to are the only two patterns of inference that are valid within the 'translated' syllogistic system:

(AA) $(\forall x)\,(Bx \to Cx),\,(\forall x)\,(Ax \to Bx) \vdash (\forall x)\,(Ax \to Cx)$.

(AE) $(\forall x)\,(Bx \to Cx),\,(\exists x)\,(Ax \,\&\, Bx) \vdash (\exists x)\,(Ax \,\&\, Cx)$.

(AA) involves only universal propositions, and (AE) contains one premiss that is universal, and one premiss and a conclusion that are particular. Of course, such a basic division is already present in syllogistic theory, and with obversion, all the 'reductions' are provable; but it took Fregean logic, with the emphasis on logical rather than grammatical form, to highlight the simplicity of the structure. The appreciation of this might well have dismantled the (grammatically sound but logically shaky) traditional edifice of moods and figures, but Aristotle himself would have been impressed with the reduction.

APPENDIX 2

Leibniz on Analysis

All proof, according to Leibniz, depends on the Principle of Identity, which states that a proposition expresses an 'identity' if the predicate is explicitly either identical with or included in the subject. Now Leibniz believed that 'always, in every true affirmative proposition, necessary or contingent, universal or particular, the concept of the predicate is in a sense included in that of the subject' (*LAC*, p. 63); so that if this inclusion could be made explicit, if it was not already, a *proof* of the proposition could be achieved. Proof thus proceeds by reducing the proposition to an 'identity' by successive applications of the rule of 'substitution of equivalents', i.e. by *analysing* each term in turn by means of a definition. As illustrations, consider the following two proofs of '2 + 1 = 3' ('Two plus one is three') and 'Logicians are thinkers', respectively:

(A) (1) $\quad 2 + 1 \quad = \quad 3$
     (2) $\quad 1 + 1 + 1 \quad = \quad 3 \qquad$ (by the def. '2 = 1 + 1')
     (3) $\quad 1 + 1 + 1 \quad = \quad 2 + 1 \quad$ (by the def. '3 = 2 + 1')
     (4) $\quad 1 + 1 + 1 \quad = \quad 1 + 1 + 1 \quad$ (by the def. '2 = 1 + 1')

(B) (1) Logicians are thinkers
     (2) Sharp-minded philosophers are thinkers
         (by the def. 'Logicians are sharp-minded philosophers')
     (3) Sharp-minded enlightened intellectuals are thinkers
         (by the def. 'Philosophers are enlightened intellectuals')
     (4) Sharp-minded enlightened stimulating thinkers are thinkers
         (by the def. 'Intellectuals are stimulating thinkers')

In both cases, (4) is an 'identity' in Leibniz's sense, and cannot itself be demonstrated, being something that is immediately *intuited* as true. (Cf. MacDonald Ross, 1984: pp. 62-3; Ishiguro, 1990: pp. 56-7.) But if it is possible to *analyse* downwards from (1) to (4), to *prove* a proposition, then it must be possible to *synthesize* upwards from (4) to (1), to *discover* (the fact expressed by) a proposition. (Cf. Kneale, 1962: pp. 332-3.) Once the basic terms are found, Leibniz believed, we can move in *either* direction, and a universal character can thus be combined with a *calculus ratiocinator* to provide *both* a logic of proof *and* a logic of discovery (cf. §2.1 above).

APPENDIX 3

Frege's Logical Notation

Frege called his logical notation 'Begriffsschrift', which literally means 'concept-script' (it has also been translated as 'conceptual notation'), reflecting his avowed aim of providing a means of capturing the 'conceptual content' ('Begriffsinhalt') of propositions (see §2.5 above). The name also formed the title of his first book, which introduced his logical system. Since I have used modern notation in discussing Frege's ideas in the present work, a brief account of Frege's own symbolism and its translation into modern notation is provided here.

Frege explains his symbolism in Part I of the *Begriffsschrift*. He starts by introducing the following symbol (§2):

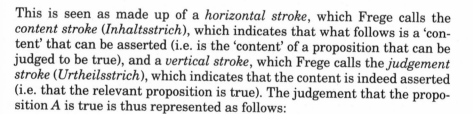

This is seen as made up of a *horizontal stroke*, which Frege calls the *content stroke* (*Inhaltsstrich*), which indicates that what follows is a 'content' that can be asserted (i.e. is the 'content' of a proposition that can be judged to be true), and a *vertical stroke*, which Frege calls the *judgement stroke* (*Urtheilsstrich*), which indicates that the content is indeed asserted (i.e. that the relevant proposition is true). The judgement that the proposition *A* is true is thus represented as follows:

In §5 Frege notes that if *A* and *B* represent judgeable contents (i.e. are propositions), then there are four possibilities to consider (anticipating Wittgenstein's introduction of *truth-tables* in the *Tractatus*, a treatise that was profoundly influenced by Frege's work):

(i)   *A* is affirmed, *B* is affirmed (i.e. both are true);
(ii)   *A* is affirmed, *B* is denied (i.e. *A* is true, *B* is false);
(iii) *A* is denied, *B* is affirmed (i.e. *A* is false, *B* is true);
(iv) *A* is denied, *B* is denied (i.e. both are false).

The following symbol is then defined as representing the judgement that *the third of these possibilities does not obtain, but one of the other three does*:

What is represented here is the assertion of the conditional proposition 'If *B*, then *A*', understood as involving the material conditional, i.e. construed as what would be formalized in modern notation as '*B* → *A*', since this is indeed equivalent to '¬(¬*A* & *B*)' (denying the third possibility). The vertical stroke that connects the upper and lower horizontal strokes Frege thus calls the *conditional stroke* (*Bedingungsstrich*). More complex symbols can then be readily constructed, such as the following:

This represents the assertion of the complex conditional proposition '*Γ* → (*B* → *A*)', which is equivalent to '¬(¬*A* & *B* & *Γ*)'. (Cf. *BS*, §5.)

Frege's definition of the conditional thus implies that from the judgements

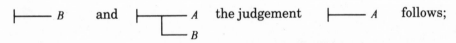

and what is involved here is *modus ponens*, the rule that licenses inferring '*A*' from '*B*' and 'If *B*, then *A*'. 'In logic', Frege writes, 'following Aristotle, a whole series of modes of inference are enumerated [cf. App. 1 above]; I use just this one – at least in all cases where a new judgement is derived from more than one single judgement'. If it is possible to manage with a single mode of inference, Frege goes on, 'perspicuity demands that this be done'. (*BS*, §6.)

Frege then defines the *negation stroke* (§7), which he represents by attaching a small vertical stroke to the underside of the content-stroke:

This is understood as *denying* (the content of the proposition) *A*, i.e. as asserting that '¬*A*' is true. Using the conditional and negation strokes, further judgements can then be represented. For example, assertion of the proposition '*A* or *B*', construing 'or' in the inclusive sense, i.e. '*A* ∨ *B*', which is equivalent to '¬*B* → *A*', can be represented as follows:

'A & B', which is equivalent to '¬(B → ¬A)', can also be readily represented (note how the *scope* of each negation sign is reflected in Frege's symbolism):

What Frege has thus specified is a system of propositional logic, with negation and the conditional as the primitive connectives, and *modus ponens* as the basic rule of inference. (Frege also makes tacit use of a rule of substitution.) Both conjunction and disjunction can clearly be defined in Frege's system (as Frege himself explains in §7); but it has to be said that, except in the case of conditional propositions, Frege's two-dimensional 'Begriffsschrift' does not render the validity of inferences in propositional logic as perspicuous as modern notation is capable of doing. Of course, it is true that any system that uses some but not all of the propositional connectives either 'deflates' or 'inflates' certain inferences. As an example of each, consider the following 'translations' of one of de Morgan's laws, '¬(A & B) ↔ ¬A ∨ ¬B', and one of the distributive laws, 'A ∨ (B & C) ↔ (A ∨ B) & (A ∨ C)', respectively:

(ML) '(B → ¬A) ↔ (B → ¬A)';
(DL) '[(C → ¬B) → A] ↔ ¬[(¬C → A) → ¬(¬B → A)]'.

But Frege's notation would certainly add to the 'inflation' of many inferences; and although the possibility of defining '&' and '∨' in terms of '→' and '¬' is instructive (Frege himself frequently emphasizes the value of making do with as few primitives as possible), the lack of simple signs for conjunction and disjunction (even if defined in terms of other connectives) must be regarded as a deficiency of the symbolism.

In §8 Frege defines a symbol for what he calls 'identity of content' ('Inhaltsgleichheit'):

$$\vdash\!\!\!-\!\!\!-\!\!\!-\ (A \equiv B)$$

This is understood as meaning that 'the symbol A and the symbol B have the same conceptual content, so that A can always be replaced by B and vice versa'. As argued in §2.5 above, Frege's criterion for sameness of conceptual content is essentially *logical equivalence*; but the problems that this raises, and the restrictions that are needed in appealing to intersubstitutability *salva veritate*, were only recognized by Frege later, in his paper 'Über Sinn und Bedeutung' (see ch. 6 above). At the time of the *Begriffsschrift*, as §8 reveals, Frege also thought that identity of content was a relation between names rather than contents, a view which he criticizes at the beginning of 'Über Sinn und Bedeutung' (see §6.1 above).

In the rest of Part I of the *Begriffsschrift* (§§9-12) Frege introduces his notation for what we now know as predicate logic. In §9 he explains his use of function-argument analysis (for details, see §5.2 above), and in §10 he defines the following symbols as '*A* has the property *Φ*' ('*Fa*' in modern notation) and '*B* stands in the *Ψ*-relation to *A*' ('*Rba*' in modern notation), respectively:

$$\vdash\!\!\!\!\!\!\!\!\!\!- \quad \Phi\,(A)$$

$$\vdash\!\!\!\!\!\!\!\!\!\!- \quad \Psi\,(A,\,B)$$

In §11 he introduces his key symbol for the universal quantifier, which involves inserting in the content stroke a concavity (*Höhlung*) in which the letter indicating the argument is placed:

This is understood as representing the judgement that 'the function [*Φ*] yields a fact whatever is taken as its argument', i.e. that everything has the property *Φ* (for all *x*, *Fx* – '(∀*x*) *Fx*' as it would be formalized in modern notation). [Frege uses italicized upper case Greek letters for function terms, lower case Gothic (old German) letters for bound variables, and italicized ordinary letters for free variables. I have replaced Frege's Gothic letters with ordinary letters in the account offered here. In modern notation, italicized upper case ordinary letters – such as *F* and *G* – are conventionally used for function terms, italicized lower case ordinary letters typically from the end of the alphabet – such as *x* and *y* – for bound variables, and italicized lower case ordinary letters typically from the beginning of the alphabet – such as *a* and *b* – for free variables, as illustrated in the inference schema '(∀*x*) *Fx* → *Fa*', reflecting the rule of universal elimination.] As Frege points out, the concavity with the letter written in it 'delimits the scope [*Gebiet*] of the generality signified by the letter' (§11). As shown in §2.2 above, appreciation of the *scope* of the quantifier is essential in formalizing statements of multiple generality, where ambiguity may be present.

In §12, Frege considers certain combinations of symbols. Using negation and the universal quantifier, existential judgements such as 'There are some things that do not have the property *X*' (understood as equivalent to 'It is not true that everything is *X*') can be represented:

The following symbol, on the other hand, is translated simply as 'There are *Λ*'s' (i.e. 'There is at least one *Λ*'):

$\vdash\!\!\!\top\!\!\!\cup\!\!\!\top\!\!\!\top$ Λ(a)

Clearly, what we have here is a definition of the existential quantifier – '($\exists x$) Fx', in modern notation, being definable as '$\neg(\forall x)\neg Fx$' – although as in the case of conjunction and disjunction, Frege does not introduce a simple sign for the existential quantifier.

Frege also shows how the four types of syllogistic proposition, as contained in the traditional square of opposition (cf. App. 1 above), are represented in his system:

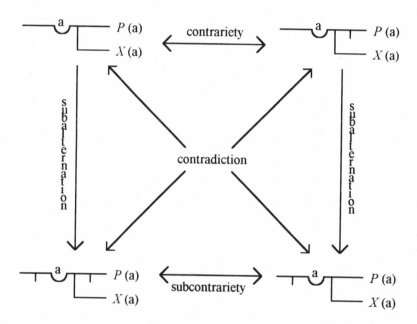

Syllogistic A, E, I and O propositions are thus formalized, in modern notation (substituting 'C' for 'X' and 'x' for 'a'), as follows:

(A) $(\forall x)\,(Cx \to Px)$;
(E) $(\forall x)\,(Cx \to \neg Px)$;
(I) $\neg(\forall x)\,(Cx \to \neg Px)$, which is equivalent to $(\exists x)\,(Cx \,\&\, Px)$;
(O) $\neg(\forall x)\,(Cx \to Px)$, which is equivalent to $(\exists x)\,(Cx \,\&\, \neg Px)$.

As noted in Appendix 1, however, although the square of opposition is reproduced in §12 of the *Begriffsschrift*, with the traditional relations marked, Frege does not make clear that contrariety, subcontrariety and subalternation are all invalidated under his formalizations. [(A) and (E) can both be true (if there are no C's); (I) and (O) can both be false (if there are no C's); and (A) does not imply (I), and (E) does not imply (O).]

Nevertheless, this aside, it is clear that, in utilizing function-argument analysis and inventing the quantifier, Frege succeeded in developing the first system of predicate logic.

In Part II of the *Begriffsschrift*, Frege shows how more complex judgements can be represented and derived in his system. All we need note here is the 'kernel' of nine propositions that Frege takes as the axioms of his system (numbered (1), (2), (8), (28), (31), (41), (52), (54) and (58), respectively, in his own account):

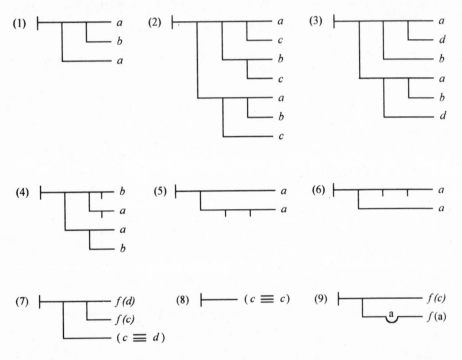

As Lukasiewicz (1934) was later to prove, the first six axioms form a complete set of axioms for propositional logic, though the third axiom can in fact be derived, using just the rules of *modus ponens* and substitution, from the first two (cf. Kneale, 1962: pp. 490-1). The other five are independent of one another (cf. n. 9 of ch. 2 above). The axioms can be formulated in modern notation as follows:

(1*) $P \rightarrow (Q \rightarrow P)$.
(2*) $[R \rightarrow (Q \rightarrow P)] \rightarrow [(R \rightarrow Q) \rightarrow (R \rightarrow P)]$.
(3*) $[S \rightarrow (Q \rightarrow P)] \rightarrow [Q \rightarrow (S \rightarrow P)]$.
(4*) $(Q \rightarrow P) \rightarrow (\neg P \rightarrow \neg Q)$.
(5*) $\neg\neg P \rightarrow P$.
(6*) $P \rightarrow \neg\neg P$.

The seventh and eighth formulae involve Frege's symbol for identity of content, and might be re-expressed thus:

(7*) $(a = b) \to (Fa \to Fb)$.

(8*) $a = a$.

(7*) is a version of the Principle of the Indiscernibility of Identicals (cf. §4.2 above; making explicit the implicit quantification over properties, and replacing the second conditional by the biconditional, gives us '$a = b \to (\forall F)$ $(Fa \leftrightarrow Fb)$'); and (8*), of course, states that everything is identical with itself. The ninth axiom, reflecting what, in a natural deduction system, is the rule of universal elimination, can be formulated as follows:

(9*) $(\forall x) Fx \to Fa$.

Frege also recognizes (*BS*, §11) what we now know as the rule of universal introduction, legitimizing the transition from a proposition involving italic letters to a universally quantified proposition (i.e. 'From Fa infer $(\forall x) Fx$' – on the understanding that 'a' is an arbitrary name and Fa does not rest on any assumption in which 'a' occurs). Here too Frege succeeded in specifying a complete set of axioms and rules for first-order predicate logic (cf. Kneale, p. 489).

What revisions to his logical system were made in Frege's *Grundgesetze*? As noted in §4.2 above, and discussed in the chapters that follow, the two fundamental developments in Frege's philosophical views between the *Begriffsschrift* and the *Grundgesetze* concerned, firstly, the bifurcation of his early notion of 'content' into 'Sinn' and 'Bedeutung', and secondly, connected with this, the clarification of his ontology, admitting, in particular, both truth-values and extensions of concepts as objects, and hence as legitimate arguments of functions; and these developments did indeed necessitate certain changes in his logical theory. The essential system of 'strokes' remained the same, though Frege talks simply of the 'horizontal' rather than the 'content' stroke (cf. *GG*, I, §5). Taking truth-values as the *Bedeutungen* of sentences involved treating sentences as names, so that what is then seen as following the horizontal stroke is a name of a truth-value (cf. *GG*, I, §§2, 5). The main change – or addition – to the notation itself concerns the introduction of a symbol, '$\acute{\varepsilon}\varPhi(\varepsilon)$', with a smooth breathing over the first occurrence of 'ε', for the *value-range* of the function $\varPhi(\xi)$; where the function is one that maps objects onto one of the two truth-values, i.e. is a concept, then what we have here is a symbol for the extension of the concept $\varPhi$. (Cf. *GG*, I, §9.) As explained in chapter 4 above, Frege defines the natural numbers by identifying them with extensions of concepts that are logically definable; and by the time of the *Grundgesetze*, he had convinced himself that the appeal to extensions was legitimate (cf. §5.5 above).

As far as the axioms and rules of his logical system were concerned, there was a certain amount of reorganization. Axiom (1) of the *Be-*

griffsschrift survives unchanged as Axiom I of the *Grundgesetze*, but Axioms (2), (3) and (4) disappear as a result of the specification of a greater number of rules. [18 rules are formulated altogether – see *GG*, I, §48 – but the last six simply concern the use of brackets, Rule 1 is a formation rule for the horizontal stroke, and Rules 9 to 12 are rules of substitution. Rules 2 to 8 are the rules of inference, in propositional and predicate logic.] Axiom (2) becomes provable by means of the rule of *amalgamation of identical subcomponents* (Rule 4; allowing e.g. the transition from 'if *P*, then if *P*, then *Q*' to the simpler 'if *P*, then *Q*'); and Axiom (3) becomes provable by means of the rule of *interchange of subcomponents* (Rule 2; allowing e.g. the transition from 'if *P*, then if *Q*, then *R*' to 'if *Q*, then if *P*, then *R*'). Axiom (4) is made redundant with the introduction of the rule of *contraposition* (Rule 3). Axioms (5) and (6), which, as Frege noted in the 'Preface' to the *Begriffsschrift*, he later realized could be combined using the symbol for identity of content (just as (5*) and (6*) above can be combined as '$\neg\neg P \leftrightarrow P$'), become derivable from Axiom IV of the *Grundgesetze*:

$$\vdash\!\!\!\begin{array}{l} \rule{1em}{0.4pt}\ (\rule{1.5em}{0.4pt}\ a) = (\rule{1.5em}{0.4pt}\ b) \\ \rule{1em}{0.4pt}_{\top}\ (\rule{1.5em}{0.4pt}\ a) = (\rule{0.5em}{0.4pt}_{\top}\ b) \end{array}$$

What this says is that either $a = b$ or $a \neq b$. Axioms (7) and (8) of the *Begriffsschrift* are replaced by Axiom III of the *Grundgesetze*:

$$\vdash\!\!\!\begin{array}{l} g\ \left(\overset{f}{\smallsmile}\!\!\begin{array}{l} f\,(a) \\ f\,(b) \end{array} \right) \\ \\ g\,(a = b) \end{array}$$

Given that both the expressions contained within the brackets (as governed by '*g*') are truth-values, what Axiom III says is that the truth-value named by the expression in the upper brackets falls under every concept under which the truth-value named by '*a* = *b*' falls (cf. *GG*, I, §20). From this it follows that if *a* = *b*, then anything that holds of *a* holds of *b*, which is Axiom (7) of the *Begriffsschrift*, and that everything is identical to itself, which is Axiom (8). Axiom (9) of the *Begriffsschrift* is retained unchanged as Axiom IIa of the *Grundgesetze*, but a corresponding version, Axiom IIb, is introduced for second-level functions:

$$\vdash\!\!\!\begin{array}{l} \rule{2em}{0.4pt}\ M_\beta(f(\beta)) \\ \underset{f}{\smallsmile}\ \rule{1em}{0.4pt}\ M_\beta(\mathfrak{f}(\beta)) \end{array}$$

What this says is that whatever holds of all first-level functions of one argument holds of any (cf. *GG*, I, §25). The nine axioms of the *Begriffsschrift* are thus condensed into the first four axioms of the *Grundgesetze*, with some additional rules formulated and with second-order quantification made official.

The most significant development, however, involved the introduction of Axiom V of the *Grundgesetze*, legitimizing value-ranges of functions (extensions of concepts). As the present work has been concerned to show, Axiom V played a central role in the evolution of Frege's philosophy: its origins lie in the central argument of the *Grundlagen* (see §5.3 above), the problem of its status motivated the distinction between *Sinn* and *Bedeutung* (see esp. §§5.4 – 5.5 above), and it was eventually held responsible by Frege for the contradiction that Russell discovered in his system (see §7.2 above). Frege formulated it as follows:

$$\vdash\!\!\!\!- \ (\,\acute{\varepsilon}f(\varepsilon) \ = \ \grave{\alpha}g(\alpha)) \ = \ (-\!\!\smile\!\!\!a\!\!\!\frown\!\!\!- \ f(a) = g(a)\,)$$

What this asserts is the equivalence between (Vb) and (Va), in effect contextually defining (Vb) by means of (Va):

(Va) The function F has the same value for each argument as the function G.

(Vb) The value-range of the function F is identical with the value-range of the function G.

In modern notation, adapting Frege's symbol for the value-range of a function, the equivalence can be expressed as follows:

(V*) $\dot{x}\,Fx = \dot{x}\,Gx \leftrightarrow (\forall x)\,(Fx \leftrightarrow Gx)$.

Frege's final axiom, Axiom VI, introduces a further new symbol, '\$\backslash\xi$', representing the function that Frege defines to replace the definite article of ordinary language. In ordinary language, definite descriptions, which Frege classifies as proper names, are formed by prefixing the definite article 'the' to a concept expression ('the *F* '). But such descriptions can readily be formed that lack a referent, or that fail to uniquely determine a single referent. Ordinary language is deficient in this respect, according to Frege, whereas in a logical language a referent must be determined for every legitimately constructed proper name. How might this be done? If we assume that concepts are sharply defined, and that extensions of concepts are objects, then any definite description of the form 'the extension of the concept *F* ' is guaranteed a unique referent. So the obvious solution is to admit only definite descriptions of this form into the logical language. But how then do we refer to 'ordinary' objects? Here the strategy is to note that for any given object $\varDelta$, there is a concept *is identical with $\varDelta$*, which clearly meets the condition of being sharply defined. So the suggestion is to *identify* the object Δ with the extension of this concept (which is itself an object). However, as discussed in §6.4 above (and see esp. n. 29 of ch. 6, which states Frege's own argument in *GG*, I, §10), there are objections to identifying objects with the corresponding extensions (i.e. with their unit classes). So what Frege does instead is introduce a function that serves the same purpose, *mapping* extensions of concepts under which only one object falls onto that object itself. More precisely, the function $\backslash\xi$ is defined in the following way:

(i)   If the argument is the extension of the concept *is identical with* Δ, i.e. $\acute{\varepsilon}(\Delta = \varepsilon)$, for any given object Δ, then the value of the function is the object Δ itself.

(ii)   If the argument is not an extension as specified in (i), i.e. is not an extension of a concept under which only one object falls, then the value of the function is the argument itself (i.e. the function maps all other objects onto themselves). [Cf. *GG*, I, §11.]

(ii) ensures that the function is defined for all objects; and (i) gives rise to Axiom VI (cf. *GG*, I, §18):

$$\vdash a = \backslash\acute{\varepsilon}(a = \varepsilon)$$

Frege's strategy might be illustrated by considering the example that Russell used to motivate his theory of descriptions:

(K)   The present King of France is bald.

If there is no King of France (i.e. in Fregean terminology, the definite description lacks a *Bedeutung*), then the proposition as a whole would seem to lack a truth-value (i.e. a *Bedeutung*). Yet (K) remains meaningful, and hence, according to Russell, *must* have a truth-value. To solve the problem, Russell suggests that (K) should be analysed as the following:

(KR)   There is one and only one King of France, and whatever is King of France is bald.

The proposition now comes out as *false* because the first conjunct is false (there is no King of France). According to Frege, however, (K) should be rewritten in his ideal logical language thus:

(KF) $\backslash$ (extension of the concept *present King of France*) is bald.

If there *is* one and only one present King of France, then the value of '$\backslash$ (extension of the concept *present King of France*)' is that person; if there is not, then the value is the extension itself. If there is no present King of France at all, in other words, then the value is the null set, and it is false that the null set is bald. (If there were somehow more than one King of France, then the value would be the set of such people, and it is equally false that this set is bald; although strictly speaking, of course, the vagueness of ξ *is bald* means that there is no genuine (i.e. logically correct) concept involved here, according to Frege; see §7.3 above.) So Frege's treatment has the same result as Russell's: propositions involving definite descriptions that fail to refer to a unique entity come out as *false*. The difference is that whilst Russell 'analysed away' the troublesome denoting phrase (cf. n. 36 of ch. 6 above), Frege ingeniously provided a replacement for it and introduced a technical device to ensure it had a referent (cf. the last two pages of §8.2 above). If, to use the term introduced in §5.3 above, Frege's central argument in the *Grundlagen*, in seeking to define the natural numbers in a logically impeccable way, relied on *conceptual ascent*, then his description function $\backslash \xi$ was required for *objectual descent* – to make the return trip from the pure logical realm of extensions of concepts to the everyday world of 'ordinary' objects.

APPENDIX 4

Chronology of Frege's Life and Works

[What little is known of Frege's life is recorded in Bynum, 1972a, on which the present chronology is based. For a much more detailed list of Frege's works, arranged chronologically, see Bibliography below.]

1848   Birth of Friedrich Ludwig Gottlob Frege on 8 November in Wismar, on the Baltic Sea. His father, Karl Alexander (b.1809), was director of a private girls' school, and his mother, Auguste Bialloblotzky, was a teacher and later principal of the school.

1864   Entered the *Gymnasium* in Wismar.

1866   Death of Frege's father.

1869   Passed his *Abitur* in the spring and immediately entered the University of Jena, where he spent four semesters, taking courses in chemistry, mathematics and philosophy.

1871   Transferred to the University of Göttingen, where he spent five semesters, taking courses in physics, mathematics and philosophy of religion.

1873   Awarded his doctorate on 12 December for his dissertation 'On a Geometrical Representation of Imaginary Forms in the Plane' (*GR*).

1874   Appointed to the post of *Privatdozent* (an unsalaried lectureship) in the mathematics faculty at the University of Jena in May, submitting his *Habilitationsschrift* on 'Methods of Calculation based on an Extension of the Concept of Magnitude' (*MC*). Had a heavy teaching load during the first few years of his career.

1878   Death of Frege's mother.

1879   Publication of *Begriffsschrift*. Promoted to *ausserordentlicher Professor* (a salaried position), on the recommendation of Ernst Abbe, his mentor at Jena. His book was, however, poorly received.

1884   Publication of *Die Grundlagen der Arithmetik*. Again, the reviews were unfavourable.

1892   Publication of 'On Concept and Object' (*CO*) and 'On Sense and Reference' (*SR*), heralding the central development in Frege's semantic views.

1893   Publication of Volume I of Frege's *magnum opus*, the *Grundgesetze der Arithmetik*. Once again, the reviews were unfavourable. One of them, however, was by Peano, which led to an exchange of letters between Frege and Peano, and through Peano, to Russell's reading of Frege's works.

1894   Review of Husserl's *Philosophie der Arithmetik*, which had the effect of converting Husserl to anti-psychologism.

1896   Promoted to the post of Honorary Ordinary Professor. The post was unsalaried, but with no administrative duties, and with a stipend arranged by Abbe from the Carl Zeiss *Stiftung* (a foundation that Abbe had helped set up), Frege acquired more time for research.

1902   Letter from Russell to Frege, dated 16 June, informing him of the contradiction in his logical system.

1903   Publication, at Frege's own expense, of Volume II of the *Grundgesetze*, including a hastily written appendix seeking to respond to Russell's paradox.

1905   Death of Frege's wife, Margaret Lieseburg (b.1856), leaving Frege with their adopted son, Alfred. (Their own children had all died young, and Alfred had been adopted around 1900.)

1910   Carnap attended Frege's course on logic. Carnap also attended later courses, including one given in 1914 on 'Logic in Mathematics'.

1911   Wittgenstein visited Frege, who recommended that he study with Russell.

1918   Retired from the University of Jena, and moved to Bad Kleinen, near Wismar. Publication of 'Der Gedanke' (*T*).

1925   Death of Frege on 26 July at the age of 77.

1935   Frege's *Nachlaß* handed over by Alfred Frege to Heinrich Scholz of the University of Münster, who was planning an edition of Frege's works. Copies were made of most of the important pieces. (For details of the history of Frege's *Nachlaß*, see the account given by H. Hermes, F. Kambartel and F. Kaulbach in *NS*, pp. xxxiv-xli / *PW*, pp. ix-xiii.)

1943   Frege's *Nachlaß* deposited in the University Library at Münster.

1944   Alfred Frege killed in action in France on 15 June.

1945   Frege's *Nachlaß* destroyed in a bombing raid on Münster on 25 March.

1950   First English translation, by J.L. Austin, of Frege's *Grundlagen* (*FA*).

1952   First English edition, by P.T. Geach and M. Black, of Frege's published philosophical writings (*TPW*).

1969   Frege's *Nachgelassene Schriften* (*NS*), based on the copies Scholz had made, finally published in German (translated into English as *PW* in 1979).

1976   Frege's correspondence (*WB*) published in German (translated into English as *PMC* in 1980).

Notes

Introduction

1. For details of the extent of Descartes' debt to scholastic philosophy, see, in particular, Gilson, 1951.

2. Cf. Rée, 1978: Part 3; Ayers, 1978: §3; MacIntyre, 1984, p. 31; and esp. Rorty, 1984: §1. Obvious examples of rational reconstructions are Strawson's *The Bounds of Sense* (1966) and Dummett's *Frege: Philosophy of Language* (1981a), and of historical reconstructions Janik and Toulmin's *Wittgenstein's Vienna* (1973) and Sluga's *Gottlob Frege* (1980).

3. Cf. Rée (1978: p. 17), who offers an historical critique of this view. Rorty (1984: §3) and Krüger (1984: §1) also denounce this view, which underpins what Rorty terms 'doxography' and Krüger calls 'problematic history' (the history of philosophical problems).

4. Cf. MacIntyre, 1984: pp. 42-4, who also emphasizes the *positive* role that the incoherences of a theory play, being the source of intellectual progress.

5. Recent work on Frege illustrates very well the difficulties involved in striking a balance between rational and historical reconstruction. Dummett (1981a, 1981b), it seems to me, does present Frege's thought too much in the form of contemporary reflections on topics that Frege treats, and one loses a clear sense of the origins and development of Frege's philosophy. Sluga (1980), on the other hand, in seeking to redress the balance, concentrates too much on the influences that there may have been on Frege (which is ironic in a series dedicated to the *arguments* of the philosophers). Baker and Hacker (1984), also in reaction to Dummett, properly focus on the evolution of Frege's thought, but here their antipathy to Frege undermines the historical sensitivity that they themselves advocate: from the vantage-point of a rather radical Wittgensteinianism, Frege is accused of one conceptual confusion after another (despite the fact that Frege was the philosopher for whom Wittgenstein had the greatest respect). Clearly, a course must be steered between these approaches; and Dummett's more recent book (1991a) provides a better example of how to do this. But here the concern is solely with Frege's philosophy of mathematics; and what I have sought to do in the present work is to provide an account of Frege's philosophy as a whole.

6. Hegel's dialectical method was first put to use in his *Lectures on the History of Philosophy*, first given at Jena (where Frege was later to teach) in 1805-6, but only published after his death. For discussion of these lectures, see Westoby, 1978.

7. In *The Idea of History*, Collingwood presents a rather extreme historicism, in which philosophy seems to have been absorbed into history. But his earlier *Essay on Philosophical Method* (1933) reflects a more balanced conception – philosophy as reasonably autonomous, but with its own essentially historical development – which is what I have tried to capture here. For an account of the rise and fall of Hegelianism in Britain, see Quinton, 1986.

8. This has taken two forms. Rorty (1980), MacIntyre (1981), Craig (1987), Taylor (1989) and Skorupski (1994), for example, offer what Rorty (1984: §2) has called 'Geistesgeschichte' (his third genre of 'history of philosophy', after rational and historical reconstructions) – sweeping accounts of whole changes in *Weltanschauung*. Hylton (1990) and Dummett (1991a), on the other hand, provide more detailed and textually focussed accounts of the work of individual philosophers. The present book is intended to fall into the latter category.

9. Cf. Taylor, 1984, on the importance of retrieving previous 'paradigms' and of appreciating the historical origins of conceptions that might now be taken wholly for granted.

10. For further criticism of Dummett's reconstruction of Frege as a philosopher of language, see Sluga, 1975; Currie, 1976; Skorupski, 1984. On Frege's lack of interest in 'linguistic meaning', cf. also Burge, 1979, 1990.

11. Cf. *SR*, p. 61; *PMC*, p. 67; *IL*, p. 193; *BSLD*, p. 198; *T*, pp. 356-7. I use 'meaning' here to refer to all those elements involved in the use and understanding of an expression. According to Frege (*PWLB*, p. 140), 'This dog howled the whole night' and 'This cur howled the whole night', for example, have the same *sense*, the difference being merely that the second has a more pejorative *tone* (to use Dummett's term here; 1981a: ch. 1).

12. The example is used, most famously, in *SR*, p. 62. For fuller discussion of the criteria roughly stated here, see §8.1.

13. The division was reinforced by Dummett's decision to publish his work on Frege's philosophy of language quite separately from his work on Frege's philosophy of mathematics – the latter, in fact, not appearing until almost two decades after the former. Collections, such as the volume edited by Klemke (1968), the three volumes edited by Schirn (1976), and the volume edited by Haaparanta and Hintikka (1986), also reinforce the division. The division is not illegitimate in itself; what is regrettable is the extent to which discussion of Frege's philosophical logic proceeds as if his logicism was entirely irrelevant. Even a book as recent as Carl's *Frege's Theory of Sense and Reference* (1994) contains no account at all of Frege's logicism. Writers on Frege's philosophy of mathematics, however, have been much better at relating it to his philosophical logic. See esp. Resnik, 1980; Wright, 1983; and Dummett, 1991a. Cf. Benacerraf, 1981, however, for the view that Frege should be seen primarily as a mathematician; and for criticism of Benacerraf's view, in particular, see Weiner, 1984.

14. The first real tract in what is now called philosophical logic is Wittgenstein's *Tractatus Logico-Philosophicus*. The initial proposal was indeed to translate his original title of 'Logisch-philosophische Abhandlung' as 'Philosophical Logic', but Wittgenstein himself rejected the term as meaningless, preferring instead the title suggested by Moore (see Wittgenstein, *LO*, p. 20; McGuinness, 1988: p. 299).

15. See §2.5. Frege himself gives this example in *GG*, I, §2, where he states that the two identity statements possess *different* senses.

16. The dilemma might also be stated by means of the use/mention distinction. Whilst the rational reconstructor *uses* certain of the philosophical ideas of the philosopher concerned, but runs the risk of using them differently, the historical reconstructor merely *mentions* them, and runs the risk of not making clear how they *can* be used. In either case, the reconstructor fails to get at what the ideas really are. There is an interesting analogy here with Russell's critique, in 'On Denoting', of Frege's conception of sense, a critique which also utilizes the use/mention distinction in aiming to show that there is no way of getting at *senses*.

17. The allusion is to Wittgenstein, *PI*, §217. Where I depart from Wittgenstein is in not resting content with saying, at the point where justifications are exhausted, 'This is simply what I do', but in turning to historical understanding for further explanation. Wittgenstein, I think, accepted too Fregean a view of the distinction between justification and historical or causal explanation. Clearly, if the latter is seen of no philosophical value, then when reasons give out, we are indeed left with the ordinary language philosopher's 'This is simply what I do'. Wittgenstein was right to insist that liberation from philosophical misconceptions involves appreciating the contingency of our linguistic practices, but this contingency can be appreciated all the more with concrete historical and scientific investigations, where this can involve literary criticism, anthropology, sociology, psychology, biology, or any other discipline that enables us to place our ideas or practices in broader perspective.

18. There are certainly interpretations, by philosophers who regard themselves as Fregeans, that are based on only a selective reading of Frege's texts. An obvious example is the Evans/McDowell interpretation of Frege's conception of the sense of proper names; see n. 19 to ch. 6. I discuss the issues involved here in §§ 6.3 and 6.4. The revision of Frege's views may be in the right direction, but more explanation is required of the passages that conflict with the interpretation.

19. Equally, there is no such thing as *the* theory of meaning for a natural language. Our linguistic activities will always outflank any particular theory that is offered – which is not to say that the development of such a theory may not influence the way we do conceive or use language. There is a form of linguistic creativity, in other words, *pace* Fregeans and Chomskians, that precisely does *not* involve the following of rules antecedently given or theoretically hypothesized.

1. The Logical Background

1. Tr. in Holmes, 1980: p. 88.

2. Tr. in Ackrill, 1981: p. 80.

3. On the background to syllogistic theory, see Lloyd, 1979: ch. 2. For a fuller account of the development of Aristotelian logic itself, see Kapp, 1942; and esp. Kneale, 1962: chs. 1-2.

4. See, for example, *Phaedrus* 265-6; *Philebus* 16ff.; *Sophist* 218ff.; *Politicus* 258ff.

5. Cf. Ross, 1949: pp. 25-7; Kneale, 1962: pp. 9-10, 67-8.

6. Cf. Patzig, 1968: §4. In fact, the point is even stronger in Greek than in English, since word-order is flexible in Greek and there can be *more* occasions on which it is unclear which term is the subject and which the predicate.

7. This salient transitivity is seen as characteristic of first figure or 'perfect' syllogisms; cf. Patzig, 1968: pp. 51-2; Kneale, 1962: p. 73. Of course, (BB) exhibits this transitivity as clearly as (BB″), which is why, for us, it represents *Barbara* more perspicuously. The point here is only to explain the traditional ordering of the premisses.

8. For criticism of the Lukasiewicz-Patzig interpretation, see Smiley, 1973: pp. 136-9; Corcoran, 1974a: §1; Lear, 1980: pp. 8-10. Smiley and Lear also argue that such an interpretation fails to do justice both to Aristotle's distinction between ostensive and *per impossibile* syllogisms and to his theory of the 'reduction' of syllogisms; cf. §1.2.

9. This assumes that the system is construed as a *natural deduction* system, i.e. where there are only rules of inference and no axioms; see n. 11 below. It is as a natural deduction system that Smiley (1973) and Corcoran (1974a) have reconstructed syllogistic theory.

10. In calling perfect syllogisms the 'axioms' of the system, I use the term in its general sense – as indicating those (usually self-evident) assumptions or principles that are explicitly taken for granted in constructing the relevant theory. In a natural deduction system, what are here counted as 'axioms' are reformulated as *rules*; but there is no reason why this should cause any problems. *Barbara*, for example, straightforwardly gives rise to the rule 'From *Abc* and *Aab*, deduce *Aac*' (which can then be used – naturally enough! – to 'prove' *Barbara* itself). As to the implied self-evidence of the axioms, elsewhere Aristotle writes that it is 'intuitive reason' (*nous*) that grasps 'the first principles', that is 'of the limiting premisses, for which no reason can be given' (*Nicomachean Ethics*, VI 6-8). Cf. *Posterior Analytics*, I 2-3.

11. Arguably, *ecthesis* is an important third method; see Lukasiewicz, 1957: §19; Patzig, 1968: §30; Corcoran, 1974a: p. 128, n. 20. For the two examples that follow, cf. Lear, 1980: pp. 5-6.

12. Cf. Lukasiewicz, 1957: §§17-19; Patzig, 1968: §§28-9; Smiley, 1973; Corcoran, 1974a: §4; Lear, 1980: pp. 5-6.

13. Cf. Smiley, 1973: pp. 137-8. My own formulation of the reply to the criticism is influenced by the way Wittgenstein expressed his early conception of logic – see e.g. *NB*, p. 109; *TLP*, 6.126-6.127.

14. See esp. the recent reconstructions by Smiley (1973) and Corcoran (1974a). As they both admit, their reconstructions are only *approximations* to syllogistic theory, aimed particularly at avoiding the misconstruals of Lukasiewicz. Modern defenders of the traditional view, Smiley (1982: p. 15) writes, 'are developing systems approximating to *the original system about which Aristotle theorised*, while [Lukasiewicz] has invented a system approximating to *the metatheory of the original*'. This is not illegitimate in itself, but it must not be used as a stick with which to beat Aristotle.

15. The only qualification to make here would be to note Aristotle's own failure to recognize the fourth figure and the *subaltern* moods (see App. 1). But syllogistic theory itself, taken as including these, is perfectly coherent. Indeed, it is also, in the logical sense, 'complete' (cf. Corcoran, 1974a: §5.1; Clark, 1980: ch. 3; Lear, 1980: ch. 2), although this should not be taken to suggest that Aristotle himself understood the notion of a completeness proof.

16. Cf. n. b of the Loeb tr.; n. 4 of the Oxford tr. For an account of Aristotle's understanding of hypothetical syllogisms, see Lear, 1980: ch. 3.

17. Cf. Lukasiewicz, 1957: §6; Kneale, 1962: pp. 139, 737.

18. I thus agree here more with Ackrill (1981: p. 94) than with Lear (1980: pp. ix, 13).

19. Cf. Kneale, 1962: p. 115. For a full analysis of the supposed rivalry, see Mueller, 1969; and in particular, Frede, 1987a. Cf. also Brunschwig, 1980; and Barnes, 1980.

20. Lear (1980: pp. 77-84) provides a detailed criticism of Aristotle's argument that demonstration must proceed from non-demonstrable premisses (cf. also Barnes, 1975b: pp. 106-12); but I am not convinced that once Aristotle's *epistemological* conception of proof is recognized, there is anything inconsistent about his argument – though the conception itself may not be to our (modern) taste.

21. Cf. Barnes, 1975a, p. 77: 'the theory of demonstrative science was never meant to guide or formalise scientific research: it is concerned exclusively with the teaching of facts already won; it does not describe how scientists do, or ought to, *acquire* knowledge: it offers a formal model of how teachers should *present and impart* knowledge'. Cf. Kapp, 1931: p. 42; Weil, 1951: pp. 89, 100; Owen, 1965: p. 26. I return to the general issue in §5.1.

22. The same problem arises in interpreting Aristotle's discussion of what has been termed 'relative' necessity – necessity 'given certain conditions', as Aristotle himself calls it (30b32-3) – which Aristotle misleadingly treats as attaching to the individual proposition deduced in a syllogism, rather than construing the necessity (logical necessity) as attaching to the whole inference (which would bring it more into line with his 'absolute' necessity). On this, see Patzig, 1968: ch. 2; and cf. Kneale, 1962: pp. 90ff.

23. The point is made by Ackrill (1981: p. 86), though he does not use it to suggest any explanation of Aristotle's understanding of conversion.

24. Aristotle's conception of identity, particularly in the area of his metaphysics, has provoked much debate, focussing on the question as to the connection between *sameness* and *oneness*; see e.g. White, 1971, and Miller, 1973. I make no attempt to address this larger issue, confining myself purely to 'logical identity'. But it is worth noting the following passage from the *Metaphysics*, where the idea of identity as involving the unmediated and mutual transition between two things (propositions or concepts) is also suggested: 'being and unity are the same and are one thing in the sense that they are implied in one another as principle and cause are, not in the sense that they are explained by the same definition' (1003b22-5).

25. It should be emphasized that even a 'necessary conversion' need not count as 'immediate'. This is clearly consistent with Aristotle's understanding of logical necessity as 'necessity given certain conditions' (see n. 21 above), since any number of 'mediating assumptions' can be included in these 'conditions'. What is wrong is just the idea that one such 'mediating assumption' could be the very rule itself, since an infinite regress would otherwise threaten. If the transition from *Iab* to *Iba* required the rule '*Iab* → *Iba*' *as an additional assumption*, then why wouldn't the transition from *Iab* and '*Iab* → *Iba*' to *Iba* in turn require the rule '(*Iab* & (*Iab* → *Iba*)) → *Iba*', and so on *ad infinitum*? However, as was illustrated in §1.3, Aristotle is sensitive to infinite regress considerations, so it would be uncharitable to accuse him of this particular confusion. The epistemological explanation being offered, therefore, seems the only reasonable interpretation. The rule '*Iab* → *Iba*' is not an *additional* 'assumption', but only an 'assumption' in the sense that it does not itself count (according to Aristotle) as 'primitive and immediate'.

26. This connection between sameness of proof and sameness of meaning is also suggested in *Prior Analytics*, I 46, where Aristotle writes: 'since it is clear that "it is not-white" and "it is not white" differ in meaning, and that one is an affirmation and the other a negation, it is evident that the method of proof is not the same in both cases' (52a24-7).

27. In *Prior Analytics*, I 46, Aristotle states: 'It makes no little difference in establishing or refuting a proposition whether we suppose that "not to be so-and-so" and "to be not-so-and-so" mean the same or something different' (51b5-7); and he correctly notes, for instance, that ' "not to understand the good" and "to understand the not-good" are not the same' (51b22-3). Similar remarks about the 'meanings' of terms occur throughout Aristotle's work, though it is the *Topics* and the *Metaphysics* that contain the most sustained treatment of semantic issues. In particular, Aristotle's interest in *ambiguity* has been widely recognized, and Owen (1960) has been especially influential in stimulating discussion of what he termed Aristotle's conception of 'focal meaning'. However, this is not to say that the issue as to exactly what Aristotle meant by 'meaning' is uncontroversial. Irwin (1982) has suggested that the Greek word '*semainein*' should more accurately be rendered as 'signify' rather than 'mean', and has argued that Aristotle's concept of signification is *not* a concept of meaning: 'what a word signifies is not what it means, but the nature, essence, property correlated with it' (p. 248). Aristotle's inquiry into the signification of words, he concludes, 'is not concerned with sense, communication, translation or linguistic competence, but with the discovery of the real

properties there are and their relation to words' (p. 265). If this is right, then *a fortiori* Aristotle cannot be attributed a semantic conception of sense. However, whilst Irwin's claim may be right as a general (and corrective) thesis, there do seem to be cases where it is neither misleading nor unhelpful to regard Aristotle as referring to 'meaning' (as in fact I have just been assuming). But whatever position one adopts on this general issue, it does not, I believe, affect the argument that I have been developing, which has been more concerned with Aristotle's understanding of 'identities' within his logical system.

28. For an excellent account of the history of logic up to Frege, see Kneale, 1962: chs. 1-6.

29. This is certainly the conventional wisdom, although, strictly speaking, it may be incorrect, since application of the rule of substitution (not always explicitly recognized) arguably appeals to a type of syllogistic reasoning. Consider, for example, the following: All arguments of the form '$P, P \rightarrow Q \vdash Q$' are valid; this is an argument of the form '$P, P \rightarrow Q \vdash Q$'; therefore this argument is valid.

30. Cf. Mates, 1953: ch. 2; Kneale, 1962: ch. 3, §4; Graeser, 1978; Frede, 1987b, 1987c, and esp. 1994.

31. Cf. Kneale, 1962: p. 260; and esp. Geach, 1972: §1.5.

32. Descartes, *OR*, 'Second Set of Replies', p. 111. Cf. *RDM*, Rule Four, pp. 18-19. For detailed discussion of Descartes' critique of syllogistic theory and his conception of analysis and synthesis, see Gaukroger, 1989. I return to the issue in §5.1.

33. The most important of Leibniz's logical works have been collected and translated by Parkinson (Leibniz, *LP*). In his introduction (1966: pp. xix-xx), Parkinson notes that Leibniz's belief, that only supplementation and not expansion of traditional logic was needed to accommodate relational arguments, was consciously opposed to the view of the Hamburg logician Joachim Jungius (1587-1657), who had not only recognized and classified certain types of non-syllogistic arguments but had also argued that 'new ways of reasoning' would have to be invented (cf. Leibniz, *LP*, p. 15). It took Frege to finally show that Jungius was right here rather than Leibniz. On Leibniz's *characteristica universalis*, see §2.1; and on Leibniz's conception of analysis and synthesis, see App. 2.

34. It was Kant, in fact, who was responsible for the dissemination of the term 'formal logic', and Kant naively thought that, as a body of doctrine, logic had been essentially completed by Aristotle (cf. *CPR*, B viii-ix). I discuss the Kantian distinctions, and Frege's revision of their criteria, in §§3.4, 5.1 and 5.2.

35. Applying Kant's official criterion, *all* truths turn out to be analytic, on Leibniz's view (see §5.1 and App. 2), which suggests that we need to treat cautiously any imposition of the Kantian framework on Leibniz's thought. Cf. Ishiguro, 1990: pp. 10, 15, 173-4.

36. See Frege, *BLC, BLF, ACN* (on Boole; see §2.2); *CES* (on Schröder); *PCN* (on Peano). It should be noted here that Peirce (1883, 1885), independently of Frege, can also be credited with invention of the quantifier, but he did not develop the comprehensive theory that Frege produced (cf. Kneale, 1962: ch. 6, §5). Frege and Peirce seem to have remained unaware of each other's achievements, although given that few of their contemporaries appreciated their logical work, this is hardly surprising. (Peirce's earlier papers on Boolean algebra are mentioned at the end of Schröder's 1880 review of Frege's *Begriffsschrift*, but this would only have classified Peirce as one of the Booleans in Frege's mind.)

37. For details of these 19th-century movements, see Sluga, 1980: chs. 1-2.

38. The extent of this influence is, however, controversial. See §3.3 and nn. 31-6 to ch. 3.

2. Frege's 'Begriffsschrift'

1. The reviews are repr. in Frege, *CN*, App. 1.

2. For details of the history of these papers, see Bynum, 1972a: §§8-9. Frege also wrote a short piece called 'Applications of the "Conceptual Notation" ' (*APCN*), but this simply gives some examples of how mathematical relations can be represented in his 'Begriffsschrift'.

3. The idea of a 'universal character' was first articulated by Bacon in 1605, and systems were actually devised by, amongst others, George Dalgarno and John Wilkins, both of whom Leibniz knew. The idea of a scientifically structured language was put forward by Descartes (in a letter to Mersenne dated 20 November 1629), in answer to the objection that an international language would have to contain many different words, and hence be impractical. For it to work, Descartes thought, the basic terms would have to correspond to 'the simple ideas in the human imagination out of which all human thoughts are compounded', the discovery of which, however, would have to await the 'true philosophy' (*DL*, p. 13). For further details, see Cohen, 1954. For an account that is itself written in a 'scientifically structured' language (Ogden's Basic English), see Nidditch, 1962: ch. 3.

4. For details, see App. 2; and for Leibniz's own discussion of the workings of his *characteristica universalis*, see Leibniz, *LP*, and the first three papers in *LPW*. Frege's knowledge of Leibniz's idea of a logical language appears to have come through a paper by Trendelenburg (1867), mentioned in the n. to the 'Preface' to *BS*. For discussion of this, see Sluga, 1980: ch. 2, §4; and for more on the influence of Leibniz on Frege, see Kluge, 1980: ch. 6, pp. 231-62.

5. Having asked his opinion on the issue of an international language, and received a reply (which has not itself been preserved), Couturat writes back to Frege: 'I am altogether in agreement with you: it is for scientific, commercial and utilitarian purposes that we require an international language, in a domain where the expression of *facts* and *ideas* must *not* be invested with a national character, and where it is already *in fact* largely international' (*PMC*, p. 11). The letter certainly suggests that Frege approved the project, although it also indicates that certain limits were recognized. Couturat mentions in particular that works of literature could only be inadequately translated (though he thinks – surely mistakenly – that it could be done better than into another national language; *PMC*, p. 12).

6. This is especially true of Frege's own idiosyncratic two-dimensional concept-script (explained in App. 3), which John Venn (1880) in his curt review of the *Begriffsschrift* dismissed as 'cumbrous and inconvenient'. No doubt, in Frege's insistence against Peano that logical rigour rather than universal comprehension was the more important goal, there is a measure of underlying indignation about the failure of his own notation to become adopted by logicians.

7. As mentioned in n. 3 above, Descartes had raised just this problem – that an ideal notation presupposes a completed science or 'true philosophy'. This had failed to worry Leibniz, however, whose comment on the passage was: 'although this language depends on the true philosophy it does not depend on its perfection' (quoted by Cohen, 1954: p. 52). Leibniz's own reply to the objection is thus similar to Frege's – there is nothing to stop a scientific notation being gradually developed as our knowledge itself improves.

8. For Frege's suggestion that he had 'discovered' the True and the False, see e.g. *PW*, p. 194. I discuss Frege's ontology in ch. 7.

9. Frege himself speaks of the 'completeness' of his system of logic, though it was left to Lukasiewicz (1934) to *prove* the completeness of Frege's propositional calculus. He also proved the redundancy of the third axiom, deriving it from the first two. The remaining five axioms are all independent of each other; cf. Thiel, 1968: p. 21; Bynum, 1972b: p. 73. It is true that Frege remarks in the 'Preface' to the *Begriffsschrift* that he later noticed that the last two axioms can be combined into one, but this depends on the introduction of Frege's symbol for identity of content. Cf. App. 3.

10. I say more about the role of function theory in the development of Frege's logic in §§3.1-3.3, and about its importance in the emergence of his notion of 'conceptual content' in §5.2.

11. It should be noted here that Frege himself uses only the universal quantifier, expressing '$(\exists x) (Ax \ \& \ Bx)$' as '$\neg(\forall x) \ \neg(Ax \ \& \ Bx)$' or '$\neg(\forall x) (Ax \rightarrow \neg Bx)$' (in modern notation). Given the interdefinability of the two quantifiers, there can be no objection to using both here; although it should be borne in mind that Frege himself depends on just three logical constants – negation, the material conditional, and the universal quantifier. See App. 3 for details of Frege's own symbolism.

12. Strictly speaking, and as Russell (from *POM* to *PM*) would have put it, 'x is an *A*' represents a *propositional function*, which takes objects as arguments ('x' being replaced by a singular term), yielding propositions as values. Frege's own position is more complex. In his early work, *judgeable contents (beurtheilbare Inhalte)* were taken as the values; but once the distinction between *Sinn* and *Bedeutung* had been formulated, the True and the False were seen as the values, the *thought* expressed by the proposition being the *mode of presentation* of the truth-value. See ch. 6.

13. Boole's example, the difficulty it generates for his own system, and Frege's advance over Boole on this issue, are discussed in Dudman, 1976a, a paper to which I am here indebted.

14. See e.g. *BS*, §§6, 12, 22; *BLC*, p. 38. Sluga is thus wrong to allege that 'In the whole body of Frege's writings there is not a single indication that he ever ... spent any time investigating Aristotelian logic' (1980: p. 52). Frege was well aware of the syllogistic modes of inference, and reports that some of his formulae were specifically introduced to cater for them (*BLC*, p. 38). Nevertheless, Sluga is right in stating that 'there is no criticism of the theory of the syllogism' (ibid.). As we suggested in §1.2, there is nothing *wrong* with syllogistic theory, considered as a formal system; it is just that it has limited applicability. Frege simply replaced it with a more powerful logic, and the development of this was prompted not by worries about syllogistic theory as such but by his desire to provide a firmer foundation for arithmetic. As we shall see in chs. 3 and 4, without his invention of the quantifier, the logical analysis of mathematical propositions (where multiple generality predominates) would have been impossible, and it was logicism that provided Frege's overriding motivation.

15. At the deepest level, of course, Frege himself assumes that what I called (in §2.2) *atomic* propositions are of subject-predicate form, or in more Fregean terms, are of the form '$F(a)$', where 'a' denotes an object and '$F(\ )$' a concept. For the strongest defence of the claim that, at the most fundamental level, the subject/predicate distinction *cannot* be discarded, see Strawson, 1953; 1959: Part II; 1961; 1970; 1974.

16. Frege's insistence on the difference between *asserting* and merely *entertaining* a proposition (cf. n. 21 below) may well have led, as it did in the case of Lukasiewicz and Patzig after him, to the construal of syllogisms as *conditionals* (ironically, so that they could then be *asserted* within his concept-script). However, in the light of the clarification offered in §1.1, I shall continue to characterize syllogisms here as *sequents*.

17. I make one important assumption here – that the syllogistic O-proposition is construed as 'Some *A*'s are not *B*' rather than 'Not all *A*'s are *B*', preserving its intuitive connection with 'Some *A*'s are *B*' (as captured in the traditional rules of *obversion*). As I explain in App. 1, if we in fact *give up* this assumption, there is an alternative (though less satisfying) way out of the dilemma to the 'presupposition' strategy pursued in this section. Angell (1986) has also pointed out the difficulties in assigning existential import to syllogistic propositions; and he rightly shows that the source of the differences between traditional and modern logic lies in the modern logician's use of the truth-functional material conditional. But this is not to say that syllogistic theory cannot coherently be seen as *presupposing* that all terms have reference. Angell mentions this Strawsonian interpretation, but immediately dismisses it as challenging 'the universality of the law of the excluded middle' (p. 12). But for Aristotle, a purported statement in which there is reference-failure fails to *say* anything, so that it is not, strictly speaking, a statement at all, and hence cannot be considered as a counterexample to the law of excluded middle. The assumption common to *both* the apparent objection to Fregean logic *and* the Fregean's objection to syllogistic theory is that the logical formalizations must be seen as *context-independent* (i.e. as encapsulating once and for all the existential import that each syllogistic proposition is viewed as carrying or not), and it is just this assumption that needs to be discharged to avoid the dilemma, as I go on to argue.

18. The issue involved here was the subject of the classic debate between Russell (*OD*; *MSR*) and Strawson (1950); and the line I have taken is Strawsonian. After making the crucial distinction between a sentence and its use (§II), Strawson goes on: 'Meaning (in at least one important sense) is a function of the sentence or expression; mentioning and referring and truth or falsity, are functions of the use of the sentence or expression' (1950: p. 9). However, this is not to say that one may not *recommend* that 'true' or 'false' be used in a more Fregean or Russellian way, as Strawson himself later recognized (cf. 1964, 1969). The point of taking the Strawsonian line in this case is to respond to the charge of *incoherence* in syllogistic theory – the Fregean analysis is in no way *intrinsically* superior. This was also part of Strawson's motivation; cf. 1950; pp. 9-20, 26-7; 1952: ch. 6.

19. This raises a whole set of issues that are only properly taken up in chs. 7 and 8; but the key point here is just to respond to the charge of incoherence in syllogistic theory.

20. It would be interesting to explore further here the relationship between Frege's and Leibniz's logic. For in distinguishing between *existential* and *essential* propositions, and characterizing the latter in conditional terms – analysing 'All *A*'s are *B*', for example, as 'In all possible worlds, if anything is an *A*, then it is a *B*' – Leibniz may be regarded as anticipating Frege's own analysis, though it should be noted that Leibniz did not interpret the conditional truth-functionally. On Leibniz's views here, see Ishiguro, 1990: ch. 3, §1; chs. 8-9; and cf. Mates, 1986: ch. 3, §3; chs. 5-6.

21. The best example of this is perhaps Frege's judgement stroke, specifically introduced to indicate when an *assertion* is being made (see App. 3). It illustrates very well the philosophical problems involved in Frege's project of *decontextualism*. There is nothing *incoherent* about the introduction of a symbol to make normally *contextual* aspects of the meaning of a proposition more explicit (it is no doubt an essential aim for a logician to have). But that it is not to say that the symbol cannot itself be abused, so that one can never *avoid* counting on a 'meeting of minds' (to adopt Frege's own phrase; cf. *LM*, p. 207). If someone is unsure whether something I have said is being asserted by me or not, I can say 'I assert that ...', but of course someone then has to understand that I am asserting *that*. For discussion of Frege's views on assertion, see Bell, 1979: ch. 3; and Dummett, 1981a: ch. 10; and for a recent sermon on the need for (decontextualist) signs of mood, which he calls 'tropics', see Hare, 1989. I take up the more general problem concerning the very idea of *context-independent thoughts* in the final two chapters.

22. As Morris Zapp, one of David Lodge's fictional objects (see e.g. *Small World*), might have put it, every decontextualization is a recontextualization. It was presumably Frege's primary interest in mathematics that made the project of decontextualism seem so entirely plausible – for mathematics itself, of course, can be applied in many other scientific contexts. Indeed, as we shall see in ch. 3, arithmetic was seen as governing *everything thinkable*. However, to simply suggest that all discourse must be seen as relativized to particular contexts, whether scientific or fictional, is not in itself to solve all the problems. The issue is far more complex, since there are plenty of meaningful sentences that appear to *span* contexts. For sensitive discussion of some of the difficulties here, see Walton, 1973, 1978; Lewis, 1978; and Evans, 1982: ch. 10.

23. See esp. Frege, *CO* and *CES*; and for an account of the *subter* and *sub* relations that Frege distinguishes in this latter paper (i.e. subsumption and subordination, respectively), see Bell, 1979: pp. 33ff.

24. 'All whales are mammals', of course, might well be regarded as an *analytic* truth, a mark of which being that mere inspection of its 'content' verifies it, i.e. establishes it as true (I make use of this point at the beginning of §4.1); but Frege's considerations are obviously meant to apply to *all* propositions of the form 'All *A's* are *B*', irrespective of their analytic or synthetic status. (Frege's argument is more plausible in German, since the proposition taken is 'Alle Walfische sind Säugethiere'.) Frege's crucial thought is further elucidated in *RH*: 'It should be clear that someone who utters the proposition 'All men are mortal' does not want to state something about a certain chief Akpanya whom he may never have heard of' (p. 205; cf. *LM*, pp. 213-14). This passage and that from the *Grundlagen* are noted by Wiggins (1980: §X), in the context of developing a treatment of such quantifiers as 'most' that preserves a certain parallelism with the treatment of 'all'. Wiggins, in fact, distinguishes what we may term the *conditional* analysis of universal propositions ('everything is such that it is if-*A*-then-*B*') from the *subordination* analysis ('the concept *A* is subordinate to the concept *B*'), suggesting that it was only Frege's drive for maximum simplicity (utilizing propositional logic in the predicate calculus) that led him to assimilate the two (§XIII; cf. §2.2 above). The preferred strategy of *binary quantification* that the subordination analysis suggests (as far as homogenizing the treatment of 'all' and 'most' is concerned) is also explained and pursued by Davies, 1981: ch. 6, §2; and for further discussion of universal quantification, see Peacocke, 1986: ch. 3. The importance of the subordination analysis for Frege will emerge in §5.3.

25. See Frege's letter to Husserl, dated 9 December 1906, where he writes: 'If a form of expression, like the one containing "all", is to be used as a fundamental form in logical considerations, it is not feasible to use it so as to express two distinguishable thoughts at the same time' (*PMC*, p. 71). Since, according to Frege, it is a separable thought that there exist objects falling under the subject and predicate concepts, it should be neither part of what is meant nor presupposed. However, as I go on to show, Frege himself presupposes that *particular* propositions carry existential import, so that he does appear to be somewhat confused about the nature of presupposition. This might in turn be taken to reflect a tension both in his conception of quantification – cf. Stevenson, 1973 – and in his conception of existence, between his 'official' construal of existence in terms of the second-level concept '( ) is instantiated' (see e.g. *GL*, §53; *CO*, pp. 48-9; explained in §4.1) and his 'presupposition' doctrine of the non-emptiness of *object-names* – cf. n. 4 to ch. 4; and for fuller discussion of which, see Haaparanta, 1986.

26. Consider the following two informal analyses of 'All *A's* are *B*', an Aristotelian and a Fregean construal, respectively: (i) 'Take the class of (existent) *A's* – each one is a *B*'; (ii) 'Take the class of all (existent) things – if any one of them is an *A*, it is also a *B*'. Which represents the 'simplest' thought? (ii) corresponds to the *conditional* Fregean analysis (see n. 24 above), but even on the *subordination* analysis, since we would now be talking about concepts, it could still be argued that the thought involved is more sophisticated. At any rate, the issue of 'simplicity' is by no means straightforward. I also assume here that syllogistic theory is best construed as presupposing that *all* terms have existential import (the 'simplest' construal?), as argued in App. 1.

27. Indeed, for Frege, logical inference itself was seen as only proceeding from *truths* – see e.g. *PWLA*, p. 3; *LM*, pp. 204, 244-5; *FGII*, pp. 318, 335; *N*, pp. 375-6; *CT*, pp. 402-3; *LG*, p. 261. Frege has been frequently condemned for holding such a view, but, as in the case of Aristotle (see §1.3), recognizing Frege's *epistemological* interests goes some way towards mitigating the criticism.

28. Of course, even the 'relatively simple' intuition that '*P* and *Q*' and '*Q* and *P*' 'mean' the same is only simple relative to practices governed by classical propositional logic. There is not always an obvious match betweeen the use of 'and' in ordinary language and the use of '&' as symbolizing conjunction in classical logic. 'Diana married Charles and became pregnant', for example, does not mean the same as 'Diana became pregnant and married Charles'. Conjunction is only commutative if the conjuncts are logically independent. Note, however, that 'Diana married Charles in Summer 1981 and Diana became pregnant in Autumn 1981' and 'Diana became pregnant in Autumn 1981 and Diana married Charles in Summer 1981' *are* equivalent (although the latter may not be a natural way to put things), which Frege would take to show that 'decontextualizing' is required to represent propositions in a logically correct way. This only reinforces the point argued in this section – that what semantic intuitions we have are shaped by the logic we learn, even though this logic is in turn only possible on the basis of such intuitions. It also illustrates the main theme of this book – that senses are 'made' or 'crystallized' in the process of developing and using a logical system.

29. Venn diagrams, and the similar Euler diagrams, are not of course suitable for representing every kind of logical relation. Frege himself comments on their limitation (*CES*, pp. 212, 216, 228; cf. *PMC*, p. 63). But the point here is only to indicate their *potential* for exhibiting 'content' (as Frege also implicitly recognizes; cf. *BLC*, p. 33, lines 19-21). The use of the phrase 'pictorial content' alludes to Wittgenstein, who (at the time of the *Tractatus*) would also have treated the two propositions as identical in sense, characterizing this relationship as the picturing of the same state of affairs.

30. As in the case of Aristotle, we might well have doubts about attributing to Boole a conception of logical equivalence merely on the basis of acknowledging 'mutual transition' between two propositions. But Boole, unlike Aristotle, does at least have an appreciation of the conditional as a propositional connective, and there is no indication that he thought that the logical relationships between *Eab* and *Eba*, and between *Iab* and *Iba*, were *different* in any way. So it is fair to grant him *some* kind of conception of logical equivalence.

31. Baker and Hacker (1984: ch. 5, §5) have also emphasized the importance of the underlying semantic insight, but they have, I think, underestimated the role that the logical context plays in bringing the insight to prominence. They suggest, for example, that it is misguided to even look for a *criterion* for 'conceptual content'. It may well be true that certain semantic intuitions have to be seen as lying at the base of a logical system, but this is not to say that the rationale for these *cannot* be given in terms of the working of that system.

32. The allusion to Descartes here is not inappropriate. For whilst the Cartesian Circle may be harder to deal with satisfactorily, the essential strategy is the same. In both cases we have to recognize certain intuitions to get the ball moving, but those intuitions are reinforced and their status guaranteed once the wider picture is appreciated.

33. Given Frege's conception of a logical system as a system of *truths*, in which inference is just the transition from one truth to another (cf. n. 27 above), all the propositions of the system would turn out to have the same 'conceptual content'!

34. See Frege's letter to Husserl dated 9 December 1906 (*PMC*, p. 70). I discuss this in §8.1.

35. This example is given by Frege himself in *GG*, I, §2, where he explicitly states that they do not possess the same 'Sinn'. The point is even stronger in the case of pairs of propositions such as '4 = 2 + 2' and '3 = 2 + 1', where 'cross-identifications' are illegitimate. These would certainly not be regarded as 'cognitively equivalent', a fact which turns out to be crucial in the argument developed in §5.3.

36. The notion of 'logical content' is clearly semantic, whilst Frege's 'official' notion of 'Sinn' will turn out to be epistemic. But since even here there is room for more than one possible notion (see ch. 8), and I shall generally use the term 'epistemic' in relation to a very fine-grained notion, I talk of 'cognitive content' here to avoid prejudging the issue.

3. Frege's Critique of Mathematical Reason

1. Philolaus, *On the World*, tr. in Barnes, ed., *Early Greek Philosophy*, p. 217. Philolaus was a Pythagorean, and although there is disagreement over whether Philolaus himself wrote these words, they can be taken as representative of early Pythagoreanism.

2. Cf. Kline, 1972: p. 139; 1980: p. 105-6. (Kline, 1980 is a popularization of Kline, 1972.)

3. For details of the history of arithmetic from the ancient Greeks to the Renaissance, see Kline, 1972: chs. 3, 6, 9; 1980: ch. 5, pp. 103-13.

4. Cf. Kline, 1972: ch. 13; 1980: ch. 5, pp. 113-18.

5. Cf. Kneale, 1962: pp. 61-2; Kline, 1972: p. 139; 1980: p. 108.

6. Cf. Kline, 1972: ch. 13, §§3-4; 1980: pp. 121-3. What Kline calls 'numerical coefficients' and 'literal coefficients' I here call 'numerical variables' and 'schematic letters', respectively.

7. We could, of course, also consider the interval immediately before t_n, or the interval from $t_n - \delta t$ to $t_n + \delta t$, but the proposal here makes for the easiest exposition.

8. For an account of Newton's invention of the calculus, see Kline, 1972: ch. 17, pp. 359-65; 1980: pp. 134-5; Kitcher, 1984: ch. 10, §§1-2.

9. Leibniz's remark is made in a letter to des Bosses dated 3 March 1706; quoted in Ishiguro, 1990: p. 85. Ishiguro (1990: ch. 5) provides a convincing defence of the coherence of Leibniz's conception of the infinitesimal calculus, though she recognizes the ambiguity in Leibniz's use of the sign 'dx' (p. 95); cf. also Kline, 1972: ch. 17, §4; Kitcher, 1984: pp. 234-7.

10. See Berkeley, *PHK*, §§123-132; and esp. his later work of 1734, the full title of which is worth noting: *The Analyst; Or, A Discourse Addressed to an Infidel Mathematician. Wherein It is examined whether the Object, Principles, and Inferences of the modern Analysis are more distinctly conceived, or more evidently deduced, than Religious Mysteries and Points of Faith*; with a motto taken from Matthew, ch. 7, v.5: 'First cast out the beam out of thine own Eye; and then shalt thou see clearly to cast out the mote out of thy brother's Eye'.

11. For Weierstrass' example, see Kline, 1972: p. 956; Temple, 1981: p. 142. Bolzano seems to have been the first to discover such an example, in 1834, but his work was not published until nearly a century later; cf. Kline, 1972: p. 955.

12. See d'Alembert's entries under 'Différentiel' and 'Limit'.

13. For an account of Cauchy's work and Weierstrass' refinement of it, see Kitcher, 1984: ch. 10, §§4-6.

14. Cf. Kline, 1972: ch. 32; 1980: pp. 159-60. Frege himself attacks such postulatory activity in *GL*, §102. See the beginning of §4.4.

15. Cf. Kitcher, 1984: pp. 241-2.

16. Cf. Kline, 1972: pp. 983-5; Temple, 1981: pp. 13-15. As Temple notes, what both Weierstrass' and Cantor's theories really define are equivalent representations of a real number. 'Strictly speaking', he remarks, a Weierstrassian or Cantorian real number should be defined as 'a class of equivalent representations, each with the same limit'. This is essentially Frege's move; and I discuss Frege's own critique of Cantor in §4.5.

17. Dedekind seems careful not to *identify* an irrational number with its corresponding cut (he explicitly rejects such an identification in a letter of 1888; cf. Kline, 1972: p. 986). Mathematicians (e.g. Temple, 1981: p. 16) have often taken Dedekind as proposing this identification, however, seeing it as an improvement on Cantor's theory, which involves a multiplicity of representations of a real number (cf. n. 16 above).

18. On the significance of Dedekind's theory in the history of analysis, see Kitcher, 1984: ch. 10, §7.

19. For an account of Cantor's theory of sets and transfinite numbers, see Kline, 1972: ch. 41, §§7-8; 1980: pp. 199-203; Temple, 1981: ch. 4.

20. For details of the history of geometry, see Kline, 1972: chs. 4, 14-15, 23, 35-9, 42; 1980: pp. 78-88, 95-7, 180-2, 192-6.

21. Bynum (1972a: §4) records what little is known of Frege's university education; and Sluga (1984) offers a (debatable) account of the early influences on Frege. See App. 4 for a chronology of Frege's life and works.

22. Gauss was not the first; Wessel and Argand, in particular, preceded him. But he was, perhaps, the most influential in encouraging the acceptance of complex numbers. Cf. Kline, 1972: ch. 27, §3.

23. Cf. *GR*, p. 55, where Gauss is specifically mentioned. Gauss is, in fact, the only person Frege refers to in *GR* (his name also appears on p. 19). The Gaussian influences on Frege are indicated in Sluga, 1984: §§3-4.

24. I have quoted this paragraph in full, because the concept of direction is precisely the example that Frege uses in his central argument in *GL*, where he defines 'the direction of line *a*' as 'the extension of the concept "parallel to line *a*" '. See §4.2.

25. For details of Frege's application, see Bynum, 1972a: §5.

26. I have here translated 'Grösse' (which appears in the title of this work) as 'magnitude' rather than 'quantity', which is how it is rendered (more awkwardly in places) in *CP*. In the translations that follow, taken from *CP*, I have simply made the appropriate substitutions. Cf. n. 31 to ch. 4.

306 Notes to pp. 75-77

27. Sluga (1980: ch. 2, §3; 1984: §4) has suggested that in his early dissertations Frege held a Kantian rather than Gaussian view of geometry; but the evidence is really too slight to justify this. It seems more likely that Frege had simply not committed himself at this early stage in his life.

28. In the last two years of his life, twenty years after he first became aware of the fatal flaw in his logicist project, Frege reverted to the traditional view of arithmetic, seeing it as based not on logic but on geometry. See the last five pieces in *PW* (*DECN, PWN, SKM, NA* and *NAFA*).

29. The post of *Privatdozent* was an unsalaried lectureship. Frege was promoted to *ausserordentlicher Professor*, a salaried position, on the publication of *BS* in 1879; and was probably offered a full Ordinary Professorship in 1896, though he accepted only an Honorary Ordinary Professorship, which was unsalaried but without administrative duties, which freed him more for research. He retired from the University of Jena in 1918. Cf. Bynum, 1972a: §§5, 8, 15, 17. For further biographical details, see App. 4.

30. Cf. Bynum, 1972a: §6. The pieces are repr. in *CP*, pp. 93-100, amounting to just 5 published pages in 5 years. Any assessment of Frege's research potential, on this basis, would have been wide of the mark!

31. Amongst Frege scholars, it is Sluga (1976: §4; 1977: §§3-4; 1980: ch. 2, §5; 1984: §§ 7, 9; 1986: §5) who has most persistently argued that Lotze's influence on Frege was much stronger than has been generally recognized; and it does seem clear both that Frege knew of Lotze's work and that there are similarities. Dummett (1981b: App. 2; 1981c; 1982), however, has been critical of Sluga's claims, suggesting that Lotze's work is too nebulous to have made any impact on Frege. The truth is no doubt somewhere in between. Frege would undoubtedly have been receptive to some of Lotze's ideas, but his own development of those ideas is so much more rigorously pursued, and the ideas so much more comprehensively integrated, that all we really need note, in any modest account of Frege's philosophy, are the relevant points of contact.

32. The piece is *KSL*, incorrectly located in *NS* and *PW* by the editors, but convincingly illuminated by Dummett, 1981c.

33. Cf. Lotze, *Logik*, §28, p. 47: 'an appropriate symbol for the construction of a concept is not the equation $S = a + b + c + d$ ..., but best the designation $S = F(a, b, c, ...)$, which mathematical expression merely indicates that $a, b, c, ...$ must be combined in a way that is precisely given in any particular case, but that is highly variable in general, in order to yield the value of S'. Cf. §110.

34. In support of his thesis concerning Lotze's influence on Frege, Sluga (1980: pp. 52-8) quotes the testimony of Bruno Bauch, one of Frege's colleagues at Jena, who wrote that Frege's work was 'not independent of Lotze's'. But Bauch's essay, which appeared in vol.1 of *Beiträge zur Philosophie des Deutschen Idealismus* in 1918, was composed not only as a tribute to the impact of Lotze's work in German philosophy but also as an introduction to Frege's own paper 'Der Gedanke' (*T*), which follows it, and hence may well have exaggerated the extent of Lotze's influence. Frege, who in any case can hardly have been sympathetic to the goals of the new journal, would have been relatively unfamiliar to its intended readership. The construal of concepts as functions was one of the points of connection singled out by Bauch; but, unlike Frege, Lotze offered no function-argument analysis of traditional syllogistic propositions; and as we saw in ch. 2, it was this that initiated the revolution in logic.

35. Cf. Lotze, *Logik*, §112, p. 138, where Lotze writes that 'one must not after all completely forget that calculation at any rate also belongs to the logical activities, and that it is only a separation for the practical purposes of education that has let the full entitlement of mathematics to a home in the general realm of logic be overlooked'. Cf. §18, quoted in the next note.

36. In §18 of his *Logik*, Lotze speaks of the vast structure of mathematics that has developed, 'which forbids any attempt to reincorporate it into general logic'. However, he goes on, 'it is necessary to expressly point out that all calculation is a kind of thinking, that the fundamental concepts and principles of mathematics have their systematic place in logic, that we must in the end preserve our right, wherever the situation later demands it, to safely return to the results which in the meantime mathematics has achieved, as an independently developing branch of general logic' (p. 34). It is unclear from this to what extent Lotze thinks that mathematical developments take place *outside* logic; but in any case it hardly justifies attributing him the full-blown logicist thesis. As Sluga (1980: p. 58) suggests, the following remark by Frege in 1885 can be read as a response to Lotze: 'no sharp boundary can be drawn between logic and arithmetic. ... If we were to allot the most general basic propositions and perhaps also their most immediate consequences to logic while we assigned their further development to arithmetic, then this would be like separating a distinct science of axioms from that of geometry. Of course, the division of the entire field of knowledge into the various sciences is determined not merely by theoretical but also by pragmatic considerations; and by the preceding I do not mean to say anything against a certain pragmatic division: only it must not become a schism, as is at present the case to the detriment of all sides concerned.' (*FTA*, pp. 112-13.)

37. For an explanation of Frege's concept-script, see App. 3. The only point to note here, if a comparison is made, is that Frege uses Gothic (old German) letters for bound variables, and ordinary italic letters, such as x and y, for free variables; whereas I have used (more conventionally) x and y, etc. for bound variables, and a, b, etc. for free variables.

38. Cf. *BS*, §27, formula 77. We should note here that (PA) involves quantification over functions, i.e. presupposes second order predicate logic. Frege did not at the time of *BS* distinguish between first order and higher order quantification, and his derivation of formula 77 requires amendment; see Bynum's n. to this derivation, *CN*, pp. 174-5, and n. 88 of his 'Editor's Introduction', 1972b: §8/ *CN*, p. 72.

39. Cf. *BS*, §28, formula 93. On the necessary amendment to its derivation, see Bynum's n. to the text, *CN*, p. 183 (cf. n. 38 above). In demonstrating informally the validity of the converse relation in what follows, by considering the property of *following a in the f-series*, cf. Currie, 1982: p. 38.

40. Frege gives the following example: let F be the property of being a heap of beans, and f be the procedure of removing one bean. Then the result is obtained – this is the traditional Sorites paradox – that one bean and even no beans at all is a heap of beans. The property of being a heap cannot, therefore, be hereditary in the f-series; and this is due, Frege suggests, to the vagueness of the concept *heap*, which allows some values of 'x is a heap' to be indeterminate (cf. *BS*, §27). I return to the issue in §7.3.

41. To say that a relation is many-one is not to say that, for any member of the f-series, there is necessarily more than one (immediate) predecessor, but merely that, for any member, there is only one result of applying f, i.e. that any member has a unique (immediate) successor. Similarly, to say that a relation is one-many is merely to say that any member has a unique (immediate) predecessor. There is nothing paradoxical, then, about a one-one relation being both many-one and one-many.

42. As Frege later put it in *GL*, 'Only by means of this definition of following in a series is it possible to reduce the transition from n to $(n + 1)$, which is apparently peculiar to mathematics, to the general laws of logic' (§80; cf. §91).

43. Cf. Bynum, 1972a: §8; cf. n. 29 above.

44. Quoted by Bynum, 1972a: p. 16.

45. Aside from the three short articles, *APCN, SJCN* and *ACN* (see the introd. to ch. 2), the only pieces that Frege published between 1879 and 1884 were a two page review of a book on analytic geometry (*CP*, pp. 101-2) and two papers read (like *APCN* and *ACN*) to the *Jenaische Gesellschaft für Medicin und Naturwissenschaft*, one on analytic geometry (repr. in *CP*, pp. 103-7) and the other on Leibniz's and Huygens' correspondence with Papin (repr. in *BSA*). Most of Frege's research time between 1881 (after *BLC* and *BLF* had been written) and 1884 was therefore devoted to work on *GL*.

46. For Leibniz's view, see App. 2; and on the need for caution in characterizing it, see n. 35 to ch. 1. For Kant's view, see *CPR*, B14-17, A163-5/B204-6; *PFM*, §2; and for Mill's view, see *SL*, II v-vi, III xxiv. I make no attempt to do justice here to either Kant's view or Mill's view; but for discussion of the former, see Parsons, 1971; Kitcher, 1975; and of the latter, see Resnik, 1980: ch. 4; Skorupski, 1989: ch. 5.

47. For details of Leibniz's account, see App. 2.

48. According to Frege, our conceptions even of small numbers do not consist in having ideas; cf. §§58-60, discussed in §4.1. For Leibniz too, our conceptual capacities outstrip our self-conscious awareness of ideas, but Leibniz's insight here was obscured by the issue of innateness (see esp. *NE*, 'Preface'; I i), and he did not in any case draw the Fregean distinction between concepts and ideas.

49. Cf. Kant, *CPR*, B15-16; *PFM*, §2. I return to Kant's conception of analysis in §5.1.

50. What we might call Frege's argument from the equal treatment of numbers can, of course, be played both ways. Kant could reply that since the apprehension of the truth of simple formulae such as $7 + 5 = 12$ relies upon intuition, then it must *in principle* be possible for intuition to provide the means of determining the truth of complex formulae. In fact, however, if we consider formulae that are even simpler than Kant's paradigm example, Frege's argument can be reinforced. For it does seem absurd to regard $2 = 1 + 1$, for example, as a synthetic truth. If anything is an analytic truth, it is surely this.

51. Mill talks of 'physical facts' in the paragraph immediately preceding that from which we have just quoted. In view of Frege's own later distinction between 'Sinn' and 'Bedeutung', it is worth noting what Mill says here (which Frege must obviously have read): 'The expression "two pebbles and one pebble", and the expression, "three pebbles", stand indeed for the same aggregation of objects, but they by no means stand for the same physical fact. They are names of the same objects, but of those objects in two different states: though they *de*note the same things, their *con*notation is different.' (*SL*, II vi 2, p. 256.)

52. (AN) does not itself provide us with a criterion for the analyticity of the general logical laws and definitions themselves. Clearly a different criterion is needed here. I return to this issue in ch. 5.

53. In II viii of Locke's *Essay*, the *locus classicus* for the distinction between primary and secondary qualities, number is listed amongst the primary qualities. The idea seems to be that every material thing has, objectively, a number because it is composed of a determinate number of 'corpuscles' ('physical units'). But it still needs to be made clear that the 'primary quality' here is not number in general but *number of corpuscles*. Of course, if the idea of an ultimate building block is problematic, then it is even more obvious that numbers can only be ascribed to something *relative* to a specified unit (e.g. molecule, atom, electron, or quark); which is Frege's point.

54. I have changed Frege's own example of skat to that of bridge, which may be more familiar to (English-speaking) readers today.

55. It is important to recognize that, at least within a Kantian framework, 'empiricism' can be associated with either 'realism' or 'idealism' – Locke, for example, being an empirical realist, and Berkeley an empirical idealist. Frege's attack on psychologism can thus be construed as an attack on empirical idealism (but see n. 56 below). Given the Kantian opposition between empiricism and transcendentalism, the question then becomes whether Frege is a transcendental realist or a transcendental idealist. See n. 59 below.

56. Frege himself (§25) quotes a passage from *NTV*, §109; but I have here substituted a more familiar passage from *PHK*. Berkeley goes on to remark that no idea can be found that answers to the word 'unity' (§13), and since he later defines number as a *collection of units*, it follows that there are no ideas, according to Berkeley, corresponding to number terms (§120). 'In *arithmetic* therefore we regard not the *things* but the *signs*' (§122), which suggests that Berkeley himself should be attributed not a psychologistic but a formalist conception of number. But it remains the case that Berkeley believed that 'number is entirely the creature of the mind' (cf. also *NTV*, §109), a view that overcompensates for the errors of empirical realism.

57. Repudiation of psychologism is also a theme in Lotze's work (see e.g. *Logik*, §18; and cf. Sluga, 1977: p. 230; 1980: pp. 53-4); but once again it must be noted that Frege would already have been predisposed to this (neo-Kantian) feature of Lotze's thought.

58. Cf. *GG*, 'Introd.', p. xviii/ *BLA*, p. 16. *GG*, pp. xiv-xix contains a more sustained attack on psychologism than Frege provided in *GL*, but the essential points remain.

59. This is one of the passages that is often taken to suggest that Frege was a transcendental idealist about number (cf. Sluga, 1980: p. 120; Resnik, 1980: pp. 163-4). But Frege's remark is meant to apply to *everything* that is 'objective', which *includes* the 'actual'. On the assumption, then, that he was undoubtedly a realist about the 'actual', this passage at any rate does not support the suggestion. (Cf. Dummett, 1982, esp. §8.) On Frege's realism, cf. also Sluga, 1975; 1977; Dummett, 1976; Currie, 1978; 1981; 1983.

60. Cf. also Frege's later works, *OCN*, *SN* and *RT*. For more detailed discussion of Frege's critique of abstractionism, see Dummett, 1991a: ch. 8.

61. We should note that on the 'set theory' Frege here discusses, sets are *composed* of their members, so that, for example, 1 = {1}. If 'units' are identical, then, all numbers turn out to be equivalent to 1!

62. The argument just presented develops a suggestion – indexing the units – actually made by Jevons (1874: p. 182), which Frege demolishes, in his usual fashion, by *reductio ad absurdum*.

4. The Logicist Project

1. Some of the problems raised by Frege's construal were discussed in §2.4, and I return to the issue in §5.3.

2. A sortal concept is a concept that *sorts* into the objects that fall under it, which can then be counted. Cf. Strawson, 1959: pp. 167-70; Wiggins, 1980: pp. 7-8, 73-4; Wright, 1983: §1. Wiggins, 1980, esp. chs. 2-3, provides the most sustained treatment to date of sortal concepts.

3. The paradox is mentioned by Sainsbury, 1988, pp. 147, 153.

4. It might be thought that Frege's presupposition here is incompatible with his doctrine that existence is a second-level concept; but of course, within the predicate calculus, $Fa \rightarrow (\exists x) Fx$, and although, for any given a, the converse does not necessarily hold, $(\exists x) Fx$ does imply that there is at least one proper name that yields a true substitution-instance of 'Fx'.

5. See esp. §§ 6.3 and 7.1. Treatment of the issues requires consideration of the distinction between *Sinn* and *Bedeutung*, which had not at this time been formulated. For further discussion of the relevance of Frege's linguistic considerations to ontological questions, see esp. Dummett, 1981a: chs. 4, 14; Wright, 1983: chs. 1-2; Hale, 1984.

6. The circularity in the reasoning here should be clear. If logicism is correct, then numbers are logical objects, but it is just this that needs to be established for logicism to be correct.

7. In the same way, if I say, truly, 'This book belongs to me', then it is not the book itself that is a property of me (though it is, of course, my property!); rather, the property that I am being attributed is the property of *possessing this book*. 'This book' is only an element in the predicate.

8. The *attributive* use of adjectives is often distinguished from the *predicative* use. In 'Bombur is a large dwarf', for example, 'large' is being used attributively. Bombur is only large for a dwarf – he is not large compared to a human; so the sentence cannot be analysed (without qualification) as 'Bombur is large and Bombur is a dwarf'. 'Bombur is a 5-stone dwarf', on the other hand, *can* be analysed as 'Bombur is 5-stone and Bombur is a dwarf'. Here '5-stone' is being used predicatively. In practice, of course, the distinction is not always easy to apply – consider e.g. 'Bombur is a lazy dwarf' or 'Bombur is a hungry dwarf'. But in cases such as 'Jupiter has four moons', there is no doubt that the adjective is being used attributively.

9. The distinction between *adjectival* and *substantival* uses of numbers words is taken from Dummett, 1991a: ch. 9, which provides a helpful discussion of the issue.

10. As we shall see in chs. 7 and 8, Frege regarded all objects – abstract as well as concrete – as 'independent', an assumption that generated many of the problems in his philosophy.

11. Cf. n. 10 above. I return to the issue of Frege's contextualism at the end of §5.3, and address it more fully in §8.2.

12. We can, of course, offer the following definition: $m = n$ iff $(\forall F) [(\exists_m x) Fx \leftrightarrow (\exists_n x) Fx]$. (Cf. Wright, 1983: p. 37.) But once again, from Frege's point of view, this involves use of the expressions '$\exists_m x$' and '$\exists_n x$', which have not themselves yet been adequately defined.

13. It is clear, throughout his writings, that by 'Gleichheit' – 'equality' – Frege means 'identity' (cf. e.g. *BS*, §8, and his first n. to *SR*); and I have generally used 'identity' here, though 'equality' and its cognates (esp. 'equation' for 'Gleichung') often in direct translation. In *GL*, §63, Frege simply uses the phrase 'eindeutige Zuordnung', by which he means what is now called a 'many-one relation', 'beiderseits eindeutige Zuordnung' being his expression for 'one-one correlation'. But, as the expression itself suggests, the latter is readily defined in terms of the former (cf. §3.3 and n. 41 to ch. 3). Austin translates 'gleichzahlig' as 'equal', but it is better translated as 'equinumerous', despite Austin's stylistic worries (see his n. to *FA*, §68; p. 79). The use of 'equal' has confused at least one commentator. In her 'feminist reading' of Frege, Andrea Nye writes: 'To say that one concept is equal to another – and here we are close to the problem of number – is to say that their value-ranges are equal. ... Given that the universe of discourse must include every object, concepts are equal when they carve out of that totality correlatable sets of objects. To say that a bachelor is an unmarried man is to say that there is a one-one correlation between bachelors and unmarried men. To say that two concepts are equal is to say that they have the same number. To say that two concepts are equivalent is to assert a numerical equivalence.' (1990: p. 134; cf. p. 146.) As an obvious counterexample, consider the concepts 'married woman' and 'married man'. The two are *equinumerous*, since the objects that fall under them can be correlated one-one, but *not equal*, since their extensions are different. It is ironical that 'equality' should have been confused here with mere 'pairing'.

14. On the legitimacy of Frege's geometrical analogy, cf. Dummett, 1991a: ch. 10, pp. 115-17.

15. Commentators are divided as to exactly what 'Leibniz's Law' is. Some treat it simply as (SV) (e.g. Mates, 1986: p. 123), some identify it with the Principle of the Indiscernibility of Identicals (e.g. Ishiguro, 1990: p. 17; Wiggins, 1980: p. 19), some (less commonly) with the Principle of the Identity of Indiscernibles (e.g. MacDonald Ross, 1984: p. 53), and some with both Principles (e.g. Dummett, 1991a: p. 112). (SV) as it stands requires modification, since it involves use/mention confusion; and I here simply stipulate that by 'Leibniz's Law' I refer to the biconditional (LL) which incorporates *both* Principles.

16. Frege's appreciation of the point was manifested first, and most fully, in *SR*; see §§ 6.2 and 6.5.

17. The phrase seems to have been first used by Wright, 1983: §14.

18. See also §107, quoted at the beginning of §5.5; and on the assumption, cf. n. 24 to ch. 5.

19. I return to this issue in §§4.5, 5.3, 5.5 and 7.2.

20. This is one of the central insights that motivates Wright, 1983, in his own reconstruction of Frege's arguments. As Dummett (1991a: p. 123) notes, Frege does, in fact, himself derive all his theorems from the original contextual equivalence without further appeal to his explicit definition.

21. I return to the issue of Frege's understanding of extensions in §7.2.

22. Cf. *GL*, §§82-3. Frege provides only a sketch here; a fuller proof is given in *GG*, I, §§114-19.

23. *GL*, §78. The formal proofs are presented in Part II of *Grundgesetze* (vol. I, §§53-179; vol. II, §§1-54), which has not as yet been translated into English (Part I has been translated as *BLA*; and for those sections of Part III that have been translated, see n. 36 below). A useful summary of the main theorems derived in Part II, however, is provided in Currie, 1982: pp. 55-7.

24. The formalism here is what Dummett (1991a: p. 178) has suggested should be better called 'postulationism', to distinguish it from more sophisticated forms, both those that Frege attacks in the *Grundgesetze* (vol. II, §§86-137), and those that have subsequently been developed. For discussion of Frege's critique of formalism, see Resnik, 1980: ch. 2; Dummett, 1991a: ch. 20.

25. *GL*, §94; cf. §74, quoted in §4.3. I return to the issue of Frege's understanding of concepts in §7.1.

26. Cf. *GG*, II, §§56-65 (*FDI*, pp. 139-50), where Frege objects very strongly to what he calls in §57 'mathematicians' favourite procedure, piecemeal definition'.

27. Cf. Ishiguro, 1990: ch. 5, §6.

28. Most of Frege's remarks are contained in his 1885 review of H. Cohen's *Das Prinzip der Infinitesimal-Methode und seine Geschichte*, which attacks Cohen for construing the infinitesimal as an 'intensive magnitude', whereas, argues Frege, it should be understood purely arithmetically (*RHC*, p. 110). Infinitesimals may be granted 'objectivity' ('Objektivität'), but not 'reality' ('Realität'): 'I do not find that the infinitesimal has an intimate connection with reality' (*RHC*, p. 111). In his later, 1892 review of Cantor's work, he mentions that 'Mr. Cantor deals with the question whether there are actually infinitely small numerical quantities and gives a negative answer to the question for those infinitesimals that can be mapped as limited rectilinear continuous distances', and comments that 'The main part of the proof, which is not carried out, I accept as valid' (*RGC*, p. 180). None of this is incompatible with a belief that infinitesimals are *logical objects*, but Frege's positive views are by no means specified.

29. The only mention of the real numbers worth noting is in §19, where Frege discusses Newton's conception of number as a relation between magnitudes. Frege does indeed later adopt this view for the case of real numbers, but purges it of (Newtonian) geometrical interpretation. Frege merely remarks here that 'operations with negative, fractional and irrational numbers can all be reduced to operations with the natural numbers', leaving it open how this is to be done.

30. See n. 36 below for the main divisions in Frege's account of the real numbers in vol. II of *GG*. The translations from this work that follow are my own.

31. Frege's term translated here as 'natural number' is 'Anzahl' (translated in *FA*, *BLA* and *FR* as 'Number', with a capital 'N'), which is now explicitly distinguished from the more general term 'Zahl' – the *Anzahlen* (natural or cardinal numbers) being contrasted with the (corresponding) *reelen Zahlen* (real numbers). The distinction was anticipated at *GG*, I, §§41-2, but played no significant role either there (i.e. in *GG*, I) or in *GL*. Once again I have translated 'Grösse' as 'magnitude' rather than 'quantity' (cf. n. 26 to ch. 3). Frege indicates in §160 that he understands the word as synonymous with 'Quantität', but partly because the two words are nevertheless different, I have preferred 'magnitude' here, which in most contexts makes better sense. Dummett (1991a) uses 'quantity', whilst Currie (1986) uses 'magnitude'.

32. The applicability of numbers is also stressed in Frege's critique of formalism: 'it is applicability alone which elevates arithmetic from a game to the rank of a science. So applicability necessarily belongs to it. Is it good, then, to exclude from arithmetic what it needs in order to be a science?' (*GG*, II, §91/ *FF*, p. 167.)

33. Frege first introduces this notion in his *Habilitationsschrift*, which, as we saw in §3.2, was concerned with how the concept of magnitude is extended as it frees itself from geometry, and reveals itself to be dependent on general properties of addition. A magnitude of a certain kind, Frege writes, is 'a property in which a group of things can agree with a single thing of the same kind independently of the internal constitution of the group'; and a 'magnitude domain' ('Grössengebiet') is a domain comprising all possible magnitudes of a given type. Not only such magnitudes as lengths, but also, in general, and this is Frege's key idea, any kind of *operation*, can form a magnitude domain. (*MC*, pp. 56-8.) For a much fuller account of Frege's theory of the real numbers, see Currie, 1986; Simons, 1987; and Dummett, 1991a: ch. 22. What follows here is the barest of sketches.

34. Russell wrote to Frege telling him of the paradox on 16 June 1902; see *PMC*, pp. 130-1. I discuss the paradox in §7.2. For reconstructions of Frege's logicist project that seek to circumvent the paradox that Frege himself failed to resolve, see Bostock, 1974; Wright, 1983; Cocchiarella, 1986.

35. For Frege's writings during this period, see Bibliography. The three most important papers were *FC*, *CO* and *SR*, introducing the developments mentioned in the next paragraph, and discussed in the chapters that follow. For biographical details of this period, see Bynum, 1972a: §§12-16.

36. This is reflected in the fact that Part III of *GG* is itself divided into two parts, the first entitled 'Critique of Theories of the Irrational Numbers' (§§55-164), and the second 'Theory of Magnitude' (§§165-245). The subdivisions of the former are as follows: (a) 'Principles of Definition' (§§55-67; tr. as *FDI* in *TPW*); (b) 'Cantor's Theory of the Irrational Numbers' (§§68-85); (c) 'The Theories of the Irrationals of E. Heine and J. Thomae' (§§86-137, containing his attack on formalism; tr. as *FF* in *TPW*); (d) 'The Construction of New Objects by R. Dedekind, H. Hankel, O. Stolz' (§§138-47; most of it tr. as *FDII* in *TPW*); (e) 'Weierstrass' Theory' (§§148-55); (f) 'Review and Outlook' (§§156-9); (g) 'Magnitude' (§§160-4).

37. Cf. Frege's comment on Russell's theory (a refined version of Cantor's and Dedekind's theories) in a letter to Russell dated 21 May 1903: 'When you define an irrational number as a class of rational numbers, it is, of course, something different from what I call an irrational number according to my definition, although there is naturally a connection. It seems to me that you need a double transition: (1) from [natural] numbers to rational numbers, and (2) from rational to real numbers in general. I want to go at once from [natural] numbers to real numbers as relations of magnitudes.' (*PMC*, p. 156.)

38. Cantor, 1883: p. 567; quoted by Frege, *GG*, II, §68. I have here translated 'Fundamentalreihe' as 'fundamental sequence', and the verb 'zuordnen' as 'assign'.

39. Cf. Russell's critique of Cantor's theory in *POM*, §269: 'There is absolutely nothing in [Cantor's] definition of the real numbers to show that *a* is the real number defined by a fundamental series whose terms are all equal to *a*. The only reason why this seems self-evident is, that the definition by limits is unconsciously present, making us think that, since *a* is plainly the limit of a series whose terms are all equal to *a*, therefore *a* must be the real number defined by such a series.' (p. 285.) However, what is true, Russell goes on, is this: 'Connected with every rational *a* there is a real number, namely that defined by the fundamental series whose terms are all equal to *a* .... The limit of a series of rationals either does not exist, or is rational; in no case is it a real number. But in all cases a fundamental series of rationals *defines* a real number, which is never identical with any rational.' (Ibid.) Russell's own strategy is to *identify* the real numbers with the fundamental sequences themselves: 'I conclude, then, that an irrational actually *is* a segment of rationals which does not have a limit; while a real number which would be commonly identified with a rational is a segment which does have a rational limit' (§270, p. 286).

40. This is the refinement mentioned in n. 16 to ch. 3: a real number is the class of all fundamental sequences with the same limit; just as, on a Fregean account, a natural number is the class of all classes equinumerous to a given class. Cf. Dummett, 1991a: p. 267.

41. Cf. Dummett, 1991a: pp. 249-50. As suggested in n. 17 to ch. 3, Dedekind avoids *identifying* real numbers with cuts; but this just leaves the exact relationship between the two unclear. For a comparison of Frege's and Dedekind's theories, see Kitcher, 1986.

42. Cf. Quine, 1963: pp. 81-3; Resnik, 1980: p. 229.

43. Of course, any set theory such as Zermelo's or von Neumann's has a broad range of applicability, but it does not, as it were, have its general applicability built into it. Compare Frege's conception of a theory of real numbers, governing everything that is measurable; see §4.4.

44. See §7.2 for discussion of Russell's paradox.

45. For further criticism of Benacerraf's argument, see Resnik, 1980: pp. 228-33; Dummett, 1991a: ch. 5; and esp. Wright, 1983: §15.

46. *GL*, §69; see the beginning of §5.5. Dedekind had appreciated a similar problem in his own account of the natural numbers. In a famous passage from the preface to *Was sind und was sollen die Zahlen?* (1888), he remarked: 'I feel conscious that many a reader will scarcely recognise in the shadowy forms which I bring before him his numbers which all his life long have accompanied him as faithful and familiar friends' (p. 33).

5. Analysis and Definitions

1. Plato does not himself explicitly distinguish between 'unconscious knowledge' and 'full-blown knowledge', and these terms must not be understood in any Freudian sense, but, like Aristotle after him (see §1.3), he does tend to use the verb *eidenai* when talking about what we already or ordinarily know and reserve the term *epistēmē* for 'scientifically tethered' knowledge.

2. Cf. n. 1 above. The distinction between 'true opinion' and 'knowledge' can be accepted, in other words, without endorsing the more mystical elements of Plato's doctrine of recollection. We can allow that there is some sense in which, in coming to 'properly know' something, we are *reminded* of what we already believe, but still maintain that there was an earlier period of genuine learning.

3. For Aristotle's conception of *scientific deduction*, see *Posterior Analytics*, I 2; discussed in §1.3. Cf. also Gaukroger, 1989: pp. 16-17; 74-5.

4. See Descartes, *RDM*, Rule Four, p. 17; *OR*, 'Second Set of Replies', p. 111. Leibniz alludes to Descartes' suggestion here in e.g. *USA*, p. 17; *NE*, pp. 488-9.

5. Cf. Gaukroger, 1989: ch. 3, esp. p. 83.

6. Leibniz, *MKTI*, p. 26. According to Descartes, a perception is 'clear' if it is 'present and accessible to the attentive mind – just as we say that we see something clearly when it is present to the eye's gaze and stimulates it with a sufficient degree of strength and accessibility', and 'distinct' if it is both clear and 'so sharply separated from all other perceptions that it contains within itself only what is clear' (*PP*, I 45). Locke's criteria are very similar to Descartes' (cf. *Essay*, II xxix 4); and Leibniz also criticizes Locke's account in the relevant passage of the *New Essays* (i.e. II xxix).

7. See Leibniz, *MKTI*. I formulate the criteria here for *concepts*, rather than ideas. Leibniz himself does not distinguish the two, but in the light of Frege's own distinction, this is the preferable formulation. Cf. n. 48 to ch. 3.

8. Cf. *NE*, pp. 488-9. According to Leibniz, algebra was only part of a more general *characteristica universalis*, which it was his aim to develop (see §2.1). For further discussion of Descartes' and Leibniz's views on the relationship between truth and proof, see Hacking, 1986.

9. See esp. Leibniz, *PNG*, §§4, 13. For the fullest account of Leibniz's ideas here, see McRae, 1976; and on 'confused ideas', see Wilson, 1977; Parkinson, 1982.

10. Kant, *CPR*, A271/B327. The remark is particularly unfair to Leibniz. See e.g. *NE*, p. 49, where Leibniz admits that 'the senses are necessary for all our actual knowledge', though they are not sufficient. Cf. Parkinson, 1982.

11. See App. 2. We should note that, in offering a criterion for analytic truth, Kant ignores cases of 'analytic falsehood'. Clearly, in a 'false judgement' the predicate B cannot be contained in the subject A, but this does not necessarily make it synthetic, since if not-B is contained in A, then the original proposition can be regarded as 'analytically false'. (Cf. Bennett, 1966: ch. 1, §2.) For Kant, though, 'judgement' consists in asserting that a proposition is true, just as it does later for Frege, so that there cannot actually be any 'analytically false judgements'.

12. According to Leibniz, in other words, all truths are 'analytic' for God, who is the true judge of the matter. Kant remarks: 'the question is not what we *ought*

to join in thought to the given concept, but what we *actually* think in it, even if only obscurely' (B17). The last two clauses exhibit the tension.

13. On the distinction between the logical and the phenomenological criterion, see Beck, 1967. Beck himself accused Kant of failing to appreciate the difference, although Kant does discuss them separately (see also *PFM*, §2). But since, except in the case of Leibnizian 'identities' (see App. 2), the same objection can be raised to both, they clearly have something in common. Cf. Allison, 1983: pp. 74-5.

14. On the centrality of the explicative/ampliative contrast, as opposed to Kant's 'official' criteria, see Allison, 1983: ch. 4, §3.

15. Cf. e.g. Kant, *CPR*, A4/B8: 'Mathematics gives us a shining example of how far, independently of experience, we can progress in *a priori* knowledge.'

16. According to Leibniz, the 'perfect' or 'complete' notion of an individual substance contains *all* its predicates (cf. e.g. *DM*, §8; *PT*, p. 89); so that even existential judgements turn out to be 'analytic'.

17. Frege's criterion is also deficient on the realist assumption that there may be true propositions that cannot be proved (cf. Dummett, 1991a: p. 24). But Gödelian worries about incompleteness had not emerged at this point, and although Frege held the weaker realist view that the truth of a proposition is independent of its being held to be true (cf. e.g. *GG*, I, p. xv), he appears not to have contemplated the possibility that there might be true propositions that *cannot* be proved.

18. Throughout his life, Frege was adamant that, as he put in *GG*, 'the laws of truth are not psychological laws, but boundary stones set in an eternal foundation, which our thought can overflow but not dislodge' (I, p. xvi). However, by the time of *GG*, Frege no longer chose to express this by talking of the *analyticity* of arithmetic, as we shall see in §5.5.

19. Cf. *FGI*, p. 274; *FGII*, p. 294; *LM*, pp. 210-11, where they are termed 'constructive definitions' (see §5.5).

20. For further discussion of Frege's *Grundlagen* conception of fruitfulness, see Dummett, 1991a: ch. 4.

21. The allusion is to what has been called Wittgenstein's *Grundgedanke* in his early work – that (in relation to the logical constants) there are *no* logical objects (cf. *NB*, pp. 37, 120; *TLP*, 4.0312, 4.441, 5.4).

22. Frege writes: 'Does the proposition "The Earth has two poles" mean the same as [*Ist der Satz ... gleichbedeutend mit*] "The North Pole is different from the South Pole"? Obviously not. The second proposition could hold without the first, and the first without the second.' (*GL*, §44.)

23. I introduce this term with Quine's notion of *semantic ascent* (1960: §56) in mind, characterized as the shift from the *material* to the *formal* mode of speech, to use (with Quine) the terminology of Carnap (cf. 1937: §§63-4). Quine writes: 'It is the shift from talking in certain terms to talking about them. It is precisely the shift that Carnap thinks of as divesting philosophical questions of a deceptive guise and setting them forth in their true colors .... The strategy of semantic ascent is that it carries the discussion into a domain where both parties are better agreed on the objects (viz., words) and on the main terms concerning them.' (1960: pp. 271-2.) Replacing reference to words by reference to concepts, what we have here is a fine characterization of Frege's own project, as will emerge in what follows.

24. This assumption follows from Frege's views on the determinacy of sense (see e.g. *PMC*, p. 100; *GL*, §§54, 74; *FC*, p. 33; *GG*, §56; *LM*, p. 229; and esp. *CSR*, pp. 122-5). Any genuine concept sharply divides objects into those that fall under it and those that do not. Grasp of such a concept, then, involves knowing that it has a determinate extension. In *GL*, Frege only acknowledges this assumption in the n. to §68 and at the very end (§107); see §5.5.

25. Axiom V was not responsible on its own for the paradox; also required was the assumption that each concept had to be defined for all objects, *including* the extension of that concept itself (extensions themselves being objects of the domain). See §§ 7.1 and 7.2.

26. Alternative translations of 'Werthverlauf' are 'course-of-values' and 'graph'. 'Graph' is inappropriate, since the notion of a function has been generalized, and as we saw in ch. 3, Frege was insistent that our logical and arithmetical knowledge outstrips our powers of geometrical intuition. But both renderings at least have the virtue of indicating that Frege has in mind a set of *pairings* of arguments with values, and not just the range of values themselves. But I have used the more straightforward term 'value-range' here, and simply note that it is to be understood in the way just indicated. In the specific case of *extensions*, objects are paired with one or other of the truth-values, so that if we then take the set of all objects that a certain concept pairs with the True, the result is the 'extension' of that concept as traditionally conceived.

27. Frege's conception of how the appeal to extensions avoids the Caesar problem was, at the time of *GL*, rather vague; and it is only in *GG*, I, §10 that the issue is finally confronted. See §§6.4 and 7.2.

28. This was a requirement frequently stated by Frege; see the refs. given in n. 24 above.

29. Strictly speaking, we also require that *everything* be definable as an extension, so that any object can – in principle – be distinguished from every other. But if Frege's *Grundgedanke* is legitimate, then this can be done (cf. *GG*, I, §10; discussed in §6.4), since the following transition can be effected *for any X*:

(Xa) *X* is identical with *Y*.

(Xe) *X* is the extension of the concept 'is identical with *X*'.

30. I return to this in ch. 8. On the controversial issue of Frege's contextualism, see e.g. Dummett, 1981a: ch. 19; 1991a: chs. 15-17; 1995; Resnik, 1976; 1979; 1980: pp. 161-71; Wright, 1983: ch. 1.

31. I say more about Frege's appeal to extensions in §§5.5 and 7.1, and discuss the problems with Axiom V in §§5.4 and 7.2.

32. See Langford, 1942. For discussion of Moore's conception of analysis, see Ayer, 1971: ch. 9, §§A-B; Baldwin, 1990: ch. 7.

33. See esp. Russell, *PLA*, Lectures 1-2, 5-6; *LA*; Wittgenstein, *TLP*, 3.25 – 4.0031, 4.11 – 4.1213; *PR*, §§1-9; *PI*, §§81, 89-133.

34. In criticizing the central argument of *GL*, Husserl writes: 'what this method allows us to define are not the contents [*Inhalte*] of the concepts of direction, shape, number, but their *extensions* [*Umfänge*]' (1891: p. 122). In an earlier passage, discussing the definition of equinumerosity in terms of one-one correlation, he makes clear that he understands 'content' epistemically: 'The possibility of one-one correlation between two pluralities does not constitute their equinumerosity, but only *guarantees* it. The knowledge that their numbers are equal by no means requires the knowledge of their possible correlation, let alone that both [items of knowledge] are identical' (p. 105). For further discussion of the dispute between Frege and Husserl, see Dummett, 1987; 1991a: ch. 12.

35. The structure here is very similar to that of Sanchez's dilemma. In both cases the underlying assumption is that the 'meaning' of an expression is exhausted by the thing it designates (object or idea); and it is this assumption that needs to be repudiated.

36. The distinction first appears in *FC*, delivered as a lecture in January 1891 and published that same year (see below). Since Husserl's book was only itself published in 1891, and there is no indication of any communication between Frege and Husserl before this time, it cannot be the case that the distinction was prompted in the first place by the need to respond to Husserl's objections, though we can certainly suggest that it was Frege's own awareness of the problem of the status of his definitions that played a crucial role in motivating the distinction.

37. (De), in other words, is intended to be analytic, whilst (Di) is merely synthetic. Considered as 'derivations', as represented in §5.3, although (De) and (Di) would both result from (Db) and (Dd), in the case of (De) it is only the left-hand side of each identity statement that is taken, the syntheticity of (Db) and (Dd) thus 'cancelling out', whereas (Di) results from combining the left-hand side of (Db) with the right-hand side of (Dd), the syntheticity therefore being retained.

38. It might perhaps be suggested that Frege's thought was that sameness of *Bedeutung* would suffice for analyticity, whilst 'epistemic sense' would accommodate informativeness. Certainly, demonstrating sameness of *Bedeutung* – that truth is transmitted along a chain of inference – is enough to show that a theorem follows from a set of axioms, but for this to be shown to be *analytic*, the axioms must themselves be analytic, and this cannot be clarified without a notion of 'semantic sense'. However, Frege himself appears to have abandoned talk of 'analyticity' by the time the *Sinn/Bedeutung* distinction was operative; see §5.5 and n. 48 below. (The term 'analytic' is used at the beginning of *SR*, but only in relation to Kant.)

39. This is suggested by the brief notes that Scholz, the collector of Frege's *Nachlass*, made on one of Frege's lost manuscripts, dating from just after *GL* (see item no. 47 in the catalogue printed in Veraart, 1976: p. 95). For details of this, see Burge, 1984: §II.

40. Compare 'The point of intersection of lines *a* and *b* is identical with the point of intersection of lines *b* and *c*', where *a*, *b* and *c* are the lines connecting the vertices of a triangle with the midpoints of the opposite sides (*SR*, p. 57); as well as the more familiar 'The Morning Star is the Evening Star'. See §6.1.

41. The standard translation of these terms is potentially misleading, since 'constructive definitions' are only constructive in the sense of playing an abbreviatory role in the 'building up' of a system (they are not 'fruitful' in Frege's earlier sense), and 'analytic definitions' (literally, 'analysing definitions'), in so far as they are different from 'constructive definitions', are not 'analytic' in the Kantian sense, except where they are more correctly regarded as 'axioms' (as explained in what follows).

42. See e.g. *GL*, pp. vi-viii, §§3, 17; *RC*, p. 109; *OLI*, p. 136; *LM*, pp. 241-2.

43. It is tempting to say here that the purpose of logical analysis is to *make sense*; but Frege himself would have been uneasy about this way of putting it. On his view, determinate senses are already there; it is just that they are not clearly associated with the appropriate sign, so that what analysis does is to *make the connection*. But I return to the issue in ch. 8.

44. Cf. *GG*, II, §146 (*TPW*, pp. 159-60), where Frege specifically states that Axiom V is not to be regarded as a definition.

45. Again, cf. *GG*, II, §146, where Frege assumes that we already know what identity is in general, just as he did so in the central argument of *GL* (cf. §63). What is therefore being shown is *sense-identity*.

46. This was just the point made in §4.3. With (De) in place, the equivalence between (Da) and (Db) is reinstated, and Frege's logicist project is off the ground.

47. The argument is then that 'the well-known properties of numbers' can indeed be derived (cf. *GL*, §70), as sketched in ch. 4.

48. In *GG*, I, for example, he talks of gaining 'a basis for judging the epistemological nature of the law that is proved' (p. vii). But the fundamental laws of arithmetic are characterized as *logical*, not analytic. Even when he refers to his earlier work, he studiously avoids using the term 'analytic', as in the opening sentence of the introduction: 'In my *Grundlagen der Arithmetik* I sought to make it plausible that arithmetic is a branch of logic and need take no grounds of proof from either experience or intuition' (p. 1). Cf. also n. 38 above.

6. *Sinn* and *Bedeutung*

1. For caution in using Kantian language here, see nn. 38 and 48 to ch. 5.

2. Certainly, the concept of direction is generally acquired before the concept of parallelism. A child, for example, learns the use of phrases such as 'in this direction' long before they explore the geometrical properties of lines.

3. See e.g. *BS*, §2 (cf. §§3, 9), where Frege talks of 'circumstances' (*Umstände*) as being the contents of possible judgement. Cf. Dummett, 1981b: pp. 176f.; Currie, 1984: §2. Dummett comments on the debate between Grossmann (1969: ch. 1), who had criticized Frege for not including states of affairs in his ontology, and Kluge (1970), who had argued that they *were* included. The right answer seems to be that they were included at the time of *BS*, but were later regarded as *true thoughts*, inhabiting the realm of sense rather than *Bedeutung*. I return to the issue in §7.5.

4. For the most sympathetic discussion of Leibniz's understanding, see Ishiguro, 1990: ch. 2.

5. Qualifications are needed here, as Wittgenstein's critique of his own earlier *Tractatus* view shows. The suggestion, for example, that every sentence represents or *pictures* a 'state of affairs' must, at the very least, be restricted to indicative sentences. But since other sentences such as questions and imperatives can be seen as derivative from a corresponding indicative, we might still allow that every sentence can be *correlated* with a 'state of affairs'. The realism implicit in talk of 'states of affairs' might also be regarded as illegitimate in certain kinds of discourse (e.g. fictional discourse), although the phrase could be granted a metaphorical use. Even in what Frege would regard as 'scientific' discourse, negative, existential and general statements, not to mention counterfactual conditionals and modal propositions, have presented particular problems to the 'state of affairs' or 'situation' theorist, although attempts have been made to overcome them (most notably, recently, by Barwise and Perry, 1983). That there is a case for arguing that Frege *should have* taken the *Bedeutungen* of sentences as 'facts' or 'states of affairs' will emerge in the next two chapters (see esp. §8.3; cf. also Yourgrau, 1987: §2), but the main point in the present section is just to show that Frege provides no compelling reason in *SR* for identifying the *Bedeutungen* of sentences with truth-values rather than with, say, 'states of affairs'.

6. Only true ('scientific') sentences present actual states of affairs: to account for false sentences, we must regard them, as Wittgenstein did in *TLP*, as presenting *possible* states of affairs. Frege appears to come close to a more Tractarian view on p. 63 of *SR*, where he writes that 'By the truth-value [= *Bedeutung*] of a sentence I understand the circumstance [*Umstand*] that it is true or false'. But what he meant here was not the circumstance that makes the sentence true or false, but the (bare) circumstance of it being true or false.

7. See esp. Tugendhat, 1970. My notions of 'veritable content' (for sentences) and 'veritable value' (for names; see §6.3) are also close to Tugendhat's notion of 'truth-value potential'. Cf. also Gabriel, 1984.

8. Compare the point made here with what was said in §5.4 in relation to the propositions (De) and (Di).

9. Such a view is arguably implicit in e.g. *BS*, §9; cf. Baker & Hacker, 1984: esp. ch. 6, §3. But for caution in reading too definite a view into Frege's early thought, see Dummett, 1984: §1.

10. As in the case of construing numbers as extensions of concepts (see §5.5), Frege admits that his views here may seem counterintuitive: 'I do not fail to see that this way of putting it may at first seem arbitrary and artificial, and that it would be desirable to establish my view by going further into the matter. Cf. my forthcoming essay "Über Sinn und Bedeutung" ' (*FC*, p. 29, n.).

11. For further criticism of Frege's doctrine, see Dummett, 1981a: ch. 12; Potts, 1982; and for a more sympathetic account, see Burge, 1986.

12. The notion of 'veritable value' here corresponds to Dummett's notion of 'semantic value' (see esp. 1981b: ch. 7), but I use the term 'veritable value' to make explicit the connection with the notion introduced earlier of 'veritable content'. Cf. n. 7 above.

13. For the distinction between 'reference' and 'referent', see Dummett, 1981a: pp. 93-4. 'Reference' signifies the *relation* between the expression and its referent; and relations can clearly remain even if one or more of the relata cease to exist. For example, I am still the eldest grandson of my maternal grandfather, even though he died 15 years ago. On reference without referents, cf. also Dummett, 1981a: p. 410.

14. For further discussion of the need for this distinction, see Dummett, 1981b: ch. 7.

15. This has induced some critics of Frege, notably, Kripke (1980), to use the apparently simple proper names 'Hesperus' and 'Phosphorus' instead (replacing 'the Evening Star' and 'the Morning Star', respectively); but it is clear that these should be treated as disguised definite descriptions.

16. Frege uses the metaphor of senses as *routes* to referents in e.g. *OCN*, p. 85, senses indicating 'different ways in which it is possible for us to arrive at the same thing'. Cf. Dummett, 1981a: p. 96.

17. A Kantian influence might well be suggested here: on a transcendental idealist conception, an object is 'presented' to consciousness precisely by being 'determined'. Geometrical points, for example, do not exist independently of 'modes of determination' – they are 'presented', say, as intersections of lines. And in the empirical realm, compare Frege's imagined case of 'Afla' and 'Ateb' ('Alfa' and 'Beta' backwards) – two names for the same mountain, but reflecting opposite directions from which the mountain is viewed. 'An object can be determined in different ways, and every one of these ways of determining it can give rise to a special name, and these different names then have different senses; for it is not self-evident that it is the same object which is being determined in different ways.' (*PMC*, p. 80.) My only point in distinguishing modes of determination from modes of presentation is to sharpen the discussion of senses without referents.

18. In cases such as this, the answer to Wittgenstein's question in 4.243 of *TLP*, as quoted at the beginning of this chapter, is therefore 'No'. But Wittgenstein is wrong to imply there that this is the correct answer in all cases, at least as we ordinarily use the term 'understand', and unless it is made explicit that the category of 'names' does not include definite descriptions. The issue will become clearer in what follows.

19. For the alternative interpretation – that Frege understood senses as fundamentally requiring referents – see esp. Evans, 1982: ch. 1 (and cf. McDowell, 1984); and for criticism of Evans, see Bell, 1990. Evans' interpretation is also incompatible with Frege's later insistence on the distinctness of the realms of sense and of reference (see §7.5). However, as I go on to argue in the next section, Frege *should* have held such a view in the case of simple names.

20. For an interpretation of Frege that does take typographical distinctness as the criterion for difference of sense, see Wienpahl, 1950.

21. The conception of the sense of a proposition as given by its truth-conditions, regarded by later philosophers (from the early Wittgenstein to Dummett, Davidson and other contemporary semantic theorists) as one of Frege's most fundamental ideas, follows naturally from this, although the conception itself only really emerges in Frege's own work in *GG*, I, §32.

22. Examples of this latter class are 'Hesperus' and 'Phosphorus'; cf. n. 15 above.

23. This follows from (PDS), as formulated in §6.2, and discussed further in ch. 8.

24. What counts as an 'analytic' truth will thus vary from person to person (cf. §§5.1-5.2), providing further justification for Frege's abandonment of the notion of 'analyticity' (cf. nn. 38 and 48 to ch. 5).

25. It may well have been the line of thought first sketched in §67 of *GL*, then, that prompted Frege to deny that *senses* were of any concern to the (mathematical) logician, motivating the response he gave to Husserl's objections that we discussed in §5.4 (*RH*, pp. 199-200). As we argued, however, and as will be clearer shortly, considerations of sense *are* important.

26. The first position received its classic statement in Wittgenstein's *TLP* (see esp. 2.0123, 3.203, 3.26, 3.3411, 4.243, 6.232, 6.2322), and was later attacked by Wittgenstein himself in *PI* (see esp. §§37-79). Kripke (1980) was instrumental in destroying the second position – using modal considerations to demonstrate the inadequacy of any attempt to identify the sense of a name with the sense of some corresponding definite description. However, Kripke's own positive account is no less problematic: the extrusion of the epistemological dimension that his causal theory of reference involves generates similar difficulties to those that affected Wittgenstein's *Tractatus* view. For criticism of Kripke, see Dummett, 1981a: App. to ch. 5; 1981b: ch. 9; App. 3; Evans, 1982: ch. 3; McCulloch, 1989: ch. 4.

27. *GG*, I, §10 is one of the most difficult passages in Frege's work. For helpful discussion, see Dummett, 1981b: pp. 402-27; and for a response to Dummett, see Moore & Rein, 1986.

28. To formulate (Xb), we would need to introduce another new expression, 'the identicant of *X*', defined in the standard contextual way:

(Xa) *X* is identical with *Y*.

(Xb) The identicant of *X* is the same as the identicant of *Y*.

In this case, however, there is no new abstract object: the identicant of *X* just is *X*. (Xc) is straightforward:

(Xc) The concept *is identical with X* is coextensive with the concept *is identical with Y*.

On the (questionable) assumption, then, that (Xa) is 'cognitively equivalent' to (Xc), (Xe) can be derived (cf. §5.3).

29. *GG*, I, §10, n./ *BLA*, p. 48, n. 17. The proof that the generalization does not hold if the object is already given as a value-range can be stated as follows. Using Frege's notation for extensions, '$\acute{\varepsilon}\Phi(\varepsilon)$' representing 'the extension of the concept Φ', Axiom V can be formulated thus:

(V) $(\forall a) [\Phi(a) = \psi(a)]$ iff $\acute{\varepsilon}\Phi(\varepsilon) = \acute{\alpha}\psi(\alpha)$.

The suggestion is to characterize every object Δ as the extension of the concept *is identical with* Δ, i.e. stipulating that $\acute{\varepsilon}(\Delta = \varepsilon)$ be the same as Δ. But now consider the case where Δ is already given as a value-range, say, as $\acute{\alpha}\Phi(\alpha)$. Taking '$\acute{\varepsilon}(\Delta = \varepsilon)$ $= \Delta$', and substituting in, we have:

$\acute{\varepsilon}(\acute{\alpha}\Phi(\alpha) = \varepsilon) = \acute{\alpha}\Phi(\alpha)$.

By Axiom V, this is equivalent to:

$(\forall a)\,[(\acute{\alpha}\Phi(\alpha) = a) = \Phi(a)]$.

However, as Frege then notes, this refers to the True 'only if $\Phi(\xi)$ is a concept under which one and only one object falls, namely $\acute{\alpha}\Phi(\alpha)$'. For in this case, if $a = \acute{\alpha}\Phi(\alpha)$, then both '$\acute{\alpha}\Phi(\alpha) = a$' and '$\Phi(a)$' will refer to the True, so that '$(\acute{\alpha}\Phi(\alpha) = a) = \Phi(a)$' will refer to the True; and if $a \neq \acute{\alpha}\Phi(\alpha)$, then both '$\acute{\alpha}\Phi(\alpha) = a$' and '$\Phi(a)$' will refer to the False, so that '$(\acute{\alpha}\Phi(\alpha) = a) = \Phi(a)$' also refers to the True. But in every other case, there will be some values of a for which '$(\acute{\alpha}\Phi(\alpha) = a) = \Phi(a)$' will refer to the False, i.e. where $a = \acute{\alpha}\Phi(\alpha)$ and does not fall under the concept Φ, or $a \neq \acute{\alpha}\Phi(\alpha)$ and does fall under the concept Φ. So, as Frege concludes, 'our stipulation cannot remain intact in its general form.' (*BLA*, pp. 48-9.) Even before the emergence of Russell's Paradox, this result should already have alerted Frege to the danger of regarding an extension of a concept as on the same ontological level as the objects that fall under that concept. What Frege does instead, in *GG*, I, §11, is introduce a function, represented by '\$\xi$', that *maps* extensions of concepts under which one and only one object falls onto that object itself; see App. 3.

30. That Frege should be seen as providing a *Bedeutung* to numerical terms is emphasized by Weiner, 1990: ch. 3. I return to the issue in §8.5.

31. See §4.5 and ch. 5, where the problem was revealed as an instance of the paradox of analysis.

32. On the tension in Frege's conception of the domain involved in his formal system, cf. Dummett, 1981b: p. 418; Moore & Rein, 1986: n. 9.

33. That understanding the sense of a proper name involves *knowing which* object is referred to has been most powerfully argued by Evans (1982). Evans calls the principle involved here 'Russell's Principle': 'a subject cannot make a judgement about something unless he knows which object his judgement is about' (p. 89; cf. p. 65). Russell formulates his own 'fundamental epistemological principle' slightly differently: 'Every proposition which we can understand must be composed wholly of constituents with which we are acquainted' (*KAKD*, p. 159; *PP*, p. 32); but if we rephrase Russell's talk of propositions *containing* the objects that the propositions are about, and we substitute Russell's problematic notion of *acquaintance* by Evans' theoretically far more richly developed notion of having *discriminating knowledge*, whilst still insisting on the underlying point of agreement – that, at the fundamental level, thinking about an object requires that the object exist (this is the heart of Evans' Russellian account), then the term 'Russell's principle' appropriately honours the connection. All that is being brought out here, then, is the idea that having discriminating knowledge of an object involves knowing *what kind of object* it is, an idea that is implicit in Evans' own account (see esp. ch. 4).

34. The saying/showing distinction was one of the fundamental ideas of Wittgenstein's early philosophy, where it originated in Wittgenstein's articulation of his objections to Russell's theory of types, which he regarded as an attempt to *say* what could only be *shown* (see *NB*, p. 122; cf. pp. 109-10). The idea was then generalized: logical propositions *show* the logical properties of language and the world, but *say* nothing (cf. *NB*, p. 108; *TLP*, 6.11, 6.12). Incorporating the idea into his picture theory of language, Wittgenstein wrote: 'A proposition *shows* its sense. A proposition *shows* how things stand *if* it is true. And it *says that* they do so stand.' (4.022.) Furthermore, 'What *can* be shown, *cannot* be said' (4.1212). It was this

distinction that Dummett utilized in remarking that, 'for Frege, we *say* what the referent of a word is, and thereby *show* what its sense is' (1981a: p. 227). McDowell (1977) and Evans (1982: ch. 1), in particular, have developed this idea (building also on Davidson's work – see esp. Davidson, 1967), in arguing that a theory of sense (theory of meaning) can be based on a theory of reference (theory of truth), so long as the axioms that assign referents to terms do so in an appropriate way, *showing* the sense of the terms. Evans (p. 16, n. 14) also recognizes the need to distinguish (SMI) and (MIS); cf. Dummett, 1975, p. 130. But neither he nor McDowell stress enough, I think, that knowledge of the sense of *simple* names can be exhibited in any number of different ways, although McDowell is sensitive to the importance of context in determining the appropriate way to specify the referent of a given term. Wiggins (1976) offers an account of sense, which is similarly motivated but even more austere than McDowell's, which fits better the case of simple names, but looks less plausible in the case of names that clearly can be treated as disguised definite descriptions. For an alternative account of sense, which, by way of contrast, offers too rich a conception, playing down the distinction between (SMI) and (MIS) by identifying the sense of a name with the whole stock of knowledge that speakers of a language can draw upon in using the name, see Luntley, 1984.

35. On the importance of 'hints' and 'illustrative examples', see *CO*, pp. 42-3, 45, 54-5; *LM*, p. 207. I return to this in §8.5. That at some point we must allow that understanding the sense of a name involves knowing which object is referred to, to avoid the infinite regress in the analysis of propositions, was fundamental to the logical atomism that Russell and Wittgenstein developed (albeit in their different ways) in the 1910s, as reflected, for example, in Russell's 'fundamental principle' quoted in n. 33 above.

36. $a/a = 1$ for all $a \neq 0$, and $0/a = 0$ for all $a \neq 0$; but clearly without the restriction (excluding $a = 0$), we would have a contradiction ($1 = 0$). Conveniently forgetting the restriction is what enables mathematicians to perform their favourite party trick, 'proving', say, that $4 = 5$. For we are asked to agree to the following two arithmetical generalizations: (1) $a \times 0 = 0$; (2) $a = b \leftrightarrow c \times a = c \times b$. But then from the identity '$0 = 0$', by (1) we can derive '$0 \times 4 = 0 \times 5$', from which by (2) we can conclude '$4 = 5$'. For a useful (if provocatively conventionalist) discussion of the philosophical issues raised here, see Ambrose, 1959.

37. It was precisely this thought that motivated Russell's theory of descriptions, the central point of which, as Russell himself put it, was that 'a phrase may contribute to the meaning of a sentence [in fact, to both its sense and truth-value] without having any meaning at all in isolation [i.e. a referent]' (*MPD*, p. 64).

38. Frege's conviction that senses are objective, grounded in the conception of senses as objects, was no doubt also a major motivation. For if both senses and referents are objects, then it is natural to suppose that they can exist independent of one another (indeed, according to Frege, they inhabit quite separate realms; see §7.5).

39. See esp. Dummett, 1981a: p. 267; 1981b: pp. 87-9.

40. Russell himself translates 'Bedeutung' as 'denotation' and 'Sinn' as 'meaning', which is especially confusing now, given that the translation of 'Bedeutung' in the current Blackwell edition of Frege's works is 'meaning'. (This translation is avoided in my forthcoming new Blackwell selection of Frege's works, *The Frege Reader*.) Here I have simply replaced Russell's 'meaning' by 'sense'.

41. Dummett later admits (1981b: pp. 89-90, 98) that his earlier dismissal of the suggestion that the indirect sense of 'Aristotle' is simply the customary sense of 'the sense of "Aristotle" ' (1973/ 1981a: p. 267) was too curt; and in responding to the objections that Heidelberger (1975) raised to his earlier account, Dummett in the end concludes that 'no definite preference' can be given to his account: 'it depends to which conception of sense we are appealing' (1981b: p. 99).

42. I make no attempt here to say more about these 'well-established ways'. For detailed discussion of some of the issues involved, see Evans, 1982: ch. 11; and McCulloch, 1989: ch. 8.

43. In 'On Denoting', Russell raises two main objections to Frege's conception of sense (cf. p. 49). One is the problem of specification that we have been discussing; the other is the problem of whether senses are indeed objects. For if the sense ('meaning') and referent ('denotation') of an expression are independently existing objects (cf. n. 38 above), then there is no way of maintaining the *logical* relation that is still supposed to hold between them. However, on the supposition that senses are *abstract objects*, contextually defined, Russell's second objection can be answered, but only by abandoning Frege's conception of the separate realms of *Sinn* and *Bedeutung*. This will become clear in §8.4.

44. Dummett, 1981b: pp. 87-100, esp. pp. 96-100, where Dummett remarks that 'the theory of indirect sense is in any case a needless and unjustifiable complication' (p. 98).

7. Language, Logic and Paradox

1. Both Marshall (1953, 1956) and Grossmann (1961), for example, denied that Frege applied the distinction to functional expressions; Dummett (1955) and Jackson (1962) suggested that it did apply.

2. In *BS*, Frege certainly did regard the 'content' of a proper name as the object referred to (see §6.1 above); and several passages in *GL* might be taken to indicate an *intensionalist* view of concepts. He writes, for example: 'The content of a concept diminishes as its extension grows; if the latter becomes all-embracing, then the content must be lost entirely' (§29). His talk of *abstracting* concepts in §48 and of 'splitting up' content to yield new concepts in §64 also suggests an intensionalist view. Set against this, however, is the important n. to §68 (see §4.5), where Frege implies that he can refute the claim that concepts can have identical extensions without themselves coinciding. But he provides no argument for this in *GL*; and clarification of his views had to wait until the early 1890s.

3. This is the central objection raised by Benno Kerry, to whom *CO* was written as a response. Kerry was *Privatdozent* in philosophy at the University of Strasburg, and had written a series of articles in the *Vierteljahrsschrift für wissenschaftliche Philosophie* (in which *CO* also subsequently appeared), two of which, in particular, had criticized Frege's views in *GL* (cf. *PW*, p. 87, editors' n.).

4. See §4.1. The idea of an eliminative strategy only properly surfaced as such with the arrival of Russell's theory of descriptions in 1905. See the remark by Russell quoted in n. 37 to ch. 6. I return to the issue of Frege's non-eliminativism towards the end of §8.2.

5. The term 'concept-correlates' is taken from Wells, 1951: §12.

6. In *CSR*, for example, Frege talks of 'the *Bedeutung* of the expression "the concept *equilateral triangle*" ', but adds in parentheses 'if there is one in this case' (pp. 119-20).

7. See §6.2 in the case of identity statements; and §6.4 in the case of names.

8. On the importance of Axiom V, cf. *GG*, II, §147; quoted in §5.3. I have made minor revisions to the translation in *PMC*, to accord with the terminology I have adopted in this book.

9. As we suggested in ch. 5, the distinction between *Sinn* and *Bedeutung* was arguably intended to provide justification here, but it fails to do so.

10. Cf. *GG*, II, App.: 'Hardly anything more unfortunate can befall a scientific writer than to have one of the foundations of his edifice shaken after the work is finished. This was the position I was placed in by a letter of Mr. Bertrand Russell, just when the printing of this volume was nearing its completion. It is a matter of my Axiom (V). I have never disguised from myself its lack of the self-evidence that belongs to the other axioms and that must properly be demanded of a logical law. And so in fact I indicated this weak point in the Preface to Vol. I (p. vii). I should gladly have dispensed with this foundation if I had known of any substitute for it.' (*FRP*, p. 214.)

11. It is often thought that there are more extensions that do not fall under the concept whose extension they are than there are those that do (see e.g. Sainsbury, 1988: p. 109), but if we allow that for every 'positive' predicate there is a corresponding 'negative' predicate (e.g. 'horse' and 'non-horse'), then there are, of course, exactly the same number of each.

12. The more usual formulation of the paradox is given in terms of classes. A class either belongs to itself (e.g. the class of non-horses, or the class of classes) or does not belong to itself (e.g. the class of horses, or the class of non-classes). Consider now the class of all classes that do not belong to themselves. Does this class belong to itself or not? If it does, then it does not; and if it does not, then it does. Frege himself gives this alternative formulation in *GG*, II, App./ *FRP*, p. 215.

13. The point is not simply that Frege *quantifies* over numbers, which presupposes that they are objects of the domain, but that this is necessary in order to prove that there is an infinite sequence of natural numbers, i.e. that every natural number has a successor. As explained in §4.3, each number is defined in terms of the set of its predecessors – def. (Nn+1) – and it is this definition that implies that every number has a successor. For detailed discussion, see Dummett, 1991a: pp. 131-40.

14. The two most controversial axioms were the axiom of infinity and the axiom of reducibility. The former, stating that there are infinitely many objects in the universe, had had to be introduced since Russell had rejected the (Fregean) view that classes were objects and his theory of types had blocked the unrestricted formation of classes of classes (cf. Russell, *IMP*, ch. 13; Sainsbury, 1979: ch. 8, §5). The latter, stating that for any function there is a formally equivalent *predicative* function, had had to be introduced to *restore* some of what the theory of types had outlawed (cf. Russell, *PM*, pp. 55-60, 161-7; *IMP*, ch. 17; Sainsbury, 1979: ch. 8, §10). Neither axiom, as Russell himself accepted, could strictly count as a *logical* truth.

15. Cf. Russell, *MPD*, pp. 60-2; and on Cantor's paradox, see also e.g. Russell, *TTN*, pp. 138-9; *STC*, pp. 179-80. Russell himself reports that the theory of descriptions was his 'first success' in his resolution of the paradoxes (*MPD*, p. 60; cf. *ABR*, p. 155), but this oversimplifies the development of his views. Not only did he provide the first sketch of his theory of types in *POM*, as I go on to indicate, but he shortly afterwards also tried out rejecting classes altogether. Since this early attempt still generated a contradiction, however, he returned to a realistic conception until his theory of descriptions convinced him of its dispensability. The development of Russell's solution to the paradox may be traced in the following works: *POM*, App. B; *TTN*; *STC*; *ISSL*; *MLTT*; *TLT*; *PM*, Introd.: ch. 2. I provide only the barest sketch here; but for further details, see Lackey, 1973: introd. to Part IV of Russell, *EA*; Sainsbury, 1979: ch. 8, §7; Kilmister, 1984: ch. 3; and esp. Grattan-Guinness, 1977.

16. See e.g. Russell, *PLA*, p. 253; *IMP*, p. 182; *LA*, p. 326.

17. If Ramsey (1925) is right, then the paradoxes should be divided into two groups, the logical and the semantic, the 'simple theory of types' being sufficient for solving the paradoxes of the first group (which includes Russell's own paradox), and the 'ramified theory of types' being required to resolve the semantic paradoxes. For detailed discussion, see Ramsey, 1925: ch. 2; Quine, 1963: §§34-5; Copi, 1971; and Sainsbury, 1979: ch. 8, §§6-9; 1988: ch. 5.

18. See Quine, 1955; Geach, 1956. Axiom V, as it stands, is inconsistent even in a domain of just one object – where that object is the extension of the concept '( ) is the extension of a concept under which it does not fall'. It is clear that (V_c') is consistent in a domain of just one object, since in the paradoxical case, that object is precisely what is excluded in the axiom. In such a domain, (V') only holds in a trivial sense.

19. The two truth-values are introduced as objects in *GG*, I, §2. For further discussion of the inconsistency in Frege's system, see Boolos, 1993; Clark, 1993; and esp. Dummett, 1991a: chs. 17-18; 1994.

20. The solution was first offered by Dummett, 1981a: pp. 216-17. Making use of the second-level predicate '( ) is something which everything either is or is not', (CHC) can then be legitimately expressed as 'A horse is something which everything either is or is not'. For further discussion of the paradox, see Diamond, 1979; 1984: §3; Dudman, 1976b: §2; Mendelsohn, 1981; Wiggins, 1984; Wright, 1983: ch. 1, §iv.

21. Clearly, what counts as a heap of X's will depend on what X is. A heap of rocks may require fewer rocks to be a heap than a heap of beans requires beans, which may in turn require fewer than a heap of sand requires grains of sand. So we should strictly speak of *rockheaps, beanheaps, sandheaps*, and so on. But since a paradox can be formulated whichever type of heap we take, I shall ignore this difference here.

22. Cf. Sainsbury, 1988: p. 26, where it is simply explained as follows: 'If two people differ in height by no more than 0.1 in., then both or neither are tall; if two collections of sand differ in number by at most one grain, then both or neither are heaps'.

23. *BS*, §27; see n. 40 to ch. 3.

24. It is hard to see how (NB) could be *false*, which would imply that there is a sharp dividing line and hence that the concept is not vague after all, which has led some people (e.g. Sainsbury, 1988: ch. 2) to reject the reasoning. But in rejecting the reasoning, modus ponens is not shown to be *false* either (how could it?), but rather, on the assumption of a degrees of truth theory (as favoured by Sainsbury), as simply inapplicable; though what we have is an *analogue* of modus ponens, which admits propositions with degrees of truth. 'Rejecting' is ambiguous between 'taking as false' and 'not taking at all', and the Sorites paradox precisely shows the importance of recognizing the latter notion. We can reject (NB), then, without taking it as false; it is simply that it too is inapplicable in certain cases. As I go on to show, the paradox can be defused by treating (NB) as *neither true nor false*. For a more formal account of what is essentially the intuitionistic solution to the Sorites paradox, see Mott, 1994. This is clearly not the place to consider all the possible responses to the paradox; but for an excellent survey and critique of the various solutions that have been offered, as well as a controversial defence of the 'Epistemic' view, which does treat (NB) as false, see Williamson, 1994.

25. Cf. Sainsbury, 1988: p. 33.

26. Sainsbury (1988: p. 31) defines the *positive extension* of a predicate as the set of objects that definitely possess the relevant property, the *negative extension* as the set of objects that definitely lack the property, and the *penumbra* as the set of objects that neither definitely possess nor definitely lack the property. A vague predicate is then one for which this last set is not empty. Of course, the notion of a *penumbra* is itself vague; but this does not mean that there are not clear penumbral and non-penumbral cases.

27. The second principle is the *principle of simplicity*, intended to rule out contextual definitions of the kind considered and rejected in *GL*. Definitions must *uniquely determine* the relevant object. See *GG*, II, §66.

28. This statement is essentially a reformulation of the paradox of analysis, transposed to the level of comparing definitions themselves. If the original definition is correct (i.e. complete), then any subsequent redefinition cannot be informative; and if any subsequent redefinition *is* informative, then the original definition cannot be correct. Frege himself remarks: 'If it is known, a definition is at least superfluous; if it is not known, it cannot serve for the purpose of definition. This is so obvious, and yet people sin against it so often!' (*GG*, II, §59/ *FDI*, p. 143.) What is noticeable here is the abandonment of his earlier conception of the fruitfulness of definitions (see esp. *GL*, §88; discussed in §5.2). This is a retrograde step; for the obvious response to Frege's critique is to argue (in this case inverting Frege's *Grundlagen* analogy) that in new contexts (e.g. moving from the natural to the rational numbers), original definitions can be reformulated to carve out new content within the same basic boundary lines.

29. Bell (1979: pp. 46-7) extends Frege's argument in a similar way to show that the domain must be widened to include *non-objects* as well! For, assuming that italic letters do range over all objects and not just numbers, we should surely make this explicit too:

if a is an object and b is an object then $a + b = b + a$.

But this can be transformed into the following:

if $a + b \neq b + a$ and a is an object, then b is not an object.

30. 'X has between 0 and 100 hairs on his head' can, of course, be analysed into a disjunction of 'elementary propositions' – 'Either X has 0 hairs on his head or X has 1 hair on his head ... or X has 100 hairs on his head'; whilst there is no unique truth-functional analysis of 'X is bald'. But again, there is no reason why the impossibility of such an analysis should necessarily imply that it lacks a truth-value on a particular occasion of use. This whole question occupied Wittgenstein in his own later critique of his *Tractatus* conception of elementary propositions and determinacy of sense; see esp. *PI*, §§65-108.

31. What is at issue here is the problem of *higher-order vagueness*. For recent discussion, see Hyde (1994) and Tye (1994).

32. Of course, the use of proper names, even those as unusual as 'Gottlob Frege', is contextually dependent as well; so there is no sharp division between names and demonstratives. But I return to this shortly.

33. Kaplan (1979) uses the term 'character' and Perry (1977) uses the term 'role'.

34. On 'timelessness', Frege writes: 'The present tense is used in two ways: first, in order to indicate a time; second, in order to eliminate any temporal restriction, where timelessness or eternity is part of the thought – consider for instance the laws of mathematics' (*T*, p. 358). I return to the issue of timelessness in the next section; but see esp. n. 57 below.

35. I discuss the criterion for sameness of thought involved here – which raises many problems, which I have deliberately glossed over in the way I have formulated the argument – in §8.1.

36. The analogy between proper names and indexicals is instructive here: in neither case can their sense be explained by a 'description theory'. Evans (1981) uses this as the basis of his critique of Perry (1977), a critique to which I am indebted in the present section.

37. The same applies to our use of other indexicals: described from a third person point of view, what John Perry realizes is that *he* is making the mess. But the fact that we can preserve the indexicality when moving from a first person to a third person perspective suggests that there is nothing essential about the *first person* perspective. As Frege himself argues, as we shall see, the 'same thought' can be captured from different perspectives by using different indexicals.

38. Cf. Evans, 1981: p. 86. Although the emphasis Evans places on the role of *keeping track* of objects represents a fundamental insight into the nature of thoughts, Evans does not, I think, appreciate the impulse to leave the realm of 'ordinary' indexicals that such tracking involves, an impulse which Frege himself felt, as I go on to show.

39. See e.g. Evans, 1981: §5; McGinn, 1983: ch. 5; Noonan, 1984: §3. McGinn notes an ambiguity in the first sentence here, between what he calls the 'AE thesis', which maintains that everyone has their own unique mode of presentation of themselves, and the 'EA thesis', which maintains that there is one mode of presentation shared by everyone who thinks about themselves. McGinn suggests that the text permits no decisive disambiguation (p. 60); but Frege's general conception of sense makes it perfectly clear that it could not have been the EA thesis that he had in mind, since if the reference of a term changes, then so too does the sense. An EA thesis might look plausible if *linguistic role* were involved, but this possibility is ruled out here by the talk of 'mode of presentation'. In any case, as I go on to argue, the question as to whether there is a primitive and irreducible sense of 'I' for each person should be separated from the question as to whether I-thoughts are communicable.

40. Evans writes: 'it is the inference from shareability to objectivity which is of paramount importance to Frege, rather than shareability itself. Since an unshareable thought can be perfectly objective – can exist and have a truth-value independently of anyone's entertaining it – there is no clash between what Frege says about 'I'-thoughts and this, undeniably central, aspect of his philosophy.' (1981: p. 89.) Evans admits that Frege does emphasize that thoughts must be graspable by more than one person, but suggests that this is merely 'a slight overstatement' of his position (ibid.).

41. See also e.g. *N*, p. 376: 'The being of a thought may also be taken to lie in the possibility of different thinkers' grasping the thought as one and the same thought.'

42. Ideas, according to Frege, include all the constituents of the inner world – sense-impressions, imaginings, sensations, feelings, moods, inclinations, wishes – except decisions (*T*, p. 360). Frege goes on to argue that *thoughts* are not ideas, but since decisions have been allowed to inhabit the inner world whilst not being ideas, the question must arise as to why thoughts are not treated in the same way. There are obvious similarities. Decisions, like thoughts, are not something we *have*; they are something we *make*, just as thoughts are something we *grasp*. So decisions too do not, strictly speaking, have an *owner*: they have a *maker*. Can I make someone else's decision for them? Can two people make the same decision? If the answer to these two questions is 'Yes', then, if Frege's argument concerning thoughts is right, decisions too must inhabit a different realm from ideas – the same realm as thoughts, or yet a 'fourth realm'?

43. Cf. *T*, pp. 360-3. Frege's argument here simply rehearses his earlier anti-psychologistic polemic, the concern now being with thoughts rather than numbers; cf. esp. *GL*, §§26-7; *GG*, I, p. xviii/ *BLA*, p. 16.

44. At the epistemological level, 'conceptual contents' might indeed have been regarded as 'thoughts', but since these were not, even at the time of *BS*, regarded as psychological entities, and the sense/reference distinction had not yet been drawn, their identity conditions would presumably have been dependent on those of 'states of affairs'. But the unclarity here is precisely what Frege's sense/reference distinction was intended to remove. I return to the issue in §8.1.

45. The crudity of Frege's views here should make us wary of seeing Frege as in any significant way a Kantian. Frege does not even allude to any of those difficulties in Kant's theory of the self – concerning the relationships between the noumenal self, the phenomenal self, and the transcendental unity of apperception, between inner and outer sense, and between the conflicting demands of Kant's theoretical and practical philosophy. The attempted resolution of these difficulties was precisely what gave rise to the great 19th-century tradition of German idealism, but Frege himself, having come to philosophy through mathematics and logic, remained largely outside this tradition. In his basic metaphysical outlook, Frege does not so much move forward from Kant as look backward to Plato.

46. In discussing the example of pain himself, Frege writes that 'not only a thing but also an idea may be a common object of thought for people who do not have the idea' (*T*, p. 367). On Frege's view (see n. 42 above), pain counts as an idea, and any idea that can be externally manifested is a legitimate object of thought. But such a conception is only plausible on the assumption that I infer that someone else is in pain on the basis of their behaviour by argument from analogy. I know from my own case that being in pain (i.e. having the idea of pain) results in the appropriate behaviour, and infer backwards in the case of other people. So at best, other people's ideas can only be *indirect* objects of thought. In fact, however, the argument from analogy is notoriously open to sceptical attack. I can never really *know* what someone else's ideas are; I can only *suppose* that they have similar ideas to me. To see the tension in Frege's account, we need only take the example of ideas of oneself. I might argue by analogy that the ideas that others have of themselves are similar to the idea that I have of myself; but Frege clearly thinks here that such an idea is unique and private. So why is it not the same for all ideas?

47. In 'Negation', after the remark quoted in n. 41 above, Frege goes on: 'In that case the fact that a thought had no being would consist in several thinkers' each associating with the sentence a sense of his own; this sense would in that case be a content of his particular consciousness, so that there would be no *common* sense that could be grasped by several people' (*N*, p. 376). This suggests that there *are* subjective senses, but ones that are actually to be identified with ideas (contents of consciousness). However, Frege should not really talk here of 'senses' at all; and he *is* explicit that there are no 'subjective thoughts' – they have no being.

48. As n. 46 should suggest, this assumption is actually problematic on Frege's account. Frege talks of the *probability* being 'very great, so great that it is in my opinion no longer distinguishable from certainty' (*T*, p. 368); but this would hardly be enough to satisfy the determined sceptic. Once again, what we have here is a very *pre-Kantian* (Cartesian/Humean) conception.

49. Care is needed in the formulation of this point. Thoughts, on Frege's view, are independent of any person *thinking* the thought, but on the conception of senses as modes of presentation (see §§6.3-6.4), some will certainly depend on the *existence* of a person or persons. The thought that Dr. Lauben is wounded, for example, cannot (arguably) be expressed if there is no such person as Dr. Lauben, but it is not necessary that *Dr. Lauben* give expression to the thought.

50. 'Self-subsistent' ('selbständig') was the term Frege used (esp. in *GL*) in characterizing numbers as objects. In 'Der Gedanke' he only uses the term to characterize *people* – as 'independent owners' ('selbständigen Träger') of ideas (*T*, p. 367). 'Unabhängig' is the term Frege uses instead to describe the independence of thoughts. But given his conception of a 'third realm' of thoughts, he clearly regards independence, of whatever kind, just as he did in the case of numbers, as implying 'self-subsistence'.

51. See the n. to the second sentence of the passage quoted (*T*, n. 8); and cf. *T*, p. 363, n. 7: 'A person sees a thing, has an idea, grasps or thinks a thought. When he grasps or thinks a thought he does not create it but only comes to stand in a certain relation to what already existed – a different relation from seeing a thing or having an idea.'

52. Frege goes on to deny that *sense-perceptions* are involved in thinking, which might initially seem to conflict with the claim that thinking involves ideas, but Frege has already made clear that sense-perceptions are not the only contents of consciousness (see n. 42 above), and he in fact argues that there must be some *non-sensible* contents that enable us to think thoughts (*T*, pp. 369-70).

53. This conception received its classic statement in Wittgenstein's *TLP*, which was influenced by Frege's antipsychologism – see esp. 4.11-4.116, 5.551-5.552. However, Frege's own view of thoughts does make psychological investigation more difficult, if not impossible, for thinking is seen as directed not towards the ordinary objects of the 'first realm' but to the timeless entities of a 'third realm'.

54. As Dummett remarks (1986: p. 253), what leads Frege astray here is the failure to recognize the distinction between the *object* and the *content* of a mental act, and the consequent assumption that thoughts, in being the contents of mental acts, are thereby the objects of mental acts. For an illustration of the importance of resisting the temptation to construe ways of thinking as relations to thoughts, see my 'Mistakes and Mismatches' (1987), which was a reply to Rudebusch (1985). I accept with Rudebusch (1987) that the clarification I offered represents a repudiation of Frege's own Platonistic tendencies, and I would be more hesitant now in calling it Fregean.

55. As I envisage these positions, Hume and Mach would count as phenomenalists, Leibniz and Kant as noumenalists, and Plato and Meinong as semainomenalists. My introduction of the term 'semainomenalism' is prompted by the ancient Stoic conception of *semainomena* – the things signified or expressed by words, of which the most important were *lekta*, which, as we suggested in §1.5, can be seen as distant ancestors of Fregean *thoughts* (for refs., see n. 30 to ch. 1). For attempts to play down Frege's semainomenalism, see Sluga, 1977, 1980; Ricketts, 1986; Weiner, 1990: chs. 4-5; all of whom are criticized by Burge, 1992, who provides a fairer account, I think, of the role of Platonism in Frege's philosophy.

56. The similarities to Leibniz's philosophy are striking here. On a Leibnizian view, there is a sense too in which contingent truths are *made necessary* by 'cashing out' their implicit indexicality – in particular, their relativization to the actual world. According to Leibniz, the truth expressed by 'Caesar crossed the Rubicon' is contingent because it is only a truth of the actual world; but his essentialism suggests that the statement 'In the actual world, Caesar crossed the Rubicon' comes out as necessary. The crossing by Caesar of the Rubicon is an essential part of the actual world: the actual world would not be that world if that event had not happened. In choosing to actualize our world, as the best of all possible worlds, God must presumably himself have had 'timeless' thoughts (since he was outside the realm of the indexical). But the issues here are controversial in

Leibnizian scholarship; for discussion, see Mates, 1986: chs. 4-8; Ishiguro, 1990: ch. 9.

57. Although Frege himself uses the terms 'timeless' (*'zeitlos'*) and 'eternal' (*'ewig'*) synonymously (see e.g. *T*, pp. 358, 370), they should really be distinguished (in the same way as 'necessary' and 'universal' should be distinguished). To say that a truth is *eternal* is to say that it is true at all times, whereas to say that a truth is *timeless* is to deny that it makes sense to say that it is true at any time. '3 is a prime number', for example, expresses a timeless, not an eternal, truth. It makes as little sense to say that it is true at a certain time as to say that it is true at a certain place or for a certain person: it is true independently of when or where or by whom it is said. So it equally makes no sense to say that it is true at *all* times. 'The world exists', on the other hand, arguably expresses an eternal but not a timeless truth: if time itself came into existence with the big bang, and depends on (change in) the world, then the statement is indeed true at all times. Carruthers (1984) provides a powerful critique of the conception of *eternal thoughts*, but wrongly dismisses the view that it was timelessness rather than eternity (as just distinguished) that Frege really meant. As we have just seen, the key point about Frege's conception of thoughts is that any 'complete' expression involves cashing out all indexicality, and this applies to 'eternal' thoughts as well. The truth expressed by 'The world exists', for example, is only 'eternal' at the temporal level; more fully articulated, e.g. by 'The world exists at all times', its timelessness, at the transcendent level, becomes evident. But this is not to say, of course, as I go on to argue, that the conception of *timeless* thoughts is any less problematic. For if thoughts are indeed timeless, then how can they be *grasped*, something that does occur *at* times?

58. As mentioned in n. 46 above, Frege did claim that someone else's ideas were legitimate objects of thought, so that he would presumably argue that I *can* know whether someone else grasps the thought I express. But it is not at all obvious that Frege is entitled to the underlying claim.

8. The Crystallization of Sense

1. To specify a criterion in terms of *provable* material equivalence is to allow different notions of 'logical content' depending on the logical system within which the proofs are given. But since Frege himself thought that there was only *one* correct system of logic, this would not have been perceived as a problem by him. We should also note that such a criterion does not provide for the 'content' of the axioms and definitions upon which proof depends – just as Frege's criterion for analyticity did not so provide. Proof may also require formalization, and no criterion is provided here either for judging the legitimacy of the formalizations. On the notion of 'logical content', cf. Salmon (1992), who also advocates a three-way distinction, though his own discussion is not rooted in the detailed historical account that is needed to properly elucidate the source of the distinction in Frege's work.

2. Even this is not uncontroversial; see §8.2.

3. I ignore here the complication introduced by Frege's conception of indirect senses; on which see §6.5.

4. Van Heijenoort (1977a, 1977b) has also been concerned with the lack of any precise definition of Frege's conception of *Sinn*, and also discusses the two passages just quoted, though he appears not to appreciate the qualifications that I go on to note (see the last few lines of 1977b: p. 105). On the tension, cf. also Currie, 1982a; Simons, 1992a; Picardi, 1993.

5. See e.g. *PWLB*, p. 141; *PMC*, pp. 80, 153. Evans (1982: pp. 18-19) refers to these passages in offering his own criterion for sense, which may account for the inadequacy of that criterion. Evans fails to appreciate the problems surrounding its application to logical propositions that I go on to discuss.

6. This may be charitable. As we saw in §2.5, Frege's criterion for sameness of 'conceptual content' in *BS* was also open to the objection that all logical truths turn out to possess the same 'content', and whilst Frege drops this early notion of 'content', he never explicitly rejects it for this reason.

7. A simple modification of (SEE) might be offered to take care of this – that anyone who recognizes the content of one as true must *thereby* immediately recognize the content of the other as true. But see n. 13 below. In his last published paper, *CT*, Frege does raise the question as to whether 'If *A*, then *A*', for example, has a 'content' at all, and gives an ambivalent answer (p. 405); but it is clear that he did not pursue the line later taken by Wittgenstein in *TLP* in regarding all logical truths as having the same cognitive status, namely, as all being *senseless*.

8. As noted in n. 6 above, however, Frege never explicitly remarks on the similarly inconsistent implications of his criterion for sameness of 'content' in *BS*, though the notion of 'content' is indeed later officially dropped. But this is not to say, as the formulations of (SLE) and (SEE) show, that the term 'content' ('Inhalt') is never again used; and it arguably *is* intended to refer to the *thought* expressed by a proposition (i.e. whatever it is that is judged to be true). I return to this shortly.

9. Of course, if there are doubts about whether something is self-evident, then it cannot *be* self-evident – unless we can suggest that it has not been properly understood, which, as we shall see, is a line that might be taken.

10. Formulating the first criterion like this brings the notion of sense much closer to the notion of *Bedeutung*, which only reinforces the argument offered in §6.2, that Frege's arguments underdetermine what is to count as the *Bedeutung* of a sentence. The obvious alternative would have been to take *Bedeutung* as semantic sense, leaving the notion of epistemic sense to account for informativeness.

11. For a similar criterion, see Dummett, 1991a: p. 171. Dummett stresses the importance of 'immediate recognition' here; and in the light of the point made in n. 7 above, we might also stress the importance of immediately recognizing the second proposition as true *if* the first is recognized as true, i.e. that the second must be recognized as true *in virtue of* recognizing the first as true. Being offered an epistemic rather than semantic conception of sense brings us back full circle to Aristotle. As we saw in §1.4, Aristotle regarded *Eab* and *Eba* as 'identical' because the transition from one to the other was immediate, whereas the transition from *Iab* to *Iba* required mediation by the first rule of conversion.

12. On the significance of this point, see Bell, 1994: pp. 158-61. However, as I suggest in §8.4, what is wrong is not so much the introduction of abstract objects as the assumption that such objects are 'independent'.

13. Even this qualification may be inadequate. Take, for example, the two sums '280984 + 210288 = 491272' and '280985 + 210288 = 491273'. Neither is self-evident, yet I can immediately recognize that one is true if I recognize that the other is true (since the sum only differs by one). In response, it might be argued that there is *no* immediate recognition here – that some kind of *working out* is still required, however simple it may be. But this threatens to overly limit the possible cases of 'immediate recognition', making the criterion useless. Perhaps we should rule out the application of the criterion to *all* logical and arithmetical truths; but we would then be left with no specification of a notion of sense relevant to Frege's logicism. However, even this restriction fails to remove all possible counterintuitive implications. Consider the series of propositions generated by *conceptual ascent*, as elucidated in §5.3 – e.g. (Da), (Dc), (Df), ..., which are not themselves logical truths. Frege would regard all these as expressing the same sense; yet whilst I may be able to immediately recognize that (Dc) is true if I recognize that (Da) is true, and that (Df) is true if I recognize that (Dc) is true, I may need to *work out* that (Df) is true if (Da) is true, i.e. by going through (Dc). What this points to, of course, is a general problem with the appeal to 'immediate recognition', a problem which underlies Sorites paradoxes. I may perceive *a* and *b* to be the same, and *b* and *c* to be the same, but not perceive *a* and *c* to be the same. Transitivity thus fails, and we are left with a context-dependent notion of identity. I return to the issue in §8.4.

14. Cf. Dummett, 1991a: pp. 171-2. The problem is acute if we accept what Dummett (1981b: ch. 17) has called the *transparency* of thought: I cannot grasp the thoughts expressed by two propositions without knowing whether they are the same or not. But consider, for example, 'No philosophers are logicians' and 'No logicians are philosophers' (cf. §2.5). On first being asked, many people, who 'understand' the sentences perfectly well, do *not* 'immediately recognize' that these express the same thought. Have they therefore failed to grasp that thought?

15. I formulate the principle here in terms of 'content' rather than 'meaning', which is what is more often used. What Frege in fact says is that the 'Bedeutung' of a word is dependent on the 'Sinn' of a sentence, but he also uses both these terms in *GL* synonymously with 'Inhalt'.

16. I have found just two occasions where Frege later appeals to contextual considerations. In *WF* (p. 110), he remarks that the expression 'the number *n*' 'must be considered in a context'; and in *FGII* (p. 306), in relation to the use of letters in mathematics, he writes: 'it is only in the context of a proposition that they have a certain task to fulfil, that they are to contribute to the expression of the thought. But outside of this context, they say nothing.' But Frege's concern is with schematic letters, which, like the syncategorematic terms recognized by traditional logicians, do indeed have no meaning on their own. However, whilst the context principle, as it relates to names, is never again mentioned, there is an extent to which it continues to underlie Frege's logicist project, as we noted at the end of §5.3. Axiom V, in particular, encapsulates the assumed legitimacy of at least one kind of contextual definition. It has also been argued that the context principle informs Frege's notorious proof of referentiality in *GG*; but the issue is both complex and controversial. For discussion, see Parsons, 1965; Martin, 1982; Resnik, 1986; Moore & Rein, 1986; Dummett, 1981b: ch. 19; 1991a: chs. 17-18; 1995. In the present section, I am less concerned with the role of the context principle in Frege's logicist project than with the apparent tension between his contextualism and compositionalism as it relates to the issue of analysis.

17. Another reason that the context principle could not be reformulated again in relation to *Bedeutung* is that in conceiving the *Bedeutung* of a sentence as its truth-value, Frege thereby conceives the sentence itself as a name – referring to the object that is the truth-value. For criticism of the assimilation of sentences to names, see esp. Dummett, 1981a: chs. 12, 19; Sullivan, 1994. On the technical side, the issue relates to Frege's proof of referentiality mentioned in the previous n.

18. The first sentence of the passage quoted is not to be taken to suggest that concepts are parts of thoughts, arrived at by dividing up thoughts. It is the *senses* of concept expressions that Frege regards as parts of thoughts; though what role concepts themselves then play is left mysterious. See §7.1; and for further discussion of Frege's understanding of concepts, see Dummett, 1981a: chs. 7-8; 1981b: chs. 8, 13.

19. Cf. *LM*, p. 225. I return shortly to the sentence omitted from the quotation from *CT*, a sentence which does not correspond to anything in *LM*.

20. That Frege is the founder of modern semantic theory has been the message of Dummett's work, in particular. But in its application to ordinary language, truth-conditional semantics was only developed by Wittgenstein in *TLP*. On the recognition of 'linguistic creativity', cf. Wittgenstein, *TLP*, 4.002. It is tempting to speculate on the possible relationship between Frege and Wittgenstein here. We know that they met in the period 1911-12 (see Wittgenstein, *LR*, p.17/ *NB*, p. 121; cf. McGuinness, 1988: pp. 73-6, 164) and corresponded from 1913 to 1920 (see Frege, *WB*, pp. 264-8; *BLW*). Frege does not himself express his astonishment about what language can do until 1914 (when *LM* was composed), and the assumed isomorphism between thought and language, which is fundamental to Wittgenstein's early philosophy, is arguably an aberration on Frege's part, given his lifelong conviction that ordinary language is inherently deficient. So did Wittgenstein prompt Frege into saying something in conflict with his deeper beliefs?

21. Cf. Wittgenstein's conception of simple objects in *TLP*, which also cannot exist outside states of affairs. Wittgenstein endorses the context principle at 3.3.

22. See e.g. *CT*, his last published paper, where the doctrine is extended to propositional connectives (pp. 390-1), and *PMC*, p. 55, his last recorded letter.

23. Dummett, 1981b: ch. 17; cf. 1989: §2.

24. It is at this point that Frege's use of the Greek letters as argument place-holders becomes significant, for the order of the variables is relevant in the specification of a relation, just as it is if represented as '*Rab*'.

25. My own conjecture is that Frege, had he realized the need for a paper 'On Relation and Object', would have regarded (HLC) and (CHH) as concerned with the same relation, it being a deficiency of language (though presumably not just of ordinary language here) that they can be represented either as '*Rab*' or '*R'ba*'. Even if criteria of identity for relations are given, extensionally, in terms of sets of ordered pairs, then since each pair is ordered the other way for the inverse relation, the problem remains. However, since Frege would presumably have regarded the transition from *Rab* to *R'ba* as 'immediate' (if we understand the notion of an inverse relation at all), he would have taken them as expressing the same *sense*, and hence *a fortiori* as having the same reference.

26. See esp. Dummett, 1989; a reply to Bell, 1987.

27. *CO* is very much concerned with these worries (see §7.1 above); but the issue was regarded as a problem of ordinary language. Frege had no doubts that we could *think about* concepts being instantiated or not.

28. On the notion of a 'degenerative decomposition', cf. Dummett, 1981b: ch. 15, pp. 288-90.

29. As suggested in n. 13, this raises a problem for Frege's criterion for sameness of sense. There are obvious similarities with Frege's method for generating the natural numbers, yet in spinning them all out (quite literally!) from *nothing*, he clearly did think that 'content' can be added in the process.

30. This was indeed in response to just those difficulties that Frege's system generated. Cf. ch. 6, n. 37; ch. 7, nn. 4, 15.

31. This is essentially why Axiom V, asserting the equivalence of (Va) and (Vb), had to be explicitly formulated as an axiom; see §§5.3, 5.5, 7.2 above.

32. A similar modification of (TIS) is, of course, trivial.

33. In his later work, with the distinction between *Sinn* and *Bedeutung* in place, the principle, more precisely, becomes one concerning the logical priority of thoughts over the *senses* of concept words.

34. Had *Bedeutung* been taken as semantic sense, understood as in Wittgenstein's *Tractatus* as the possible state of affairs pictured, then there would indeed be dependence. Cf. n. 21 above.

35. Frege himself suggests this three paragraphs later; quoted in §7.5 above. I return to this shortly.

36. As noted in n. 54 to ch. 7, a distinction is often drawn between the *object* and the *content* of a mental act; but I am here mapping this onto the distinction between 'content' and the thought itself, respectively.

37. If it did, then the whole of this book would be invalidated, since I have been attempting to explain in English ideas and beliefs that Frege himself expressed in German! Since Kripke (1979), in particular, however, doubts have been raised about whether it *is* possible, at least in certain cases, to capture, in a different language, the thought that someone expresses by the use of a sentence. But I am far from convinced that the Fregean can make no response to Kripke's own puzzle; cf. Taschek, 1988.

38. 'Beleuchtung' or 'Färbung' are the terms that Frege uses. For refs., see introd., n. 11.

39. The thesis that language has logical priority over thought has often been regarded as characteristic of analytic philosophy, but in recent years has come under increasing attack. The interpretation of Frege has been at the centre of the battleground, as the dispute between Dummett and Evans shows; see esp. Dummett, 1988. Although his ideas lend themselves to the language-first camp – as their development in the work of Wittgenstein and Dummett, in particular, shows – Frege should perhaps be regarded more as a philosopher of thought than as a philosopher of language, to use Dummett's own distinction (1981b: ch. 2). Dummett has argued that being the former amounts to being the latter, but given Frege's hostility to ordinary language, qualifications are needed here. Although Frege is undoubtedly sensitive to problems of language, as we have seen in this book, it would certainly be wrong to call him a philosopher of ordinary language. Cf. §0.2 above.

40. Cf. *CO*, pp. 42-3; *GG*, I, p. 4 (*TPW*, p. 131/ *BLA*, p. 32); and esp. *LM*, p. 207; *PMC*, pp. 36-7. Cf. also Wittgenstein, *TLP*, 3.263.

41. For a useful short account of the 'chemical revolution', upon which I have drawn here, see Perrin, 1990.

42. Ordinary speech is, in fact, quite resistant to scientific advance. Think, for example, of our continuing to say 'The sun rises in the east', even though science shows that it is strictly speaking false (in so far as it presupposes an outdated model of the heavens). But as Leibniz remarked, a Copernican can rightly speak of the rising of the sun, providing this is 'sanely understood' (*ENS*, §12). A correct analysis, then, need not change what we actually *say*.

43. Such a response might be seen as lending support to a *structuralist* view of arithmetic. Dedekind (1888) and Benacerraf (1965), in their different ways, offer a structuralist view. For discussion of these, see Dummett, 1991a: chs. 5, 23.

44. As Cantor showed, there is *no* one-one correlation between the set of natural numbers, whose cardinality Cantor denoted by '$\aleph_0$', and the set of real numbers, which led him to assign the next transfinite number, $\aleph_1$, to the latter set. Cf. §3.1 above.

45. There were, of course, important differences between Frege's and the early Wittgenstein's conceptions of logic, which we might characterize by saying that whilst, for Frege, logic was *transcendent*, in its relation to ordinary language, for

Wittgenstein, logic was *immanent*. Although Wittgenstein remarked in *TLP* that 'All philosophy is a "critique of language" ' (4.0031), he also insisted that 'all the propositions of our everyday language, just as they stand, are in perfect logical order' (5.5563), the point being that this logical order is only revealed as such when the propositions have been fully analysed. But Wittgenstein nevertheless believed in the absoluteness of the (Fregean) logic that was seen as underlying ordinary language.

46. For Wittgensten's own distinction between 'describing' and 'explaining', see e.g. *PI*, §§109, 120, 124-6. I do not, however, see what I have been doing here as *incompatible* with Wittgenstein's 'descriptive philosophy', since by 'explanation' Wittgenstein generally meant 'logical justification'. But as I argued in the introduction, what is needed is a more *historical* form of philosophizing (*diachronically* and not just *synchronically* 'descriptive philosophy'), which can be seen as furthering Wittgenstein's project of demythologizing our conception of logic by embedding and developing his insights in the richer framework of an historical narrative.

Bibliography

This bibliography contains all works referred to in the text (except in a small number of minor cases, where details can be found in other works referred to in the same context), by either year of publication or abbreviation, as indicated below in parentheses immediately after the name(s). Included is a full list, arranged chronologically, of all Frege's works published in English, though only those pieces referred to in the text are specifically picked out from the collections in which they are contained. Unless otherwise indicated, references given in the text are to the relevant publication (edition, collection or translation) *first* named in the bibliography. Where the reference is solely to the original German edition of a work, or the reference to an English translation is omitted (as in the case of Frege's *Begriffsschrift*, *Grundlagen* and *Grundgesetze*, in particular), any translations are my own (in the latter case, the translations are taken from my forthcoming *Frege Reader*).

Ackrill, J.L. (1981), *Aristotle the Philosopher* (OUP)

Allison, Henry E. (1983), *Kant's Transcendental Idealism* (Yale Univ. Press)

Ambrose, Alice (1959), 'Proof and the Theorem Proved', in Ambrose (1966), pp. 13-25; orig. in *Mind* 1959

———, (1966), *Essays in Analysis* (George Allen & Unwin)

Angell, R.B. (1986), 'Truth-Functional Conditionals and Modern vs. Traditional Syllogistic', *Mind* 95, pp. 210-23

Aristotle, *Categories* and *De Interpretatione*, tr. J.L. Ackrill (OUP, 1963)

———, *Prior Analytics*, tr. H. Tredennick, Loeb Classical Library, vol. 1 (Harvard/Heinemann, 1938); tr. R. Smith (Hackett, Indianapolis, 1989); also tr. A.J. Jenkinson, *The Works of Aristotle Translated into English*, vol. 1 (OUP, 1928)

———, *Posterior Analytics*, tr. J. Barnes (OUP, 1975)

———, *Topics*, tr. W.A. Pickard-Cambridge, *The Works of Aristotle Translated into English*, vol. 1 (OUP, 1928)

———, *Sophistici elenchi*, tr. E.S. Forster, Loeb Classical Library, vol. 3 (Harvard/Heinemann, 1955)

———, *Metaphysics*, tr. W.D. Ross, *The Works of Aristotle Translated into English*, vol. 8 (OUP, 1908, 1928); Books Γ, Δ, and also tr. C. Kirwan (OUP, 1971)

———, *Nicomachean Ethics*, tr. W. David Ross, rev. J.L. Ackrill & J.O. Urmson (OUP, 1980)

Ayer, A.J. (1971), *Russell and Moore: The Analytical Heritage* (Macmillan)

Ayers, Michael (1978), 'Analytical Philosophy and the History of Philosophy', in Rée, Ayers & Westoby, pp. 41-66

Baker, G.P. & Hacker, P.M.S. (1984), *Frege: Logical Excavations* (Blackwell)

Baldwin, Thomas (1990), *G.E. Moore* (Routledge)

Bar-Hillel, Yehoshua (1965), ed., *Logic, Methodology, and Philosophy of Science* (North-Holland, Amsterdam)

338 Bibliography

Barnes, Jonathan (1975a), 'Aristotle's Theory of Demonstration', in Barnes et al. (1975), pp. 65-87
———, (1980), 'Proof Destroyed', in Schofield et al. (1980), pp. 161-81
———, (1987), ed., *Early Greek Philosophy* (Penguin)
Barnes, J., Schofield, M. & Sorabji, R. (1975), eds., *Articles on Aristotle*, vol. 1: Science (Duckworth)
———, (1979), eds., *Articles on Aristotle*, vol. 3: Metaphysics (Duckworth)
Barwise, Jon & Perry, John (1983), *Situations and Attitudes* (MIT Press)
Beaney, Michael (1987), 'Mistakes and Mismatches: a Reply to Rudebusch', *Mind* 96, pp. 95-8
———, (*FR*), ed., *The Frege Reader* (Blackwell, forthcoming 1997; see also under Frege, *FR*)
Beck, Lewis W. (1967), 'Can Kant's Synthetic Judgments Be Made Analytic?', in Wolff (1967), pp. 3-22; orig. publ. in *Kant-Studien* 47 (1955-6), pp. 168-81
Bell, David (1979), *Frege's Theory of Judgement* (OUP)
———, (1987), 'Thoughts', *Notre Dame J. Formal Logic* 28, pp. 36-50
———, (1990), 'How "Russellian" Was Frege?', *Mind* 99, pp. 267-77
———, (1994), 'Objects and Concepts', *Proc. Aris. Soc. Supp.* 68, pp. 149-66
Bell, D. & Cooper, N. (1990), eds., *The Analytic Tradition* (Blackwell)
Benacerraf, Paul (1965), 'What numbers could not be', in Benacerraf & Putnam, pp. 272-94; orig. in *Phil. Rev.* 1965, pp. 47-73
———, (1981), 'Frege: The Last Logicist', in French et al., pp. 17-35
Benacerraf, P. & Putnam, H. (1983), eds., *Philosophy of Mathematics*, 2nd ed. (CUP)
Bennett, Jonathan (1966), *Kant's Analytic* (CUP)
Berkeley, George, (*NTV*) *An Essay towards a New Theory of Vision*, 4th ed. (1732; 1st ed. 1709), in *BPW*
———, (*PHK*) *A Treatise Concerning the Principles of Human Knowledge*, 2nd ed. (1734; 1st ed. 1710), in *BPW*
———, *The Analyst* (Dublin and London, 1734)
———, (*BPW*) *Philosophical Works*, ed. M.R. Ayers (J.M. Dent & Sons Ltd, London, 1975)
Black, M. (1965), ed., *Philosophy in America* (George Allen & Unwin, London)
Boole, George (1847), *The Mathematical Analysis of Logic* (Cambridge and London); repr. in *Studies in Logic and Probability*, ed. R. Rhees (Watts & Co., London, 1952)
———, (1854), *The Laws of Thought* (London and Cambridge); repr. as *Collected Logical Works*, vol. 2 (Open Court, Chicago & London, 1940)
Boolos, George (1993), 'Basic Law (V)', *Proc. Aris. Soc. Supp.* 67, pp. 213-33
Bostock, David (1974), *Logic and Arithmetic: Natural Numbers* (OUP)
Brunschwig, Jacques (1980), 'Proof Defined', in Schofield et al. (1980), pp. 125-60
Burge, Tyler (1979), 'Sinning against Frege', *Phil. Rev.* 1979, pp. 398-432
———, (1984), 'Frege on Extensions of Concepts, from 1884 to 1903', *Phil. Rev.* 1984, pp. 3-34
———, (1986), 'Frege on Truth', in Haaparanta & Hintikka, pp. 97-154
———, (1990), 'Frege on Sense and Linguistic Meaning', in Bell & Cooper, pp. 30-60
———, (1992), 'Frege on Knowing the Third Realm', *Mind* 101, pp. 633-50
Bynum, Terrell Ward (1972a), 'On the Life and Work of Gottlob Frege', in Frege, *CN*, pp. 1-54
———, (1972b), 'Editor's Introduction', in Frege, *CN*, pp. 55-80

Cantor, Georg (1883), 'Grundlagen einer allgemeinen Mannichfaltigkeitslehre', *Mathematische Annalen* 21, pp. 545-91; repr. in *GA*

——, (*GA*) *Gesammelte Abhandlungen: mathematischen und philosophischen Inhalts*, ed. E. Zermelo (Berlin, 1932)

Carl, Wolfgang (1994), *Frege's Theory of Sense and Reference* (CUP)

Carnap, Rudolf (1937), *The Logical Syntax of Language* (Harcourt, New York)

Carruthers, Peter (1984), 'Eternal Thoughts', in Wright (1984), pp. 1-19

Church, Alonzo (1965), 'The history of the question of existential import of categorical propositions', in Bar-Hillel (1965), pp. 417-24

Clark, Michael (1980), *The Place of Syllogistic in Logical Theory* (Nottingham Univ. Press)

Clark, Peter (1993), 'Basic Law (V)', *Proc. Aris. Soc. Supp.* 67, pp. 235-49

Cocchiarella, Nina (1986), 'Frege, Russell and Logicism: A Logical Reconstruction', in Haaparanta & Hintikka, pp. 197-252

Cohen, L. Jonathan (1954), 'On the Project of a Universal Character', *Mind* 63, pp. 49-63

Collingwood, R.G. (1933), *Essay on Philosophical Method* (OUP)

——, (1946), *The Idea of History* (OUP; rev. ed. 1993)

Copi, Irving M. (1971), *The Theory of Logical Types* (London)

Corcoran, John (1974), ed., *Ancient Logic and its Modern Interpretations* (D. Reidel, Holland)

——, (1974a), 'Aristotle's Natural Deduction System', in Corcoran (1974), pp. 85-131

Craig, Edward (1987), *The Mind of God and the Works of Man* (OUP)

Currie, Gregory (1976), 'Was Frege a Linguistic Philosopher?', *Brit. J. Phil. Sc.* 27, pp. 79-92

——, (1978), 'Frege's Realism', *Inquiry* 21, pp. 218-21

——, (1981), 'The Origin of Frege's Realism', *Inquiry* 24, pp. 448-54

——, (1982), *Frege: An Introduction to his Philosophy* (Harvester)

——, (1982a), 'Frege, Sense and Mathematical Knowledge', *Aus. J. Phil.* 60, pp. 5-19

——, (1983), 'Interpreting Frege: A Reply to Michael Dummett', *Inquiry* 26, pp. 345-59

——, (1984), 'Frege's Metaphysical Argument', in Wright (1984), pp. 144-57

——, (1986), 'Continuity and Change in Frege's Philosophy of Mathematics', in Haaparanta & Hintikka, pp. 345-73

Davidson, Donald (1967), 'Truth and Meaning', in Davidson (1984), pp. 17-36; orig. in *Synthese* 17, pp. 304-23

——, (1984), *Inquiries into Truth and Interpretation* (OUP)

Davies, Martin (1981), *Meaning, Quantification, Necessity* (Routledge)

Dedekind, R. (1872), *Continuity and Irrational Numbers*, tr. W. Beman, in *ETN*

——, (1888), *Was sind und was sollen die Zahlen?*, tr. W. Beman, in *ETN*

——, (*ETN*) *Essays on the Theory of Numbers*, ed. & tr. W. Beman (Dover, New York, 1963; orig. publ. 1901)

Descartes, (*RDM*) *Rules for the Direction of the Mind*, in *PWD*, vol. 1

——, (*PP*) *Principles of Philosophy*, in *PWD*, vol. 1

——, (*OR*) *Objections and Replies*, in *PWD*, vol. 2

——, (*DL*) *Letters*, in *PWD*, vol. 3

——, (*PWD*) *The Philosophical Writings of Descartes*, 3 vols., tr. J. Cottingham, R. Stoothof, D. Murdoch & A. Kenny (CUP, vol. 1 1985, vol. 2 1984, vol. 3 1991)

Diamond, Cora (1979), 'Frege and Nonsense', in Diamond & Teichman, pp. 195-218

——, (1984), 'What does a Concept Script do?', in Wright (1984), pp. 158-83
Diamond, C. & Teichman, J. (1979), eds., *Intention and Intentionality* (Harvester)
Dudman, Victor H. (1976a), 'From Boole to Frege', in Schirn (1976), vol. 1, pp. 109-38
——, (1976b), *'Bedeutung* for Predicates', in Schirn (1976), vol. 3, pp. 71-84
Dummett, Michael (1955), 'Frege on Functions: A Reply', *Phil. Rev.* 64, pp. 96-107; repr. in Klemke (1968), pp. 268-83
——, (1975), 'Frege's Distinction between Sense and Reference', in Dummett (1978), pp. 116-43; also in Moore (1992), pp. 228-56
——, (1976), 'Frege as a Realist', in Dummett (1991b), pp. 79-96; orig. in *Inquiry* 19, pp. 455-68
——, (1978), *Truth and Other Enigmas* (Duckworth)
——, (1981a), *Frege: Philosophy of Language*, 2nd ed. (Duckworth; 1st ed. 1973)
——, (1981b), *The Interpretation of Frege's Philosophy* (Duckworth)
——, (1981c), 'Frege's "Kernsätze zur Logik" ', in Dummett (1991b), pp. 65-78; orig. in *Inquiry* 24 (1981), pp. 439-48
——, (1982), 'Objectivity and Reality in Lotze and Frege', in Dummett (1991b), pp. 97-125; orig. in *Inquiry* 25 (1982), pp. 95-114
——, (1984), 'An Unsuccessful Dig', in Wright (1984), pp. 192-216; repr. in Dummett (1991b), pp. 158-98
——, (1986), 'Frege's Myth of the Third Realm', in Dummett (1991b), pp. 249-62); orig. in *Untersuchungen zur Logik und zur Methodologie* 3, pp. 24-38
——, (1987), 'Frege and the Paradox of Analysis', in Dummett (1991b), pp. 17-52
——, (1988), 'The Relative Priority of Thought and Language', in Dummett (1991b), pp. 315-24
——, (1989), 'More about Thoughts', in Dummett (1991b), pp. 289-314; orig. in *Notre Dame J. Formal Logic* 30, pp. 1-19
——, (1991a), *Frege: Philosophy of Mathematics* (Duckworth)
——, (1991b), *Frege and Other Philosophers* (OUP)
——, (1994), 'Chairman's Address: Basic Law V', *Proc. Aris. Soc.* 94 (1993-4), pp. 243-51; response to Boolos (1993) and Clark (1993)
——, (1995), 'The Context Principle: Centre of Frege's Philosophy', in Max & Stelzner, pp. 3-19
Evans, Gareth (1981), 'Understanding Demonstratives', in Evans (1985), pp. 291-321; also in Yourgrau (1990), pp. 71-96; orig. in Parret & Bouveresse
——, (1982), *The Varieties of Reference*, ed. John McDowell (OUP)
——, (1985), *Collected Papers* (OUP)
Everson, Stephen (1994), ed., *Language: Companions to Ancient Thought 3* (CUP)
Frede, Michael (1987), *Essays in Ancient Philosophy* (OUP)
——, (1987a), 'Stoic vs. Aristotelian Syllogistic', in Frede (1987), pp. 99-124
——, (1987b), 'Principles of Stoic Grammar', in Frede (1987), pp. 301-37; orig. in Rist (1978), pp. 27-75
——, (1987c), 'The Origins of Traditional Grammar', in Frede (1987), pp. 338-59
——, (1994), 'The Stoic notion of a *lekton*', in Everson (1994), pp. 109-28
Frege, Gottlob, *(GR)* 'On a Geometrical Representation of Imaginary Forms in the Plane' (1873), in *CP*, pp. 1-55
——, *(MC)* 'Methods of Calculation based on an Extension of the Concept of Quantity [Magnitude]' (1874), in *CP*, pp. 56-92
——, *(RS)* 'Review of H. Seeger, *Die Elemente der Arithmetik*' (1874), in *CP*, pp. 93-4
——, *(KSL)* '[17 Key Sentences on Logic]' (1876/77), in *PW*, pp. 174-5
——, *(BS) Begriffsschrift, eine der arithmetischen nachgebildete Formelsprache*

des reinen Denkens (Halle: L. Nebert, 1879), tr. in *CN*, pp. 101-203; also tr. S. Bauer-Mengelberg, in van Heijenoort (1967), pp. 5-82; most of Part I (§§1-12) also tr. in *TPW*, pp. 1-20, and in *FR*

———, (*APCN*) 'Applications of the "Conceptual Notation" ' (1879), in *CN*, pp. 204-8

———, (*PWLA*) 'Logic' (1879 ... 1891), in *PW*, pp. 1-8

———, (*BLC*) 'Boole's logical Calculus and the Concept-script' (1880/81), in *PW*, pp. 9-46

———, (*BLF*) 'Boole's logical Formula-language and my Concept-script' (1882), in *PW*, pp. 47-52

———, (*SJCN*) 'On the Scientific Justification of a Conceptual Notation' (1882), in *CN*, pp. 83-89

———, (*ACN*) 'On the Aim of the "Conceptual Notation" ' (1882), in *CN*, pp. 90-100

———, (*DPE*) '[Dialogue with Pünjer on Existence]' (< 1884), in *PW*, pp. 53-67

———, (*GL*) *Die Grundlagen der Arithmetik, eine logisch mathematische Untersuchung über den Begriff der Zahl* (Breslau: W. Koebner, 1884), tr. as (*FA*) *The Foundations of Arithmetic* by J.L. Austin, with German text, 2nd ed. (Blackwell, 1953; 1st ed. 1950); selections also tr. in *FR*

———, (*RHC*) 'Review of H. Cohen, *Das Prinzip der Infinitesimal-Methode und seine Geschichte*' (1885), in *CP*, pp. 108-11

———, (*FTA*) 'On Formal Theories of Arithmetic' (1885), in *CP*, pp. 112-21

———, (*OLI*) 'On the Law of Inertia' (1891), in *CP*, pp. 123-36

———, (*FC*) 'Function and Concept' (1891), in *TPW*, pp. 21-41; also in *CP*, pp. 137-56; and in *FR*

———, (*OCN*) 'On the Concept of Number' (1891/92), in *PW*, pp. 72-86

———, (*CO*) 'On Concept and Object' (1892), in *TPW*, pp. 42-55; also in *PW*, pp. 87-117; in *CP*, pp. 182-94; and in *FR*

———, (*SR*) 'On Sense and Meaning [Reference]' (1892), in *TPW*, pp. 56-78; also in *CP*, pp. 157-77; and in *FR*

———, (*RGC*) 'Review of Georg Cantor, *Zur Lehre vom Transfiniten*' (1892), in *CP*, pp. 178-81

———, (*CSR*) '[Comments on Sense and Meaning [Reference]]' (1892-1895), in *PW*, pp. 118-25; also in *FR*

———, (*GG*) *Grundgesetze der Arithmetik* (Jena: H. Pohle, Band I 1893, Band II 1903; repr. together, Hildesheim: Georg Olms, 1962), Introd. & §§1-52 of vol. 1 tr. as (*BLA*) *The Basic Laws of Arithmetic: Exposition of the System*, tr. & ed. with an introd. by Montgomery Furth (Univ. of California Press, 1964); selections from both vols. also tr. in *TPW*; and in *FR*

———, (*RH*) 'Review of E.G. Husserl, *Philosophie der Arithmetik I*' (1894), in *CP*, pp. 195-209; illustrative extracts also in *TPW*, pp. 79-85; extract also in *FR*

———, (*CES*) 'A Critical Elucidation of Some Points in E. Schröder, *Vorlesungen über die Algebra der Logik*' (1895), in *CP*, pp. 210-28; also in *TPW*, pp. 86-106

———, (*WN*) 'Whole Numbers' (1895), in *CP*, pp. 229-33

———, (*PWLB*) 'Logic' (1897), in *PW*, pp. 126-51; extract also in *FR*

———, (*PCN*) 'On Mr. Peano's Conceptual Notation and My Own' (1897), in *CP*, pp. 234-48

———, (*ASCN*) 'The Argument for my stricter Canons of Definition' (1897/98), in *PW*, pp. 152-6

———, (*SN*) 'On Mr. H. Schubert's Numbers' (1899), in *CP*, pp. 249-72

———, (*EG*) 'On Euclidean Geometry' (1899-1906?), in *PW*, pp. 167-9; extract also in *FR*

————, *(FDI)* 'Frege on Definitions – I' (*GG*, II, §§56-67; 1903), in *TPW*, pp. 139-52; also in *FR*

————, *(FDII)* 'Frege on Definitions – II' (*GG*, II, §§ 139-44, 146-7; 1903), in *TPW*, pp. 153-61; also in *FR*

————, *(FF)* 'Frege against the Formalists' (*GG*, II, §§86-137; 1903), in *TPW*, pp. 162-213

————, *(FRP)* 'Frege on Russell's Paradox' (*GG*, II, App. , pp. 253-65; 1903), in *TPW*, pp. 214-24; also in *FR*

————, *(FGI)* 'On the Foundations of Geometry: First Series' (1903), in *CP*, pp. 273-84; also in *FG*, pp. 22-37

————, *(WF)* 'What is a Function?' (1904), in *TPW*, pp. 107-16; also in *CP*, pp. 285-92

————, *(FGII)* 'On the Foundations of Geometry: Second Series' (1906), in *CP*, pp. 293-340; also in *FG*, pp. 49-112

————, *(SLPM)* 'On Schoenflies: *Die Logischen Paradoxien der Mengenlehre*' (1906), in *PW*, pp. 176-83

————, *(IL)* 'Introduction to Logic' (1906), in *PW*, pp. 185-96; extract also in *FR*

————, *(BSLD)* 'A brief Survey of my logical Doctrines' (1906), in *PW*, pp. 197-202; extract also in *FR*

————, *(RT)* 'Reply to Mr. Thomae's Holiday *Causerie*' (1906), in *CP*, pp. 341-45

————, *(LM)* 'Logic in Mathematics' (1914), in *PW*, pp. 203-50; extract also in *FR*

————, *(BLW)* 'Briefe an Ludwig Wittgenstein aus den Jahren 1914-1920', ed. A. Janik, in McGuinness & Haller, pp. 5-33

————, *(MBLI)* 'My basic logical Insights' (1915), in *PW*, pp. 251-2; also in *FR*

————, *(T)* 'Thoughts' (1918), Part I of *LI*, in *CP*, pp. 351-72, and in *FR*; also in Salmon & Soames, pp. 33-55; also tr. A.M. & M. Quinton, *Mind* 65 (1956), pp. 289-311, repr. in Strawson (1967), pp. 17-38, and in Klemke (1968), pp. 507-35

————, *(N)* 'Negation' (1918), Part II of *LI*, in *CP*, pp. 373-89; also in *FR*

————, *(NLD)* '[Notes for Ludwig Darmstaedter]' (1919), in *PW*, pp. 253-57; also in *FR*

————, *(CT)* 'Compound Thoughts' (1923), Part III of *LI*, in *CP*, pp. 390-406

————, *(LG)* 'Logical Generality' (> 1923), in *PW*, pp. 258-62

————, *(DECN)* '[Diary Entries on the Concept of Number]' (1924), in *PW*, pp. 263-4

————, *(PWN)* 'Number' (1924), in *PW*, pp. 265-6

————, *(SKM)* 'Sources of Knowledge of Mathematics and the mathematical natural Sciences' (1924/25), in *PW*, pp. 267-74; extract also in *FR*

————, *(NA)* 'Numbers and Arithmetic' (1924/25), in *PW*, pp. 275-7; also in *FR*

————, *(NAFA)* 'A new Attempt at a Foundation for Arithmetic' (1924/25), in *PW*, pp. 278-81

————, *(TPW)* *Translations from the Philosophical Writings of Gottlob Frege*, ed. Peter Geach & Max Black, 3rd ed. (Blackwell, 1980; 1st ed. 1952)

————, *(BSA)* *Begriffsschrift und andere Aufsätze*, ed. I Angelelli (Hildesheim: Georg Olms, 1964)

————, *(KS)* *Kleine Schriften*, ed. I. Angelelli (Hildesheim: Georg Olms, 1967), tr. as *(CP)* *Collected Papers on Mathematics, Logic, and Philosophy*, ed. B. McGuinness, tr. M. Black et al. (Blackwell, 1984)

————, *(NS)* *Nachgelassene Schriften*, ed. H. Hermes, F. Kambartel & F. Kaulbach (Hamburg: Felix Meiner, 1969), tr. as *(PW)* *Posthumous Writings* by P. Long & R. White (Blackwell, 1979)

————, *(FG)* *On the Foundations of Geometry and Formal Theories of Arithmetic*, tr. & with an introd. by Eike-Henner W. Kluge (Yale Univ. Press, 1971); letters and papers by Frege now contained in *PMC* and *CP*

———, (*CN*) *Conceptual Notation and related articles*, tr. & ed. with a biog. & introd. by T.W. Bynum (OUP, 1972)

———, (*WB*) *Wissenschaftlicher Briefwechsel*, ed. G. Gabriel, H. Hermes, F. Kambartel, C. Thiel & A. Veraart (Hamburg: Felix Meiner, 1976), abr. for English ed. by B. McGuinness & tr. as (*PMC*) *Philosophical and Mathematical Correspondence* by H. Kaal (Blackwell, 1980); selections also in *FR*

———, (*LI*) *Logical Investigations*, ed. P.T. Geach, tr. P.T. Geach & R.H. Stoothoff (Blackwell, 1977); now contained in *CP*

———, (*FR*) *The Frege Reader*, ed. M. Beaney (Blackwell, forthcoming 1997)

French, P.A., Uehling, T.E. & Wettstein, H.K. (1981), eds., *Midwest Studies in Philosophy* VI (Univ. of Minnesota Press)

Gabriel, Gottfried (1984), 'Fregean Connection: *Bedeutung*, Value and Truth-Value', in Wright (1984), pp. 187-91

Gaukroger, Stephen (1989), *Cartesian Logic* (OUP)

Geach, P.T. (1956), 'On Frege's Way Out', *Mind* 65, pp. 408-9; repr. in Geach (1972), pp. 235-7; also in Klemke (1968), pp. 502-4

———, (1972), *Logic Matters* (Blackwell)

Gilson, Etienne (1951), *Etudes sur le rôle de la pensée médiévale dans la formation du système cartésien* (Paris: Vrin)

Graeser, Andreas (1978), 'The Stoic Theory of Meaning', in Rist (1978), pp. 77-100

Grattan-Guinness, I. (1977), *Dear Russell – Dear Jourdain* (Duckworth)

Grossmann, Reinhardt (1961), 'Frege's Ontology', *Phil. Rev.* 70, pp. 23-40; repr. in Klemke (1968), pp. 79-98

———, (1969), *Reflections on Frege's Philosophy* (Evanston)

Haaparanta, Leila (1986), 'Frege on Existence', in Haaparanta & Hintikka, pp. 155-74

Haaparanta, Leila & Hintikka, Jaakko (1986), eds., *Frege Synthesized* (D. Reidel, Holland)

Hacking, Ian (1986), 'Leibniz and Descartes: Proof and Eternal Truths', in Kenny (1986), pp. 47-60

Hale, Bob (1984), 'Frege's Platonism', in Wright (1984), pp. 40-56

Hare, R.M. (1989), 'Some Sub-Atomic Particles of Logic', *Mind* 98, pp. 23-37

Hegel, *Lectures on the History of Philosophy*, tr. E.S. Haldane & F.H. Simson, 3 vols. (RKP, 1955; orig. publ. 1892-6)

Heidelberger, H. (1975), 'Review of Dummett, *Frege: Philosophy of Language*', *Metaphilosophy* 6, pp. 35-43

Holmes, George (1980), *Dante* (OUP)

Hooker, Michael (1982), ed., *Leibniz: Critical and Interpretive Essays* (Manchester Univ. Press)

Husserl, Edmund (1891), *Philosophie der Arithmetik*, in *Gesammelte Werke*, Band 12 (Den Haag: Martinus Nijhoff, 1970)

Hyde, Dominic (1994), 'Why Higher-Order Vagueness is a Pseudo-Problem', *Mind* 103, pp. 35-41

Hylton, Peter (1990), *Russell, Idealism, and the Emergence of Analytic Philosophy* (OUP)

Irwin, T.H. (1982), 'Aristotle's concept of signification', in Schofield & Nussbaum, pp. 241-66

Ishiguro, Hidé (1990), *Leibniz's Philosophy of Logic and Language*, 2nd ed. (CUP; 1st ed. Duckworth, 1972)

Jackson, Howard (1962), 'Frege on Sense-Functions', *Analysis* 23, pp. 84-7; repr. in Klemke (1968), pp. 376-81

Janik, A. & Toulmin, S. (1973), *Wittgenstein's Vienna* (Simon & Schuster, New York)

Jevons, W.S. (1874), *The Principles of Science* (London)

Johnson, W.E. (1892), 'The Logical Calculus', *Mind* 1, pp. 3-30, 235-50, 340-57

——, (1921-4), *Logic* (CUP; Part I, 1921; Part II, 1922; Part III, 1924)

Kant, Immanuel, *(CPR) Critique of Pure Reason* (1781 and 1787), tr. Norman Kemp Smith (Macmillan, 1929)

——, *(PFM) Prolegomena to Any Future Metaphysics* (1783), tr. Paul Carus, rev. James W. Ellington (Hackett, Indianapolis, 1977); also tr. P.G. Lucas (Manchester Univ. Press, 1953)

Kaplan, David (1979), 'On the Logic of Demonstratives', in Salmon & Soames, pp. 66-82; pp. 66-71 repr. in Kaplan (1990), pp. 34-8; orig. in *J. Phil. Logic* 8, pp. 81-98

——, (1990), 'Thoughts on Demonstratives', in Yourgrau (1990), pp. 34-49

Kapp, E. (1931), 'Syllogistic', in Barnes et al. (1975), pp. 35-49

——, (1942), *Greek Foundations of Traditional Logic* (New York)

Kenny, A. (1986), ed., *Rationalism, Empiricism, and Idealism* (OUP)

Keynes, J.N. (1906), *Studies and Exercises in Formal Logic*, 4th ed. (London; 1st ed. 1884)

Kilmister, C.W. (1984), *Russell* (Harvester)

Kitcher, Philip (1975), 'Kant and the Foundations of Mathematics', *Phil. Rev.* 1975, pp. 23-50

——, (1984), *The Nature of Mathematical Knowledge* (OUP)

——, (1986), 'Frege, Dedekind, and the Philosophy of Mathematics', in Haaparanta & Hintikka, pp. 299-343

Klemke, E.D. (1968), ed., *Essays on Frege* (Univ. of Illinois Press)

Kline, Morris (1972), *Mathematical Thought from Ancient to Modern Times* (OUP)

——, (1980), *Mathematics: The Loss of Certainty* (OUP)

Kluge, E.-H. W. (1970), 'Reflections on Frege', *Dialogue* IX, pp. 401-9

——, (1980), *The Metaphysics of Gottlob Frege* (Martinus Nijhoff, The Hague)

Kneale, William & Martha (1962), *The Development of Logic* (OUP)

Krüger, Lorenz (1984), 'Why do we study the history of philosophy?', in Rorty et al., pp. 77-101

Kulstad, M. (1977), ed., *Essays on the Philosophy of Leibniz* (Rice Univ. Studies, Houston)

Kripke, Saul A. (1979), 'A Puzzle about Belief', in Salmon & Soames, pp. 102-48; orig. in Margalit (1979), pp. 239-83

——, (1980), *Naming and Necessity* (Blackwell, 1980; orig. publ. 1972)

Lackey, Douglas (1973), 'Editorial Introductions' to Russell, *EA*

Langford, C.H. (1942), 'The Notion of Analysis in Moore's Philosophy', in Schilpp (1942), pp. 321-42

Lear, Jonathan (1980), *Aristotle and Logical Theory* (CUP)

Leibniz, *(USA)* 'Of Universal Synthesis and Analysis', in *LPW*, pp. 10-17

——, *(DM)* 'Discourse on Metaphysics', in *PE*, pp. 35-68; selections in *LPW*, pp. 18-47

——, *(MKTI)* 'Meditations on Knowledge, Truth, and Ideas', in *PE*, pp. 23-7

——, *(PT)* 'Primary Truths', in *LPW*, pp. 87-92; *PE*, pp. 30-4

——, *(ENS)* 'Explanation of the New System', in *LPW*, pp. 125-32

——, *(NE) New Essays on Human Understanding*, tr. & ed. P. Remnant & J. Bennett (CUP, 1981)

——, *(PNG)* 'Principles of Nature and of Grace', in *LPW*, pp. 195-204; *PE*, pp. 206-13

——, (*LS*) *Selections*, ed. Philip P. Wiener (Charles Scribner's Sons, New York, 1951)

——, (*LP*) *Logical Papers*, tr. & ed. G.H.R. Parkinson (OUP, 1966)

——, (*LAC*) *The Leibniz-Arnauld Correspondence*, ed. & tr. H.T. Mason (Manchester Univ. Press, 1967)

——, (*LPW*) *Philosophical Writings*, ed. & tr. Mary Morris & G.H.R. Parkinson (J.M. Dent & Sons Ltd, London, 1973)

Lemmon, E.J. (1965), *Beginning Logic* (Nelson)

Lewis, David (1978), 'Truth in Fiction', *Amer. Phil. Quar.* 15, pp. 37-46

Lloyd, G.E.R. (1979), *Magic, Reason and Experience* (CUP)

Locke, John, *An Essay concerning Human Understanding*, 4th ed., ed. P.H. Nidditch (OUP, 1975)

Lodge, David (1984), *Small World* (Penguin)

Lotze, Hermann (1874), *Logik* (Leipzig; 2nd ed. 1880)

Lukasiewicz, Jan (1934), 'On the History of the Logic of Propositions', in McCall (1967), pp. 66-87

——, (1957), *Aristotle's Syllogistic* (OUP)

Luntley, Michael (1984), 'The Sense of a Name', in Wright (1984), pp. 80-97

MacDonald Ross, G. (1984), *Leibniz* (OUP)

MacIntyre, Alasdair (1981), *After Virtue: a study in moral theory* (Duckworth)

——, (1984), 'The relationship of philosophy to its past', in Rorty et al., pp. 31-48

Margalit, A. (1979), ed., *Meaning and Use* (D. Reidel)

Marshall, William (1953), 'Frege's Theory of Functions and Objects', *Phil. Rev.* 62, pp. 374-90; repr. in Klemke (1968), pp. 249-67

——, (1956), 'Sense and Reference: A Reply', *Phil. Rev.* 65, pp. 342-61; repr. in Klemke (1968), pp. 298-320

Martin, E. (1982), 'Referentiality in Frege's *Grundgesetze*', *Hist. and Phil. of Logic* 3, pp. 151-64

Mates, Benson (1953), *Stoic Logic* (Univ. of California Press, 2nd pr. 1961)

——, (1986), *The Philosophy of Leibniz* (OUP)

Max, Ingolf & Stelzner, Werner (1995), eds., *Logik und Mathematik* (de Gruyter, Berlin)

McCall, Storrs (1967), ed., *Polish Logic, 1920-1939* (OUP)

McCulloch, Gregory (1989), *The Game of the Name* (OUP)

McDowell, John (1977), 'On the sense and reference of a proper name', in Platts (1980), pp. 141-66; Moore (1992), pp. 111-36; orig. in *Mind* 1977, pp. 159-85

——, (1984), '*De Re* Senses', in Wright (1984), pp. 98-109

McGinn, Colin (1983), *The Subjective View* (OUP)

McGuinness, Brian (1988), *Wittgenstein: A Life* (Duckworth)

McGuinness, B. & Haller, R. (1989), eds., *Wittgenstein in Focus – Im Brennpunkt: Wittgenstein*, Grazer Philosophische Studien 33/34 (Amsterdam: Rodopi)

McRae, Robert (1976), *Leibniz: Perception, Apperception, and Thought* (Univ. of Toronto Press)

Mendelsohn, Richard L. (1981), 'Frege on Predication', in French et al., pp. 69-82

Mill, John Stuart, (*SL*) *A System of Logic*, in *Collected Works*, vol. 7 (Univ. of Toronto Press, 1973)

Miller, Fred D. (1973), 'Did Aristotle have the concept of identity?', *Phil. Rev.* 82, pp. 483-90

Moore, A.W. (1992), ed., *Meaning and Reference* (OUP)

Moore, A.W. & Rein, Andrew (1986), '*Grundgesetze*, Section 10', in Haaparanta & Hintikka, pp. 375-84

Moravcsik, J.M.E. (1967), ed., *Aristotle: A Collection of Critical Essays* (Anchor, New York)

Mott, Peter (1994), 'On the Intuitionistic Solution of the Sorites Paradox', *Pacific Phil. Quar.* 75, pp. 133-50

Mueller, Ian (1969), 'Stoic and Peripatetic Logic', *Archiv für Geschichte der Philosophie* 51, pp. 173-87

Nelson, Everett J. (1946), 'Contradiction and the Presupposition of Existence', *Mind* 55, pp. 319-27

Nidditch, P.H. (1962), *The Development of Mathematical Logic* (Routledge)

Nietzsche, Friedrich (1886), *Human, All Too Human*, tr. R.J. Hollingdale (CUP, 1986)

Noonan, Harold (1984), 'Fregean Thoughts', in Wright (1984), pp. 20-39

Nye, Andrea (1990), *Words of Power* (Routledge)

Olby, R.C., Cantor, G.N., Christie, J.R.R. & Hodge, M.J.S. (1990), eds., *Companion to the History of Modern Science* (Routledge, 1990)

Owen, G.E.L. (1960), 'Logic and Metaphysics in Some Earlier Works of Aristotle', in Barnes et al. (1979), pp. 13-32; also in Owen (1986), pp. 180-99; orig. publ. 1960

———, (1965), 'The Platonism of Aristotle', in Barnes et al. (1975), pp. 14-34; also in Owen (1986), pp. 200-20; orig. in *Proc. Brit. Acad.* 50 (1965), pp. 125-50

———, (1986), *Logic, Science and Dialectic*, ed. Martha Nussbaum (Duckworth)

Parkinson, G.H.R. (1966), 'Introduction' to Leibniz, *LP*, pp. ix-lxv

———, (1982), 'The "Intellectualization of Appearances": Aspects of Leibniz's Theory of Sensation and Thought', in Hooker (1982), pp. 3-20

Parret, H. & Bouveresse, J. (1981), eds., *Meaning and Understanding* (Berlin)

Parsons, Charles (1965), 'Frege's Theory of Number', in Black (1965), pp. 180-203

———, (1971), 'Kant's Philosophy of Arithmetic', in Walker (1982), pp. 13-40; orig. publ. in 1971

Pascal, *Pensées*, tr. A.J. Krailsheimer (Penguin, 1966)

Patzig, Günther (1968), *Aristotle's Theory of the Syllogism*, tr. J. Barnes (D. Reidel, Holland)

Peacocke, Christopher (1986), *Thoughts: An Essay on Content* (Blackwell/Aris. Soc.)

Peirce, C.S. (1883), 'The Logic of Relatives', in *Collected Papers*, vol. III: Exact Logic, ed. C. Hartshorne & P. Weiss (Harvard Univ. Press, 1933), pp. 195-209

———, (1885), 'On the Algebra of Logic: A Contribution to the Philosophy of Notation', in *Collected Papers*, vol. III, pp. 210-49

Perrin, Carleton E. (1990), 'The Chemical Revolution', in Olby et al., pp. 264-77

Perry, John (1977), 'Frege on Demonstratives', *Phil. Rev.* 86, pp. 474-97; also in Yourgrau (1990), pp. 50-70

———, (1979), 'The Problem of the Essential Indexical', *Noûs* 13, pp. 3-21; repr. in Salmon & Soames, pp. 83-101

Picardi, Eva (1993), 'A Note on Dummett and Frege on Sense-Identity', *European Journal of Philosophy* 1, pp. 69-80

Plato, *Euthydemus*, tr. W.R.M. Lamb, Loeb Classical Library, vol. 4 (Harvard/Heinemann, 1924)

———, *Meno*, tr. W.K.C. Guthrie, in *Protagoras and Meno* (Penguin, 1956); also tr. W.R.M. Lamb, Loeb Classical Library, vol. 4 (Harvard/Heinemann, 1924)

———, *The Republic*, tr. D. Lee (Penguin, 1955, 1974)

———, *Phaedrus*, tr. W. Hamilton (Penguin, 1973)

———, *Philebus*, tr. J.C.B. Gosling (OUP, 1975); also tr. R.A.H. Waterfield (Penguin, 1982)

——, *Sophist*, tr. B. Jowett, in *The Dialogues of Plato Translated into English*, vol. 3 (OUP, 1st ed. 1871, 4th ed. 1953)

——, *Politicus* (Statesman), tr. B. Jowett, in *The Dialogues of Plato Translated into English*, vol. 3 (OUP, 1st ed. 1871, 4th ed. 1953)

Platts, Mark (1980), ed., *Reference, Truth and Reality* (Routledge)

Popkin, Richard H. (1979), *The History of Scepticism from Erasmus to Spinoza* (Univ. of California Press)

Potts, Timothy C. (1982), 'The Interpretation of Frege', *Theoretical Linguistics* 9, pp. 133-60

Prior, A.N. (1962), *Formal Logic*, 2nd ed. (OUP; 1st ed. 1955)

——, (1976), *The Doctrine of Propositions and Terms* (Duckworth)

Quine, W.V.O. (1955), 'On Frege's Way Out', *Mind* 54, pp. 145-59; repr. in Klemke (1968), pp. 485-501

——, (1960), *Word and Object* (MIT Press)

——, (1963), *Set Theory and Its Logic* (Harvard Univ. Press)

Quinton, A.M. (1986), 'Absolute Idealism', in Kenny (1986), pp. 124-50

Ramsey, Frank P. (1925), 'The Foundations of Mathematics', in Ramsey (1931), pp. 1-61; Ramsey (1978), pp. 152-212

——, (1931), *The Foundations of Mathematics* (Routledge)

——, (1978), *Foundations* (Routledge); rev. ed. of Ramsey (1931)

Rée, Jonathan (1978), 'Philosophy and the History of Philosophy', in Rée, Ayers & Westoby, pp. 1-39

Rée, J., Ayers, M. & Westoby, A. (1978), *Philosophy and its Past* (Harvester)

Resnik, Michael (1976), 'Frege's Context Principle Revisited', in Schirn (1976), vol. 3, pp. 35-49

——, (1979), 'Frege as Idealist and then Realist', *Inquiry* 22, pp. 350-7

——, (1980), *Frege and the Philosophy of Mathematics* (Cornell Univ. Press)

——, (1986), 'Frege's Proof of Referentiality', in Haaparanta & Hintikka, pp. 177-95

Ricketts, Thomas G. (1986), 'Objectivity and Objecthood: Frege's Metaphysics of Judgment', in Haaparanta & Hintikka, pp. 65-95

Rist, John M. (1978), ed., *The Stoics* (Univ. of California Press)

Rorty, Richard (1980), *Philosophy and the Mirror of Nature* (Blackwell)

——, (1984), 'The historiography of philosophy: four genres', in Rorty et al., pp. 49-75

Rorty, R., Schneewind, J.B., & Skinner, Q. (1984), eds., *Philosophy in History* (CUP)

Ross, W.D. (1949), 'Introduction' to *Aristotle's Prior and Posterior Analytics* (OUP), pp. 1-95

Rudebusch, George (1985), 'Plato on Sense and Reference', *Mind* 94, pp. 526-37

——, (1987), 'Beaney on Mistakes', *Mind* 96, pp. 545-7

Russell, Bertrand, (*POM*) *The Principles of Mathematics*, 2nd ed. (George Allen & Unwin, 1937; 1st ed. 1903)

——, (*OD*) 'On Denoting', in Russell, *LK*, pp. 41-56, and *EA*, pp. 103-19; orig. in *Mind* 1905

——, (*TTN*) 'On Some Difficulties in the Theory of Transfinite Numbers and Order Types' (1905), in Russell, *EA*, pp. 135-64

——, (*STC*) 'On the Substitutional Theory of Classes and Relations' (1906), in Russell, *EA*, pp. 165-89

——, (*ISSL*) 'On "Insolubilia" and their Solution by Symbolic Logic' (1906), in Russell, *EA*, pp. 190-214

——, (*MLTT*) 'Mathematical Logic as based on the Theory of Types', in Russell, *LK*, pp. 59-102; orig. in *Amer. J. Maths.* (1908)

——, (*TLT*) 'The Theory of Logical Types' (1910), in Russell, *EA*, pp. 215-52

——, (*KAKD*) 'Knowledge by Acquaintance and Knowledge by Description', in Russell, *ML*, pp. 152-67; orig. publ. in *Proc. Aris. Soc.* 1910-11

——, (*PP*) *The Problems of Philosophy* (OUP, 1967; orig. publ. 1912)

——, (*ML*) *Mysticism and Logic* (George Allen & Unwin, 1917)

——, (*PLA*) 'The Philosophy of Logical Atomism', in *LK*, pp. 175-281; orig. in *Monist* 28 & 29 (lectures delivered in London in 1918)

——, (*IMP*) *Introduction to Mathematical Philosophy* (George Allen & Unwin, 1919)

——, (*LA*) 'Logical Atomism', in *LK*, pp. 321-43; orig. in *Contemporary British Philosophy*, First Series (London, 1924)

——, (*LK*) *Logic and Knowledge*: Essays 1901-1950, ed. R.C. Marsh (George Allen & Unwin, 1956)

——, (*MSR*), 'Mr Strawson on Referring', in Russell, *MPD*, pp. 175-80; *EA*, pp. 120-6; orig. in *Mind* 1957, pp. 385-9

——, (*MPD*) *My Philosophical Development* (George Allen & Unwin, 1959)

——, (*ABR*) *Autobiography* (Unwin Paperbacks, 1978; first publ. in 3 vols. 1967-9)

——, (*EA*) *Essays in Analysis*, ed. Douglas Lackey (George Allen & Unwin, 1973)

Russell, B. & Whitehead, A.N., (*PM*) *Principia Mathematica* (CUP, 1910-13; 2nd ed. 1925)

Sainsbury, R.M. (1979), *Russell* (Routledge)

——, (1988), *Paradoxes* (CUP)

Salmon, Nathan (1992), 'On Content', *Mind* 101, pp. 733-51

Salmon, N. & Soames, S. (1988), eds., *Propositions and Attitudes* (OUP)

Schilpp, P.A. (1942), ed., *The Philosophy of G.E. Moore* (New York)

Schirn, Matthias (1976), ed., *Studien zu Frege* (Frommann, Stuttgart-Bad Cannstatt), 3 vols.

Schofield, M., Burnyeat, M. & Barnes, J. (1980), eds., *Doubt and Dogmatism* (OUP)

Schofield, Malcolm & Nussbaum, Martha Craven (1982), eds., *Language and Logos*: Studies in ancient Greek philosophy presented to G.E.L. Owen (CUP)

Schröder, E. (1880), 'Review of Frege's *Begriffsschrift*', tr. in Frege, *CN*, pp. 218-32

Simons, Peter (1987), 'Frege's Theory of Real Numbers', *History and Philosophy of Logic* 8, pp. 25-44; repr. in Simons (1992)

——, (1992), *Philosophy and Logic in Central Europe from Bolzano to Tarski: Selected Essays* (D. Reidel)

——, (1992a), 'Why Is There So Little Sense in Grundgesetze?', *Mind* 101, pp. 753-66

Skorupski, John (1984), 'Dummett's Frege', in Wright (1984), pp. 217-29

——, (1989), *John Stuart Mill* (Routledge)

——, (1994), *English-Language Philosophy 1750-1945* (OUP)

Sluga, Hans (1975), 'Frege and the Rise of Analytic Philosophy', *Inquiry* 18, pp. 471-87

——, (1976), 'Frege as a Rationalist', in Schirn (1976), vol. 1, pp. 27-47

——, (1977), 'Frege's Alleged Realism', *Inquiry* 20, pp. 227-42

——, (1980), *Gottlob Frege* (Routledge)

——, (1984), 'Frege: the early years', in Rorty, Schneewind & Skinner, pp. 329-56

——, (1986), 'Semantic Content and Cognitive Sense', in Haaparanta & Hintikka, pp. 47-64

Smiley, T.J., (1962), 'Syllogism and Quantification', *J. Sym. Logic* 27, pp. 58-72

——, (1973), 'What is a Syllogism?', *J. Phil. Logic* 2, pp. 135-54

——, (1982), 'The Schematic Fallacy', *Proc. Aris. Soc.* 1982-83, pp. 1-17

Spinoza, *Ethics* (1677), ed. with a rev. tr. G.H.R. Parkinson (J.M. Dent & Sons Ltd, London, 1989)

Stevenson, Leslie (1973), 'Frege's Two Definitions of Quantification', *Phil. Quar.* 23, pp. 207-23

Strawson, P.F. (1950), 'On Referring', in Strawson (1971), pp. 1-27; also in Moore (1992), pp. 56-79; orig. in *Mind* 59, pp. 320-44

——, (1952), *Introduction to Logical Theory* (Methuen, London)

——, (1953), 'Particular and General', in Strawson (1971), pp. 28-52; orig. in *Proc. Aris. Soc.* 1953-4, pp. 233-60

——, (1959), *Individuals* (Methuen, London)

——, (1961), 'Singular Terms and Predication', in Strawson (1971), pp. 53-74; also in Strawson (1967), pp. 69-88; orig. in *J. Phil.* 58 (1961), pp. 393-412

——, (1964), 'Identifying Reference and Truth-Values', in Strawson (1971), pp. 75-95; orig. in *Theoria* 30, pp. 96-118

——, (1966), *The Bounds of Sense* (Methuen, London)

——, (1967), ed., *Philosophical Logic* (OUP)

——, (1969), 'Meaning and Truth', in Strawson (1971), pp. 170-89

——, (1970), 'The Asymmetry of Subjects and Predicates', in Strawson (1971), pp. 96-115

——, (1971), *Logico-Linguistic Papers* (Methuen, London)

——, (1974), *Subject and Predicate in Logic and Grammar* (Methuen, London)

Sullivan, Peter M. (1994), 'The Sense of "A Name of a Truth-Value" ', *Phil. Quar.* 44, pp. 476-81

Taschek, William (1988), 'Would a Fregean be Puzzled by Pierre?', *Mind* 97, pp. 99-104

Taylor, Charles (1984), 'Philosophy and its history', in Rorty et al., pp. 17-30

——, (1989), *Sources of the Self* (CUP)

Temple, George (1981), *100 Years of Mathematics* (Duckworth)

Thiel, Christian (1968), *Sense and Reference in Frege's Logic*, tr. T.J. Blakeley (D. Reidel, Holland; first publ. 1965)

Thom, Paul (1981), *The Syllogism* (Philosophia Verlag, München)

Thompson, M. (1953), 'On Aristotle's Square of Opposition', *Phil. Rev.* 62, pp. 251-65; repr. in Moravcsik (1967), pp. 51-72

Trendelenburg, A. (1867), 'Über Leibnizes Entwurf einer allgemeinen Charakteristik', *Historische Beiträge zur Philosophie*, vol. 3, pp. 1-47

Tugendhat, Ernst (1970), 'The Meaning of "Bedeutung" in Frege', *Analysis* 30, pp. 177-89; repr. in German in Schirn (1976), vol. 3, pp. 51-65

Tye, Michael (1994), 'Why the Vague Need *Not* be Higher-Order Vague', *Mind* 103, pp. 43-5

Van Heijenoort, J. (1977a), 'Sense in Frege', *J. Phil. Logic* 1977, pp. 93-102

——, (1977b), 'Frege on Sense Identity', *J. Phil. Logic* 1977, pp. 103-8

——, (1967), ed., *From Frege to Gödel: A Source Book in Mathematical Logic, 1879-1931* (Harvard Univ. Press)

Venn, John (1880), 'Review of Frege's *Begriffsschrift*', *Mind* 5, p. 297; repr. in Frege, *CN*, pp. 234-5

Veraart, Albert (1976), 'Geschichte des wissenschaftlichen Nachlasses Gottlob Freges und seiner Edition. Mit einem Katalog des ursprünglichen Bestands der nachgelassenen Schriften Freges', in Schirn (1976), vol. 1, pp. 49-106

Von Neumann, John (1923), 'On the Introduction of Transfinite Numbers', in van Heijenoort (1967), pp. 346-54

Walker, Ralph C.S. (1982), ed., *Kant on Pure Reason* (OUP)

Walton, Kendall L. (1973), 'Pictures and Make-Believe', *Phil. Rev.* 82, pp. 283-319

——, (1978), 'Fearing Fictions', *J. Phil.* 75, pp. 5-27

Wedin, Michael V. (1978), 'Aristotle on the Existential Import of Singular Sentences', *Phronesis* 23, pp. 179-96

Weil, E. (1951), 'The Place of Logic in Aristotle's Thought', in Barnes et al. (1975), pp. 88-112

Weiner, Joan (1984), 'The Philosopher behind the Last Logicist', in Wright (1984), pp. 57-79

——, (1990), *Frege in Perspective* (Cornell Univ. Press)

Wells, Rulon S. (1951), 'Frege's Ontology', in Klemke (1968), pp. 3-41; orig. in *Review of Metaphysics* 4, pp. 537-73

Westoby, Adam (1978), 'Hegel's History of Philosophy', in Rée, Ayers & Westoby, pp. 67-108

Wienpahl, Paul D. (1950), 'Frege's *Sinn und Bedeutung*', in Klemke (1968), pp. 203-18; orig. in *Mind* 59, pp. 483-94

White, Nicholas P. (1971), 'Aristotle on Sameness and Oneness', *Phil. Rev.* 80, pp. 177-97

Wiggins, David (1976), 'Frege's Problem of the Morning Star and the Evening Star', in Schirn (1976), vol. 2, pp. 221-55

——, (1980), *Sameness and Substance* (Blackwell)

——, (1980a), ' "Most" and "all": some comments on a familiar programme, and on the logical form of quantified sentences', in Platts (1980), pp. 318-46

——, (1984), 'A Running Repair to Frege's Doctrine and a Plea for the Copula', in Wright (1984), pp. 126-43

Williamson, Timothy (1994), *Vagueness* (Routledge)

Wilson, Margaret D. (1977), 'Confused Ideas', in Kulstad (1977), pp. 123-37

Wittgenstein, Ludwig, (*NB*) *Notebooks 1914-1916*, 2nd ed., ed. G.H. von Wright & G.E.M. Anscombe, tr. G.E.M. Anscombe (Blackwell, 1979; 1st ed. 1961)

——, (*TLP*) *Tractatus Logico-Philosophicus*, tr. D.F. Pears & B. McGuinness (RKP; 1961, 1974); orig. tr. C.K. Ogden (RKP, 1922)

——, (*LO*) *Letters to C.K. Ogden*, ed. with an introd. by G.H. von Wright (Blackwell, 1973)

——, (*PR*) *Philosophical Remarks*, ed. R. Rhees, tr. R. Hargreaves & R. White (Blackwell, 1975)

——, (*PI*) *Philosophical Investigations*, 3rd ed., tr. G.E.M. Anscombe (Blackwell, 1978; 1st ed. 1956)

Wolff, R.P. (1967), ed., *Kant: A Collection of Critical Essays* (Macmillan)

Wright, Crispin (1983), *Frege's Conception of Numbers as Objects* (Aberdeen Univ. Press)

——, (1984), ed., *Frege: Tradition and Influence* (Blackwell, 1984); orig. publ. in *Phil. Quar.* 34, no. 136, Special Issue: Frege (July 1984), pp. 183-430

Wu, Joseph S. (1969), 'The Problem of Existential Import', *Notre Dame J. Formal Logic* 10, pp. 415-24

Yourgrau, Palle (1987), 'The Path Back to Frege', in Yourgrau (1990), pp. 97-132; orig. in *Proc. Aris. Soc.* 87, pp. 169-210

——, (1990), ed., *Demonstratives* (OUP)

Zermelo, Ernst (1908), 'Investigations in the Foundations of Set Theory I', in van Heijenoort (1967), pp. 199-215; orig. in *Mathematische Annalen* 65, pp. 261-81

Index